LORENZO GHIBERTI

BY RICHARD KRAUTHEIMER

IN COLLABORATION WITH

TRUDE KRAUTHEIMER-HESS

PRINCETON, NEW JERSEY

PRINCETON UNIVERSITY PRESS

1970

COPYRIGHT © 1956, 1970, BY PRINCETON UNIVERSITY PRESS

All Rights Reserved

L.C. CARD 56-8383

ISBN 0-691-03820-1

Second Printing, with corrections and new preface, 1970

PUBLICATION OF THIS BOOK HAS BEEN AIDED

BY GRANTS FROM

THE BOLLINGEN FOUNDATION AND THE JOHN SIMON GUGGENHEIM MEMORIAL FOUNDATION

PRINTED IN THE UNITED STATES OF AMERICA

BY PRINCETON UNIVERSITY PRESS, PRINCETON, NEW JERSEY

LORENZO GHIBERTI

VOLUME II

PRINCETON MONOGRAPHS
IN ART AND ARCHAEOLOGY
XXXI

PUBLISHED FOR THE
DEPARTMENT OF ART AND ARCHAEOLOGY
PRINCETON UNIVERSITY

CONTENTS
VOLUME II

APPENDICES   335

    Appendix A. Handlist of Antiques   337

    Appendix B. The Olympiads   353

    Appendix C. Sources   359

       1. Analysis of Documents   360

       2. Transcript of Documents   366

       3. Digest of Documents   402

       4. Digest of New Documents   422

BIBLIOGRAPHY   425

ADDITIONAL BIBLIOGRAPHY   439

INDEX   441

ADDENDA AND CORRIGENDA   457

PLATES

following page

Works of Ghiberti, Plates 1-137   457

Collateral Material, Figures 1-146

APPENDICES

APPENDIX A

HANDLIST OF ANTIQUES

THIS appendix attempts to establish a handlist of motifs and types from works of ancient art upon which Ghiberti drew. In drafting this list we have imposed on ourselves several limitations:

(1). We have tried to focus the list on such works of antiquity which, either certainly or with great probability, were known in the fifteenth century and were accessible to Ghiberti. These include a few sculptures in the round such as those then assembled in and near the Lateran or otherwise scattered in Rome.[1] They include obviously sculptures still *in situ* on Roman monuments, triumphal arches and the like. But again these are comparatively few, and among them we have come to exclude the Columns of Trajan and of Marcus Aurelius. They provide no prototypes for Ghiberti's work that do not occur better on sarcophagi and, indeed, it is unlikely that the majority of their reliefs could be seen in Ghiberti's time.[2] Most important among works of ancient art known to the fifteenth century seem to have been the sarcophagi then extant in or near the churches of Rome, Pisa, Florence, and elsewhere and re-used, either as altars or tombs, during the Middle Ages or in the fifteenth century. Isa Ragusa (bibl. 434) has assembled a most valuable, though somewhat incomplete, list of such sarcophagi. To this same general group belong the few ancient sarcophagi and other reliefs walled up or otherwise inserted for decorative purposes in medieval churches or known to have been brought to such churches prior to Ghiberti's time.

Few of these sarcophagi remain *in situ* and, indeed, many have been destroyed. But this lacuna is bridged to a large degree by drawings made from such monuments in the course of the fifteenth and sixteenth centuries. We have thus made extensive use of these drawings. The best known among fifteenth century drawings after Roman sculptures are those by Pisanello scattered through European libraries and print rooms (Degenhart, bibl. 122 and 120), a group of anonymous drawings in the Ambrosiana (Vincenzi, bibl. 539; Degenhart, bibl. 120), a number of drawings attributed to Michele di Giovanni di Bartolo (Louvre, Cabinet des Estampes; Degenhart, bibl. 120), finally the sketchbooks of Francesco di Giorgio scattered through various collections and still insufficiently published (Weller, bibl. 549) and the Codex Escurialensis (Egger, bibl. 139). Among the numerous sixteenth century drawings of Roman sculptures our most important source is the sketchbook in the collection of Prince Wolfegg (Castle Wolfegg, Wuerttemberg), dated prior to 1516 and possibly as early as 1503, described and analyzed by Robert (bibl. 449). As stressed by Robert, the unique value of this sketchbook for our knowledge of antique sculpture known to the Renaissance lies in its almost exclusive limitation to sarcophagi still sheltered in Roman churches in the early sixteenth century, as is apparent from the draftsman's notes regarding their location. Since transfers of such works to churches are rare after 1450 it is reasonable to assume that they had stood there for centuries.[3]

The Codex Coburgensis (Coburg, Bavaria, Castle, Library; Matz, bibl. 310) of *ca.* 1550

---

[1] Michaelis, bibl. 328.

[2] The earliest drawings from the columns known to us date from the end of the fifteenth or the beginning of the sixteenth century. Extensive sketches could be made only at that time when an apparatus was constructed by which the artist could be hauled up to see the upper reliefs (Strong, bibl. 510; Paribeni, bibl. 390). Meyer-Weinschel's almost exclusive use of the Column of Trajan for Ghiberti's prototypes (bibl. 327) is thus even methodologically untenable.

[3] We are greatly indebted for generous advice and assistance given during the preparation of this list to Mrs. Phyllis Pray Bober, who is in charge of the *Census of Antique Works of Art known to the Renaissance,* sponsored by the Institute of Fine Arts of New York University and the Warburg Institute, London. As part of this project, Mrs. Bober is preparing an edition of the Aspertini sketchbook in London, British Museum, 1898-11-23. The early date of the Wolfegg sketchbook

was likewise suggested by Mrs. Bober. Mrs. Bober's information will be referred to as "Mrs. Bober-Census." We are likewise indebted to Mr. Cornelius Vermeule, Bryn Mawr College, who has prepared a catalogue, as yet unpublished, of the Dal Pozzo drawings at Windsor, Royal Library, and has generously made available both his catalogue and his photographs. The numbers of his catalogue correspond to the new Windsor numbers, and will be referred to as "Vermeule-Catalogue." We are most grateful also to the Warburg Institute for kindly providing us with photographs of the Wolfegg and Coburg sketchbooks, to the German Archeological Institute in Rome for their help in procuring photographs of Roman sarcophagi in Italy, and to Mr. Bernard Ashmole of the British Museum and Mrs. V. Verhoogen of the Musées Royaux in Brussels for providing us with photographs of the sarcophagus of the Ince Blundell Hall and the Brussels sarcophagus respectively.

and the Codex Pighianus (Berlin, Staatsbibliothek, at present Tübingen, Universitaetsbibliothek; Jahn, bibl. 229) of approximately the same period, are of lesser importance from our point of view. The far richer material which they reproduce no longer necessarily reflects reliefs preserved *in situ* or in churches and hence long known, but evidently largely the new Roman collections of the period, including both material transferred into them from churches, and the numerous finds made during the first half of the sixteenth century. Moreover these two sketchbooks contain no captions giving the location of the antiques, and the identification of the monuments has been laboriously sorted out by Matz and Jahn.

We have by and large refrained from using drawings or illustrations made after 1550. Exceptions are Dal Pozzo's Windsor collection of drawings and Gori's engravings (bibl. 191) after sarcophagi in Florence. Among the sarcophagi in the Camposanto in Pisa, even though they are known from Martini's engravings (bibl. 307) as a rule only those dated by medieval inscriptions, or otherwise known in the fifteenth century, have been used.

On the other hand it seemed safe to assume that Ghiberti was acquainted with works of ancient art which are reflected in the work of his contemporaries such as Donatello. Conversely reflections of such works in the second half of the fifteenth century have been excluded by and large from this list.

Since our objective was to build up a list of monuments known to Ghiberti we have concentrated primarily on the provenance of the objects and on the time when they are first recorded. We have referred to additional recordings of these objects only when they help to establish restorations relative to our problem. We have intentionally excluded the question of dating the antique sculptures.

(2). We have attempted equally to limit ourselves to specific motifs or types which Ghiberti borrowed from ancient art, and we hope thus to have avoided loose comparisons. Within this framework the comparison of details becomes of primary importance. To give one example for many: the figure of a servant girl accompanying the bride in a wedding scene is frequent on Roman sarcophagi; but the details of the dress held together on her shoulder and her hand lifting her skirt are rare and occur in only one example definitely known to the fifteenth century (see below, item 5).

(3). This attempt to be specific encounters several major obstacles.

For one, Ghiberti rarely, and never in his later years, copied verbatim an antique motif. Hence at times it is difficult to recognize the antique prototype in Ghiberti's variant. To some degree this difficulty is offset by Ghiberti's habit of distributing the elements of the prototype over different variants. The evidence, thus, is upheld by mutual buttressing.

Second, antique monuments, particularly of the class of sarcophagi, are apt, as is well known, to be stereotype. Hence exactly the same or nearly the same sequence of scenes, composition, and style may occur on several sarcophagi. Likewise, figures and motifs are often stereotype and used for different iconographic types; the same figure may appear as a muse, a *moira*, or a victory. Hence, if the motif occurs on several monuments known to have existed in the fifteenth century, the specific model used by Ghiberti can be identified only under particularly fortunate conditions. This is the case, for instance, if Ghiberti draws on a number of figures or heads from the same ancient monument, so that again the mutual buttressing of elements leads to a specific source.

Third, a number of antique monuments have demonstrably disappeared since the fifteenth century without having left any trace in fifteenth and sixteenth century drawings; an equally great number must be presumed to have been lost. For this reason we have departed in some rare instances from our guiding principle of referring primarily to monuments known to have existed in the fifteenth century: when a type or motif in Ghiberti's work very clearly reflects a work of ancient art known to us but unrecorded in the fifteenth century or proved to have been found only later, we had to assume either a missing record or the existence of an identical prototype now lost. As a result, what seem to be Ghiberti's very free variants on antique models may also well be derived from a much closer prototype either unrecorded or, indeed, unknown.

Whenever, on any grounds, reasonable doubts preclude the identification of a clearly antique motif with a specific prototype, we have thought it best to list it as "unidentified," hoping for future clarification.

The handlist, then, is decidedly of a preliminary nature. No doubt, it can and will be enlarged as time goes on. Nor is there any doubt that the number of antiques known to Ghiberti far exceeded those from which he drew individual motifs. Despite these shortcomings, the value of the list in its present state seems to us twofold, in that it presents both a preliminary contribution towards a census of antique works of art known to the early Renaissance, and a clue to Ghiberti's selective principles in approaching antiquity and to his image of ancient art.

COMPETITION RELIEF

1. *Isaac* (Pls. 2b, 26a). Derived from an antique statue, probably a torso. Exact prototype unidentified. Possibly close to the kneeling son of Niobe, Rome, Capitoline Museum (Jones, bibl. 234, pp. 121f, pl. 12) (Fig. 102).

Isaac kneels, his right shoulder drawn upward and thrust forward, his right hip protruding, his left shoulder sloping down. A nearly continuous curve runs from his right armpit to the knee, with only a slight nick at the waist; at his left side a sharp indentation at the waist breaks the line. The body is adolescent, the yet undeveloped muscles built up from small planes.

In general terms the figure recalls Lysippan or Skopasian sculptures and one is inclined to think of a prisoner with his arms tied behind his back. But none of those known to us combines the uninterrupted curve of the body on one side and the double thrust of the shoulder with the fourth century features of the adolescent body.

The outline with the continuous curve on one side and the broken one on the other corresponds in reverse to the figure of the kneeling son of Niobe in the Capitoline collection. The figure is badly restored. Originally it was a torso, with head, right hand, right leg, and left arm missing (information kindly confirmed by Dr. Pietrangeli). Both the outline of the upper part and the pose of the left thigh call Ghiberti's *Isaac* to mind. The style of the Niobid, however, lacks the sculptural treatment in small planes found in Isaac's body.

The provenance of the Niobid is far from certain. It entered the Capitoline collection under Pope Clement XII before 1750 (Jones, *loc.cit.*), though not from the Albani collection, as was the case with many other items (see inventory as published in Jones, bibl. 234, pp. 384ff, information kindly confirmed by Dr. Pietrangeli). Nothing seems to be known of its earlier history.

Of the two other Niobid statues of the same type in the Uffizi in Florence, one (Duetschke, bibl. 136, III, no. 268) was in the Valle-Rustici collection about 1550 (Aldrovrandi, bibl. 16, p. 56; Mandowsky, bibl. 292, p. 262, note 16); the other one (Duetschke, bibl. 136, III, no. 269) was found together with the rest of the group in 1583. But neither of the two Floren-

tine statues shows the strong curve of the right side that marks the Capitoline Niobid.

With the evidence available, the relationship of the Capitoline Niobid to Ghiberti's *Isaac* is possible, but it remains hypothetical at best.

Schlosser had suggested as Ghiberti's model for the *Isaac* a satyr torso, in the Uffizi. Since this torso was in the possession of the Gaddi family since the mid-sixteenth century, Schlosser surmised that it had been acquired by Monsignor Giovanni Gaddi, who in 1550 had bought some antiques from the collection of Ghiberti's great-grandson and that hence it had belonged to Lorenzo Ghiberti and, indeed, to his stepfather. But this theory cannot be proved and certainly the torso is different from the *Isaac* in outline as well as in the massive treatment of the muscles (Schlosser, bibl. 477, pp. 141ff). Another suggestion (Gruenwald, bibl. 195, pp. 155ff) referring the *Isaac* to the Ilioneus in Munich need not be discussed. Recently Van Essen (bibl. 141) has compared the *Isaac* with a figure from an Etruscan ashurn.

2. *Group of two servants* (Pl. 2a). Derived from a Pelops sarcophagus of the type now in Brussels (Fig. 103), (Robert, bibl. 448, III, 3, no. 329).

Of the two servants, one is seen from the back, clad in a tunic and short mantle, standing on his left foot, the right one raised, as if walking. Only a small part of his face is shown in profile; the other servant, visible from the shoulder up, is seen in three-quarter view.

The group corresponds to that at the left edge of the Brussels sarcophagus, representing Pelops entering Oenomaos' palace (see also below, item 47). Pelops, seen from the back in a walking stance identical with that of Ghiberti's servant, differs from that latter only in his antique costume. The youthful companion looks out from Oenomaos' palace, much as Ghiberti's second servant from the cave.

The history of the Brussels sarcophagus is unknown prior to 1840. Either it or an identical piece, now lost, must have been known to Ghiberti.

NORTH DOOR

NATIVITY

3. *Shepherd, left hand* (Pl. 27). Derived from the seated Phoebus, Phaeton sarcophagus, Florence, Museo dell' Opera di S. Maria del Fiore (Fig. 104), (Ragusa, bibl. 434, p. 62, no. 176).

The shepherd leans back slightly, his torso nude, his right upper arm and shoulder covered by the cloak, his right hand pointing in an awkward gesture towards the angel; his head turned away to the right contrasts sharply with the pose of the arm and leg. The upper part of his body, thus is apparently an insert. It recalls closely the half-reclining figure of Phoebus in the upper left corner of the Phaeton sarcophagus. The god's left arm has been switched to the right, including the covering cloak. Otherwise, the pose, including even the drapery curving along to the right side, is extremely close. The god's head is too badly damaged for comparison.

The Phaeton sarcophagus was re-used in the cathedral, its relief turned to the wall, for the burial of Piero Farnese (d.1367). The first projects for erecting his tomb date from 1395 (Paatz, bibl. 375, III, pp. 371f, and note 260), although the date of final execution is unknown. Ghiberti as a young man could still have seen the Phaeton relief.

EXPULSION

4. *Fallen youth* (Pl. 35). Possibly derived from a fallen hunter from a sarcophagus with the Wounding of Hippolytus. (The correct identification of the subject was kindly suggested by Prof. B. Ashmole.) Closest among the extant examples is the sarcophagus at Ince Blundell Hall (Fig. 105), early history not known. (Robert, bibl. 448, III, 2, 154; Ashmole, bibl. 26, no. 246, pl. 49.)

The fallen hunter lies half upright, naked, supporting himself on the ground with his right arm strongly bent. The front leg (restored from above the knee down) was slightly flexed, the other not visible, the left arm raised, grasping the chlamys to head off the boar.

Ghiberti's fallen youth is reversed in pose and his left leg more strongly flexed. His raised right arm, in the position of the fingers still indicating the grasp on the chlamys, and his nude body barely covered by the little mantle, strikingly recall the antique prototype.

ENTRY

5. *Woman, right edge* (Pl. 41). Slave girl from right edge of Marriage Ceremony, most likely from so-called Fieschi sarcophagus, S. Lorenzo f.l.m. in Rome (Fig. 106), re-used for the burial of Cardinal Guglielmo di Lavagna in 1256 (Matz-Duhn, bibl, 311, II, no. 3090; Ragusa, bibl. 434, pp. 160ff, no. 80).

The pose of the girl, bent forward and sideward, the bare arm, the hand lifting the skirt, the chiton, belted high below the breasts, the hair held by a fillet, are nearly identical with the girl on the S. Lorenzo sarcophagus. In all other examples of Roman marriage scenes traceable to at least the sixteenth century, e.g. Mantua, Palazzo Ducale, no. 186 (Duetschke, bibl. 136, IV, no. 643); Florence, Uffizi (*ibid.*, III, no. 62); Florence, Rinuccini Collection, now lost (Gori, bibl. 191, III, pl. XXIV, and Duetschke, bibl. 136, II, no. 316), the dress of the girl slips from her shoulder, a piece of drapery crosses her arm and her hand touches the arm of the bride, instead of lifting her own dress.

PILATE

6. *Group around throne* (Pl. 48). Variation on the *congiarium* or *liberalitas augusti*.

The composition, showing Pilate enthroned obliquely, the page pouring water, the Pharisees in front, Christ and his guard in the rear at the foot of the low dais, recall the traditional representation of Roman ceremonial scenes of the emperor's largesse: enthroned, the emperor is occasionally accompanied by an assistant or a goddess standing on or at the foot of the dais, and a group of citizens in front. At times an architectural setting fills the background as in Ghiberti's panel. The Roman type appears frequently on coins (e.g., Mattingly, bibl. 309, I, p. 138, pl. 42, 2) and occasionally on reliefs, such as the Sacchetti relief (Strong, bibl. 509, II, p. 144, fig. 475; Hamberg, bibl. 205, pp. 32ff).

FRAME

7. *Elderly prophetess* (Pl. 62a). Head of nurse, Phaedra sarcophagus, Pisa, Camposanto (Fig. 109), (Lasinio, bibl. 266, pl. LXXIII; Duetschke, bibl. 136, I, no. 24; Papini, bibl. 389, no. 113; Robert, bibl. 448, III, 2, no. 164; Ragusa, bibl. 434, pp. 97f, no. 39).

Re-used for the burial of Beatrix of Tuscany in 1076 (inscription) it was frequently used as a model from the time of Niccolo Pisano.

The deeply lined face, the profile view, the kerchief of Ghiberti's prophetess and of the nurse are identical. While the type is frequent on Roman sarcophagi, the exact resemblance, the fame of the Phaedra sarcophagus and Ghiberti's frequent use of it permit direct identification.

See items 8, 9, 10.

8. *Youthful prophet* (Pl. 63b). Head of standing Hippolytus, Phaedra sarcophagus, Pisa, Camposanto (Fig. 110).

The narrow bony head with the straight nose, protruding cheekbones, deepset eyes, and short, curly, disarranged hair of this prophet corresponds closely to that of Hippolytus.

See items 7, 9, 10.

9. *Prophetess* (Pl. 58a). Head of slave girl above and behind Phaedra, Phaedra sarcophagus, Pisa, Camposanto (Fig. 111).

The young face, seen in three-quarter view, looking upward, the hair parted in the middle, soft waves encircling a fillet, the slightly parted, open mouth and soft chin correspond to the girl behind Phaedra.

See items 7, 8, 10.

10. *Prophet with flying hair* (Pl. 62b). Probably derived from the companion of Hippolytus on horseback, Phaedra sarcophagus, Pisa, Camposanto (Fig. 112).

The type with broad face and bold features in general terms recalls presumed portraits of Alexander the Great and their frequent derivatives.

The companion of Hippolytus on the Phaedra sarcophagus belongs to such reflections. Given the frequent use Ghiberti made of this sarcophagus, the identification of this prophet with the companion's head is likely, even though the damaged state of the latter makes it impossible to be definite.

See items 7, 8, 9.

11. *Prophet* (Pl. 67). Caesar portrait, specific prototype not identified.

The long face, furrowed forehead, strong brows, straight nose, creases in the corner of the mouth and cheeks of Ghiberti's prophet, as well as the garment, point to a bust or full-sized figure of Caesar (Boehringer, bibl. 61, *passim*; Curtius, bibl. 111, *passim*) in military dress with *paludamentum* and *fibula*. In particular, the features are close to the Camposanto type, so called after a portrait in Pisa (Curtius, bibl. 111, pp. 202ff; Vessberg, bibl. 537, pp. 138ff), with long face and carefully arranged, full hair. Among the busts of this type again, Ghiberti's prophet is closest to two, one in Florence, Palazzo Pitti (Fig. 107), (Curtius, bibl. 110, fig. 4; Arndt-Amelung, bibl. 24, nos. 234f), the other in the Vatican, Museo Chiaramonti (Curtius, bibl. 111, p. 218, pls. 49ff; Amelung, bibl. 20, I, p. 376, no. 107). The Pitti portrait is severely restored (nose, lips, chin); the military bust is probably second half of the fifteenth century (the latter information kindly supplied by Mr. M. Weinberger). That it was known in the later fifteenth century is proved, however, by a free variation on the head, possibly from the Rossellino workshop (New York, Metropolitan Museum of Art), (Fig. 108). Indeed it has been suggested, though not quite convincingly, that around

1420 it served as model for the so-called Poggio in the Cathedral of Florence (Francovich, bibl. 166, p. 149, figs. 11, 12). The Chiaramonti bust is equally close in type, but in civilian dress. Nothing seems to be known about its early history. Both heads, however, show the hair swept to the right, rather than to the left as in Ghiberti's prophet.

Ghiberti may have drawn either on the Pitti head or on a lost Caesar bust of similar type.

12. *Prophet* (Pl. 60c). Socrates head, specific prototype unidentified.

Among the three groups of Socrates portraits as distinguished by Bernoulli (bibl. 48), the Ghiberti head is closest to the second type with "ugly expressive features," such as the head in the Vatican, Sala delle Muse, no. 514 (Amelung, bibl. 20, pl. XXII, right).

13. *Bearded and mustachioed prophet* (Pl. 61c). Barbarian, probably from battle sarcophagus, Rome, Villa Borghese (Fig. 113).

The head, seen in profile, is turned upwards. The beaked nose and narrow eyes, the mouth almost disappearing between mustache and beard, the beard tilted slightly upwards, the curly hair, covering the ears, are drawn from the first barbarian at the left in the upper tier of the Borghese sarcophagus (Fig. 115). A similar head appears on the left small side, in the figure of a prisoner of the large battle sarcophagus in Pisa.

The battle sarcophagus, now in Villa Borghese, was in the atrium of St. Peter's around 1500 (Wolfegg, f. 30v, 31; Robert, bibl. 449); the large Pisa battle sarcophagus, now in the Camposanto, was formerly in the abbey of S. Zeno in Pisa, where it had probably stood since the Middle Ages (Lasinio, bibl. 266, pls. CXII, CXIII; Duetschke, bibl. 136, I, no. 60; Papini, bibl. 389, no. 111).

See also, items 14ff.

A relatively large group of prophets' heads on the North Door recall barbarian types frequently found on Roman battle sarcophagi. Among battle sarcophagi known in the fifteenth century, the outstanding examples seem to have been the Borghese and the Pisa sarcophagi. The front of the Pisa sarcophagus is half destroyed and hence identifiable only in the over-all composition and a few heads, among them one of a bearded barbarian. But it is reflected quite closely in Bertoldo di Giovanni's bronze relief in the Bargello (Fig. 114; Bode, bibl. 57, pp. 53ff). With all due precaution it can be stated that some of the heads in that plaque recall strongly some of Ghiberti's prophets. But only one of Ghiberti's prophets (Pl. 59f), finds its counterpart on the Pisa sarcophagus alone. One other prophet (Pl. 61c) occurs both in the Pisa relief (the prisoner on the left small side) and in the Borghese example (Fig. 115). Two more (Pl. 64a, b), are found only on the Borghese sarcophagus (Figs. 116, 117). Hence, despite Ghiberti's preference in his earlier years for the Pisa collection, it seems that it was the Borghese sarcophagus, rather than the one in Pisa on which he primarily drew. It is higher in quality, and in the one prototype common to both sarcophagi the Borghese sarcophagus head is closer in detail to Ghiberti's prophet.

Given the stereotype character of the entire group, the possibility should still be considered that Ghiberti knew battle sarcophagi, now lost, which combined both the Pisa and the Borghese types with others. The appearance of several unidentifiable barbarian heads among Ghiberti's prophets suggests that the Pisa and Borghese sarcophagi were not the only ones known to him.

14. *Bearded prophet* (Pl. 64b). Barbarian, probably from battle sarcophagus, Rome, Villa Borghese (Fig. 116).

The head in profile is turned up sharply, similar to that of the naked barbarian right of center in the bottom tier of the Borghese sarcophagus. Also the details are very much alike: deep-set, narrow eyes, beaked nose, lightly waved, stringy strands of hair and long, pointed, and curved beard.

See also items 13 and 15ff.

15. *Prophet with mustache and short goatee* (Pl. 64a). Barbarian from battle sarcophagus, probably the one in Rome, Villa Borghese (Fig. 117).

The Ghiberti head, looking upward, with a goatee and mustachios, is derived in all likelihood in reverse from the second barbarian to the left in the upper tier of the Borghese sarcophagus. The badly damaged mouth and chin of the barbarian preclude a comparison of these parts; but it is evident that he shares with the Ghiberti prophet the similar tilt of the head, the deep-set eyes, the heavy brows, the strong cheekbones and, despite a different handling, the lightly waved, short hair.

See also items 13f, 16f.

16. *Bearded and mustachioed prophet* (Pl. 57e). Barbarian from a battle sarcophagus, possibly a variation in reverse on the prophet, item 13, and thus likewise related to the Borghese sarcophagus.

See items 13ff.

17. *Bearded and turbaned prophet* (Pl. 59f). Barbarian from a battle sarcophagus, perhaps the one in Pisa, Camposanto, formerly S. Zeno, copied by Bertoldo (Fig. 114).

Ghiberti's prophet is seen in profile, his face sharply molded, his beard long, the curls escaping from under the turban. Thus he recalls closely the barbarian in Bertoldo's variant on the destroyed barbarian left of the rider in the center of the Pisa sarcophagus.

See item 13.

18. *Bearded and turbaned prophet* (Pl. 61e). Barbarian from a battle sarcophagus; specific prototype unidentified.

See item 13.

19. *'Hellenistic' prophet* (Pl. 63a). Barbarian from a battle sarcophagus; specific prototype unidentified.

See item 13.

20. *Bearded and mustachioed prophet* (Pl. 60a). Barbarian from a battle sarcophagus; specific prototype unidentified.

See item 13.

SAINT MATTHEW

21. (Pl. 7). Developed from a Trecento type under the impact of orator or related figures from Roman sarcophagi. Exact prototype unidentified.

The saint stands in his shell-topped niche in a pose reminiscent of the antique orator type, his left hand holding the book, his right arm cradled in the sling of his cloak, his left leg firmly planted on the ground in a classical *contrapposto*.

The antique orator type had survived in the disguise of apostles and other saints through Early Christian and Byzantine into Italian Dugento and Trecento art. The classical features of the *Saint Matthew*, however, the shell motif of the niche, the clear *contrapposto* and the firm modeling beneath the drapery point to a revitalization of the old type under the renewed impact of antique models. No large scale antique figures of orators were known to the fifteenth century. But on Roman sarcophagi both pagan and Early Christian, the type is used to represent rhetors, actors, poets, apostles and muses.

The combination of this type with a shell niche, the conch hinged at the bottom, narrows down the choice to sarcophagi of the so-called "Asiatic" type or their Western derivatives, Early Christian (Morey, bibl. 347, type 1) or medieval. Several such sarcophagi must have been known to Ghiberti; but among these, none offers a satisfactory prototype for the *Saint Matthew*. The sarcophagus of the Camposanto (Duetschke, bibl. 136, 1, no. 61;

Lasinio, bibl. 266, pls. CXLIII, CXLIV), which on its left flank shows a muse in a pose relatively similar cannot be traced beyond 1833. Sirén (bibl. 484, pp. 117f) has suggested as possible models statues of the type of the Sophocles figure in the Lateran and an Aesculapius statue in the Villa Ludovisi. The Sophocles was found only in the nineteenth century; the Aesculapius has but the most superficial resemblance to the *Saint Matthew*.

HEROD PLAQUE (SIENA FONT)

22. (Pl. 72). The two main groups of the relief, Herod and Herodias enthroned on a high dais and the guards pushing the Baptist forward, are placed against an architectural background. The two figures seated on the dais present a variant on the *Pilate* (see item 6) and on a *congiarium* scene with two enthroned figures. The group of the Baptist and the guards is evolved from two reliefs on the Arch of Constantine, both belonging originally to an Arch of Marcus Aurelius (Hamberg, bibl. 205, pp. 89ff; Wegner, bibl. 547):

a) wounded barbarian chieftain, submitting to emperor enthroned (*clementia imperatoris*; Hamberg, bibl. 205, pl. 14), (Fig. 119).

b) barbarian prisoner brought before emperor, standing in judgment (*justitia imperatoris*; Hamberg, bibl. 205, pl. 15), (Fig. 120).

The position of the Baptist surrounded by guards recalls the prototype of the *clementia*. The steeper design of the group, however, is closer to the second scene and equally, the young warrior next to the dais who lunges forward towards the Baptist, stems from a corresponding figure in the *justitia* relief.

SHRINE OF THE THREE MARTYRS

23. *Flying angels* (Pl. 76). Derived from medieval prototypes transformed by direct reference to Roman sarcophagi with flying victories.

The antique type of flying victories had survived through the Middle Ages, transformed into flying angels supporting inscriptions (Ambrogio Lorenzetti, Good Government, Siena, Palazzo Publico) or other objects. Among the latter, the tomb of Raneri Zen, Venice, SS. Giovanni e Paolo, 1283 (Fig. 58) shows the angels not only in a position similar to Ghiberti's but also with comparable hair and with round faces turned towards the beholder.

Ghiberti revitalizes the type by direct reference to Roman sarcophagi with flying victories, supporting *clipei* with the effigy of the deceased or tablets with inscriptions. At least

two such sarcophagi were certainly known to him:

a) Cortona, Cathedral, lid of sarcophagus with Dionysos fighting the Amazons, certainly known in the early fifteenth century (Vasari-Milanesi, bibl. 533, II, pp. 339f; Ragusa, bibl. 434, pp. 48f, no. 7), (Fig. 121).

b) Pisa, Camposanto, sarcophagus from cemetery of S. Pietro in Vinculi, front (Lasinio, bibl. 266, pl. XXIX; Duetschke, bibl. 136, I, no. 152; Papini, bibl. 389, no. 108; Ragusa, bibl. 434, p. 142, no. 68), reused in the fourteenth century, as witness the coat of arms in the *clipeus*.

Three more, also at Pisa, were possibly known to Ghiberti, although two of them are first illustrated by Martini.

c) Sarcophagus of T. Aelius, probably part of the old collection (Martini, bibl. 307, pls. 34, 131; Lasinio, bibl. 266, pl. XXXVII; Duetschke, bibl. 136, I, no. 141; Papini, bibl. 389, no. 111).

d) Sarcophagus front, with Gaia and Oceanus probably part of the old collection (Lasinio, bibl. 266, pl. CXXXVII; Martini, bibl. 307, pl. 34.16; Duetschke, bibl. 136, I, no. 44; Papini, bibl. 389, no. 109).

e) Lid of an Endymion sarcophagus of different size, used 1467 for reburial; inscription and coat of arms (Lasinio, bibl. 266, pl. LXIII; Duetschke, bibl. 136, I, no. 115; Papini, bibl. 389, no. 76; Ragusa, bibl. 434, pp. 145f, no. 71).

Beyond the Trecento prototypes, the angels on Ghiberti's shrine recall the slender proportions, and the ribbonlike folds of the garments on the Roman sarcophagi. The position of the arms and the wings both turned backward, and the bared arms and shoulder specifically recall the Cortona sarcophagus lid.

GATES OF PARADISE

GENESIS

24. *Adam, Creation* (Pl. 83a). Evolved from a Trecento type and revitalized by the impact of an antique, possibly the Adonis sarcophagus, Rome, Palazzo Rospigliosi (Fig. 122).

The posture of Adam, half seated and leaning backward, his right leg slightly raised, is reminiscent in reverse of the Adam in Piero di Puccio's Creation fresco in the Camposanto in Pisa (Fig. 79).

At the same time, the right arm of Ghiberti's Adam, slightly bent, supporting the body, the hand spread out with thumb apart, the left arm stretched forward, closely recalls the wounded Adonis from the sarcophagus, Rome, Palazzo Rospigliosi, formerly Palazzo Cevoli (now called Sacchetti), traceable to about 1615 and possibly further. Drawing Windsor, Dal Pozzo Collection, no. 8046 (Vermeule-Catalogue; Robert, bibl. 448, III, 1, nos. 15, 15').

In both Uccello's *sinopia* and his fresco of the *Creation* of the Chiostro Verde (Figs. 70, 71), Adam, though in reverse, is even closer to the Adonis from the Rospigliosi sarcophagus. Comparable are the more upright position of the body and the outstretched leg in the foreground (the leg of the antique figure is bent so sharply it could easily be mistaken for an outstretched leg, broken at the knee) and—in the *sinopia*—the youthful face and the outstretched arm showing the palm of the hand. All this suggests the existence of a drawing from the Adonis sarcophagus to which Uccello adhered more closely than Ghiberti (see p. 210).

25. *Eve, Creation* (Pl. 83b). The figure of Eve is derived in reverse from the floating Nereid at the right edge of the marine sarcophagus, Vatican, *Giardino della Pigna* (Amelung, bibl. 20, I, p. 828, pl. 92, no. 34; Robert-Rumpf, bibl. 455, V, no. 116), (Fig. 124).

The sarcophagus can be traced at least to the early sixteenth century, when it was at S. Maria in Aracoeli (Wolfegg, f. 29v, 30; Coburgensis, f. 120, Matz, bibl. 310, no. 176).

The angle at which Eve floats from Adam's rib is slightly steeper than that of the Nereid. But pose and proportion of the body, including the shape of the breasts and the taut line from breast to shoulder, the closely parallel legs, the one in front covering the other at the same angle, and even the disappearance of the ankles and feet behind the body of Adam and behind the waves, respectively, are so close as to preclude mere coincidence.

26. *Adam, Expulsion* (Pl. 84). Adam is standing terrorized behind Eve, his left leg forward and sharply bent, his right leg stretched far back, his left arm reaching backward in an unmotivated gesture, his head turned backward and upward.

The curious position of Adam's arm is explained by that of the young satyr pulling the tail of his victim on the Bacchic sarcophagus from S. Maria Maggiore (London, British Museum; Smith, bibl. 499, III, pp. 301ff), (Fig. 127). The resemblance extends not only to the sharp thrust of the legs, but even to details such as their muscles and bone structure. The sarcophagus (Figs. 125-127), in S. Maria Maggiore in Rome in the fifteenth century, was one of the antiques best known to the Renaissance and frequently drawn. Earliest instances are: Anonymous, Milan, Ambrosiana, F. 237,

1407r and v (Vincenzi, bibl. 539, p. 6; Degenhart, bibl. 120, fig. 4); Polidoro da Caravaggio, Munich, Graphische Sammlung, no. 2536 (Degenhart, bibl. 120, fig. 14); Wolfegg, f. 31v, 32, 32v, 50, front; f. 47v, 48, flanks (Robert, bibl. 449, pp. 201ff; Degenhart, bibl. 120, fig. 5). See also next item.

27. *Eve, Expulsion* (Pl. 84). The posture of Eve, her very slender body slightly bent backward, her head tilted to the side and slightly upward toward the Angel, her left hand covering her genitals, her right arm bent and lifted in a gesture of terror, her feet in a kind of *entrechat*, her right foot touching the ground with the toes only, draws on several antique prototypes. In the gesture of her hand covering her genitals she recalls the type of *Venus Pudica* used frequently, from at least the thirteenth century on, for the figure of Eve in the Expulsion (Niccolo Pisano, Perugia, Fountain; Masaccio, Brancacci Chapel, see Mesnil, bibl. 325). Ghiberti may have revitalized this type by direct reference to one of the Venus statues of the Medici type known to him (see above, p. 287) and note 17.

However, he fused this gesture into an overall design drawn from a dancing maenad beating the tambourin on the S. Maria Maggiore sarcophagus, see above item 26 (Fig. 125). Eve's right leg (missing from the knee down in the model but presumably identical in position), the strong, hipshot stance and the outline of chest, abdomen, and thigh correspond in reverse; the slant of the shoulders, the slimness of the body, the tiny breasts, correspond directly to the prototype. Indeed, this maenad is reflected even more immediately in Vittorio Ghiberti's figure of Eve on the frame of the Andrea Pisano door (Fig. 128), in original position, veil and all. Also, in that later variant, Eve adopts *one* of the gestures of the *Venus Pudica*, the hand at the breast, which had been altered in Lorenzo's design.

Both Lorenzo's and Vittorio's Eves thus are variants of one maenad of which a drawing must have existed in the workshop, but both add different gestures of the *Venus Pudica*.

The dancing step of the Eve in the Expulsion at first glance recalls the *entrechat* of a restored satyr right of center on the same S. Maria Maggiore sarcophagus. But this figure already at the time of Polidoro da Caravaggio was missing except for part of one foot (Degenhart, bibl. 120), and this indicates a different pose. Thus the stance of Ghiberti's figure is either a free invention or derived from an unknown prototype.

For curiosity's sake it should be mentioned

that in the Wolfegg drawing of the sarcophagus, f. 32v (Figs. 125, 126), a male dancer to the left of the dressed maenad has been transformed into a female bacchante, covering the *pudenda* with her right hand in the gesture of a *Venus Pudica* and with her feet crossed, much like Ghiberti's Eve. This is one of several instances where Ghiberti's and the draughtsman's variants on the antique strangely coincide.

CAIN AND ABEL

28. *Abel slain* (Pl. 86a). Possibly a Trecento type, revitalized by direct reference to an antique prototype.

Abel, toppling forward, and Cain, swinging the club with both hands from behind, are presented in postures not infrequent in medieval art, e.g. Bartolo di Fredi, Old Testament scenes, S. Gimignano, Collegiata (Fig. 81; observation by Miss Mary Ann Rukavina, Institute of Fine Arts, New York University). Ghiberti's Abel, however, supporting himself on one arm with his back curved, his knee pushed forward, the toe of his other foot bent, is drawn in reverse from the collapsing Dacian in the foreground of one of the Trajanic battle reliefs inside the Arch of Constantine (Fig. 131). The barbarian in that relief is damaged, but the break on the right side of the head suggests that originally, like Abel, he may have protected his head with his free hand. Cf. already the drawing by Antonio Federighi, Munich, Graphische Sammlung, no. 36909 (Degenhart, bibl. 123, p. 136, fig. 49), where the right arm is broken, and Piero della Francesca's Battle of Constantine (Warburg, bibl. 545, I, pp. 253ff).

29. *Abel watching his flock* (Pl. 85). Variant on antique shepherd from a sarcophagus, possibly of the Endymion group, or variant on the servant in the Abraham relief, see below item 36.

30. *Cain ploughing* (Pl. 87). Derived from a ploughing peasant on a Roman relief.

While the motif existed all through the Middle Ages among the Labors of the Months, it was presented with new emphasis on an antique prototype in Andrea Pisano's relief of Agriculture, Florence, Campanile (Paatz, bibl. 375, III, p. 191; the comparison with Etruscan terracotta groups is untenable). Ghiberti's design, however, is derived directly from a Roman model, such as the ploughman among the reliefs with rustic scenes, lost, drawing Dal Pozzo, Windsor, no. 8053 (Vermeule-Catalogue), (Fig. 130), or the small figures of a ploughman with oxen frequent on Season sar-

cophagi below the medallion of the deceased; the best example known was formerly in the Giustiniani collection (Galleria Giustiniani, bibl. 183, II, pl. 100; Hanfmann, bibl. 206, II, chapter III, note 82).

NOAH

31. *Noah's shame* (Pl. 90). Noah, his body slightly raised on the right elbow, his right leg flexed forward, his left one raised and sharply bent, his left arm resting on his left thigh, is close to Bartolo di Fredi's Noah in the Old Testament cycle, S. Gimignano, Collegiata (Fig. 82; observation Miss Mary Ann Rukavina, Fine Arts Institute, New York University). Similarities include the position of the prostrate body and the pose of the legs, which are not crossed but form a kind of rhomboid pattern.

However, the languid pose of Ghiberti's Noah, his nakedness, his head and its position, reminiscent of the antique, turned towards the beholder and resting on his right shoulder, and finally the drinking bowl, recall the drunken Silenus on Bacchic sarcophagi, who is either carried on a skin, e.g. Ny-Carlsberg (Poulsen, bibl. 424, no. 777a), and Villa Medici (Cagiano de Azevado, bibl. 83; drawing Wolfegg, f. 48, then in the Della Valle collection, Mrs. Bober-Census); or drawn on a chariot, e.g. Naples, Museo Nazionale (Pietrograade, bibl. 399, fig. 10, similar to the drawings Coburgensis, f. 112, Matz, bibl. 310, no. 128, and Dosio Berolinensis, f. 13v, Hülsen, bibl. 225, pl. XIX).

Still, the differences remain considerable: in all antique examples the body is obese, the legs are crossed, the face utterly different. No exact prototype can be determined.

32. *Animals leaving Ark: elephant* (Pl. 89). The diamond pattern of the elephant is a device frequently used to indicate a net covering the elephant on Roman sarcophagi. We are indebted to Prof. Karl Lehmann for this suggestion.

Obviously no precise prototype can be established, but one might think of the large sarcophagus with the Indian triumph of Bacchus, now Rome, Palazzo Rospigliosi, in the early sixteenth century at S. Lorenzo f.l.m. (Wolfegg, f. 36v, f. 37); see below, item 39.

33. *Noah's wife in front of the Ark* (Pl. 104a). Noah's wife, second from the right, is undoubtedly drawn from the bride in a marriage scene, possibly the one on the Fieschi sarcophagus (see above, item 5). Aside from her right arm, outstretched rather than descending to grasp the hand of the groom, and the backward movement of her head, her stance is identical: seen in three-quarter view, her right foot forward, left leg slightly bent, she clasps an end of the cloak with her left hand.

34. *Noah's Sacrifice: woman seen from back* (Pl. 92). Derived from a figure, Rome, Forum of Nerva (*le colonacce*), Minerva frieze (Fig. 129).

Ghiberti's figure, slightly turned to the left, is shown advancing toward the scene, her right heel raised slightly, her right leg showing plainly through the garments, her left leg hidden by vertical folds, her cloak, gathered in a roll around the waist, her dress pulled from the shoulders toward the waist in triangular folds. The general pose as well as the fall of the drapery appear almost identically in the female figure seen from the back on the Minerva frieze (Blankenhagen, bibl. 55, no. 41), despite the stiff, angular stance of the Roman figure, the different pose of her left arm, the coarser treatment of her draperies, and the poorer quality of workmanship.

The frieze was famous all through the Middle Ages, occasionally known as *Arca Noe* (Urlichs, bibl. 527, p. 140 and *passim*).

35. *Noah's Sacrifice: Noah's son, right edge* (Pl. 92). Derived from a sarcophagus illustrating the private life of a Roman official, Los Angeles County Museum (Feinblatt, bibl. 157, figs. 1, 9, 11), in the early sixteenth century in the atrium of St. Peter's (Wolfegg, f. 25v, 26, 27v, 28).

Ghiberti's figure is a variant in reverse on the *moira* (Figs. 132, 133), assisting at the birth of a baby, on the right short side of the sarcophagus. (For the iconographical interpretation of the *moira* see Brendel, bibl. 67, p. 1ff.)

Ghiberti's figure raises his hands in prayer, his left arm is bare, the tunic fastened on the shoulder. The mantle is draped around his left hip and leg in deep folds and falls forward over the right shoulder in a cascade. He shares with the *moira* the general pose, the movement of the arms and the fall of the mantle over the shoulder. The *moira*, however, hidden, as she stands behind the kneeling nurse in the foreground on the sarcophagus, shows little of the abundant drapery which envelop both hip and leg of Noah's son.

Curiously enough, the drawing in the Wolfegg sketchbook represents the *moira* with drapery not unlike that of Noah's son (Fig. 133) and thus shows again an interpretation very close to Ghiberti's. Also it shows her as a flute player, mistaking the compass for a *tibia* and thus with both arms half-raised almost

identical to the praying gesture of Ghiberti's figure.

ABRAHAM

36. *Servant, seated, right edge* (Pl. 91a). The servant is seated low on a rock, his legs crossed, his hands holding a crook (now missing), dressed in a short sleeveless tunic, and mantle which follows his back in a long fold.

He is derived from an antique shepherd on a sarcophagus, probably of the Endymion group.

A variation of this figure is Abel, watching his flock, see above, item 29.

ISAAC

37. *Group of visiting women* (Pl. 97a). The four women are shown, one walking in from the left, one seen from the back, one standing relaxed to the right with her left hand resting on the shoulder of the one in the middle; the fourth woman, in the background between left and center figures, is so inobtrusive as to be easily overlooked. The grouping of the three others vaguely recalls the Three Graces in Siena and similar groups. Indeed, the Siena Graces, while first recorded visually around 1480 (Antonio Federighi, Munich, Graphische Sammlung, no. 36909; Degenhart, bibl. 123, fig. 48; Salis, bibl. 459, pp. 154ff, pp. 259ff) and then owned by Cardinal Francesco Piccolomini, came from the collection of Cardinal Francesco Colonna (Egger, bibl. 139, I, pp. 106f) and may have been known as early as 1425. However, the similarity between Ghiberti's women visitors and the Three Graces, based mainly on the center figure seen from the back, is probably accidental. On the other hand, there can be no doubt, that Botticelli based his three dancing Graces in the *Primavera* both on the literary image of the Three Graces "dancing, holding hands and clad in transparent drapery" as transmitted by Alberti and Seneca (Warburg, bibl. 545, I, pp. 29f and note 3; Gombrich, bibl. 189, pp. 30ff) and on the visual image of Ghiberti's group of women in the *Isaac* (see, however, Salis, *op. cit.*). Hence, to Botticelli, Ghiberti's group recalled the antique type as described by Alberti and Seneca.

38. *Visitors' group: woman carrying basket* (Pl. 97a). A woman carrying a basket on her head is traditional in Trecento painting among the visitors to Anna or Elizabeth lying in. The type, however, has been transposed by Ghiberti into a more or less free variation on an antique theme, for example, a figure of Selene on an Endymion sarcophagus, such as:

a) Rome, Palazzo Giustiniani (Robert, bibl. 448, III, 1, no. 78; Rizzo, bibl. 446, pls. VII-VIII, 3); drawing by Dosio, Berolinensis, f. 12 (Hülsen, bibl. 225, pl. XVI), (Fig. 135).

b) lost (?) sarcophagus, in the mid-sixteenth century at Palazzo Colonna (Robert, bibl. 448, III, 1, no. 86). Drawings: Oxford sketchbook, attributed to Jacopo Ripanda (information, Mrs. Bober-Census); Dosio, Berolinensis, f. 9 (Hülsen, bibl. 225, pl. XII).

Details comparable to the Selene are seen in the profile view, the double-belted chiton, the lively, sharp drapery folds of the overhanging peplum, the pose of the right arm, the veil, clutched in the right hand, crossing the forearm and billowing out in back. The step, the movement of the skirt, the left hand and the veil crossing the legs are different. Ghiberti's variant must be viewed together with another variant of his, a prophetess, based on Selene and a maenad (Pl. 125a; see below, item 54).

39. Visitors' group: woman seen from back (Pl. 97a). The woman steps briskly forward on her left leg, her right heel is raised. Her body turns to the left in a lithe movement, her face is seen in one-quarter view only, the hair taken up in a bun. Only her left arm is visible. She wears what appears to be a fifteenth century dress, long and unbelted, which glides in serpentine folds over the back and ends in zigzag drapery over her left leg. The figure seems to be a free variant on a yet unidentified antique prototype, possibly the priestess (?) seen from the back who recurs time and again on sarcophagi with the Indian Triumph of Bacchus. Among examples known to the fifteenth century, the figure at the right edge of the Rospigliosi sarcophagus (Fig. 137; see above, item 32), despite differences in drapery, may be compared to Ghiberti's visiting woman in the lithe curve of her stance, one hip protruding, her step, with one heel slightly raised, and her upper left arm pressed close to her body.

40. Visitors' group: woman to the right (Pl. 97a). The figure, in profile, bends her head slightly forward, the sleeveless dress held by a round *fibula* on her shoulder. A small veil frames the back and hangs over her left elbow. Her cloak has slipped off the hip and envelops her legs, while another part falls forward in a long cascade over her right shoulder.

Pose and dress are generally reminiscent of muses and related female allegories, but Ghiberti's figure appears rather to be a variation in reverse on the *moira* from the Los Angeles sarcophagus (Figs. 132, 133; see items 35 and 55). Both share the profile pose, including the slight slant of the leg below the curving folds

of the cloak, the bare arms, and the general type of head and arrangement of hair. The small veil and the elaboration of the lower part of the drapery are Ghiberti's own additions.

41. Blessing of Jacob: Rebecca (Pl. 97b). The mourning pose, while frequent throughout the Middle Ages (Shorr, bibl. 493) is permeated in Ghiberti's design by genuinely antique features reminiscent of female mourners of antiquity, *Pudicitia* and others: the stance, the belted peplum, the pose of the arms, the left one crossing below the breast, the hand bent down, the right raised to support the cheek, the head covered, the left leg strongly protruding through the garment, the right leg hidden behind vertical folds.

Among possible prototypes known to the Renaissance only a few compare, such as:

a) sister of Meleager, though with uncovered head, from a relief with the Death of Meleager, Villa Albani, Coffeehouse, formerly Palazzo della Valle (Coburgensis, f. 99, Matz, bibl. 310, no. 224; Robert, bibl. 448, III, 2, no. 278).

b) Iphigenia from a *cippus* showing her sacrifice, now in the Uffizi (Fig. 134), originally at Giardino di Castello and thus probably an old Medici possession (Duetschke, bibl. 136, III, no. 165). Similar are the stance, the covered head, the pose of the right arm, the bent left hand, and the stance of both legs and the drapery. The differences are minor: Iphigenia's peplum runs horizontally, instead of sloping; her left arm is held likewise horizontally and partly covered by the gown which slides from the shoulders.

JOSEPH

42. Discovery of the Cup: mourning brother (Pl. 98). Free variant on mourner from a Gathering-in of Meleager (Fig. 138), now lost, but evidently known in the early fifteenth century (Coburgensis, f. 70, Matz, bibl. 310, no. 227; Robert, bibl. 448, III, 2, no. 286).

The pose of the man, his head hidden in the folds of the cloak raised up to his face, and the fall of the cloak in large cascades, is a free variant on the figure of a mourner following the body of Meleager. Donatello seems to have used this sarcophagus and the one in Wilton House in his tabernacle at St. Peter's. (For the latter suggestion, see Robert, bibl. 448, III, 2, no. 275.)

43. Woman with bundle and small boy (Pl. 99). Variant on two figures from a Medea sarcophagus. The woman in a sleeveless, double-belted chiton gathers her skirt with her right hand. Her head is turned slightly downward and to the side. A veil crosses her breast and right arm. A small boy, walking ahead of her, toward the right, his head turned back, his short tunic lifted, carries provisions. The position of the two figures recalls a Medea sarcophagus, now lost (fragment, Turin, Museum; Duetschke, bibl. 136, IV, no. 12; Robert, bibl. 448, II, nos. 190, 190′), but known from the Coburgensis, f. 32 (Matz, bibl. 310, no. 214) (Fig. 136).

a) Medea approaching the wedding ceremony of Jason and Cresilla, running and lifting her skirt, followed by her two children, is similar to Ghiberti's woman in the turn of the head and the stance, her skirt gathered in a bundle of lively folds. Another variant on the Medea appears in the Zenobius Shrine, see item 67.

Gruenwald (bibl. 195, pp. 150ff) had suggested as a prototype for Ghiberti a Hora, balancing a pail on her head with her raised left arm. Her right arm lifts her skirt, as she appears on a *cippus* at Este, Museo Nazionale Atestino, prior to 1653 at Padua (Ursatus, bibl. 374, p. 261; Callegari, bibl. 84, p. 65).

b) "Camillus," carrying sacrificial fruits, preceding Medea, but belonging to the wedding scene of the same sarcophagus. Ghiberti has fused this motif with that of one of Medea's children bringing presents to her, from another class of Medea sarcophagi, of which several were known to the Renaissance, among them the sarcophagus drawn in Coburgensis, f. 42 (Fig. 146), now Rome, Museo delle Terme; see item 66. Similar to the child in the *Joseph* is the forward movement of Medea's son, the position of his arms and the uncovering of legs and abdomen.

MOSES

44. *Passage through the Red Sea: dancing maiden* (Pl. 103). Derived from the figure of Venus, Adonis sarcophagus, Rome, Palazzo Rospigliosi (Fig. 122); see item 24.

The maiden is clad in a double-belted chiton; behind her back a veil billows, which she grasps with both hands. The running pose, the skirt flaring over the leg and the billowing veil recall the figure on the Rospigliosi sarcophagus. The outstretched pose of the left arm is different in the antique relief.

45. *Terrified warrior, right foreground* (Pl. 102). The pose, especially the wide step of the legs, is a variation on Adam in the Expulsion who, in turn, is derived from the Bacchic sarcophagus from S. Maria Maggiore, see item 26.

46. *Man, hiding face, right foreground* (Pl. 104b). Derived from the figure of a mourner

walking behind Meleager's body, Meleager sarcophagus (Fig. 141), Rome, Villa Doria Panfili (Robert, bibl. 448, III, 2, no. 283), traceable at least to the first half of the sixteenth century. Excellent work, badly restored. The earliest drawing preserved, by an anonymous artist, first half of the sixteenth century, is a composite of several sarcophagi, incorporated into Dal Pozzo, British Museum, I, f. 81 (Robert, bibl. 448, III, 2, no. 278″); among later drawings one, attributed to Salvatore Rosa, Uffizi, no. 895 (Robert, bibl. 448, III, 2, no. 283′) is the most important.

Despite minor differences the gesture of Ghiberti's figure corresponds exactly to that of the mourner covering his face with his right hand, while clutching his cloak with his left. The gesture appears also on other Meleager sarcophagi but none is as close to Ghiberti's variant as is the Panfili example. Further proof for Ghiberti's use of this specific sarcophagus lies in his having drawn on it for two other figures, see items 49 and 50.

JOSHUA

47. *Horses of Quadriga* (Pl. 109). Derived from Quadriga, Pelops sarcophagus, Brussels, Museum (Fig. 103), (Robert, bibl. 448, III, 3, no. 329) or an exact replica; see also item 2.

The horses are all of similar type—wild, with windblown manes, slender muzzles, open mouths, without bridles, and only held by belts across their chests. They are seen, the first in three-quarter view, the second almost *en face*, the third in profile, the fourth fully frontal.

Although quadriga horses on Roman sarcophagi are frequent, this complicated composition occurs only in the Fall of Oenomaus to the right on the Brussels sarcophagus. There are only slight differences in the pose of the first two horses.

48. *Girl, second from left, foreground* (Pl. 107). The girl, in a double-belted chiton, her right hand holding the drapery of her cloak, her left hand raised in wonder, is possibly a variation on the dancing maiden from the *Moses*, see item 44.

49. *Man, carrying rock in his hands* (Pl. 108a). Variant on servant, Meleager sarcophagus, Rome, Villa Doria Panfili; see items 46 and 50 (Fig. 141).

The bearded man in Ghiberti's relief stands with both feet firmly planted on the ground, his knees slightly flexed; he carries a rock with both hands. His pose, the position of his hands and even his footgear correspond to the figure of the man who, in the Panfili sarcophagus, carries the shoulders of Meleager. His head, helmeted on the sarcophagus, is modern, as witness the unrestored drawing, Uffizi, no. 895.

The identification of this figure was made by Mr. Joseph Polzer in a seminar report in 1952, at the Institute of Fine Arts, New York University.

50. *Man carrying rock on shoulders* (Pl. 108b). Copied from servant, Meleager sarcophagus, Rome, Villa Doria Panfili (Fig. 141), see items 46 and 49.

The man in a short tunic bends forward carrying the rock on his head and shoulders, with his arms bent backward and upward. His right leg placed securely on the ground, is flexed at the knee; the left leg set back, with the foot seen *en face*, touches the ground with the toes only. The pose is copied from the servant on the Panfili sarcophagus, carrying the feet of Meleager (the legs are restored except for the left foot, seen *en face*, but their position can be ascertained through the drawing, Uffizi, no. 895). The servant's right arm and shoulder are naked; the line of the edge of the tunic baring his shoulder is recognizable in a big drapery fold across the back of Ghiberti's figure.

51. *Youth in female dress, seen from back* (Pl. 108b). The very contrast between the female double-belted peplum and the young man's head suggests an antique prototype for garment and stance of the figure. The pose, the right foot lifted and the windblown drapery have led to a comparison (Meyer-Weinschel, bibl. 327, p. 25) with bronze statuettes of victories such as those at Cassel (Bieber, bibl. 51, no. 153). While a statue of this type in 1457 was in the collection of Cardinal Pietro Barbo (Ministero della Pubblica Istruzione, bibl. 338, I, p. 5; Mrs. Bober-Census), Ghiberti's figure recalls more closely a dancing maenad from a Bacchic sarcophagus, such as the one, now at Arbury Hall, Newdgate Collection, England, which was known as early as the sixteenth century (Coburgensis, f. 52, Matz, bibl. 310, no. 146; Dal Pozzo, Windsor, no. 8012, Vermeule-Catalogue), (Fig. 139).

DAVID

52. *Warrior seen from back, center* (Pl. 114a). Barbarian battle sarcophagus, probably the one Rome, Villa Borghese (Fig. 113), formerly at St. Peter's, see items 13, 14, 15, 64.

Pose and garment of Ghiberti's warrior are nearly identical with those of a barbarian, fourth from the left, on the Borghese sarcophagus: the legs far apart, the right arm close to the body, the muscles of the calves sharply

marked, the pants hanging in loose folds, the short tunic with sleeves fastened with a belt. The head of the barbarian in the Borghese sarcophagus is missing; in the drawing Wolfegg f. 30v (see item 13) he is bareheaded, while Ghiberti's warrior wears a turban.

The half destroyed battle sarcophagus at the Camposanto in Pisa (see above, item 13), would appear to have contained a corresponding figure. Bertoldo's bronze copy shows him nude, but in a similar pose and the original still shows traces of the feet and of the shield.

FRAME

53. *Samson* (Pl. 127b). Variation on two antique prototypes.

The left leg of the Samson is pushed forward, the knee bent, the right hip thrust outward, the body lithe and muscular; the right arm coming downward, holds the ass's jawbone, the left arm is raised and embraces the column. Hair and beard are formed by tight curls, the face is small. A large veil, falling over the left shoulder and enveloping the right leg, frames the figure. The Samson recalls:

a) bronze statuettes of Zeus holding the scepter in the raised left hand and thunderbolt in the right, such as Paris, Bibl. Nat., Cabinet des Medailles, no. 14 (Babelon-Blanchet, bibl. 29, p. 8), New York, Metropolitan Museum, (Poseidon[?]), (Richter, bibl. 444, no. 20), Cassel, (Bieber, bibl. 51, no. 129), Munich, private collection (Fig. 143). Such a statuette is described in 1457 in the collection of Cardinal Barbo (Mrs. Bober-Census), Ministero della Pubblica Istruzione, bibl. 338, I, p. 4);

b) in contrast Samson leans against the column, hip thrust out sharply; also the veil is no attribute of Zeus. These departures recall the drunken Dionysos on the Bacchic sarcophagus in the Vatican (Fig. 144), (Amelung, bibl. 20, II, no. 102, pl. 24), a monument drawn by Pisanello and his circle after the 1420's (Degenhart, bibl. 122, pp. 24ff, fig. 30; *idem*, bibl. 121, pp. 7ff, figs. 15, 16).

A Samson remarkably close to Ghiberti's was drawn by Jacopo Bellini (V. Golubev, *Die Skizzenbücher des Jacopo Bellini*, Brussels, 1908-12, II, pl. LXXXVII).

54. *Prophetess* (Pl. 125a). Ghiberti's figure is a variation on two antique types.

In her main features the prophetess recalls a) the figure of a maenad from a Bacchic sarcophagus, now lost (?), formerly Rome, Palazzo Gentili (photograph German Archeological Institute, Rome, no. 36. 631; drawing Dal

Pozzo, Windsor, no. 8649, Vermeule-Catalogue), (Fig. 140).

The two figures share the frontal pose, the flaring peplum of the belted chiton, the forward position of the right leg in a dancing movement, and the fluttering drapery alongside the leg. The right leg of the maenad is naked and the lines of her skirt baring her leg can still be discerned in the drapery of Ghiberti's prophetess.

Combined with this prototype are elements from b) Selene, alighting from her chariot on an Endymion sarcophagus such as the one from the Giustiniani Collection, or the lost one, known through sixteenth century drawings, see above, item 38.

Comparable are the position of the bare arms and the movement of the veil. Held by the right hand and crossing the forearm in both Selene examples as well as in Ghiberti's prophetess and in the Visiting Woman (above, item 38) the veil in the two Ghiberti figures is drawn across the thighs, while Selene held it high over her head with her left hand. In the prophetess, this raised left arm and hand, devoid of the original meaning have been transformed into an admonishing gesture.

55. *Male prophet with raised arm* (Pl. 126a). Variation on both the *moira* from the Los Angeles sarcophagus, and the son of Noah, derived from her; see above, items 35 and 40 (Figs. 132, 133).

The prophet is clad in the sleeveless chiton of the *moira* and in her massive cloak which envelops his right hip in deep folds and falls down over his left shoulder in a cascade.

56. *Prophetess (Hannah?)*, (Pl. 127a). Mourning woman, exact prototype unidentified. Ghiberti's prophetess is similar to a figure drawn by Heemskerk as a statue, but probably part of a relief (Hülsen-Egger, bibl. 226, II, f. 65, pl. 92, p. 40).

The covered shoulders and the fall of the drapery from the right arm are comparable, the drapery to the left different.

57. *Miriam* (Pl. 129a). Derived from a maenad with tambourin on a Bacchic sarcophagus. There are countless tambourin-playing maenads on Bacchic sarcophagi; the exact pose of the Miriam, however, is less frequent. It occurs among examples known to the sixteenth century, on the Blenheim sarcophagus (Coburgensis, f. 119; Matz, bibl. 310, no. 142), and, even more similar on a lost Bacchic sarcophagus (Coburgensis, f. 195; Matz, bibl. 310, no. 140), some remnants of which are preserved in Rome, Villa Aldobrandini (Matz-Duhn, bibl. 311, II, no. 2265), (Fig. 145). The Miriam

shares with the maenad the three-quarter view of the body, combined with the frontal view of the face; the forward step of the legs, combined with the backward movement from the waist up; the movement of both arms, one arm crossing the breast; the position of both hands, holding the tambourin; the pose of both legs, the right one strongly emphasized in volume; the stance of the dancing feet; the windblown folds of the peplum and the skirt, ending in hornlike triangles; finally, the veil, crossing the right arm, billowing behind the head with the fluttering end trailing behind. The differences are all minor and mainly concern the pose of the feet. Ghiberti's figure crosses her feet in the dancing *entrechat* (cf. his Eve, see above, item 27). A third similar maenad appeared on a (lost) Bacchic sarcophagus (Coburgensis, f. 53, Matz, bibl. 310, no. 144), but there the lower parts of the body are hidden by a little satyr.

58. *Adam* (Pl. 123a). Variation on a river god or Oceanus of a type frequent also on sarcophagi, e.g. Paris sarcophagus, Rome, Villa Medici (Robert, bibl. 448, II, no. 11; Cagiano de Azevado, bibl. 83, p. 54, fig. 43), a sarcophagus frequently drawn upon in the Renaissance.

Ghiberti's *Adam*, half seated, leans with his left arm on a bundle of leaves, tied by a band in the form of a vessel. He is naked from the abdomen up, the muscles of his chest and abdomen are strongly marked. Under the mantle, his right leg is crossed over his left one. His right elbow rests on his hip, his hand, slightly raised above the thigh, holds a hoe. The god in the Paris sarcophagus is seated in almost the same pose and even details, such as the left hand falling over the opening of the amphora, are close. But gods of this type are so frequent that the one on the Medici sarcophagus can serve only as a typical example.

59. *Eve* (Pl. 122a). Derived from a Sienese Trecento prototype revitalized by direct reversion to a reclining figure of Gaia, of the type known from the Phaeton sarcophagus, Florence; see above, item 3.

Eve is supporting herself on her right elbow, her right leg stretched out in front, her left knee sharply raised; her left hand rests on her raised knee, holding a fig branch. She is fully dressed and a goat's skin covers her shoulders.

Gaia is not too frequently represented on Roman sarcophagi in exactly this position. Usually she has her legs crossed. She appears, however, in a pose similar to Ghiberti's Eve on the Phaeton sarcophagus from Florence Cathedral. Ghiberti probably had seen this sarcophagus in his youth and he may have made drawings. But the resemblances are not close enough for specific identification and Ghiberti may have drawn as well on another similar Gaia, from an unidentified sarcophagus.

60. *Noah* (Pl. 122b). Free variant on an unidentified antique prototype.

The reclining pose and the crossed, draped legs recall a river god such as the Marforio, now Rome, Capitoline Museum (Jones, bibl. 234, p. 21, no. 1, pl. I), formerly near S. Martina e Luca. Yet the fat body, the bald head, the short upturned nose and the stringy beard recall equally a Silenus, reclining in a similar pose; see above, item 31.

61. *Noah's wife* (*Puarphera*), (Pl. 123b). Derived from a figure of Gaia of the type known from a partly lost Proserpina sarcophagus (Wolfegg, f. 36v, 37; Fig. 142), remnants Paris, Louvre (Robert, bibl. 448, III, 3, no. 359). In the early fifteenth century the sarcophagus was at SS. Cosma e Damiano in Rome and used even earlier as a fountain (Robert, *loc.cit.*).

Noah's wife is leaning on her left arm, her right hand lying loosely across her body, her right leg crossing her left one and shown *en face*, in a mannered pose, her head in profile, looking down. This is exactly the pose of Gaia on the Proserpina sarcophagus, except for the nakedness of Gaia's bust and the more natural position of her crossed legs.

Botticelli in his Venus and Mars panel (London, National Gallery) while undoubtedly influenced by a relief in the Vatican (Tietze-Conrat, bibl. 519, fig. 173; Gombrich, bibl. 189, p. 47), again reverts to Ghiberti in the mannered pose of the frontally depicted left forward leg, a feature not contained in his antique model.

62. *Head* (Pl. 133a). The classical features and the long locks crowned with an elaborate wreath of vine leaves and flowers, seem to be derived from a Dionysos. Exact prototype unidentified.

63. *Head* (Pl. 132b). The sinister-looking, sharply molded head with its shock of bushy hair is probably derived from the head of a satyr. Exact prototype unidentified.

64. *Head* (Pl. 131e). Derived from a barbarian female prisoner, possibly the one on the Borghese sarcophagus (Fig. 118), see items 13ff, 52.

The head with unruly hair, one long curl dangling over the right shoulder, a shorter one over the left shoulder, is derived from a female prisoner on a battle sarcophagus. The three strands of upswept hair above the center of the forehead occur among extant battle sarcophagi only on the Borghese sarcophagus, and only in the prisoner to the right.

65. *Head* (Pl. 131d). Derived from a barbarian prisoner, probably from a battle sarcophagus. Exact prototype unidentified.

ZENOBIUS SHRINE, MAIN PANEL

66. *Two children following woman, left edge of panel* (Pl. 79a). The two boys, the first in three-quarter view, his right arm stretched forward, the second in frontal position, his head turned toward his companion, his arm also stretched forward, are variations on one of the two children of Medea bringing presents to her. Thus they appear, with a minimum of clothing, on several Medea sarcophagi. The closest one, formerly Stamperia Reale, now at the Museo delle Terme (Fig. 146), (Robert, bibl. 448, no. 199, 199') was in the mid-sixteenth century at SS. Cosma e Damiano (Coburgensis, f. 42; Matz, bibl. 310, no. 216) and already drawn in all likelihood in the fifteenth century (Milan, Ambrosiana, F237, 1707v, attributed to the circle of Pisanello; Degenhart, bibl. 120).

The same sarcophagus was used before by Ghiberti, see item 43b.

67. *Woman with child clutching her skirt* (Pl. 79a). Variant on Medea sarcophagus, see item 43a (Fig. 136).

The woman is seen in three-quarter view, her head turned back and downward. She wears a dress with an apronlike unbelted overhang; her right leg is marked underneath the garment, her left one hidden. With her right hand, she lifts the apron in an unmotivated gesture. A veil billows behind her shoulder and crosses the right arm. A child, scantily dressed in a short skirt and turning his head back toward the two other children (see item 66), clutches her skirt. The intricacies of Ghiberti's variations on antique themes are obvious in this group. In her pose, the movement of her right arm and head, the apron slightly lifted, the woman recalls the figure of Medea approaching Jason and Cresilla on the Medea sarcophagus (Coburgensis, f. 32). The child clinging to her skirt also may be compared with this model.

On the other hand, the fall of the heavy draperies gathered in Medea's hand, which Ghiberti copies in the drapery of the woman with the bundle in the Joseph panel (see above, item 43a), he has interpreted very differently in the Zenobius Shrine. The strongly marked right leg and the billowing veil likewise depart from Medea; they may be derived from any number of other antique models which Ghiberti is known to have used.

68. *Woman seen from back* (Pl. 78a). The woman is a variant on the woman seen from the back in the Noah panel; see above, item 34 (Fig. 129).

APPENDIX B

GHIBERTI'S CALENDAR OF OLYMPIADS

THIS appendix is intended for hardy souls only. Acquaintance with its contents is not required for an understanding of the book although the results, as minor elements, have been carried over into the interpretation of Ghiberti's life and of his outlook on history.

One of the headaches in interpreting Ghiberti's *Commentarii*,[1] is caused by what seems at first but a queer fad of his; that is, his substitution of a chronology of olympiads for the years of the Christian era. The obvious source for his olympiadic calendar was, as pointed out by Schlosser, Pliny's *Natural History*. Together with other information on Greek and Roman art Ghiberti literally incorporated into the first book of his *Commentarii* Pliny's dates given in years of a genuine Greek calendar of olympiads, starting in 776 B.C. and covering four years each. Yet, the difficulty starts when Ghiberti applies, in the Second and Third Commentary a calendar of olympiads which apparently does not follow a four year cycle and moreover asserts that his starting point is the foundation of Rome, a date placed by all writers of the Renaissance and by most ancient historians in 753 B.C.[2] Scattered through the history of art from Constantine to his own time Ghiberti indicates five events which he connects with this chronology of olympiads of his own.

1. The period of the *maniera greca*, the italo-byzantine style, coincides with olympiad 382. "Finita che fu l'arte (under Constantine) stettero e templi bianchi circa d'anni 600. Cominciorono i Greci debilissimamente l'arte della pictura et con molto roçeza produssero in essa . . . Dalla edificatione di Roma furono olimpie 382." (After the art [of antiquity] had come to an end, the churches stood whitewashed for about 600 years. [Then] the Greeks began very weakly the art of painting and with great crudeness produced in it. . . . This was 382 olympiads from the building of Rome.)[3]

2. Bonamico-Buffalmacco works until olympiad 408. "Fece moltissimi lavorij a moltissimi signori per insino alla olimpia 408 (418?), fiorì (in?) Etruria molto egregiamente. . . ."

(He executed a great many works for very many gentlemen; he flourished outstandingly in Etruria until the 408th [418th?] olympiad.)[4]

3. Andrea Pisano's activity coincides with olympiad 410. "Fu grandissimo statuario fu nella olimpia 410 (420?)." (He was a very great sculptor; he lived in the 410th [420th?] olympiad.)[5]

4. Gusmin, the Cologne sculptor, died in olympiad 438, at the time of Pope Martin, who occupied the papal see from 1417 to 1431. ". . . finì al tempo di papa Martino. . . . era docto et fini nella olimpia 438." (He died at the time of Pope Martin. . . . Skilled he was and he died in the 438th olympiad.)[6]

5. In olympiad 440 Ghiberti visited Rome and saw the statue of a hermaphrodite being excavated. ". . . vidi in Roma nella olimpia quattrocento quaranta una statua d'uno Ermafrodito di grandeza d'una fanciulla . . . fu trovata in una chiavica . . . sopra a sancto Celso, in detto lato si fermò uno scultore fece trarre fuori detta statua et condussela a sancta Cecilia in Trastevere oue (el) scultore lauroraua una sepultura d'uno cardinale. . . ." (I saw in Rome in the 440th olympiad a statue of a hermaphrodite of the size of a girl. It was found in a sewer . . . above S. Celso. A sculptor stopped in this locality, he had the statue drawn forth and brought it to S. Cecilia in Trastevere where the sculptor worked on the tomb of a cardinal and he had marble removed from it to make it easier to carry it into our territory [Florence].)[7]

Whatever they are, Ghiberti's olympiads cannot correspond to the genuine four-year cycle of the Greek calendar. Even if we put faith in his assurance that he calculated from the foundation of Rome in 753 B.C. rather than from 776 B.C., a calculation of olympiads of four years' length would result in such non-sensical dates as, for example, 1756-1760 *ab urbe condita* equal to 1003-1007 for Ghiberti's visit to Rome (4 x 439 – 753).

Several solutions have been suggested to solve the puzzle. Hermanin[8] proposed that possibly Ghiberti made two mistakes in his

---

[1] Ghiberti-Schlosser, bibl. 178, II, pp. 108f.

[2] *ibid.*, I, p. 35.   [3] *ibid.*

[4] *ibid.*, I, p. 38f. Schlosser has suggested correcting the date 408 to 418 and inserting *in* between *fiorì* and *Etruria*; see also, below, pp. 354, 357.

[5] *ibid.*, I, p. 43; and II, p. 164 with the substitution of

420 for 410; see also, below, p. 354.

[6] *ibid.*, I, p. 44.

[7] *ibid.*, I, pp. 61f. Schlosser had originally read *scultura* for *sepultura*, but restored the correct reading in bibl. 477, p. 159.

[8] Hermanin, bibl. 209, pp. 8of.

calculations: first, that contrary to his assertation, Ghiberti started his calendar not with 753 B.C., but in the Greek fashion with 776 B.C.; and second, that in his computation he was constantly off one hundred years. Olympiad 440 should really read olympiad 540, thus resulting, if we follow Hermanin, in a date of 1407-1411 for Ghiberti's stay in Rome. Incidentally, Hermanin in proposing this specific date for Ghiberti's visit to Rome evidently used 753 as a starting point, not 776 B.C. as he had promised; had he stuck to 776 B.C. he would have arrived at the impossible date of 1384-1388. The period 1407-1411 seems at first plausible enough for Ghiberti's trip to Rome; yet if extended to the other events mentioned within Ghiberti's chronology of olympiads, Hermanin's calculation leads to absurdities. Gusmin, for example, would have died between 1399 and 1403, if the year 753 was taken as a starting point, or even between 1376 and 1380 assuming the earlier beginning, that is, forty-one to fourteen years before Martin V ascended to the pontificate in 1417. For this and other reasons, Schlosser suggested a different solution: he proposed to calculate Ghiberti's olympiads *ab urbe condita* (753 B.C.), thus accepting Ghiberti's assertion, but to figure them at five rather than four years each.[9]

The results Schlosser obtained on this basis are, to be sure, more convincing than any previous attempts at explanation. Still, questionable points remain.

Ol. 382 = 1157. According to Schlosser this date marks for Ghiberti the beginning of the *maniera greca*. Yet, nowhere does Ghiberti suggest that his olympiad 382 coincides with the beginning of that period. On the contrary, he twice states clearly that the Byzantines "produced their crude paintings at that time."

Ol. 408 = 1287. Ghiberti makes it clear that he identifies this date with the end of Bonamico-Buffalmacco's activity. Since, however, Vasari states that Buffalmacco was born either in 1262 or in 1272 and died in 1340, Schlosser proposed to correct the olympiad figure into 418, thus arriving at a date of 1337-1341. This emendation synchronizes Schlosser's calculation of olympiads with Vasari's account, even though no textual evidence supports the correction.[10]

Ol. 420 = 1347. The passage concerning Andrea Pisano's activity reads olympiad 410 in the only extant manuscript of the *Commentarii*. Since the date 1297 resulting from Schlosser's calculation is meaningless, he suggested the emendation 420, corresponding to 1347, and interpreted it to refer to Andrea's death. Olympiad 420 is, indeed, the reading preserved in the manuscript of the Anonimo Magliabecchiano, whose history of Trecento art is based on Ghiberti's Second Commentary.[11] Schlosser's revision thus appears to be justified. This can, however, hardly be said of his interpretation, for while it is possible, though by no means certain, that the master died in 1348, Ghiberti states clearly that Andrea *lived* in olympiad 420—"fu nella olimpia 420."

Ol. 438 = 1437. Within Schlosser's calculation of olympiads the Cologne sculptor Gusmin would have died in 1437. However, this equation contradicts Ghiberti's explanatory statement that the Cologne master died during the pontificate of Martin V, 1417-1431.[12]

Ol. 440 = 1447. Within Schlosser's scheme this is the time when Ghiberti visited Rome. No other record exists of this voyage. It may have occurred, as Schlosser assumes, after the main work on the Gates of Paradise had been completed in 1447, but any other time in Ghiberti's career would be equally likely.[13]

No doubt, then, Schlosser's calculation of Ghiberti's olympiads at five years each leads to halfway possible solutions; indeed it seems to be the only sensible point of departure for establishing at least a preliminary frame of reference within which to fit both Ghiberti's calendar of olympiads and the corresponding events as recounted by him. However, ingenious though they are, Schlosser's proposals still leave a number of problems unsolved.

Any attempt to solve the puzzle should start from the fact that Ghiberti gives at least one, possibly two, unequivocal clues to his equation of olympiads and years of the Christian era. Olympiad 438 falls within the pontificate of Martin V, that is, some time between 1417 and 1431. If then we assume with Schlosser the length of an olympiad to have been five years, olympiad 438 may have begun in 1412 so as to include at least one year of Martin's pontificate, but not earlier; or it may have begun at the latest in 1431 and ended in 1436, but not later. These dates need but one slight qualification: for of course Ghiberti calculated *stile fiorentino*; that is, in his calendar the year ran from March 25 to March 24. Martin V was elected November 1417, and died February 20, 1431, that is 1430 *stile fiorentino*. The beginning of olympiad 438 then must fall at some time between March 25, 1413, and March 25,

[9] Ghiberti-Schlosser, bibl. 178, II, pp. 108ff.

[10] Vasari-Milanesi, bibl. 533, I, p. 167, and Vasari-Ricci, bibl. 531, I, p. 519, respectively; Ghiberti-Schlosser, bibl. 178, II, pp. 110, 130f.

[11] Ghiberti-Schlosser, bibl. 178, II, pp. 110, 164.

[12] *ibid.*, I, p. 44; II, pp. 110, 165.

[13] *ibid.*, II, p. 110; on p. 187, Schlosser gives the date as 1445.

1430, its end between March 24, 1418, and March 24, 1435.

The second clue is not quite so definite, but it is good enough. Ghiberti suggests that Andrea lived in olympiad 420. It seems not far-fetched to equate this date with that of Andrea's bronze door. The date inscribed on it is 1330, but the documents which Carlo Strozzi excerpted in the seventeenth century from the books of the *Calimala* stress emphatically that Andrea started work in 1329, *stile fiorentino*,[14] and it would not be surprising if Ghiberti was aware of that earlier date. Hence olympiad 420 in his calendar would cover five years somewhere within the period from March 25, 1325 or 1326, to March 24, 1335 or 1336, respectively.

Taking as a basis these two equations, the starting point of Ghiberti's calendar of olympiads can be approximately established. But one point is easily overlooked: by multiplying the figure of the olympiad by five, one arrives at its last year; in order to get its first year, the olympiad figure before multiplication must be reduced by one. Hence, from the first equation, the concordance of the beginning of olympiad 438 with a date between March 25, 1413, and March 25, 1430, and of its end between March 24, 1418, and March 24, 1435, the starting point of Ghiberti's calendar should lie between March 25, 772 B.C. (5 x 437 = 2185 − 1413) and March 24, 755 B.C. (5 x 438 = 2190 − 1435); the second equation, the coincidence of olympiad 420 with a five year period in which either the year 1329 or the year 1330 or both are contained would cut the margin further down to between 770 or 769 B.C. and 766 or 765 B.C. respectively.

The point of departure of Ghiberti's calendar would thus lie somewhere between 772 and 755 B.C. However, this calculation presupposes a correct figuring of olympiads on Ghiberti's part, including the realization that in multiplying the olympiad figure with five he had first to subtract one in order to find its first year. Yet, he possibly made the very natural mistake of assuming that the figure of the olympiad times five marked the *first* year of the respective period; Schlosser and Hermanin fell into the trap, and so did this writer in his first draft. If, then Ghiberti made the same mistake, the margin for the starting date of his calendar would shift five years. On the basis of the dates for Gusmin and Andrea Pisano, the starting date of Ghiberti's olympiads would

thus fall between 777 and 760, and possibly between the narrower limits 775 or 774 and 770 or 769.

Despite his assurances to the contrary then, Ghiberti's calendar did not begin "dalla edificatione di Roma," 753 B.C., and Hermanin's thesis is justified at least on this point.

If then, the foundation of Rome must be eliminated as a point of departure, only one earlier date appears to make sense as a starting point for Ghiberti's calculations: the date at which the Greek calendar of olympiads started, 776 B.C. Of the margins 777-760 and 775/74-770/69 B.C., as they resulted from the two equations for Andrea's and Gusmin's activity the second seems to be at variance with this assumption. Yet, whoever told Ghiberti of a calendar of olympiads had good reasons to assume that the actual starting date of the Greek calendar was not 776, but either 774 or, in all likelihood, 775 B.C.

Indeed, it was certainly not Ghiberti who went into the maze of figuring and came up with the answer 775 B.C. One of his humanist acquaintances must have told him that the Greek calendar started that year and, in the light of their sources, they were almost bound to be led to this assumption. Their primary source for calculating a calendar of olympiads would of course have been Pliny's *Natural History* where Ghiberti himself had first encountered the olympiad. Based on Pliny, it would have been easy, one would suppose, to translate a calendar of olympiads into years of the Christian era or into years from the foundation of Rome: for in discussing the razing of Corinth in 146 B.C. Pliny gave the equation of olympiads and years *ab Urbe condita*, (ol. 158,3=608 a.U.c.), starting correctly in 776 and 753 B.C. respectively and adding that he did so in order to enable the reader to make other computations on this basis.[15] Yet, in other passages (XXXIV, *19*,49; XXXV, *34*,55) Pliny's equations are loose, with divergencies up to ten years; also, through the very nature of his work, he presents scattered dates rather than a continuous chronological scheme. Whatever the reasons, Ghiberti, when reading Pliny, evidently felt unable to work out a continuous scheme beyond antiquity; consequently, he may have turned to a learned friend for advice. The best tool for building up a calendar of olympiads for the Christian era, would have been St. Jerome's continuation of Eusebius' Chronicle.[16] Well known throughout the Mid-

14 Falk, bibl. 151, pp. 40ff.
15 Pliny, bibl. 408, IX, p. 131 (XXXIV, *3*, 7).
16 *Eusebii Pamphilii Canon Chronicus interprete S. Hieronymo, P.L.*, bibl. 354, XXVII, col. 259ff.

An error of calculation slipped in during the third century tabulations leading in A.D. 382 to a divergency of four years; but within our problem this is irrelevant.

dle Ages, it gives in synoptic columns the main dates of ancient history until A.D. 382: first in Biblical computations and in years of an imaginary Assyrian calendar, later in years from the foundation of Rome, then in olympiads; finally in years from the birth of Christ and in years of the Roman emperors. The calendar of olympiads in these tables starts correctly in 776 B.C. and the olympiads are four years each. Nothing would have been simpler than to use this comparative table. But Ghiberti's humanist adviser preferred to use pagan not Christian models for his new chronology *all'antica*.

Among the ancient authors who, aside from Pliny, were known to early fifteenth century humanists, at least two used a chronology of olympiads and a continuous chronology to boot: Diodorus Siculus and Polybius. A complete manuscript of Diodorus' *World History* was first brought from Greece to Italy under Eugene IV (1431-1447) and at least in part translated by Poggio Bracciolini between 1450 and 1455.[17] Polybius' *Roman History* had survived in manuscripts throughout the Middle Ages in both European and Byzantine libraries.[18] In the second quarter of the fifteenth century it became one of the principal sources for the revived knowledge of the Roman past. Leonardo Bruni, as early as 1421, used it extensively for his *Commentarii de Bello Punico* which indeed was little more than a rewriting of Polybius' first two books.[19] Between 1452 and 1454 Niccolo Perrotti translated the first five books of Polybius and dedicated them to Nicolaus V. No doubt, at least Bruni's version was known even to Ghiberti, when he worked on his *Commentarii* and one may safely assume that his humanist acquaintances knew also the as yet untranslated portions of both Polybius' and Diodorus Siculus' works. They may possibly have known even a manuscript of Dionysius of Halicarnassus' *Roman Antiquities*, even though the work was first translated under Paul II (1464-1471).[20]

The chronology of any of these ancient historians would lend itself to an interpretation by which a calendar of olympiads would have to or might start in 775 B.C. To be sure, Polybius in his first six books appears—like a good Greek—to have used a calendar beginning in 776 B.C.; but from book VII on, he changed to a calculation of olympiads of his own invention: "he starts his years with the beginning of winter, middle or end of November, the first year of the olympiads being counted from the winter after, rather than before the festival; olympiad 1,1 starts consequently November (11) 776."[21] To a Florentine of the fifteenth century, used to the *stile fiorentino*, this meant that the last eight months of this year from March through November would coincide with the year 775 B.C. The same result would have been arrived at, if perchance either Dionysius of Halicarnassus or Diodorus Siculus had been used: Dionysius indeed must appear to any reader to have calculated his olympiads starting in 775 B.C.; the outbreak of the first Punic War, for example, in 264 B.C. is placed by him in olympiad 128,3;[22] similarly Diodorus dates the beginning of the Gallic war, 59 B.C., ol. 180; again this leads to 775 B.C. as the starting point of his calendar; for (180 − 1 =) 179 x 4 equals 716 and this added to 59, results in 775. Based on these ancient sources Ghiberti's learned friend, whoever he was, had little reason to doubt that the first year of the first olympiad coincided with 775 B.C.

Polybius may equally be the source of Ghiberti's strange assumption of olympiads of five years' length. Each book of his *Roman History*, aside from the two introductory ones, corresponds to one, or to part of one, olympiad. Yet, occasionally in the earlier books events are included preliminary to those falling into the respective olympiad. Book III, for instance, terminating with the outbreak of the second Punic War and thus known to every educated man in the Renaissance, deals with the early part of olympiad 140, equaling 220-216 B.C.; but it also recounts at some length the events that in 221 led up to the war. A reader might thus have concluded that Polybius' olympiads were five, not four years long. Ghiberti's adviser evidently jumped to this conclusion, induced perhaps, as Schlosser suggested, by a vague identification of olympiads and *lustra*, in the back of his mind.[23] On the other hand, try as I may, I cannot find any satisfactory explanation for Ghiberti's manifestly incorrect statement that his calendar of olympiads started *ab Urbe condita*, a premise forgotten in the writing. Another good chance of course, is that the phrase "della edificatione di Roma furono olimpie 382" was interpolated by the copyist of the manuscript.

17 Diodorus Siculus, bibl. 128, p. xxiii; Voigt, bibl. 541, II, p. 185. Portions of Diodorus were already known to Salutati, bibl. 465, pp. 569ff.

18 Voigt, bibl. 541, II, pp. 134f; see also Mercati, bibl. 320, pp. 22, 36.

19 Leonardo Bruni, bibl. 79.

20 Dionysius of Halicarnassus, bibl. 130, p. xli.

21 Müller, bibl. 355, I, pp. 603ff; Steigemann, bibl. 503; Susemihl, bibl. 511.

22 (127 x 4 =) 508 + 264 + 3 = 775. Cary's explanation, bibl. 130, pp. xxxf.

23 Ghiberti-Schlosser, bibl. 178, II, p. 110.

We return again to our attempt to transpose Ghiberti's calendar of olympiads into years of the Christian era, starting with 775 B.C. and figuring in olympiads of five years each. On this basis the following interpretation of the events referred to by Ghiberti suggests itself.

Ol. 382 = March 1135-March 1140. To Ghiberti these years marked the period of Byzantine painting. The question is what he had in mind when focusing on these particular years. The first thought goes, of course, to Florence, but no painting or mosaic of such early date appears to be known there or to have been known in the fifteenth century. Yet, Ghiberti may well have thought of Rome rather than of Florence when discussing the *maniera greca*. Indeed, his text favors such an interpretation: for the first chapter of the Second Commentary, the chapter which concludes with the date ol. 382 appears to deal with the situation in Rome. It begins with Constantine and Sylvester; it continues with the statement that afterwards the churches remained whitewashed for 600 years; in the concluding sentences finally it refers to Byzantine painting. The second chapter quite intentionally, it would seem, starts with the contrasting statement: "In Tuscany began the new art of painting."[24] Byzantine painting, to Ghiberti, may well have been identified with some work in Rome.

Granting this, it is anybody's guess which works in Rome represented to Ghiberti the painting of the Byzantine era. Yet, Rome possesses a group of Romanesque-Byzantine mosaics which Ghiberti certainly knew and which exactly fit the years 1135-1140: the mosaics of the façade and the apse of S. Maria in Trastevere. They are dated by inscriptions into the pontificate of Innocent II (1130-1140) and Ghiberti must have been intimately acquainted with them. When discussing the work of Pietro Cavallino he devotes considerable praise to this master's mosaics in S. Maria in Trastevere where they cover the apse wall right below the twelfth century mosaics of Innocent II in the half dome. Nothing would have been more natural for Ghiberti than to contrast in his mind Cavallini's *maniera moderna* with the *maniera greca* of the older work. Thus, the latter and its date could easily become the outstanding monument of Byzantine painting within Ghiberti's concept of the history of medieval art.

Ol. 408 = 1265-1270. To Ghiberti this date seems to signify the end of Buffalmacco's activity. Buffalmacco, may or may not be identified with the Master of S. Cecilia.[25] Yet in either case, Ghiberti's statement must contain an error: for the years 1265-1270 correspond roughly to Buffalmacco's birth date, 1262 or 1272. Various explanations offer themselves: it may be that Ghiberti's original manuscript contained the statement that Buffalmacco's activity *began* in the 408th olympiad. The omission of one single letter would cause such a reversal of the original meaning, the change from "per insino *dalla*" to "per insino *alla* olimpia 408." Tempting as this emendation seems, its strength is diminished through the position of the passage containing the date, towards the end of Ghiberti's passage on Buffalmacco. Another possibility is that the figure 408 originally read 418 as proposed by Schlosser. This version, if justified, would result in the date 1315-1320, and indeed this is the very period when Buffalmacco's frescoes in the Badia di Settimo (1315-1319) and at Porta a Faenza (1314-1315) were dated through inscriptions.[26] No doubt, these inscriptions marked Buffalmacco's activity in the mind of Ghiberti, even though they do not refer to the end of the painter's activity.

Ol. 420 = 1325-1330, the date Ghiberti gives for Andrea Pisano. Only this date tallies with the beginning of work on the bronze door, 1329 or 1330; with the olympiad figure 420 as given by the Anonimo Magliabecchiano; finally with Ghiberti's statement that the master lived at this date.

Ol. 438 = 1415-1420: the goldsmith, old master Gusmin died at the time of Pope Martin V. Since Martin was elected November 11, 1417, Gusmin must have died between that date and March 24, 1420. This date corresponds neatly to the account of Gusmin's life as given by Ghiberti: his activity in the services of Louis I of Anjou (1339-1382); the melting-up of his great golden altar for the "public needs" of the duke in 1381 and his retirement to monastic life; finally his death as an old man "at the time of Pope Martin."

Ol. 440 = 1425-1430. According to our calculation this is the date of a visit of Ghiberti to Rome, when he saw, among other things, the antique hermaphrodite being excavated and brought to the studio of a sculptor who at the time was working on the tomb of a Cardinal at S. Cecilia.[27] Schlosser placed the visit in

24 *ibid.*, I, p. 35.
25 See the latest bibliography, in Offner, bibl. 370, III, 1, pp. 39ff and Thieme-Becker, bibl. 517, XXXVII, p. 63.
26 Vasari-Milanesi, bibl. 533, I, p. 503ff.
27 Ghiberti's reference to the sculptor working at the

1447, but admittedly without grounds, save for the fact that the Gates of Paradise were cast and almost completed and that therefore Ghiberti finally had time on his hands. Yet, in 1447 Ghiberti was nearly seventy years of age, somewhat old for the not unfatiguing trip to Rome. Also Ghiberti probably was in Rome more than once, and a trip between 1425 and 1430 seems very likely. Certainly, he had just as much time for a visit of some months to Rome in the spring or fall of 1429 when the *Saint Stephen* was placed at Or San Michele and before he started in earnest work on the panels of the Gates of Paradise. The vocabulary *all'antica* as it appears in these panels manifestly testifies to a new contact with Roman monuments shortly before 1430.[28] Thus, his visit would coincide with the general spread of archeological pilgrimages to Rome

among Florentine humanists, both *literati* and artists, before and around 1430.

With the interpretation of Ghiberti's olympiad calendar herewith proposed, beginning in 775 and using a spread of five years for each olympiad, the art historical events he refers to fall neatly into place—with only a minor divergency in the Buffalmacco dates in the way. Such minor errors mean little in the application of a system of periodization at once so complicated and so unusual for a fifteenth century artist. Yet, needless to say, Ghiberti in building up a chronology of olympiads, does not simply pursue a queer whim. He is deadly serious; for him as for his fellow humanists such a calendar *all'antica* was a true manifestation of their belief in a classical antiquity come again to life.

---

tomb of a cardinal at S. Cecilia at the time of this visit to Rome is of little help. The passage cannot refer to the tomb of Adam of Eaton, Bishop of Hertford and Cardinal of S. Cecilia; he died in 1397 and his monument in S. Cecilia for stylistic reasons can hardly be later than the first decade of the fifteenth century. The next tomb there of a cardinal may well have been that planned for Antoine de Challante, who died in 1418 in Lausanne, or for Ludovico Alamandi, Archbishop of

Arles, who succeeded him in 1426 (see also Ghiberti-Schlosser, bibl. 178, II, p. 187). In any event, no cardinal's tomb is likely to have been under construction in the decade between 1440 and 1450; for Ludovico Alamandi was deprived of his title in 1440 and reinstated only in 1449, shortly before his death in 1450. (See Eubel, bibl. 142 *passim*.)

[28] See above, pp. 287ff, and Appendix A.

APPENDIX C: SOURCES
LIST OF ABBREVIATIONS

Archives and Libraries:

AOF	Archivio dell'Opera di S. Maria del Fiore, Florence
ASF	Archivio di Stato, Florence
AUF	Archivio Uffizi, Florence
BNF	Biblioteca Nazionale, Florence
BMF	Biblioteca Marucelliana, Florence
ODS	Opera del Duomo, Siena
ODF	Opera del Duomo, Florence
Magl.	Fondo Magliabecchiano, Biblioteca Nazionale, Florence
BLF	Biblioteca Laurenziana, Florence

Documents:

Libro Grande Calimala X	Libro Grande dell'Arte de'Mercatanti, segnato X
Delib. Cons. Calimala	Deliberazioni de'Consoli dell'Arte de'Mercatanti comminciato [date] all' [date]
Delib. Cons. Lana	Deliberazioni de'Consoli dell'Arte della Lana
Libro seconda e terza porta	Libro della seconda e terza porta
Strozz. LI, 1, LI, 2, LI, 3	Spoglie (Carte) Strozziane, serie seconda, LI, 1, LI, 2, LI, 3
Delib. Off. Musaico	Deliberazioni degli Offiziali del Musaico
Delib.	Deliberazioni degli Operai di S. Maria del Fiore
Uscità Calimala	Uscità dell'Arte de'Mercatanti
Stanz.	Stanziamenti degli Operai di S. Maria del Fiore
Libro deb. cred.	Libro (giallo) dei debitori e creditori
Libro doc. art.	Libro di documenti artistici
Ricordi Proveditore	Quaderno di ricordi segnato [letter], comminciato [date] e finisce l'anno [date], del proveditore dell'Arte de'Mercatanti (or di Ser Francesco Guardi, etc.)
Bast. Ser Niccolo di Ser Diedi	Bastardello di Ser Niccolo di Ser Diedi
Beni di Compagnie e Arti	Beni di Compagnie e Arti di Firenze e de'Sei di Arezzo e Cortona

1. ANALYSIS OF DOCUMENTS

THE data of Ghiberti's life and work are supported by an uncommonly rich collection of sources. First among them, both in importance and extent, ranks his autobiography as contained in the *Commentarii*.[1] The only other autobiographical source is an account book, holograph at that, concerning the purchase and maintenance of the possession he had acquired at Settimo in 1442; known to Baldinucci and then lost, it was rediscovered some twenty years ago and has since been made available *in extenso* by the owner of the manuscript, Principe Ginori-Conti (Dig. 224).[2] A small batch of letters in the Archives of the *Opera* at Siena, written in the years 1425-1427 by Ghiberti and addressed to the *Operaio* of the Cathedral of Siena and to the bronze founder Giovanni Turini, concern the two bronze reliefs for the Baptismal Font and have been published by Milanesi, Lusini, and Bacci (Docs. 154-162).[3] This correspondence was at one time collected in a *Libro di documenti artistici* which has since been dissolved into its original components. Equally personal in character, though public documents, are Ghiberti's tax declarations, his *portate al catasto*, supplemented by the *campioni*, the notary's copies with the indication of the sums Ghiberti was required to pay (Docs. 81-86a). Running from 1427 to 1451, and filed under the district in which he lived, the *Quartiere San Giovanni, Gonfalone Chiavi*, they are preserved in the Florentine State Archives, and had been published previously in part by Gaye and, with occasional misreadings, by Rufus G. Mather.[4] They give, as do all such documents, Ghiberti's personal circumstances: his age and that of his wife and his sons; his possessions, both in bank accounts and real estate; his commitments and, occasionally among his credits what was still owing him for works of art completed, but not yet paid for in full. The minutes of the meeting of the Council of the Two Hundred at which the circumstances surrounding his birth and upbringing were discussed are, of course, also highly personal. The document contained in the *Riformazioni del Grande Consiglio* for 1444 has been published with minor omissions and mistakes by Gaye (Doc. 120); more recently Aruch has published another closely related document from the Laurenziana.[5] Ghi-

berti's registration in the goldsmiths' guild and those of his son Tomaso, and old Bartolo di Michele are contained in the *Matricola* of the *Arte della Seta*, his registration in the stonemasons' guild and in the painters' confraternity, in the *Matricola* of the *Arte di Pietra e Legname* and in the *Libro della Compagnia di San Luca* respectively (Docs. 114-117, 104, 103). One minor item to be added concerns the lease of his workshop opposite S. Maria Nuova on May 12, 1445, which is in the *Archivio di Stato* filed among the papers of the notary Ser Matteo di Domenico Zafferini (Dig. 253).

Two brief notes may reflect a tradition, written or oral, which originally emanated from Ghiberti himself. They concern the cost and weight of the *Saint John* and *Saint Matthew* and of the bronze shrine of Saint Zenobius and are contained, one in an anonymous sheet of the later fifteenth century in a volume of *miscellanea* in the Archives of the Uffizi Gallery in Florence (vol. 60, formerly *Misc.* I, no. 4; Doc. 129), the other (Doc. 126) in the Biblioteca Nazionale in Florence (*Banco Rari* 228, formerly *Fondo Magliabecchiano Cl.* XVII, II, 27), in a *zibaldone* written by Ghiberti's grandson Buonaccorso di Vettorio and largely filled with notes for an architectural treatise. Both passages have been published.[6]

Important for the chronology of Ghiberti's *œuvre* are principally the documents of the guilds for which he executed his major works. All the great guilds naturally kept a variety of books in which their business was recorded. Major decisions, such as the commissioning of an expensive work of art, were discussed by the consuls, the governing body of the guild, and put into writing as a rule in Latin in the *Deliberazioni de'Consoli*, one volume of which may run over a number of years, sometimes as many as thirty. Minor decisions taken by the consuls, such as clearance for the treasurer of the guild to make payments or the like, would as a rule appear in the small *Deliberazioni e partiti de'Consoli*, or simply *partiti*; they contain the actual minutes of their meetings, and notes, as recorded either in Latin or Italian by the notary—we might say the syndic of the guild—often in an almost illegible shorthand. The *Calimala*, moreover, had the more im-

---

[1] See above, Chapters I and XX, pp. 3ff and 306ff.

[2] Baldinucci, bibl. 35, I, pp. 373ff; Krautheimer, bibl. 249, pp. 79ff; Ginori-Conti, bibl. 181, pp. 290ff.

[3] Milanesi, bibl. 356, II, pp. 119ff, doc. 85, I-IX; Lusini, bibl. 283 *passim*; Bacci, bibl. 31 *passim*.

[4] Gaye, bibl. 175, I, pp. 103ff; Mather, bibl. 308, pp. 56ff.

[5] Gaye, bibl. 175, I, pp. 148ff; Aruch, bibl. 25.

[6] Fabriczy, bibl. 147, pp. 251f; Corwegh, bibl. 109.

portant of their minutes transcribed into a clean copy in a series of *Libri Grandi*, as a rule one volume per year. Payments of the guilds would appear in their expense books, the *Uscità dell'Arte* written in Italian, and incidentally in the tax declarations of the guilds when Florence had a corporation tax (which was the case only in 1429). To supervise the commissioning and the execution of a specific work of art, the guild would appoint a special committee, as did the *Arte del Cambio* for the statue of Saint Matthew at Or S. Michele. Sometimes a standing committee was put in charge of the maintenance, completion, or decoration of a building entrusted to the care of the guild: for the *Arte della Lana* the *Operai di S. Maria del Fiore* supervised work on the Cathedral; for the *Arte di Calimala* the *Offiziali del Musaico* were in charge of the Baptistery. Like the guild itself, these committees would have their important decisions, such as the conclusion of contracts and the commissioning of specific sections of work, recorded, usually in Italian, by their notary in a separate book of *Deliberazioni*; payments would appear in their expense books, *Stanziamenti* or *Uscità*. Also the syndic of the guild, the *proveditore*, would as a rule keep a journal of his business, a *Quaderno di ricordi* or *Ricordanze*. Moreover the important provisions regarding a major work of art might be collected in a separate volume.

The most complete set extant of such documents is represented by the papers of the *Arte della Lana* and of the *Operai di S. Maria del Fiore* which are preserved, the first in the *Archivio di Stato* in Florence, the latter in the *Archivio dell'Opera di S. Maria del Fiore: Deliberazioni de'Consoli, Deliberazioni* of the *Operai, Stanziamenti* and *Ricordanze*. The documents concerning the building of the Cathedral and of the dome have been meticulously published by Cesare Guasti (bibls. 198, 199). Giovanni Poggi (bibl. 413) has edited with equal care the documents that refer to the decoration of the Cathedral, among them Ghiberti's Zenobius Shrine, his cartoons for stained glass windows, and his unsuccessful participation in the contest for a new choir enclosure. Among the papers of the *Arte del Cambio* in the *Archivio di Stato* a separate volume records all business regarding the statue of Saint Matthew; this *Libro del Pilastro* has been painstakingly edited by Alfred Doren (bibl. 133). The *Deliberazioni* of the *Consoli* of the *Arte della Lana* contain the major de-

cisions referring to the planning and casting of the *Saint Stephen* (Docs. 107, 108, 109, 110, 111, 112, 113); they were published by Passerini (bibl. 391), though with minor errors and in some cases in mere summaries. The Archives of the *Opera del Duomo* in Siena preserve a set of documents referring to the Baptismal Font in Siena in the *Libri Gialli de'-Debitori e Creditori*, the *Pergamena* and the journals (*Memoriali*) of the *Camerlengo*. These documents were published first by Milanesi (bibl. 336) and Borghesi-Banchi (bibl. 63) and again with some additional material by Lusini (bibl. 283); a final highly important supplement has been edited by Peléo Bacci (bibl. 31). Others are published *in extenso* here for the first time. Some documents of minor importance are scattered through the *Libro delli atti e emanati dai Capitani di Or S. Michele* and the *Deliberazioni de'Consoli* of the *Arte dei Rigattieri, Linaiuoli e Sarti*, vol. 20, *Deb. e Cred. 1418-1451*, both in the *Archivio di Stato*, and the latter's *Quadernuccio di cassa 1449-1452*, at the Archive of S. Maria Nuova. They concern in this sequence: a drawing for two candlesticks to be executed by the goldsmith Guariento Guarienti (Doc. 118f);[7] the frame for Fra Angelico's Linaiuoli Altar (Docs. 105f);[8] finally the shutter for the tabernacle at S. Egidio (Dig. 274).[9]

Perhaps the largest and most comprehensive set of such records was kept by the *Arte di Calimala*. The *Deliberazioni de'Consoli* and their *Deliberazioni e partiti* were supplemented by a complete set of *Libri Grandi*, each signed with a capital letter and with the date of its year; a set of running expense books, both of the guild and of the Committee in charge of the Baptistery, *Uscità dell'Arte* and *Uscità di S. Giovanni*; a set of *Quaderni di ricordi*, kept by the *Proveditore dell'Arte*; and attached to the *Deliberazioni de'Consoli*, the *Deliberazioni degli Offiziali del Musaico*. Loose documents were either from the outset or later collected in a number of convolutes, *Filze di più sorte scritture*; by the late seventeenth century at least four of these were preserved, partly in disorder, so that documents of slightly earlier or later date had slipped in. Altogether these various record books must have contained all the important documents referring to the three main works commissioned to Ghiberti by the *Arte di Calimala*: the *Saint John* at Or S. Michele and the two bronze doors for the Baptistery. The material referring to these doors was moreover collected in a separate vol-

[7] Referred to by Vasari-Milanesi, bibl. 533, II, p. 259.
[8] Gualandi, bibl. 196, p. 109.

[9] Poggi, bibl. 411, pp. 105ff.

ume, the *Libro della seconda e terza porta.* However, other volumes referring to the work on the doors may have existed outside the offices of the *Calimala,* in the *Opera di S. Giovanni,* where the *Offiziali del Musaico* did business. Only three volumes of *Deliberazioni de'Consoli* survive in the *Archivio di Stato:* January 1, 1425 (*st. c.*), through May 13, 1426; January 1, 1444, through April 22; and January 5, 1448, through April 29, 1449 (*Arti, Calimala,* vols. 18, 19, 20). The latter two contain a small amount of material concerning Ghiberti's work on his second door and these passages have been published by Heinrich Brockhaus (bibl. 69); one of the documents, which refers to Gozzoli's collaboration on the Gates of Paradise, was edited with minor omissions by Milanesi (bibl. 337). A miscellaneous *Filza* (*Arti, Calimala,* vol. 17 bis) collected from various books of the fifteenth and sixteenth centuries contains a few folios from the *Deliberazioni e partiti de'Consoli* for the years 1423, 1427, 1428, and 1449-1450, including some records referring to work on the doors. They are here published for the first time. An important stray entry in the *Denunzia dei beni* of the *Arte di Calimala* for 1429 has so far been published only in a somewhat misleading excerpt (Docs. 87f).[10]

The great majority of the rich collection of documents of the *Calimala* was apparently lost when the offices of the guild burned down in the eighteenth century; but a great many excerpts had been taken from them in the latter part of the seventeenth century by a Florentine antiquarian, the Senator Carlo Strozzi. As *proveditore* of the *Calimala,* he was in the best position to explore and draw from their archives at leisure and it is not unreasonable to suspect that occasionally he carried a few volumes of original documents home. Possibly the few papers of the *Calimala* which survived the fire were saved just because of such irregular behavior on the part of the Senator; if this suspicion is justified, it is only to be hoped that he carried home many more volumes and that these will turn up in good time. Strozzi's papers, in any case, are preserved in their great majority: excerpts from the documents of the *Calimala* and from other sources, vast numbers of original documents of miscellaneous provenance, and essays and studies of his own, fill several hundred volumes. The essays are largely distributed between the *Biblioteca Nazionale* and the *Laurenziana.* The greater

part of the original documents and of the excerpts are in the *Archivio di Stato,* but a good number have also gone to the *Biblioteca Nazionale* and some to the *Marucelliana.* They are a mine of information, largely unexplored and not even all catalogued. Two volumes in the *Archivio di Stato* contain an extensive index to Strozzi's collection of excerpts: the *Repertorio Generale delle Cose Ecclesiastiche* and *Cose Laiche* respectively. From them it appears that the many volumes of excerpts preserved represent but a fragment of what Strozzi had gathered.

The excerpts from the papers of the *Calimala,* as far as they refer to the works of art commissioned by the guild from Ghiberti, are contained together with many other items in two volumes among the *Carte Strozziane* of the *Archivio di Stato: Serie Seconda, LI, 1* and *2.* A third volume, *LI, 3,* contains only one relevant leaf, f. 153-153v, and thus, in the search for Ghiberti documents, has been frequently overlooked. Yet this one leaf is of no mean importance, for on it Strozzi had begun an index of passages from the *Libri Grandi* referring to Ghiberti's two doors for the Baptistery and to his *Saint John* for Or S. Michele.[11] The original title of the volumes is *Spoglio primo* (*secondo, terzo*) *delle scritture dell'Arte di Calimala altrimenti detta de'Mercatanti e suoi annessi fatto da me Carlo Strozzi . . . ,* their title on the cover *Fatti e Memorie dell'Arte de'Mercatanti,* and they have been quoted alternately as *Spogli Strozziani* or as *Fatti e Memorie;* we think it best to quote them simply as *ASF, Strozz. LI, 1, 2* and *3* respectively. An excerpt of part of the contents of *Strozz. LI, 1* made either by Strozzi himself or by an amanuensis is preserved among the Strozzi papers of the *Biblioteca Nazionale* (*Fondo Magliabecchiano Cl. IX, 127*). In the first half of the eighteenth century Francesco Antonio Gori copied from *Strozz. LI, 1* and *2* the passages referring to the Baptistery and among them those concerning Ghiberti's doors, and inserted them among the notes he assembled for a planned history of that building (*Marucelliana, Manoscritti, A 199 I*); these *Goriana* help to clarify some illegible passages in Strozzi and are used here for the first time. They also contain, ff. 32ff, some valuable passages copied from a lost manuscript of Strozzi's, *Descrizione dell' insigne Tempio di S. Giovanni del Senatore Strozzi.*

The general assumption so far has been that

<hr />

[10] See above, pp. 111f.

[11] Brockhaus (bibl. 69, p. 36, note 1), knew and referred to this index, but apparently misinterpreted its

content as concerning largely the *Gates of Paradise;* see above, p. 73.

the *Strozziana* in their entirety are but summaries of the original documents collected somewhat haphazardly and transcribed by Strozzi freely and with extensive explanatory insertions of his own. True, the value of the notes is not equal throughout: large parts of *Strozz. LI, 2* are but repeats, other parts free summaries of one or more entries in *Strozz. LI, 1*. On the other hand, the majority of the entries in *Strozz. LI, 1*, and some in *LI, 2* contain surprisingly large portions which are obviously culled verbatim from original documents, as witness the passages in which Strozzi breaks off with or interrupts a phrase by an *etc.* Occasionally he copied literally an entire document, such as Leonardo Bruni's letter (Doc. 52). At other times his notes appear to be faithful copies from the marginal notes in the original document in which the notary of the guild had summed up for easy reference the contents of a lengthy document. This correspondence becomes manifest from a comparison between Strozzi's formulations and these notaries' marginalia in the few cases where both the *Strozziana* and the original documents are preserved (Docs. 72, 91). Other such notary's marginalia, now lost, would appear to be recognizable among Strozzi's notes by their terse style such as "Porta di S. Giovanni terza si da a armare" (Docs. 25, 59). Occasionally Strozzi summed up the content of an important document in a phrase which, however, contains all relevant data, as witness the correspondence of his entry regarding Gozzoli's collaboration on the Gates of Paradise and the text of the original document in the *Deliberazioni de' Consoli* (Docs. 71, 94). Only in the passages culled from the *Libro della seconda e terza porta* did Strozzi apparently reword and make insertions in the original documents.

The exact nature of this *Libro della seconda e terza porta* is not quite clear. From Strozzi's notes it would appear that, in contrast to the other record books of the *Calimala*, it lacked pagination, a strange deficiency in a regular account book or journal of the fifteenth century. Likewise its chronology was apparently disordered: an entry probably from 1403 and referring to the gilding of the competition relief (Doc. 33) would follow a list of assistants' wages dated after 1407 (Doc. 31). The text is frequently interspersed with explanatory remarks or summaries: the contract for Ghiberti's second door contains a phrase to the effect that "in working on his first door he had little observed his obligation not to take on any other work"; or else, an annotation in the

agreement of 1407 refers back to the contract of 1403 "as it had been agreed above"; another states that this new agreement was made with Lorenzo di Bartolo "alone, without naming the father" (Doc. 27). In the list of assistants employed on the North Door (Doc. 31) the helpers are enumerated with their varying annual salaries and the amounts of wages received totaling ". . . fl. 113.6.2, item fl. 87.1.4, item fl. 131.7.8"; or (Doc. 30) weight and cost are computed into figures such as fl. 57.l. 1344 d.4 without transforming them into the corresponding total of roughly 390 florins. The entire book then bears the mark of a compilation and indeed it has been suggested that it was compiled long after the doors had been completed.[12] This obviously cannot be so, for why would Strozzi, faithful historian that he was, excerpt or copy a compilation of his own under a misleading title? The impression is rather that the original had been gathered while work on the doors was going on, possibly as a loose convolute, in which the *Offiziali del Musaico* had collected for easy reference in copies the important documents regarding Ghiberti's two doors (and incidentally also the bronze frame for Andrea Pisano's door). Such a convolute would naturally lack pagination and even if originally arranged in chronological order, this sequence might well have been disturbed. In fact, other *filze* used by Strozzi showed apparently the same lack of pagination and the same chronological disorder. If the *Libro* then, was such a convolute it need not have been complete and in not more than rough chronological order by the time it fell into Strozzi's hands. But it would have contained, as did the *Libro del Pilastro* of the *Arte del Cambio*, in addition to the contracts and the like, the detailed running accounts of expenses, including workers' annual salaries and actual pay received. On the basis of this convolute then, Strozzi would seem to have made excerpts of the relevant passages of the contracts and to have compiled his lists of workers and of their salaries; going back and forth and occasionally repeating an assistant's name or else computing his wages in several, rather than in one single item; taking up at a later point a forgotten entry, summing up accounts on amounts of material purchased, or sums spent up to a certain point; finally inserting, when necessary, an explanatory annotation.

Strozzi went systematically, it would seem, through the books of the guild selecting items he deemed important. Obviously, he did not

[12] Frey, bibl. 532, pp. 353f, note.

exploit all the books of the *Calimala* for his ends and certainly he was unable to complete his task. Some of the original record books may well have been missing, others may have been incomplete. One gathers this impression from Strozzi's own notes: in *Strozz. LI, 1*, excerpts from a series of *Libri Grandi* follow each other year by year from 1402 to 1406 and sporadically from then until 1416 or 1417; in the following years, until 1461 and later, one volume seems to have covered occasionally more than one year.[13] These excerpts are followed by notes from three *ricordi* covering the period 1435-1463, from the *Libro della seconda e terza porta*, from a few expense books dating 1415-1417 and from a *Filza di varie scritture*. At the end of the volume finally appear excerpts from the *Deliberazioni de' Consoli* and the *Deliberazioni degli Offiziali del Musaico*, the former apparently extant at Strozzi's time, for the years 1401-1414 in one continuous volume, for the years 1439-1459 though with gaps in a number of volumes covering from one to four years, the latter only for the period 1401-1414 as an appendix to the *Deliberazioni de'Consoli*. This sketchy list is supplemented by the fragmentary index of relevant items in the *Libri Grandi* inserted into *Strozz. LI, 3*: from this it would appear that the series of these records ran unbroken or nearly unbroken from 1402 through 1421 and perhaps through 1440, but that the following years were covered at Strozzi's time

only by scattered volumes. On the other hand this same index makes it quite patent that Strozzi never was able to finish his compilation as planned: none of the passages noted down in the index obviously for future use appear anywhere among the items he actually did enter in *Strozz. LI, 1* or 2.

The excerpts as far as Strozzi collected them give the impression of being highly trustworthy. He never fails to give carefully the exact quotation of his sources: title of the series; year or signature of volume or both; name of notary; page of item. Occasionally he may have made a mistake in nomenclature, by entering an expense book of the guild as an *Uscità di S. Giovanni* (Docs. 55, 56), but this is of little importance. Exact dates for individual items he gives only occasionally.

Not only was Strozzi unable to finish his task, but his notes appear to be preserved only in part. One volume marked XX and according to the *Repertorii Generali* crammed with entries on Florentine artists has disappeared from the *Fondo Magliabecchiano*. Other lost items are reflected in Gori's notes in the *Marucelliana* (Ms. A199 I). His copy of the *Descrizione dell' insigne Tempio di San Giovanni* contains, along with summaries of the material exploited in *Strozz. LI, 1*, a number of new items: three computations, regarding the cost of the two doors and of the bronze frame of the Pisano door, added up in Strozzi's characteristic manner and obviously based on lost

---

[13] The original sequence of the *Libri Grandi* does not come out clearly in Strozzi's excerpts. Apparently they were marked each by a capital letter and presumably the date of the year, for example C 1402. A fragmentary list in one of Strozzi's volumes (*BNF Magl. IX*, 127, c.185ff) is of considerable help. However, in his excerpt in *ASF, Strozz. LI, 3* (see our Doc. 80), Strozzi frequently gives only the signature by capital letter, e.g. L, but omits the corresponding date; second, he occasionally makes mistakes such as dating volume C, once 1402, another time 1403; third, the alphabetization has been confused by the insertion of letters accompanied by a cross, e.g. Q+, following P for 1414 and preceding Q for 1416. This indication Q+ may, then, refer to a supplement for the volume marked Q, in this case 1416, or to the volume for the preceding year, 1415, or even the succeeding year, 1417. Finally, one volume seems occasionally to have covered more than one year and at times a volume seems to have been missing by Strozzi's time.

With these reservations in mind, the following list can be tentatively established:

C = 1402 (dated by *Strozz. LI, 1*, f. 2; *Strozz. LI, 3*, f. 153 is probably erroneous)
D = 1403 (dated by *Magl. IX, 127*, c.185)
E = 1404 (dated by *Magl. IX, 127*, c.185)
F = 1405 (dated by *Magl. IX, 127*, c.186 and *Strozz. LI, 1*, f. 3)
G = 1406 (dated by *Magl. IX, 127*, c.187 and *Strozz. LI*,

1, f. 3, 3v)
I (mentioned by *Strozz. LI, 3*, f. 153, but not dated)
K = 1409 (dated by *Magl. IX, 127*, c.187)
L = 1410 (?) (mentioned by *Strozz. LI, 3*, f. 153, but not dated)
M = 1412 (?) (dated by *Magl. IX, 127*, c.187, but perhaps mistaken for 1411)
N (mentioned by *Strozz. LI, 3*, f. 153, but undated)
O (mentioned by *Strozz. LI, 3*, f. 153, but undated)
P = 1414 (dated by *Magl. IX, 127*, c.187, and *Strozz. LI, 1*, f. 5)
Q+ = 1415 (?) (mentioned by *Strozz. LI, 3*, f. 153, but undated)
Q = 1416 (dated by *Magl. IX, 127*, c.188 and *Strozz. LI, 1*, f. 5v)
T = 1421 (*sic*) (dated by *Strozz. LI, 3*, f. 153)
I = 1429 (dated by *Magl. IX, 127*, c.188 and *Strozz. LI, 1*, f. 6)
K (mentioned by *Strozz. LI, 3*, f. 153, but undated)
L = 1433 (dated by *Magl. IX, 127*, c.188, mentioned *Strozz. LI, 3*, f. 153)
M = 1436 (dated by *Magl. IX, 127*, c.189, mentioned *Strozz. LI, 3*, f. 153)
N (mentioned by *Strozz. LI, 3*, f. 153, but undated)
O (mentioned by *Strozz. LI, 3*, f. 153, but undated)
P (mentioned by *Strozz. LI, 3*, f. 153, but undated)
Q (mentioned by *Strozz. LI, 3*, f. 153, but undated)
B = 1455 (dated by *Strozz. LI, 1*, f. 9v)
F = 1461 (dated by *Strozz. LI, 1*, f. 10f)

notes of his; and, in a list of the assistants who had worked on the Gates of Paradise, a number of names which do not appear in Strozzi's extant notes.

The value of Strozzi's notes was recognized early and in consequence the references pertaining to works of art commissioned by the *Calimala* have been published several times: the excerpts from the *Libro della seconda e terza porta* by Patch and Gregori (bibl. 392) as early as 1773 and, in a reprint of this publication, by Muentz in 1890; the excerpts from that and from other books of the *Calimala*, as far as they concern the Gates of Paradise, together with the original documents regarding that door, by Brockhaus (bibl. 69); finally most of Strozzi's notes which concern the works of art commissioned by the guild including both doors of the Baptistery and the *Saint John* at Or S. Michele by Frey (bibl. 532) in his monumental, if abortive Vasari edition. None of these editions has been critical; none has attempted to use, along with Strozzi's excerpts in the *Archivio di Stato*, corroborative and supplementary material offered by the original documents or by the copies and summaries in the *Biblioteca Nazionale* and the *Marucelliana*; no attempt has been made to evaluate the various portions of Strozzi's notes or sources, nor have his excerpts in their entirety been fully exploited.

Frey's edition though the most complete so far, suffers from a number of shortcomings. It is incomplete and overlooks a considerable number of items; it is uncritical and thus repeats at times items from different sources used by Strozzi, without indicating that they refer to the same event. Likewise, to cite but one more example, the entries referring to the jambs of Andrea Pisano's door are not recognized as such and are intermingled with those concerning the frame of the Gates of Paradise. In addition Frey's dating of Strozzi's entries, often concerning years and almost without exception concerning month and day, is unreliable. Obviously a date which in Strozzi's excerpts appears two, three, or even ten lines higher up on the margin must not under any circumstances be referred to all of the following entries. Contrary, then, to Frey's procedure, the undated entries should be inserted between the preceding and the following marginal

dates, thus establishing a loose, but not a fatally wrong chronology. On the other hand, Strozzi's careful indication of the page on which an entry appears in the original document gives at times a lead regarding its chronological relationship to the nearest dated items, and even where no date closely precedes or follows, the page indication alone may place an entry early or late in the period covered by the original volume.

With all this it must be remembered that almost all the original documents are at this moment, it seems, irretrievably lost. As late as the eighteenth century a number of record books may still have survived even outside the archives of the *Calimala*: Richa[14] alluded to expense books extant at his time in the *Opera di S. Giovanni*, but it must be admitted that his account sounds much like an excerpt from Strozzi's notes, including possibly his *Descrizione*; Gori mentioned an important note referring to the preparation of a program for the Gates of Paradise which he maintained to have culled from the "Diaries of the Calimala."[15] Certainly Baldinucci in the latter part of the seventeenth century knew a great number of original papers, both public and private, regarding Ghiberti: a journal in which Ghiberti had entered his works, "beginning May 1, 1403" (Doc. 163); his household books (*libri domestici*), then in the possession of the Altoviti family; his last will, dated November 1455, drawn up by the notary Ser Santi di Domenico Naldi (Dig. 293); an estimate of his collection of antiques "valued at more than 1500 florins," a note at Baldinucci's time in the possession of Cristofano Berardi in Florence, who owned also Ghiberti's account book concerning his possession at Settimo; a journal of the notary of the Signoria, Ser Nofri di Ser Paolo Nenni, then in the possession of his family and containing an important entry referring to Ghiberti's assistants in 1407 (Dig. 25); finally a document referring to a law suit over Ghiberti's inheritance from Cione made out by Ser Pietro di Ser Michele Guidoni.[16] As late as the mid-nineteenth century Milanesi appears to have known some of these and some more documents which have meantime disappeared, not the least among them the record of Ghiberti's death and burial at S. Croce (Dig. 294).[17]

---

[14] Richa, bibl. 443, v, p. xxi.

[15] See above, p. 161 and note 3.

[16] Baldinucci, bibl. 35, I, pp. 350ff. None of the notaries' documents mentioned by Baldinucci appear to be extant among their papers in the *Archivio di Stato*.

[17] Vasari-Milanesi, bibl. 533, II, pp. 248f, note. Milanesi refers to the *Libri dei Morti* as his source for the

record of Ghiberti's death and burial; but the series of the *Libri della Grescia* (*Libri dei Morti*) extant in the *Archivio di Stato* has at present a gap between 1449 and 1457, as I am informed by Miss Eve Borsook, who, with the help of Signora Giulia Camerani of the *Archivio di Stato*, was good enough to make another check.

ASF, STROZZ., LI, 1

DOC. 1, 1402, NORTH DOOR, Dig. 4

f. 2. *Libro Grande dell'Arte de Mercatanti segnato C, dell'anno 1402*: Nencio di Bartoluccio orafo debbe fare la Porta del Metallo, c. 255.[2]

    LI, 2, f. 123v.

DOC. 2, 1405, NORTH DOOR, Dig. 17

f. 3. *Libro Grande dell'Arte de Mercatanti segnato F, 1405*: Giuliano di Ser Andrea discepolo di Lorenzo di Bartoluccio, c. 171[3]

DOC. 3, 1414, SAINT JOHN, Digs. 33, 37

f. 5. *Libro Grande segnato P, 1414*: Giuliano di Arrigo detto Pesello e compagni Dipintori[(a)] segli paga fl. 20 per parte di pagamento del lavorio fanno nel Tabernacolo dell' Arte di Orto S. Michele, c. 236

dipinge detto (?), c. 417

pittori (?) di S. Gio., c. 423[4]

    BNF, Magl., Cl. IX, 127, f. 187: breaks off at: [(a)]Dipintori

DOC. 4, 1414, SAINT JOHN, Dig. 34

f. 5. *ibidem*: Frate Bernardo di Stefano dell' Ordine de Predicatori segli paga fl. 12 per opera del lauoro del vetro a tolto a lauorare per lo Tabernacolo di O.S.M., c. 236.[5]

DOC. 5, 1414, SAINT JOHN, Dig. 35

f. 5. *ibidem*: Libbre 1884 di Mosaico si compra degli Operai del Duomo di Pisa per fl. 65[6] (pagination illegible).

DOC. 6, 1416, SAINT JOHN, Dig. 46

f. 5v. *Libro Grande segnato Q, 1416*: Frate Bernardo di Stefano . . . lavora i vetri nel tabernacolo di Orto s. Michele[7] (no pagination).

DOC. 7, 1416, SAINT JOHN, Dig. 47

f. 5v. *ibidem*: Giuliano d'Arrigo detto Pesello e Compagni Dipintori nel Corso degli Ademari lavora il fregio del vetro del Tabernacolo d'Orto Santo Michele da beccatelli in giù[8] (no pagination).

DOC. 8, 1429, EAST DOOR, Dig. 158

f. 6v. *Libro Grande segnato I, 1429*: Colonne di S. Gio si levano dinanzi alla porta di S. Gio e pongonsi a lato alla faccia di detta Chiesa 1429, c. 176.[9]

    LI, 2, f. 111; *BNF, Magl., Cl. IX, 127*, f. 188, with minor variations.

DOC. 9, 1462 [possibly 1463], EAST DOOR, Dig. 300

f. 10v. *Libro Grande segnato F, 1461*:[(a)] Vettorio di Bartoluccio dee hauere per gli stipiti soglia e altro della terza Porta [sic] di S. Gio. fl. 1060, lire 6124,[(b)] s. 15, c. 219 & 241.[10]

---

[1] Appendix C2 contains a transcript of 163 documents. They fall into three categories: unpublished documents; documents published heretofore only in excerpts; documents published heretofore with significant errors in transcription or dating. Documents outside these categories, such as those gathered by Doren, bibl. 133, Guasti, bibl. 198, 199, Poggi, bibl. 395, 397, 399 and Ginori-Conti, bibl. 181 are not included in this appendix.

The Digest, Appendix C3 contains a list of all references to Ghiberti's life and works in chronological order, a day by day account, as it were, irrespective of whether the relevant document is published in Appendix C2 or elsewhere.

In Appendix C2 the documents are listed according to archives and, within the archives, according to their classification.

Repetitions of documents contained in other manuscripts are indicated in Appendix C2 immediately following the main source. Variants from the text are referred to by notes a, b, c. Archives and *fondi* from which these repetitions are taken, are indicated only if they differ from those of the main source. (The manuscript *BMF, Collezione Gori, A 199 I*, is quoted simply as Gori.) In the Digest Appendix C3, such repetitions or variants are referred to only if providing additional information.

Relevant bibliography and discussion of the documents contained in Appendix C2 will be found in the footnotes. In the Digest, Appendix C3, bibliographical references have been limited to data based on documents either not contained in Appendix C2 or else of questionable chronology.

A list of abbreviations of archives, *fondi*, and volumes precedes Appendix C1.

[2] Frey, bibl. 532, p. 353, doc. 2.

[3] Frey, bibl. 532, p. 354, doc. 6.

[4] Frey (bibl. 532, p. 381, doc. 20) adds, perhaps from another source "per la statua di S. Giovanni, a. 1413."

[5] Frey, bibl. 532, p. 381, as first part of his doc. 21.

[6] Frey, bibl. 532, p. 381, as second part of his doc. 21.

[7] Not in Frey, bibl. 532.

[8] Frey (bibl. 532, p. 381, doc. 24) adds a second part, based on Berti's nineteenth century transcript: "si mette su la figura di S. Giov. Batt. nel detto tabernacolo."

[9] Frey, bibl. 532, p. 342, doc. 78.

[10] Frey (bibl. 532, p. 364, doc. 44), with the date 1461. Since, however, Doc. 9 must be later than Doc. 68, its date is probably 1463.

Our dating of such Strozzi documents with the terms "after" and "before" a given date is cumbersome, but inevitable in order to avoid misdatings. By referring to the nearest preceding and following dates in the margin of Strozzi's manuscripts these terms establish chronological limits. Where in our transcript such approxi-

Gori, 140v and 153, where correct date is to be found: (a)*Libro Grande G, 1462*; (b)6129.

DOC. 10, 1426, after Apr. 26; just before Dec. 29, BAPTISTERY, Dig. 127

f. 37ff. *Filza di più sorte scritture dell' Arte de Mercatanti dall'anno 1414 al 1433*, f. 38v: drawing of lintel | br. 3¼ | br. 2⅓ | br. ¼ | Per il frontespicio della Porta di S. Gio scrive Forasasso (?) da Carrara per minore spesa volendo pigliare di tre pezzi come sopra(a)11

Gori, 153v, with date 1424 or 1425: cio fu intorno al 1424 o 25; (a)come di contro

DOC. 11, 1451, Jan. 5 [or 16], EAST DOOR, Dig. 275

f. 43. *Quaderno di Riccordi segnato O comminciato 1450 e finito 1453*: Lorenzo di Bartoluccio e Vettorio suo figliolo si obbligano di dare finita interamente la terza porta di S. Gio fra venti mesi con certe condizioni nel qual tempo(a) devono tenere a lavorare quattro maestri buoni e tre non cosi perfetti, e un ragazzo, c. 132.12

(a)Only first part until *tempo* legibile in *LI*, *1*, dated Jan. 5; repetition of first part in *LI, 2, 113*, dated Jan. 16.

Reconstruction of whole entry after Gori, 153, dated Jan. 16, 1451.

DOC. 12, 1452, after Apr. 18 and before Aug. 22 [probably June 16], EAST DOOR, Dig. 281

f. 44v. *ibidem*: Lorenzo di Bartoluccio è dichiarato avere bene indorato la 3a porta di S. Gio, c. 147.13

Gori, 153 and 142 with date June 16, 1451; summary of this and following entry in *LI, 2, 113* with date June 16, 1451.

DOC. 13, 1452, after Apr. 18, before Aug. 22 [probably after June 16], EAST DOOR, Dig. 282

f. 44v. *ibidem*: Lorenzo di Bartoluccio e Vettorio suo figliolo è dichiarato che interamente habbino finite la terza porta di S. Gio, c. 149.14

LI, 2, 113 for summary of this and previous entry; also *LI, 2, 114v*, with date June 16, 1451.

DOC. 14, 1452, after Aug. 22 [probably Dec. 12-18], SOUTH DOOR, Dig. 285

f. 45. *ibidem*: Alla Porta del Battesimo di S. Gio si faccia li stipiti da lato e soglia e cornice e cardinale in modo che la risponda all' altre due che sono fatte, c. 154.15

LI, 2, 113; Gori, 153

DOC. 15, 1452, after Aug. 22 [after Dec. 12-18; before Feb. 12, 1453], EAST DOOR, Dig. 287

f. 45. *ibidem*: A Lorenzo di Bartoluccio se gli da una casa e bottega appresso S. Maria Nuova dove s' è lavorato la Porta di S. Gio per fl. 218.3.4 che restava havere per la fattura di detta porta, c. 155.16

DOC. 16, 1452, after Aug. 22 [probably Feb. 12, 1453], SOUTH DOOR, Dig. 288

f. 45. *ibidem*: A Lorenzo detto s' alluoga a fare gli stipiti e altro della porta del Battesimo, c. 155.17

LI, 2, 113v, with date 1452; Gori, 153v.

DOC. 17, 1453, after May 9, EAST DOOR, Dig. 290

f. 45. *ibidem*: Fregio di Marmo si fa intorno alla Porta dinanzi di S. Gio, c. 158.18

LI, 2, 113v; Gori, 141v, dated 1453; *ibid.*, 153v.

DOC. 18, 1445, after Jan. 7; shortly before June 1, EAST DOOR, Dig. 252

mate dates are followed by more precise indications, placed in brackets, these dates are based either on a dated document referring to the same event or on conclusions obtained from other relative material.

11 Brockhaus, bibl. 69, p. 39; Frey, bibl. 532, p. 357, doc. 1 with erroneous date April 22, 1423. The revised date results from the pagination of the original *filza*. As excerpted by Strozzi, c.38 contains entries dating from Nov. 23, 1423 to April 26, 1426; c.38v begins with Doc. 10 followed by an entry dated Dec. 29, 1426.

12 Frey, bibl. 532, p. 362, doc. 28 and Brockhaus, bibl. 69, p. 45, both give only the first part. The entry is nearly identical with the last part of our Doc. 44.

13 Unpublished. The approximate date results from the nearest entries preceding and following; the specific date results from doc. 47, the first part of which refers to the same event.

14 Frey, bibl. 532, p. 361, doc. 21 with date of April 13, 1452. The date is probably slightly later than doc.

11 and precedes doc. 75 of July 13, 1452.

15 Frey, bibl. 532, p. 363, doc. 37, with date of August 22. Frey mistakenly brings all the documents relating to the frame around the Andrea Pisano door, i.e., the south portal, under the heading "third door," i.e., *Porta del Paradiso*. See our Doc. 74.

16 Frey, bibl. 532, p. 363, doc. 36, with date of August 22, 1452. The pagination of the *Quaderno O*, excerpted by Strozzi, contradicts Frey's dating: c. 153 (Doc. 14)= after August 22; c. 158 (Doc. 17)= after May 9, 1453. Ghiberti evidently received the house after the decision had been taken to decorate the Andrea Pisano door, i.e., Dec. 12-18 (Doc. 74) and before it is commissioned to him and Vittorio on Feb. 12, 1453.

17 Frey, bibl. 532, p. 363, doc. 38 with date August 22, 1452. The approximate date results from the nearest entry preceding it; for the correct date see Doc. 50.

18 Unpublished. The date results from the nearest entries preceding and following.

f. 48. *Quaderno di Riccordi segnato M comminciato 1° Gennaio 1444 e finisce l'anno 1449 del Proveditore dell' Arte de Mercatanti*: Fiorini 2000 di Monte dell'Opera di S. Giouanni si vendono[(a)] per pagare l'Ottone che si fa venire di Bruggia, c. 136[19]

Gori, 162v: [(a)]vendino

DOC. **19**, 1445, after June 1; shortly before Oct. 7, EAST DOOR, Dig. 254

f. 48v. *ibidem*: Ottone lb. 14623 si fa venire da Bruggia e sono posto in Firenze fl. 1135, c. 138[20]

DOC. **20**, 1447, Aug. 7, EAST DOOR, Dig. 259

f. 49v. *ibidem*: 7 agosto Lorenzo di Bartoluccio M.° delle Porte di S. Gio è dichiarato havere finito le dieci storie e se gli paga il resto di fl. 1200 prezzo convenuto con lui della fattura di esse, c. 148[21]

LI, 2, 113v; Gori, 141v, 153v.

DOC. **21**, 1447, after Aug. 7; before Apr. 22, 1448, CANDELABRA, Dig. 260

f. 49v. *ibidem*: Candellieri due di rame coperti d'argento si fanno a S. Gio. per Maso di Lorenzo di Bartoluccio, c. 151.[22]

LI, 2, 114, dated 1447

DOC. **22**, 1447, after Aug. 7; before Apr. 22, 1448 [probably Jan. 24], EAST DOOR, Dig. 263

f. 49v. *ibidem*: Piu[(a)] pregi fatti con Lorenzo di Bartoluccio e Vettorio suo figlio per i fregi, teste 24[(b)] che hanno a stare nei compassi, cornici[(c)] . . . soglia etc. della terza porta di S. Gio[(d)], c. 152[23]

LI, 2, 114: [(a)]Pregi fatti; [(b)]24 teste; [(c)]supplements: stipiti, cardinale; [(d)]adds: 1447; Gori, 153v.

DOC. **23**, 1436 [1437?], Apr. 4, EAST DOOR, Dig. 198

f. 61f. *Quaderno di Ricordi segnato K cominciato 1° marzo 1434 (=1435) e finisce l'anno 1440, del Proveditore dell'Arte de Mercatanti*: Historie dieci e pezzi 24 di fregi delle porte di S. Gio gettati si comincino a nettare[(a)] per Lorenzo di Bartoluccio e un suo figliolo e Michelozzo di Bartolomeo, c. 87[24]

Gori, 153v; *LI*, 2, 114: [(a)]rinettare

DOC. **24**, 1439, July 4, EAST DOOR, Dig. 208

f. 63v. *ibidem*: 4 Luglio concordia con Lorenzo di Bartoluccio per le Porte di S. Gio al quale si paghi per lavoro fatto su dette Porte egli, il figlio ed altri da dì 1° Genn.° 1437[(a)] a tutto Giugno passato fl. 180 rogatu Ser Francesco. Le Storie erano all'hora in questo termine.
Una Storia di Caino e Abel finita a fatto
Una Storia di Moise perla Legge, manca poco d'essere finita
Una Storia di Giacob et Esau, finita
Una Storia di Giuseppe del Grano per metà finita
Una Storia di Salomone erano fatti i Casamenti e un pezzo da piè le figure da lato ritto quasi per 1/4
Due delle spiagie [?] fattone solo il fogliame, c. 103.[25]

Gori, 153v f: [(a)]1438

DOC. **25**, 1439, after July 17, before Oct. 3 [probably July 18], EAST DOOR, Dig. 209

f. 64. *ibidem*: Porta di S. Gio terza si da a armare, c. 103[26]

Gori, 154, with date July 17

DOC. **26**, 1403, Nov. 23, NORTH DOOR, Dig. 8

f. 79ff. *Libro della seconda e terza porta di Bronzo della Chiesa di S. Gio. Battista di Firenze*: Si da a fare la seconda Porta di S. Gio a Lorenzo di Bartolo, e a Bartolo di Michele suo padre Orafi, con che Lor.zo debba lavorare in sui[(a)] Compassi di sua mano le figure, alberi e simili cose de compassi con che possa torre in suo aiuto Bartolo suo padre e altri sufficienti maestri che gli parra.
Deve ogn' anno dar compiuti tre Compassi et il tempo cominci il p.°[(b)] di Dicembre. Non devono mettere se non la loro fatica, a tutte

19 Frey, bibl. 532, p. 360, doc. 15, as Jan. 3. The date results from the nearest entries preceding and following.

20 Frey, bibl. 532, p. 360, doc. 16, with date of Jan. 3. The revised date results from the nearest entries preceding and following.

21 Frey, bibl. 532, p. 360, as last part of his doc. 17. See our Doc. 42.

22 Frey, bibl. 532, p. 370, doc. 43, with date of August 7, 1447. The correct approximate date results from the nearest entries preceding and following.

23 Frey, bibl. 532, p. 361, as second part of his doc. 18 with date of August 7, 1447. The event referred to is evidently identical with the new agreement of Jan. 24, 1448 (see our Doc. 44). The excerpt Doc. 79 precedes the above by one page in the original quaderno. The preceding paragraph in Frey, starting "e piu prezzi fatti," and identical in content with our Doc. 22, could not be identified in any of the different variants of the entry.

24 Frey, bibl. 532, p. 359, doc. 5; for the probable date 1437, see p. 164.

25 Frey, bibl. 532, pp. 359f, doc. 7, with slight variations; Brockhaus, bibl. 69, pp. 39f, with erroneous date 1437.

26 Frey, bibl. 532, p. 360, as first part of his doc. 8. See our Doc. 59 which refers to the same event and is dated July 18.

l'altre cose deve pensare l'Arte. Devino havere per fattura di d.a Porta quello sara giudicato da Consoli e Off.li di Mosaico et a buon conto se gli possa dare sino in fl. 200 l'anno.

Furono eletti a sollecitare la d.a Opera Matteo di Gio. Villani, Palla di Nofri delli Strozzi e Nicolo di Luca di Feo.[27]

Gori, 154v: [a]su; [b]dì; *LI, 2,* 114, summary; *BNF, Magl. IX, 127,* f. 197

DOC. 27, 1407, June 1, NORTH DOOR, Dig. 22

f. 79f. *ibidem*: Non osservando Lorenzo di Bartolo di dare compiuto ogn'anno i tre Compassi come di sopra era convenuto si fa di nuovo l'infra scritta convenzione con Lorenzo di Bartolo solo senza nominare il padre [la quale, cancelled]. Seguiti il d.o Lorenzo il lavorio cominciato della d.a porta [la quale canceled] e finche non sara finito non possa pigliare a fare altro lavoro senza Licenza de Consoli e finito che sia deva aspettare un altro (?) anno per vedere se dall' Arte gli verra (?) esser dato a fare altro lavoro.

f. 79v. Deva havere per suo Magisterio fl. 200 l'anno.

Deva ogni giorno che si lavora lavorare di suo mano tutto il dì come fa chi sta a provisione e scioperandosi lo sciopero gli debbe essere messo a conto e scritto in su un libro fatto a posto.

Deva il d.o Lorenzo lavorare di sua mano in su Cera e Ottone e massimamente in su quelle parti che sono di piu perfezione come Capelli, ignudi, e simili.

Deva trovar lui i lavoranti; ma il salario gli deva essere stabilito da Consoli.

Non deva mettere se non la sua fatica e Magisterio, e ogni materia e instrumenti gli deve essere dato dall'Arte.[28]

Gori, 154v f

DOC. 28, 1404-7, NORTH DOOR, Dig. 24

f. 79v. *ibidem*: Hebbe Lorenzo di Bartolo in tutto il tempo della prima conuenzione fra lui e suoi lauoranti fl. 882, l. 260, d. 66 a oro, e resto havere fl. 200.

Suoi lavoranti nel tempo della prima convenzione furono.

Bandino di Stefano

Giuliano di Ser Andrea
Donato di Niccolo di Betto Bardi
Jacopo d'Antonio da Bologna
Domenico di Gio
Maso di Christofano
Michele di Nicolai
Bernardo di Piero
Michele detto (?) [a]Scalcagna
Giovanni di Francesco
Antonio di Tommaso, nipote di Bandino[29]

Gori, 155: [a]dello

DOC. 29, 1403 (=1404)-1415, NORTH DOOR, Dig. 39

f. 79v. *ibidem*: Hebbe il d.o Lorenzo per il lavorio della d.a Porta dell'anno 1403 al 1415 lb. 5564 d. 11 d'ottone.[30]

Gori, 155v

DOC. 30, 1403 (=1404)-1424 (?), NORTH DOOR, Dig. 108

f. 79v. Costo l'ottone per la d.a porta detto ottone di Ritaglio[a] l. 831[b] l. 11 parte a s. sei la lb. e parte a s. sei e mezzo. Costo il carbone e le legne fl. 57, l. 1344, d. 4. Si consumò nella d.a Opera lb. 1739 d.[oncie] 8 di cera e lb. 69 d.[oncie] 4 se ne dette ai lavoranti in falcole per tornare la sera a casa.[31]

Gori, 155f.

DOC. 31, after 1407 [presumably before 1415], NORTH DOOR, Dig. 41

f. 8of. *ibidem*: Lavoranti alla d.a Porta dopo la seconda convenzione furono con il d.o Lorenzo.

Bandino di Stefano a fl. 75 l'anno. Ebbe in tutto fl. 87.l.12. d. o (?).

Giuliano di Ser Andrea a fl. 75 l'anno. Hebbe in tutto fl. 179.13.10, item fl. 120 incirca.

Donato di Niccolo di Betto Bardi a fl. 75 l'anno. Hebbe in tutto fl. 8.4.0.

Maso di Christofano in prima a fl. 55 e di poi a fl. 75 l'anno. Hebbe in tutto fl. 113.6.2 item fl. 87.1.4 e fl. 131.7.8.

Domenico di Gio a fl. 38 l'anno, hebbe in tutto fl. 38.

Bernardo di Piero a fl. 26 l'anno. Hebbe in tutto fl. 6.5.4.

---

[27] Frey, bibl. 532, pp. 353f, doc. 4.

[28] Frey, bibl. 532, pp. 354ff, doc. 7. Our Docs. 27-32 have been presented by Frey as one single document, all under the date June 5, 1407.

[29] Frey, bibl. 532, pp. 354ff, doc. 7 with erroneous figures and date of June 5, 1407. Clearly this entry refers to the entire period of the first contract.

[30] The document manifestly refers to the entire period 1404-1415, contrary to Frey, (bibl. 532, pp. 354ff,

doc. 7) who brings it under June 5, 1407.

[31] It is unclear whether these three items or any one of them refer to the period of 1404-1424 or, like the preceding one, to the period 1404-1415, or possibly to the period 1415-1424. Frey, bibl. 532, pp. 354ff, doc. 7, gives the document under June 5, 1407, and with misreadings: [a]*adorato*; [b]*881.*

While the reading l(=lire)831 is clear in both Strozzi and Gori, it may yet be a *lapsus calami* for fl.

Nanni di Franc.o a fl. 24 l'anno. Hebbe in tutto fl. 11.

Franc.o di Gio. detto Bruscaccio a fl. 25 l'anno. Hebbe in tutto fl. 3.18.2.

Cola di Liello di Pietro da Roma. Hebbe in tutto fl. 13.19.2 a fl. 48 l'anno.

Franc.o di Marchetto di Verona a fl. 4 il mese. Hebbe in tutto l.13 d. 4 d'oro.

Giuliano di Gio. da Poggibonsi per fanciullo fl. 6 l'anno. Hebbe in tutto fl. 6.

Maestro (?) Antonio di Domenico (?) di Cicilia a fl. 5 il mese. Hebbe in tutto fl. 3.13.6.

Bartolo di Michele a fl. 75 l'anno. Hebbe in tutto fl. 197.1.7.

Bernardo di Piero Ciuffagni a fl. 45 l'anno. Hebbe in tutto fl. 14.13.—.

Domenico di Gio. a fl. 48 l'anno. Hebbe in tutto fl. 147.16.6, item fl. 67.1.1.

Zanobi di Piero a fl. 16 l'anno. Hebbe in tutto fl. 66.15.11.

Niccolo di Lor.o a fl. 25 l'anno. Hebbe in tutto 21 [sic].

Jacopo di Bartolomeo fanciullo a fl. 6 l'anno e di poi a fl. 9. Hebbe in tutto fl. 20.10.[b]

Giuliano di Monaldo a fl. 18 l'anno. Hebbe in tutto fl. 16.14.3.

Pagolo di Dono garzone di bottega a fl. 5 l'anno e di poi a fl. 7. Hebbe in tutto fl. 20.10.—.

Matteo di Donato a fl. 60 l'anno hebbe in tutto fl. 190 incirca e dipoi a fl. 75 l'anno, hebbe fl. 190 incirca.

Bartolo di Niccolo a fl. 75 l'anno. Hebbe in tutto fl. 64.13.11.

Bartolo di Michele a fl. 50 l'anno. Hebbe in tutto fl. 48.18.9.

Niccolo di Baldovino a fl. 8 l'anno. Hebbe in tutto fl. 7.12.5.

Pagolo di Dono a fl. 25 l'anno. Hebbe in tutto fl. 31.1.7.[32]

Gori, 154v with several minor variants, the only important ones being that [a]Maso di Cristofano's last two wages are added to Donatello's and that [b]Jacopo di Bartolomeo is credited with fior. 16 total wages.

DOC. 32, 1424, April 19, NORTH DOOR, Dig. 105

[32] Frey, bibl. 532, pp. 354ff, doc. 7, with date June 5, 1407. However, this list clearly is a summary which may refer either to the period 1407-1424, or more likely to part of it such as 1407-1415.

[33] Frey, bibl. 532, pp. 354ff, doc. 7.

[34] Frey, bibl. 532, pp. 356f, doc. 8, with date June 5, 1407 (?). The passage refers to both the gilding of the competition relief and the subsequent change of program. Frey dated it, questioningly, June 5, 1407. Yet, by that time work on the New Testament panels was well advanced. The change of program must have been made before work got under way, and thus probably

f. 80v. *ibidem*: La detta Porta fu compiuta del Mese d'Aprile 1424 a dì 19 del d.o Mese si puose e rizzò alle Porti [sic] di S. Gio[33]

Gori, 156

DOC. 33, no date [possibly 1402-3], COMPETITION RELIEF, Dig. 6

f. 80v. *ibidem*: Dorassi il Compasso della Storia d'Abramo del testam.o vecchio per fare prova di diversi Maestri e pigliare che meglio facesse. Deliberossi poi di(?) mettere nella Porta sopradetta il Testamento Nuovo e si riserbo la detta Storia per metterla nell' altra Porta se Testamento Vecchio vi si facesse. Vi si messe d'oro in dorare d.a Storia fl. 12.3.—.[34]

Gori, 156; *LI*, 2, 141

DOC. 34, no date [ca. 1420], NORTH DOOR, Dig. 81

f. 80v. *ibidem*: Michelozzo di Bartolomeo lavorò piu tempo alla d.a seconda Porta a fl. 75 l'anno.[35]

Gori, 156

DOC. 35 [April 19, 1424], NORTH DOOR, Dig. 105

f. 80v. *ibidem*: La d.a seconda Porta fu messo alla Porta di S. Gio.[a] risguarda verso S. Maria del fiore.[36]

Gori, 156: [a]che

DOC. 36, 1424 (=1425), Jan. 2, EAST DOOR, Dig. 110

f. 81. *ibidem*: Si da a fare la terza Porta di Bronzo della Chiesa di S. Gio a Lorenzo di Bartolo di Michele, excellente maestro con che finche non sarà finita, non possa pigliare a fare altro lavoro; il che nel fare la seconda porta haveva poco osservato, e per sua fatica e opera deve havere quello sara giudicato da consoli etc. [sic]. Se gli paghi a buon conto a ragione di fl. 200 l'anno. Michelozzo di Bartolomeo che lavora in su d.a Porta se gli paghi fl. 100 l'anno.[37]

LI, 2, 141; Gori, 142, 156

in 1403. In fact, the tenor of the phrase which refers to the gilding has been interpreted to mean that the gilding was part of the competition (Rossi, bibl. 452, pp. 334ff).

[35] Frey, bibl. 532, p. 357, doc. 9, as of June 5, 1407 (?). Since Michelozzo was not born until 1399 the date is erroneous.

[36] Frey, bibl. 532, p. 357, doc. 10. The date of April 19, 1424, derives from our Doc. 32.

[37] Frey, bibl. 532, p. 357, doc. 2, without the Michelozzo passage which he quotes under p. 359, doc. 6, and dates 1437.

DOC. **37**, 1437, EAST DOOR, Dig. 200

f. 81. *ibidem*: Lorenzo di Bartolo possa tenere al lavoro della d.a Porta Michelozzo sudetto, Vettorio, figliolo di d.o Lorenzo, e altri tre.[38]

Gori, 156

DOC. **38**, 1440, EAST DOOR, Dig. 219

f. 81. *ibidem*: Si delibera di comprare in Fiandra per fare d.a Porta lb. 17000 d'ottone fine.[39]

Gori, 156

DOC. **39**, after 1440; before June 24, 1443 [possibly 1442],[(a)] EAST DOOR, Dig. 240

f. 81. *ibidem*: Matteo di Fran.o d'Andrea da Settignano lavorante della d.a Porta se gli paghi l. 14 il mese.[40]

Gori, 156v with date[(a)] 1442

DOC. **40**, 1443, June 24,[(a)] EAST DOOR, Dig. 241

f. 81. *ibidem*: Restando a farsi ancora di dieci storie che andavano nella terza porta quattro, si conviene con Lorenzo di Bartolo, che egli per compiemento di dette dieci storie per suo magisterio e fatica, garzoni con legne e carboni habbia fl. 1200 o più e meno all'arbitrio degli officiali, con obligo di finire ogni sei mesi la terza parte, che ne egli ne suoi figliuoli possino torre a fare altro lavoro in d.o tempo, ma deva continuamente tenere a lavorare in d.a porta Tommaso e Vettorio, suoi figliuoli etc. [sic].[41]

Gori, 156v, with date[(a)] 1442

DOC. **41**, after June 24, 1443; before Aug. 7, 1447 [possibly 1445], EAST DOOR, Dig. 255

f. 81. *ibidem*: Francesco di Papi se gli da a fare il telaio della d.a porta.[42]

Gori, 156v

DOC. **42**, 1447, Aug. 7, EAST DOOR, Dig. 259

f. 81. *ibidem*: Si delibera di pagare fl. 1200 a Lorenzo di Bartolo per havere finite le storie delle porte, conforme a che era tenuto.[43]

Gori, 156v

DOC. **43** [before Jan. 24, 1448], EAST DOOR, Dig. 262

f. 81. *ibidem*: Si paghi al d.o Lorenzo di Bartolo per fattura delle spranghe fl. 125.[44]

Gori, 156v

DOC. **44**, 1448, Jan. 24, amended 1451 [Jan. 5 or 16], EAST DOOR, Digs. 263, 275

f. 81, 81v. *ibidem*: Si da a fare a L.o di Bartolo il restante della terza Porta cioè 24 spiaggie gettate gl'una di nettatura solamente, per insino si possa dorare, fl. 25, perche siamo chiari, si penera (?)[(a)] a nettare l'una per un buono maestro mesi tre e mezzo o poco meno; e per provisione del tempo vi mettera Lorenzo, mettiamo fl. 3 dell'una. In tutto si fece l'una fl. 28; montano in tutto fl. 672.

Ventiquattro teste, che s'hanno a fare di cera e le forme a gettare e nettare secondo nostra informazione facevamo, si habbia Lorenzo per il tutto sino si possa dorare, fl. 300 a spese dell' Arte di Carboni e Cera.

A Gettare e fare di Cera la Cornice sopra il cardinale, facemmo n'habbia d.o Lorenzo per insino sara cavata dalla forma e del fuoco, a spese dell'Arte fl. 60.

A Gettare e fare di Cera e forme del Cardinale e della soglia e d'uno stipide e d'un altro che n'ha gettato e fatto la forma fra tutto fl. 320.

A fare le forme di Cera e gettare circa di 12 pezzi di spiaggie, che sara l'una braccie cioè 2⅛ o circa per mettere negli stipidi e cardinali d'intorno[(b)] alla porta di fuori, dove saranno i fogliami e animali e debbono essere piu belli di quelli che sono nella Porta fatta, fl. 30 l'una; in tutto fl. 360.

A scarpellare un fregio di poco rilievo dentro alli stipiti e Cardinali d'intorno alla porta che sara braccie 25½ o circa fl. 140.

Per il getto fatto da Lorenzo dell'ultimo telaio della porta e condottolo fino a questo dì, fl. 100.

Tutte le sopradette cose si danno a fare a Lorenzo di Bartoluccio e a Vettorio suo figliuolo, le quali [dovevano canceled] l'anno 1450 non havendo[(c)] finite, di nuovo se gli alluogano per haverle finite in venti mesi da cominciare il dì primo febbraio 1450 (= 1451).[45]

Gori, 156v; 139

[38] Frey, bibl. 532, p. 359, doc. 6.
[39] Frey, bibl. 532, p. 360, as first part of his doc. 11.
[40] Frey, bibl. 532, p. 360, as second part of his doc. 11, with erroneous date of 1440. The approximate date results from the nearest entries preceding and following. The date 1442 is given by Gori.
[41] Frey, bibl. 532, p. 360, doc. 12.
[42] Frey, bibl. 532, p. 360, doc. 13, with erroneous date June 24, 1443. The approximate date results from the nearest entries preceding and following, the probable date 1445 from Doc. 19.

[43] Frey, bibl. 532, pp. 360f, first part of doc. 17. See our Doc. 20.
[44] Frey, bibl. 532, p. 361, doc. 19, with date of Jan. 28. The date results from the silence of Doc. 44 regarding these cross bars.
[45] Frey, bibl. 532, pp. 361f, doc. 20, misread: ᵃponera; ᵇd'un terzo; ᶜparte havendo. The last part of the document is identical with the dated Document 11 and covers a new agreement. Frey assumed, erroneously, that the agreement of 1448 became active only at that late date.

DOC. **45**, 1452 [Mar. 19], EAST DOOR, Dig. 278

f. 81v. *ibidem*: Bilichi della 3 a porta si danno a fare a Tinaccio fabbro, figliuolo di Piero.[46]

Gori, 139 as March 19, 1451 (=1452)

DOC. **46**, 1452, Apr. 2, EAST DOOR, Dig. 279

f. 81v. *ibidem*: Essendo finito la terza porta di S. Gio., si da a indorare a Lorenzo di Bartoluccio e a Vettorio suo figliuolo per fl. 100 di lor magisterio e fatica a tutt'altre spese dell'Arte per doverla haver' finita il dì 20 di Giugno prossimo.[47]

Gori, 142 with date 1451; 139 with date 1452, April 2.

DOC. **47**, 1452, June 16, EAST DOOR, Dig. 280

f. 81v, 82. *ibidem*: Il di 16 di Giugno fù dichiarato essere la d.a Porta finito del tutto indorare. Si paga fl. 884 d'oro e l. 99, s. 3, d. 8 per oro comprato per dorare la d.a Porta.[48]

Gori, 139

DOC. **48** [July 13, 1452], EAST DOOR, Dig. 283

f. 82. *ibidem*: Porta terza di bronzo essendo del tutto finita, si ponga alla porta di S. Gio, che risguarda verso Santa Maria del Fiore.[49]

Gori, 139

DOC. **49** [after Dec. 12-18, 1452; before Feb. 12, 1453], EAST DOOR, Dig. 287

f. 82. *ibidem*: Bottega si da a Lorenzo di Bartoluccio e Vettorio, suo figliuolo, posta parte nel popolo di Santa Maria in Campo e parte nel popolo di San Michele Visdomini per fl. 270, che restavano creditori per la fattura della porta di S. Gio. terza, nella qual bottega havevano lavorato la d.a terza porta.[50]

Gori, 139

DOC. **50**, 1453, Feb. 12, SOUTH DOOR, Dig. 288

f. 82. *ibidem*: Stipiti, cardinale, soglia e grado della porta del Battesimo di S. Gio. si danno a fare a Lorenzo di Bartoluccio e Vettorio suo figliuolo.[51]

Gori, 139 with date Feb. 12, 1453 (=1454)

DOC. **51**, 1457, Feb. 11, SOUTH DOOR, Dig. 297

f. 82. *ibidem*: A Vettorio di Lorenzo di Bartoluccio si paga a conto del magisterio de sopra detti stipiti e altro fl. 100. Item fl. 50.[52]

Gori, 139v

DOC. **52**, 1424 [June ?], EAST DOOR, Dig. 106

f. 82, 82v. *ibidem*: A tergo: Spettabili huomini Niccolo da Uzzano e Compagni, deputati etc. [sic] Intus vero [sic]:

Spectabiles etc. [sic]. Io considero che le 20 historie della nuova porta le quali avete deliberato che siano del vecchio testamento, vogliono avere due cose principalmente: l'una che siano illustri, l'altra che siano significanti. Illustri chiamo quelle che possono ben pascere l'occhio con varietà di disegno, significanti chiamo quelle che abbino importanza degna di memoria. Presupponendo queste due cose, ho eletto secondo il giudicio mio 20 historie le quali vi mando notate in una carta. Bisognerà che colui, che l'ha a disegnare, sia bene instrutto di ciascuna historia, si che possa ben mettere e le persone e gl'atti occorrenti, e che habbia del gentile, si che le sappia bene ornare. Oltra all'historie 20 ho notato otto profeti come vedrete nella carta. Hora (?) dubito punto (?) che quest'opera, come io ve l'ho disegnata riuscira excellentissima. Ma bene vorrei essere presso a chi l'harà a disegnare per fargli prendere ogni significato, che la storia importa. Raccomandomi a Voi Vostro Lionardo d'Arezzo. [See scheme on p. 373.]

Gori, 140f, with the explanatory notes: "Copia di lettera rinchiuso drento a detto Libro della seconda e terza porta di S. Gio.," and in the margin: "Bellissima Memoria finora non saputa."

DOC. **53**, 1416, SAINT JOHN, Dig. 48

f. 91. *Uscita d'Arte de Mercatanti 1416*: Tabernacolo si fa a Orto S. M[ichele], c. 7 e si paga a Frate Bernardo di Stefano, frate di S. M[aria] Novella per parte del Lavorio del

---

[46] Frey, bibl. 532, p. 363, doc. 29.

[47] Frey, bibl. 532, p. 363, doc. 30.

[48] Frey, bibl. 532, p. 363, as first part of his doc. 32. See Doc. 12.

[49] Frey, bibl. 532, p. 363, as second part of his doc. 32, with date of June 16. This entry is essentially identical with the dated one of July 13, 1452, Doc. 73.

[50] Frey, bibl. 532, p. 363, doc. 34, with date of June 16, 1452. Regarding the date, see Docs. 15, 75.

[51] Frey, bibl. 532, p. 364, doc. 40, with date of June 16. The date 1453 (=1454), as it appears on f. 82 and in the copy in Gori, 139, must be revised into 1452 (=1453). Doc. 16, which refers to the same event, was extracted from c. 155 of *Quaderno O*. Since c. 158 of the same quaderno is dated after May 9, 1453 (see Doc. 17), the above entry must be earlier.

[52] Frey, bibl. 532, p. 364, doc. 42.

Scheme from Doc. 52

Come Dio crea il cielo e le stelle	Dio fa l'huomo e la femina	Adam et Eva intorno al albore mangiano il pome	Come sono cacciati del Paradiso dall'Angelo
Cain uccide Abel suo fratello	Ogni forma d'animale entra nell'Arca di Noe	Abraham vuole immolare Isaac per command.o di Dio	Isaac da la benedizione a Jacob credendo che sia Esau
E fratelli di Josef il [?] vendono per invidia	Il sogno di Faraone di 7 vacche e 7 spighe	Josef riconosce i fratelli venuti per lo grano in Egitto	Moise vede Dio nelle spine ardenti
Moise parla a Faraone e fa segni miracolosi	Il mare diviso et il popolo di Dio passante	Le leggi date da Dio a Moise nel monte ardente buccina sonante	Aron immolante sopra l'altare in abito sacerdotale con campanelle e melagrane intorno a vestimenti
Il popolo di Dio passa il fiume Giordano et entra in terra della promissione con l'arca federis.	Davit uccide Golia in presenza del re Saul	Davit fatto re con letizia del popolo	Salamone giudica intra le due femine la questione del fanciullo
Samuel Profeta	Natan Profeta	Helia Profeta	Heliseo Profeta
Isaia Profeta	Jeremia	Ezechiel	Daniel[53]

vetro fà a d.o Tabernacolo. c. 7. Si mette su la figura del S. Gio.(a) c. 7[54]

LI, 2, 115v: (a)Batt. nel d.o tabernacolo

DOC. **54**, 1413, SAINT JOHN, Dig. 31
f. 93. *Uscita dell'Arte, 1413*: Figura(a) si fa per il Pilastro di O. S. M. c. 5[55]
Gori, 173: (a)di bronzo

DOC. **55**, 1415, SAINT JOHN, Dig. 42
f. 101. *Uscita di S. Gio., 1415*: A Albizzo di Piero Maestro per parte della sua provisione del Tabernacolo fa a Orto S. Michele fl. 7, c. 12[56]

DOC. **56**, 1417, Nov. 28, SAINT JOHN, Dig. 56
f. 101. *Uscita di S. Gio., 1417*: Alla figura di S. Gio. a dì 28 di Novembre fl. 5 d'oro pagammo per d.a poliza [?] a Lorenzo di Bartoluccio proprio dette per oro e altro lavorio a

comprato per la d.a figura, c. 20[57]
LI, 2, 115: summary

DOC. **57** [after 1455], PROPERTY, Dig. 295
f. 115ff. *Filza 2 a dell'Arte de Mercatanti di Partiti e Deliberazioni de Consoli dall' 1425 al 1438* [sic]: Consoli possono dare licenza a Vettorio di Lorenzo di Bartoluccio di poter transmutare un podere presso a Careggi il quale Lor.o compro dall'Opera di S. Gio. a vita sua della moglie e di Tommaso e Vettorio suoi figlioli i quali Lor.o e Tom.so di puoi erano morti purche (?) trovano da venderlo bene e possino ancora d.i consoli venderlo libero per doppo [sic] la morte di d.o Vettorio con alcune condizioni, c. 14[58]

DOC. **58**, 1423, NORTH DOOR, Dig. 102
f. 118v. *ibidem*: Porte di S. Gio, Cardinale e stipiti si fanno conforme al disegno di Lo[ren]zo di Bartoluccio, c. 281[59]

[53] Frey, bibl. 532, pp. 357ff, doc. 3, with date of 1425; Brockhaus, bibl. 69, p. 37. For date, see Dig. 106.
[54] Frey, bibl. 532, pp. 380f, doc. 16, quoted from LI, 2, 115v, but with erroneous date of 1412. Repeated, Frey, p. 381, doc. 25, last part only, with correct date of 1416.
[55] Frey, bibl. 532, p. 381, doc. 17.
[56] Frey, bibl. 532, p. 381, doc. 23.
[57] Frey, bibl. 532, p. 381, doc. 26, without month and day.
[58] Unpublished. The document must date from after Ghiberti's death in 1455.
[59] Unpublished.

DOC. **59**, 1439, July 18, EAST DOOR, Dig. 209

f. 123. *Filza 4a dell'Arte de Mercatanti di Peti-zioni e altre scritture dal 1434 al 1461*: Tinac-cio di Piero e Piero di Francesco segli da a fare l'armatura del getto del telaio della terza porta di bronzo di S. Gio, c. 255[60]

DOC. **60**, 1403, Sept. 3, NORTH DOOR, Dig. 7

f. 183ff. *Deliberazioni de Consoli dall' 1401 al 1414*: Porta di Metallo si delibera che si faccia per la Porta dinanzi della Chiesa di S. Gio. che risguarda S. M[aria] del fiore, c. 35[61]

DOC. **61**, before Jan. 12, 1404 [probably Nov. 23, 1403],[(a)] NORTH DOOR, Dig. 8

f. 184. *ibidem*: Porta di Bronzo: Si da a fare a Lorenzo di Bartoluccio Orefice, c. 38[62]

   Gori, 33: [(a)]l'anno 1404

DOC. **62**, 1405, after Aug. 31; before Feb. 11, 1406, NORTH DOOR, Dig. 15

f. 184v. *ibidem*: Lorenzo di Bartoluccio fa la Porta di Metallo e sono nominati i suoi lavor-anti, c. 65[63]

DOC. **63**, 1407, on or before June 3, SAINT JOHN, Dig. 23

f. 185. *ibidem*: Pilastro dell'Arte nel Palazzo d'O.S.M. si orni e per questo s'eleggi[e] [?] tre Offi.li, c. 77[64]

DOC. **64**, 1408, after Dec. 24; before May 2, 1409, NORTH DOOR, Digs. 26, 27

f. 185v. *ibidem*: Porta di Metallo S. Gio. lavor-anti, c. 95 hore che i lavoranti devino havere di vacanza, c. 109[65]

DOC. **65**, 1403 (=1404), Jan. 30, NORTH DOOR, Dig. 10

f. 185v. *Delib. degli Offiziali di Musaico*: Porta di Bronzo si da a fare a Lorenzo di Bartolo Orefice, c. 113[66]

DOC. **66** [1404-1415?], NORTH DOOR, Dig. 40

Lavoranti, c. 114, 115, 116, 117, 118, 119, 120, 121, 122, 123[67]

DOC. **67**, 1454, after Apr. 23; before Apr. 29, 1456, EAST DOOR, Dig. 292

f. 191. *Libro di Provisioni del 1420 al 1470*: Non si possa spendere danari per l'opera di S. Gio. se prima non sara deliberato per i con-soli officiali di mosaico e Proveditori delle porte di S. Gio. fuorche per i salari ordinari, c. 28[68]

DOC. **68**, 1462, after July 5; before March 13, 1463 (=1464), SOUTH DOOR, Dig. 299

f. 192v. *ibidem*: Porte di S. Gio[(a)] erano for-nite[(b)] e solo restava fare il pregio con Vettorio di Lorenzo di Bartoluccio che l'haveva fornite, e particolarmente si doveva restare d'accordo degli stipiti, cardinale, cornice, scaglione e soglia che ultimamente haveva fatto per dette porte, c. 48[69]

   LI, 2, 119v and Gori, 143: [(a)]l'anno 1462; [(b)]finite; Gori, 143 ends after finite

DOC. **69**, 1463 (=1464), before March 13, DOORS, Dig. 301

f. 192v. *ibidem*: Proveditori delle Porte di S. Gio. havendo finito l'officio loro per essere finite le porte, i quali dovevano intervenire negli stanziamenti da farsi delle spese di detta chiesa, però si delibera, che per l'avvenire si stanzino solamente per [illegible] de consoli e offiziali di mosaico, c. 48[70]

DOC. **70**, 1440, after Dec. 7; before Jan. 4, 1441, EAST DOOR, Dig. 217

f. 199ff. *Deliberazioni 1439 e 1440*: Porte di S. Gio si fabbricano, c. 47[71]

[60] Frey, bibl. 532, p. 360, doc. 9; Brockhaus, bibl. 69, p. 40.

[61] Frey, bibl. 532, p. 353, doc. 3.

[62] Unpublished. The pagination points to a date prior to Jan. 12, 1404; for the exact date, Nov. 23, 1403, see Doc. 26.

[63] Unpublished. The date results from the nearest dated entries preceding and following.

[64] Unpublished. The date results from the nearest dated entries preceding and following.

[65] Unpublished. The date results from the nearest dated entries preceding and following.

[66] Frey, bibl. 532, p. 354, doc. 5.

[67] Unpublished. An approximate date can be estab-lished from the following entries: on c. 113, dated Jan. 30, 1404; on c. 118, dated May 28, 1406; on c. 120, dated Jan. 30, 1409.

[68] Unpublished. The date results from the nearest dated entries preceding and following.

[69] Frey, bibl. 532, p. 364, doc. 45, with date of July 5, 1462 and reference to *Porte del Paradiso*. The correct date results from the nearest dated entries preceding and following.

[70] Frey, bibl. 532, p. 364, doc. 46, with date of July 5, 1462. The correct date results from the nearest dated entries preceding and following. Docs. 68 and 69 must be close in date as evident from the pagination of the *Libro di Provisioni*, excerpted by Strozzi.

[71] Frey, bibl. 532, p. 360, doc. 10, with the erroneous date of Dec. 7, 1439. The correct date results from the nearest entries preceding and following.

DOC. 71, 1444, after Jan. 3; before Feb. 24 [Jan. 24], EAST DOOR, Dig. 246

f. 203. *Deliberazioni de Consoli 1443 e 1444*: S. Gio. Porta di Bronzo Vettorio di Lor[en]zo di Bartolo M.stro delle d.e Porte in nome di suo padre conduce per tre anni a lavorare a d.a Porta Benozzo di Leso (?) Pittore po.lo di S. Friano, c. 8[72]

Gori, 141v

DOC. 72, 1449, Sept. 22, EAST DOOR, Dig. 273

f. 206. *Deliberazioni de Consoli dall'anno 1447 al 1451*: Porta di S. Gio di bronzo scarpellatori elezione, c. 73[73]

DOC. 73, 1452, July 13, EAST AND NORTH DOORS, Dig. 283

f. 209ff. *Deliberazioni de Consoli dall'anno 1452 al 1454*: Pratica circa il rizzare e porre la porta di bronzo nuovamente fatta nella chiesa di S. Gio. Si delibera stante la sua bellezza, che si metta alla porta di mezzo, che risguarda S. Maria del Fiore e che[(a)] quella che era in d.o luogo si ponga alla porta verso la colonna e case dell'Opera, c. 17[74]

LI, 2, 119v: [(a)]la porta che era prima in d.o luogo si ponga . . . ; Gori, 143, identical.

DOC. 74, 1452, Dec. 12-18, SOUTH DOOR, Dig. 285

f. 209v. *ibidem*: S. Gio. Stipiti, cardinale e soglia si faccia fare alla porta di d.a chiesa, che e vicino al Battesimo nel modo e forma che stanno le altre porte di d.a chiesa, c. 33[75]

LI, 2, 119v; Gori, 143, with date 1452

DOC. 75, 1453, Apr. 9-26, EAST DOOR, Dig. 289

f. 210. *ibidem*: Casa si consegna per fl. 250 a M.o Lorenzo di Bartoluccio Maestro d'Intaglio [?] e Vettorio suo figliuolo che ultimamente havevano fatto la Porta del Bronzo per fl. 250

che era per il resto di quando havevano havere per d.a manifattura, c. 53[76]

DOC. 76, 1453, May 14-26, EAST DOOR, Dig. 291

f. 210. *ibidem*: Scaglione di bronzo si mettono dalla porta di mezzo verso l'Opa., c. 58[77]

DOC. 77, 1456, April 3 and following months, EAST DOOR, Dig. 296

f. 213f. *Deliberazioni e altro de Consoli dall'anno 1455 al 1459*: Vettorio di Lorenzo di Bartoluccio se gli paga danari per fare gli stipiti scaglione e soglia della porta di S. Gio., c. 17, 19, 32, 42, 79[78]

DOC. 78, 1458, after Nov. 21; through April 1459, SOUTH DOOR, Dig. 298

f. 217v. *ibidem*: Bronzo si faccia venire per le porte e stipiti di S. Gio., c. 192, 215, 221, 228[79]

ASF, STROZZ., LI, 2

DOC. 79, 1447, after Aug. 7; before Apr. 22, 1448 [probably before Jan. 24], EAST DOOR, Dig. 261

f. 114. *Quaderno di Riccordi segnato M dal 1444 al 1449*:[(a)] Fregi della terza Porta di S. Gio. si rigettano[(b)] per Lorenzo di Bartoluccio, c. 151[80]

Gori, 153v: [(a)]gives the source; [(b)]rigettino

ASF, STROZZ., LI, 3

DOC. 80, Digs. 5, 9, 11, 16, 38

f. 153. Nencio di Bartoluccio f. 30 lib. C 1403[81] 270; Libr. D 178 fl. 100.

Spese per la Porta del Metallo che si fa lib. D 183 fl. 3 l. 87 s. 13; lib.o E 173, 174, 226; lib.o F 150, 157, 281; G 126, 131, 156, 158, 159, 166, 176; J 91, 93, 94, 97, 98, 130, 139.

Figura del Pilastro d'O.S.M. F 97; K 96, 27,

[72] Frey, bibl. 532, p. 360, doc. 14, as Jan. 3, 1444. The approximate date results from the nearest entries, preceding and following, the exact date from the original document (Doc. 99).

[73] Brockhaus, bibl. 69, p. 45; Frey, bibl. 532, p. 362, doc. 27, with the date of Sept. 12. The date 1449 is confirmed by the original document, Doc. 95; c. 73 in Strozzi's excerpt corresponds to c. 73v in the original document.

[74] Frey, bibl. 532, p. 363, doc. 35, with date of June 16; Brockhaus, bibl. 69, p. 45. See Doc. 48 for the same event.

[75] Frey, bibl. 532, pp. 363f, doc. 39. Frey fails to realize that this document refers to the Andrea Pisano door and not to Ghiberti's second door. The date results from the nearest entries preceding and following. See also Doc. 14.

[76] Unpublished. The date results from the nearest entries preceding and following. See the earlier Docs. 49 and 15.

[77] Unpublished. The date results from the nearest entries preceding and following.

[78] Frey, bibl. 532, p. 365, doc. 41.

[79] Frey, bibl. 532, p. 364, doc. 43, with date of November 21, 1458. The correct date results from the last dated entry preceding, November 21, 1458, and the entries on c. 215 and c. 228, dated February and April 28, 1459, respectively.

[80] Frey, bibl. 532, p. 361, as first part of his doc. 18. The approximate correct date results from the pagination in the original *Ricordo M*: c. 148=Aug. 7, 1447 (cf. Doc. 20); c. 152=Jan. 24, 1448 (cf. Docs. 22 and 44).

[81] Error of Strozzi's. The *Libro Grande C* corresponds to the year 1402.

104, 123, 126, 131, 138; L 88, 90, 102[?] . . . ,
103, 107, 110, 121, 134; M 23, 88, 89, 91, 92, 98,
102, 107, 120, 130; N 68, 78, 80, 81, 82, 92, 97,
100, 102, 104, 120; P 6.z[?],8.y, 79, 80, 81, 82,
100, 103, 112.y, 113.z, 181, 182, 183, 184, 185,
187, 188, 199, 200, 201, 202, 203, 204, 207, 229,
235, 236, 374, 375, 376, 377, 380[?], 381, 391,
392, 393, 394, 395, 396, 397, 398, 399, 400, 407,
409; O 8, 87, 89, 90, 98, 99; Q+ 5, 172, 173, 174,
176, 177, 178, 190, 191, 197, 231, 232, 247, 248,
252, 256, 262, 264, 266, 272, 274, 275, 276, 279,
280, 367, 272 [sic], 376, 378, 380, 382, 383, 386,
402; T 173, 176, 177, 180, 186, 187, 190, 191,
207, 272, 275, 276, 279, 281, 363; T 1421. 187,
188, 189, 193, 196, 202, 207, 209, 210, 212, 213,
217, 222, 223, 225, 233, 234, 240, 243, 245, 246,
247, 249, 258[?], 300, 304, 306, 308, 322, 323,
325, 326, 330, 338, 352, 355, 356, 357, 358; G
256, 258, 259, 266, 268, 271, 272, 297, 298, 301,
307, 316, 319, 323, 330, 332, 333, 335, 341, 352.
Terza Porta 337, 338, 365, 373, 166, 169, 182,
198; K 177, 178, 179, 188; L 263, 264, 265.
Seconda Porta J 165, 166, 167 [canceled], 171,
190; L 271.
Terza M 286, 287, 288; N 310, 311, 312, 313;
O 164; P 184, 185, 186; Q[?] 162, 163[?], 164.[82]

ASF, CATASTO

DOC. 81, 1427, July 9, TAX DECLARATION,
Dig. 138

*ASF, Quartiere di San Giovanni, Gonfalone
Chiavi, Portate al Catasto, 1427, vol. 58, c. 199,
199v*

+XPUS MCCCCXXVII a di VIIII di luglo
Dinanzi a voi signori ufficiali del chatasto del
comune di firenze sustanze inchariche per
me
Lorenzo di bartolo orafo lavora le porte di
sco. giovanni ghonfalone delle chiavi [h]o di
prestanzon fl. II s. XVI d. X le sustanze sono
queste cioe
una chasa posta nel popolo di sco. anbruogio
di firenze nella via borgho allegri confinata
da primo via da secondo zanobi di jachopo
de rosso da terzo tomaso di bartolone granaiu-
olo detto bolliera (?) e piu altri confini a
detta chasa con piu maseritie a uso di me e
della mia famiglia. . . .   fl.
uno pezzo di terra posto nel popolo di sco.
donato in fronzano da primo via da secondo
labadia di valonbrosa da terzo Nanni di nicholo e piu altri confini cioe lavoratia ulivata e
vignata
Lavorala Nanni di nicholo dame di fitto
l'anno soma una dolio [d'olio] . . .   fl.
truovomi in bottega II istorie dottone per

una fonte di battesimo le quali o fatto per a
Siena le quali due storie sarano per amici
comuni a stimare penso averne pellomeno
quatro cento o circa de quali o auti fl. 290
restero avere fl. cientodieci . . . .   fl. 110
truovomi ancora in bottegha una chasetta
dottone fatta per chossmo demedici stima di
fl. CC° circha della quale o avuti gia piu
tempo per ispese sono ite in essa fl. CXXXV
Resto avere ancora fl. LXV . . .   fl. 65
In sul monte del chomune di firenze mi truovo
iscritti in me fl. 714½ di monte dotto [d'otto][a]
percento de quali ve [v'e] posto la conditione di
fl. 100 per fl.L gli resto a dare cioe al bancho
d'isau e compagni . . . .   fl.
Resto avere da frati di sca maria novella fl. 10
della sepoltura ch'io feci pel gienerale . . . fl. 10
da giuliano di piero Maestro di murare detto
scanbella   fl. 5
+XPUS a di VIIII di luglio 1427
Incharichi a me Lorenzo di bartolo orafo
Lorenzo sopradetto detta [d'età] danni [d'an-
ni] XLVI o circha
La marsilia mia donna detta danni XXVI o
circha
tomaso mio figliulo deta danni X o circha
vetorio mio figlouolo deta danni VIIII o circha
[H]o debito con piu persone come apresso
diro
Antonio di piero del vaglente e compagni
orafi   fl. 13
Nichola di messer veri de medici   fl. 10
Domenicho di tano coltriciaio   fl. 9
Nicholo charducci e compagni ritaglatori fl. 7
Papi d'andrea legnaiuolo   fl. 16
Mariano da ghanbassi Maestro di murare   fl. 7
Papero di meo dassettignano   ) sono miei
Simone di nanni da fiesole   } garzoni in
Cipriano di bartolo da pistoia) bottega fl. 48
Antonio chiamato el mastro sarto   fl. 15
Domenicho di lippo coltriciaio   fl. 2
Allessandro d'Alessandri e compagni   fl. 4
Duccio adimari e compagni Ritaglatori   fl. 8
Antonio di giovanni cartocaio   fl. 3
Isau d'agnolo e compagni   fl. 50
L'opera di sca crocie   fl. 6
Lorenzo da brucianese fornaciaio e
   compagni   fl. 3
Meo lastraiuolo a sco pulinare   fl. 5
Pippo . . . chalzolaio a le porte (?)   fl. 8
(in different handwriting:)
Chiavi a di X di luglo
Lorenzo di bartoluccio orafo . . . l. 3 s 10 d 10
. . . questo a libro (?) c. 423
(in the first hand:)
scritta di lorenzo di bartolo orafo[83]

---

[82] Unpublished. For the date of the *Libri Grandi*, see
above, p. 364, note 13.

[83] Autograph. Mather, bibl. 308, pp. 56f, misread
detto for [a] *d'otto*.

DOC. 81a, *ibidem, Campione, 1427, vol. 80,* c.423v

Repeats the same items, adding the tax assessment for items not specified in the *Portata* and deducts 200 fiorini per dependent (*bocca*), thus arriving at the tax due:

... chonposto per gli uficiali in fl 1 s VIII[84]

DOC. 82, 1431, Jan. 26, TAX DECLARATION, Dig. 162

ibidem, Portate al Catasto, 1430, vol. 386, c. 192, 192v

+XPUS MCCCCXXX a di XXVI di giennaio
Dinanzi a voi signori uficiali del chatasto del comune di firenze sustantie e incharichi per me Lorenzo di bartolo orafo lavora la porta di sco giovanni quartier di sco giovanni ghonfalone delle chiavi le sustanze son queste.
O di catasto fl 1. s. VIII [inserted]
Una Casa posta nel popolo di sco anbruogio di firenze in via borgho allegri confini da primo via da secondo zanobi di jacopo di rosso vaiaio da terzo tomaso di bartolone da rovezano e piu altri confini a detta casa con piu altre maseritie a uso di me e della mia famiglia
uno pezzo di terra posto nel popolo sco donato in fronzano da primo via da secondo labadia di valleonbrosa da terzo nanni di nicholo di fio e piu altri confini la detta terra lavora arotto (?) nani di nicholo e damene di fitto una soma dollio detta terra vignata ulivata e lavoratia
45 pechore tielle [tienele] neri di piero dello popolo di sco bartolo a pomino a mezo pero e mezo danno
In sul monte del chomune di firenze mi truovo iscritti in me fl. MCCCVII[(a)] dotto percento e quali ve posto una conditione dico in alesandro di giuliano torrig[i]an[i] di fl. CC laquale conditione e per 80 fl. mi presto el detto alesandro e quali denari e .. (?) pel banco d'agnolo d'isau martellini
O avere dal arte di chalimala franciessca fl. dugiento ottanta e quali denari o avanzati colla detta arte come aparisce peloro libri
O avere da giuliano di piero del banbaccio fl. cinque maestro di murare[(b)]

+XPUS MCCCCXXX a di gienaio a di XXVI
Incharichi di lorenzo di bartolo orafo
Lorenzo sopradetto detta d'anni 49 o circa
La marsilia mia donna detta d'anni 30 o circa
Tomaso mio figluolo deta d'anni 13
Vetorio mio figliuolo deta d'anni 12
o debito con piu persone
Allexandro di giuliano torrigiani fl. ottanta   fl. 80

Filippo di nicholo da fiesole fl. settantacinque   fl. 75
Nichola di messer veri fl. dodici   fl. 12
L'erede d'Agnolo d'Isau Martellin fl. otto
                                                          fl. 8
Antonio sarto chiamata el mastro fl. sedici fl. 16
Al fondaco di spinello adimari fl. tre   fl. 3
A pippo chalzolaio fl. quatro   fl. 4
A Jacopo ... legnaiuolo da sco tomaso
fl. tre   fl.(c) 3[85]
repeated:
ibidem, Portate al Catasto, 1430, cod. 388, c. 170, 170v
Evidently a revised second *Portata*, with the following additions: in ending the list of *sustanze*: [(b)]avere le paghe di detti fl. MCCCVII di prestanze; in ending the list of *incarichi*:
[(c)]a l'opera (?) di sca croce per uno luogho di sepultura   fl. 15
a frate francesco frate di detta chiesa per
le spese e muratura di detta sepultura fl. 6
avere (?) la detta opera per uno ... (?) ibi
dalloro   fl. 5 d 2
A francesco di pagholo orafo e compagni
                                               fl. 2 d 2
Andrea di ser laudo e compagni   fl. 1 s 2[86]

DOC. 82a, *ibidem, Campione, 1430, cod. 409,* c. 191v, 192

DOC. 83, TAX DECLARATION, 1433, May 29, Dig. 179

ibidem, Portate al Catasto, 1433, cod. 481, c. 149, 149v

+XPUS MCCCCXXXIII a di XXVIIII di maggio
Inanzi a voi ufiziali del chatasto del comune di firenze sustantie e incharichi per me lorenzo di bartolo orafo lavoro la porta di sco giovanni ghonfalone delle chiavi o di chatasto s. sedici
le sustantie mie sono queste
una chasa posta nel popolo di sco anbruogio di firenze in via Borgho allegri Confini da primo via da secondo zanobi de rosso vaiaio da terzo tomaso di bartolone da rovezzano e piu altri confini a detta chasa co[n]masseritie a uso di me e della mia famiglia
uno podere a vita di me e della mia donna e dei miei figluoli posto nel popolo di sco piero a chareggi confini da primo via da secondo ugolino ruccellai da terzo chola di nicholo d'arezzo e molti piu altri confini. Eb[b]i el detto podere dall arte di chalimala avea la detta arte di fitto del detto podere fl. 34 tenealo a fitto bartolo del manzuolo e rimase

---

in sudetto podere el quale e [è]con terra lavoratia vignito [vigniato] e ulivato con piu altri
frutti in su detto podere e chon chasa da
lavoratore e non da oste

uno pezzo di terra a sco donato in fronzano
laquale mi chosto fl. XIIII confini da primo
via da secondo labadia a vallenbrosa da terzo
nanni di fio tiella a mezo da me el detto nanni
ane [hane] in mia parte istaia due di grano
b[arili] tre di vino

[H]o circa di venti pecore le quali tiene a
mezo neri di piero da matamorelli (?) del
popolo di sco bartolo a pomino

In sul monte del comune di firenze mi truovo
iscritti fl. 984 dotto percento o in sudetto monte
le page sostenute di fl. M e quali i vende (?)
antonio di nicho Barbadori d'otto percento .

o in sudetto monte pagati a riavere i miei
chatasti da marzo nel 1432 insino a detto di di
sopra

[H]o avere dall'arte di chalimala circha di fl.
cento[(a)] e quali o avanzati colla detta arte

da giuliano di piero del bambaccio fl. cinque
XPUS MCCCCXXXIII a di XXVIIII di maggio

Incharichi di Lorenzo di bartolo orafo gho-
falone delle chiavi. Io lorenzo sopradetto
deta danni XXXX [canceled] LII o circa la
marsilia mia donna deta danni XXXIII o
circa tommaso mio figluolo deta danni sedici
vettorio mio figluolo deta danni quindici

[H]o debito con piu persone

a filippo di nicholo da fiesole a dare circa
    di fl. XXXVIII   fl. 38
antonio chiamato el mastro sarto circa di
    fl. XVI   fl. 16
a giuliano di ser andrea ista a sco. sebbio
    circa di fl. X   fl. 10
alla ghabella del sale per nanni di bartolo
    di latino del popolo della pieve di piti-
    ano fl. XX e quali promisi a nicholo
    carduci proveditore della detta ghabella
                 fl. 20
al fondaco di nicholaio degli allesandri fl.
    XVIII o circa   fl. 18
a simone di nanni da fiesole lavora mecho
    fl. XVI   fl. 16
a papero di meo da settignano lavora
    meco fl. X   fl. 10
a papi d'andrea legniaiuolo a sco. tomaso
    fl. II   fl. 2
a chola di nicolo d'arezo fl. tre   fl. 3
a guarente orafo per una promessa per
    mano di nanni da fiesole circa di fl. III fl. 3
antonio del maestro gherardo circa di fl.
    II½   fl. 2½[87]

[87] Autograph, unpublished.
[88] Mather, bibl. 308, p. 57 transcribed this copy in-

ibidem, cod. 479, c. 143, 143v
copy of previous document with some minor
mistakes.[88]

DOC. 84, 1442, Aug. 30, TAX DECLARATION, Dig. 237

ibidem, Campione, 1442, cod. 627, c. 214, 214v
In nomine domini MCCCCXXXXII a di 30
dagosto Quartiere scto giovani Gonfalone
chiavi

Dinanzi da voi s[ignori] dieci huficiali della
conservazioni e augumentazione della nuova
gravezza del comune di firenze per me si ra-
porta [in margin in different hand: Lorenzo
di Bartolo detto Bartoluccio maestro delle
porte]

Lorenzo di bartolo Maestro delle porte di scto
giovanni dj firenze Le mie sustanzie e beni in-
frascripttj cio e

Una chasa e suoi edifizj posta in firenze nel
popolo dj scto ambruogio Luogo detto via
borgallegri con una casetta allato alla sopradetta Laquale conperai da mona pagola donna
che fu dj tomaso di bartolone da rovezano le
quali io habito da primo via da secondo zanobi
de rosso vajaio da terzo sengnia di ser Lucha e
da quarto le chase di scto ambruogio e via
. . . fl.

[in margin in different hand . . . (?) una chassa
donna pagola di tomaso del bartolone (Gᵒ)
chiavi c. 196]

Uno pezzo di terra lavoratja e un pocho di
vignja la quale comperai da nani di nicholo e
una mezza chasa per non divisa da[l]lavoratore
posta nel popolo dj scto donato in fronzano
e da primo e secondo vja da terzo labadja di
valenbrosa Lavora la detta terra e vignja e
abita la detta chasa il sopradetto nanj di nicholo costommj fiorini trentacinque rende in
parte

grano staia due
vino barili sei
oljo uno mezo barile

Uno podere posto nel popolo dj scto piero a
chareggj e chasa da lavoratoj e da primo e
secondo e terzo vja e da quarto cola d'arezzo[e]
el veschovo di fiesole Lavoralo michelino di
matteo mjo lavoratore rende in parte lenfra-
scritte chose

Grano staja venti
Vino congnja (?) tre
Oljo barili quatro
fichi sechi staia due
Mandorle staio uno

Conperai detta possessione dall'arte de merchatanti a vjta di me e della mia familglia

stead of the autograph original, erroneously inserting
at [(a)] fl. 1000 instead of cento.

dipoi torna a detta arte ebesi per prezzo di
fiorini trecentosesanta

Tre prezzetti [sic] di terra lavoratia con al-
chuno uljvo da primo e secondo e terzo via e
quarto cosimo de medici posti in detto populo
e luogo detto monte piano lavorale il sopradetto lavoratore e rende

Grano staia sei

Oljo orge mezo

costomj fiorinj sessanta

Uno podere chon chasa da singnjore [e] da[l]la-
voratore posto nel popolo della pieve a sep-
timo dj stajora cinquanta confinato da primo
e secondo e terzo e quarto vja E un pezzo di
terra dj stajora quatordjcj chon chasa da[l]la-
voratore posto in detto luogo e in detto popolo
da primo e secondo via terzo e quarto l'arte
de merchatantj Lavoralo papj dj gustino rendemi i sopradettj terrenj in parte

Grano staja trenta

biada e fave staja otto

Vino barili cinque

Uova serque quatro

Conperaj dettj terrenj dalle rede dj sandro
biliotti costomj fiorinj trecento cinquanta

Ritrovami nel secondo chatasto avere in sul
monte fl. MCCCVII de qualj nessuno mj
ritruovo oggj avere ne dj nessuna fatta [nessun
affatto ?] de qualj danarj no [n'ho] comperato

Le sopradette chose e parte pagate mje gravezze

Boche e eta

Lorenzo deta dannj sesantadue

La dona sua deta dannj quarantaquatro

Maso deta dannj ventjsej   } suoj

Vettorjo deta dannj ventjcinque } filgluiolj

Rjtruomj [sic] avere dj graveza uno fl. s. 9 d. 11

Io vettorjo filgluiolo del sopradetto Lorenzo
meto qui da pie Cento sessanta fiorinj di
monte i qualj danarj dichono in me Ma non
sono mj ipso (?) sono di mona lisa donna che
fu di betto de rugieri G[onfalone] L[eone]
d'oro e chosi si contera pella sua scritta[89]

DOC. 85, 1447 [after Feb. 28, before Mar.
25], TAX DECLARATION, Dig. 258

ibidem, Portate al Catasto, 1446, cod. 682,
c. 825, 825v

1446

Q.S.G.G. chiavi

Djnanzi da voj singnjorj ufizjalj elettj a porre
la nuova gravezza del **popolo di firenze** raporto
per me si fa

Lorenzo di cione di ser bonachorso ghibertj
altrimentj chiamato Lorenzo di bartoluccjo
maestro d'intalgljo

Nella diecina ebbj   fl. 1

Nel dispiacente ebbj   fl. 1 s. 3 d. 2

Nel primo chatasto ebbj   fl. 1 s. 8

Una chasa per mjo abitare posta nel popolo
di scto anbruogj° di firenze luogo detto vja
borgallegrj che da primo vja e secondo zanobi
di hiachopi del rosso vajajo a terzo foio (?)
pantolini a quarto sengnja di ser Lucha di ser
sengnja cholla detta chasa era una chasetta
della quale per istretezza di chasa ho fatto
d'ongnj chosa una la quale si compero da
mona pagola donna fu di tommaso di bartolone da rovezzano fl. 115 charta fatta per mano
di ser Luigj di ser michele guidi nell'anno
1438

Un podere posto nel popolo di scto piero a
chareggj che da primo vja e secondo da
terzo chosimo di giovannj de medicj da quarto
chardjnale dalbulletta da quinto meastro
ugoljno medicho da pisa e piu altri confini.
El quale podere mj fu asengnjato dall arte de
merchatantj dall anno 1431 e del mese dagosto
el quale [h]o a vita dime [e] della mia famjlglja
di poj torna a detta arte chostomi fl. 370
sichome apare charta fatta per mano di ser
franciescho guardi notajo fiorentino ollo (ho
lo) afittato nel presente anno a donato di
njcholo natj (?) chon alquante masseritje
Rendemi di fitto l'anno dal sopradetto

L'anno . . . .   fl. 38

Un pezzo di terra lavoratja posta nel popolo
di scto donato in fronzano che da primo vja
e secondo la badia di valenbrosa La quale
terra fu achatastata per me Lorenzo rendevamj
in detto chatasto soma 1 [una] d'oljo di fitto
chostomi fl. dieci Rendemi ogi

Oljo . . . . barile mezo

Grano . . . . st[aia?] 2

Un pezo di terra vingnjata posta in detto
popolo di scto donato in fronzano che da
primo vja e secondo betto di calcagnio (?) a
terzo il piu detto Lorenzo chonparossi dall
anno 1442 dal mese d'aprile fu comperato per
vettorjo mio filgljuolo carta fatta per ser luigi
di ser michele guidi chonperossi da nanni di
nicholo Lavorala e detto nanni di nicholo
sopradetta terra e vingnia chosto fl. 35 Rende
l'anno in parte

Vino . . . . barili 6

Un podere posto nel popolo della pieve di
scto guljano a settjmo chon chasa per nostro
abitare e chasa da lavoratore Conperalo dall
anno 1441 a di 2 di gennajo da biliotto di
sandro biljotti insieme chon una chasetta dove
si fa la vendemja chosto fl. 360 sichome appare
charta di ser Jachopo salvestrj Rende in parte
lanno

---

[89] Not autograph; published by Mather, bibl. 308,
p. 58 as a *Portata* with misprinted date 1432. In the
margin throughout illegible assessment notes by different hand. *Portata* not traceable.

Grano staja	st 36
Biada e fave	st 6
Noci staio	st 1
Vino barilj sei	b. 6
Caponi pajo uno	
polastri pajo uno	
Uova serque quatro	

Un pezo di terra vingnjata posta in detto popolo dalla pieve che da primo e secondo vja
a terzo Maestro gabrielle giudeo a quarto
bartolomeo t[r]onciavegli (?) La quale conperaj d'agustino di franchiescho del popolo
della badja di settjmo chosto fl. 70 charta fatta
per mano di ser Luigj di ser michele guidi
sotto di tre di dicembre 1444 Rende in parte
a me

Vino barili trenta	b. 30

Un pezzo di terra vingnjata posta nel popolo
di scto cerbazzo a pelago che da primo vja a
secondo la badia di valonbrosa a terzo fiume
di vicsano (?) a quarto l'erede di piero fabro
la quale Riconperaj dell anno 1446 a di 15
d'agosto d'antonio di piero chasella chostomi
fl. 50. Carta fatta per ser romolo di ser guido
e piu le chasolari con detta vingnja posto nel
popolo di scto chimanti (?) a pelago e dentro
nel chasteluccio che da primo via a secondo
muro chastellano a terzo altri Rendemi detta
vingnja nel presente anno barilj cinque di
vino Lavorala bartolo di domenjcho da pelago
Rende

Vino barili cinque	b. 5

Creditj di monte

fiorini cinqueciento trenta di monte comune
e qualj dicono in me Lorenzo e vettorjo mio
filgljuolo abiamoglj vendutj per soperire a
nostri bisognj vendevonsj sotto di 27 prossimo
passato

Una chasa e botega posta al chanto alla palglia
che da primo e secondo via a terzo matteo
cosmi palgljaiuolo e quarto antonio di ser
giovannj bonaiutj La quale chasa e botega e
chonsengnjata per dota dela Madalena filgljuola di antonio di ser giovanni predetto
E donna di vettorjo mio filgljuolo l'entrata
della quale debbe essere di detto vettorjo
marito di detta madalena tiella[tienela]a pigione piero di francescho marja spetiale danne
di pigione l'anno

fiorini cinquanta	fl. 50

Carta fatta per mano di ser antonio pugi
notajo fiorentino sotto di ventotto di febrajo.[90]

DOC. 86, 1451, Aug. 14, TAX DECLARATION,
Dig. 276

*ibidem, Portate al Catasto, 1451, cod. 718,
c. 297, 297v*

Dinanzi da voj singnjorj ufizialj aporre la
nuo[va] graveza Raportasi per me
Lorenzo di cione di ser bonacorso ghiberti
altrimenti chiamato Lorenzo di bartoluccjo

Ebbj di graveza nella diecina fl. 2 s. 10 d. 9	
fu sgravato	s. 10 d. 4

Una chasa per mjo habitare posta nel popolo
di scto anbruogjo luogo detto vja borgo al-
legrj con una chasetta laquale chonperaj da
mona pagola donna che fu di tomaso di bartolone da rovezano charta fatta per mano di
ser luigi di ser michele guidi che da primo
vja secondo zanobi di jachopo vaiaio da terzo
sengnia quarto vja pantoljno tutta a mjo uso.
Un podere posto nel popolo di scto piero a
chareggj a mja vita da primo secondo vja terzo
chardinale dalbulletta quarto antonjo del
rosso chaljzaio ollo [ho lo] afittato one [hone]
di fitto fl. trentotto

Una chasetta da lavoratore chon aja e pergola
intorno e orto chon vingnja allato alla chasa
jnsieme chon un pocho di terra vavevo [v'ha-
vevo] insino (?) nel primo chatasto insieme
con un pezo di terra salvaticha postj nel
popolo di scto donato in fronzano luogho
detto labonafalda da primo via secondo andrea di baldo terzo rede (?) di cantino farsat-
taio laquale chasa vingnja e terra conperaj da
nanni di nicholo di detto popolo empta da
goro di bruno da baroncelli sichome apare
charta per mano di ser luigi e di ser domenicho
di ser santi tiella [tienela] afito detto nicholo
di nanni damene di fitto lire sedici chosto-
[rono] detti beni fl. quarantacinque

Un podere chon chasa per mjo abitare e da
lavoratore posto nel popolo di scto guljano
a settimo chon terra lavoratia e parte vignjata
Insieme con una chasetta dove si fa la vendemja con altra chasa di staiora 68 o circha
in tutto, da primo l'arte de merchatanti secondo terzo quarto via luogo detto pantanaccjo
Rende in parte

Grano staia	36
vino b (arili)	6
Fave staia	6
Caponi paio uno	
Uova serque	4

Conperaj detto podere da biljotto di sandro
di biliotto sichome appare charta per mano
di ser iachopo salvestrj.
Un pezo di terra vingnjata posta in detto
popolo e[l]luogo detto in pantano che da
primo secondo vja terzo maestro gabriello
gudeo e quarto nicholo tronciavelli (?) con-
perata da quintino di cecho charta fatta per
mano di ser luigj di ser michele guidi Lavora
detto podere e vignja guljano gustini con con-

---

[90] Not autograph; Mather, bibl. 308, pp. 58f. *Campione* not extant.

ditione che dalla detta vignja mi debba dare barili dodicj di vino e talgliare e riporre a ongni sua spesa ognj anno staioro uno di detta vingnja

Un pezo di terra vingnjata posta nel popolo di scto cerbazzjo a pelago la quale conperaj d'antonjo di piero chasella insieme con un chasolare posto nel chastello vecc[h]io di pelago

Rende barilj sej di vino

Una chasa posta al chanto alla palglia che da primo secondo vja terzo antonjo di ser giovanni quarto matteo chasini (?) fummj consengnjata [consegnata] in dota di vettorjo mjo figljuolo e pella [per la] madalena sua donna filgljuola d'antonio di ser giovannj bonaiutj e suocero di detto vettorjo tiella [tienela] a pigione batista e jachopo filgljuolj furono di piero spetiale danone di pigione fl. cinquanta.[91]

DOC. 86a

ibidem, Campione, cod. 719, c. 515, 515v repeats the above, including the assessments

DOC. 87, 1429, TAX DECLARATION CALIMALA, Dig. 157

ASF, Portate al catasto, 1429, cod. 291, Beni di Compagnie e Arti di Firenze e de Sei di Arezzo e Cortona, portata, Arte di Chalimala, c. 5ff

(c. 5
. . . Beni e possessioni donati alla detta arte per Piero di Francesco Broccardi . . . .
c. 6
Incharichi [h]anno i detti beni . . .)
c. 6v
Seghuono incharichi sopra e beni di Piero di Francesco detto
Lopera di San giouanni di firenze a in diposito dalla detta kagione fl. MDCCC de quali fl. DCCC sono della donna fu del detto Piero e costano lanno a kagione di fl. 7 per c[ent]o perche cosi ne da larte allej. E fl. M costano fl. 6 per c[ent]o. Et detti denari si tolsono quando si gitto el telaio della porta di san giouanni per ottone e altre spese bisognorono torre a un tratto montano l'anno fl. ciento sedicj d[oro]   fl. 1800
c. 24
(Entrata dell'opera di san giouanni battista di firenze . . .
a la detta opera di spese . . . .)
a di spese dinteressi di fl. 1800 chella detta opera a in diposito dalla commessione di piero di francescho brocchardi de quali fl. 800 sono

della donna del detto piero e costano fl. 7 per-c[ent]o che chosi ne da larte allej e fl. M co-stano fl. 6 perc[ent]o. J detti denari dicono si tolsono per conperare ottone per lo getto del telaio della porta di san giouanni e per altre cose bisongnorono   fl. 116
c. 24v
. . . seguono incharichi dellopera di san Gio-uanni detto. . . .
Et piu dicono [h]anno di spesa per la terza porta che e comminciata [a gittare cancelled] e che non si puo immaginare il costo costa solo il maestro lanno fl. 200 . . .[92]

DOC. 88, 1429, TAX DECLARATION CALIMALA, Dig. 157

ibidem, cod. 293, Danari uno per lira della Mercanzia e Arti e Compagnie della Citta di Firenze e Beni patrimoniali dei religiosi, Campione, c. 4ff

(c. 4
beni e possessioni lasciati alla detta arte per piero di francesco brocchardi. . . .
c. 5
debitori appartenenti a detto lascito . . .)
Lopera di san giouanni a in diposito della detta kagione fl. 1800. . . .
c. 5v
Incharichi appartenenti a detto lascito di piero brocchardi. . . .
E piu anno dincharicho le prestanze ovvero chatastj di Mona chaterina donna fu di piero detto perche era creditore di detta kagione di fl. 800. Ella [E la] detta mona chaterina e morta e detti denari restano all arte e sono messi alle sustanze di detta kagione in somma di fl. 1800 a in diposito lopera di san giouanni e stimano tocchi appaghare l'anno fl. 20 che sono a kagione di fl. 7 perc[ent]o fl. 285, s. 14, d. 3. . . .
c. 10v
Incharichi alla detta hopera. . . .
Et piu [h]a debito la detta arte colla [e]redita di piero brocchardi fl. 1800 e chon piu persone fl. 260 come appare al detto libro c. 24 in tutto   fl. 2060
Et piu dichono anno di spesa nella 1/3 porta di san giouanni che chomminciata e non pos-sono albitrare per momento (?) dache solo il maestro chosta o mmo (?) fl. 200   fl. (sic)[93]

ASF, ARTI

DOC. 89, 1449, [Sept. 22], EAST DOOR, Dig. 272

ASF, Arti, Calimala, vol. 17 bis, Petizioni e

---

[91] Perhaps autograph; Mather, bibl. 308, p. 39.

[92] Unpublished. Summaries Brockhaus, bibl. 69, p. 39 and Frey, bibl. 532, p. 359, doc. 4.

[93] Unpublished. Summaries Brockhaus, bibl. 69, p. 39: Frey, bibl. 532, p. 359, doc. 4.

Deliberazioni, 1422-1518,[94] f. LXXIIIv (part f)

MCCCCXLVIIII . . . (in margin: Datur Cera Laurentio) Item suprascripti consules absente et presentibus dicto Angelo Uzzano Bartholomeo de Alexandriis et Leonardo de Acciaulis duobus ex tribus offitialibus musayci sci Johannis prouiderunt et stantiauerunt Quod possit et debeat dari et ordinetur Laurentio bartoluccij magistro januae quae fit pro Eccl. s. Johannis patroni (?) pro parte eius quod debet habere pro sua mercede laborerij dicte januae librarum mille et usque in libras mille cere de cera operae s. Johanis que cera computetur ei flor. auri novem et quarta parte alterius flor. pro quolibet centenario.

DOC. 90, 1449, Sept. 22, EAST DOOR, Dig. 273

ibidem, f. LXXIIIv (part f)
(in margin: M. simonis)
Item suprascripti uffitiales musayci deliberaverunt et stantiaverunt simoni Johannis scarpellatori super telario dicte januae ll [lire] quinquaginta Eidem debite pro Residuo sui salarij mercedis et provisionis III mensium (?) per totam diem XVIIII mensis Julij preteriti proximi.[95]

DOC. 91, 1449 [Sept. 22], EAST DOOR, Dig. 273

ibidem, f. LXXIIIv
(in margin: Electio dicti simonis)
Item reconduxerunt in dictum laborerium dictum simonem ad usum talem mercedis (?) pro tempore quo offitialibus dicte januae placuerit

Item locauerunt Simoni Johannis de fesolis Matteo Francisci de settignano Domenico Antonii Salviati	omnibus simul cooperandibus (?) laborerij scarpelli restantis de dicta janua pro pretio in totum flor. trigintaquinque ad [illegible] pro floreno

Item Quod dentur dicto Simoni fl. sexaginta auri qui denari componentur ad eius computum pro pretio declarando per Johannem protomagistrum.[96]

DOC. 92, 1423, March 30, NORTH DOOR, Dig. 101

ibidem, no pagination (part h)
Adi XXX di marzo 1423. . . . Die XXX martij. . . .
Super facto dorandi januam. Quod erat magis considerandum et extimandum honor et fama quam expensa et ideo (?) ipsa doretur.

DOC. 93, 1428, Sept. 1, EAST DOOR, Dig. 150

ibidem, no pagination (part i)
Adi primo di settembre MCCCCXXVIII. . . .
Lopera e chiesa di san Giouanni e in disordine per le sopra spese che vi si fanno piu chel conuenuto. E percio (?) se tenuto pratica di crescer l'entrata. Et formossene prouisione in palagio e non si ottenne

DOC. 94, 1444, Jan. 24, EAST DOOR, Dig. 246

Calimala, vol. 19, Deliberazioni de Consoli, gen. 4, 1444-aprile 22, 1444, c. 8f
(in margin: pro Laurentio Bartoli)
. . . vigesimo quarto mensis januarii presentibus testibus . . (?) Lionardo de Altovitis et Benedetto Bernardi de Auricellis . . .
Constituti in dicta curia in presentia mei francisci notarii et scribe dicte artis et testium suprascriptorum. Vectorius filius Laurentij bartoli magistrj januarum sancti Johannis vice et nomine ditti Laurentii sui patris et Benozius Lesis pictor populi Sancti Fridiani de Florentia et inter se ad invicem fuerunt et remanserunt in hanc concordiam et convenerunt de infrascripta locatione et conduttione, vz. Quod dittus Vectorius suo nomine conduxit dittum benozium et dittus benozius locavit se ad laborandum et se personaliter exercendum cum omni sua industria et magisterio in labo-

---

[94] The volume, unpublished, consists of a number of fragments without continuous pagination in the following sequence:

  a) two folios, March 26, 1517, marked f. 125, 126
  b) one folio, August 26, 1508, marked f. 161
  c) six folios, 1501-1508, marked f. 162-167
  d) three folios, 1501, marked f. 173-175
  e) four folios, 1501, marked f. 196-199
  f) sixteen folios, May 1, 1449-January 14, 1449, marked f. LXV-LXXX, remnants of a volume *Deliberazioni de Consoli.*
  g) two folios, unknown year, April 10-30, possibly 1423 or 1426, since Niccolo da Uzzano is consul. Probably also from a volume *Deliberazioni de Consoli.*
  h) two folios, 1423, March 30-April 20
  i) two folios, 1428, before September 1-September 22
  j) two folios, 1423, before March 30-April 20
  k) four half folios with *petizioni,* XVI century
  l) four folios, December 29, 1428, fragment of a no-

tary's diary.
  m) one folio *petizioni*
  n) two folios, February 14, 1427-March 1, fragment of a notary's diary (containing notice referring to Cosimo de' Medici acting as executor for the will of Andrea de Scholaribus, bishop of Varadin, Hungary).
  o) one folio *petizioni*
  p) one folio, September 10, 1428 to November 12, from a notary's diary.
  q) four folios, unknown year, December 10 through October 22.
  r) two folios, *petizioni,* unknown year
  s) ten folios, matriculae, 1517

[95] The date results from the identity of Doc. 90 to Doc. 72. See following note.

[96] The date of month and day results from the identity of the item referred to in the above and in Strozzi's excerpt in Doc. 72.

rerio hostiorum ianue Sancti Johannis que fiunt per dictum Laurentium bartoli diebus et horis debitis et usitatis in similibus laboreriis per tempus et terminum trium annorum initiandorum die primo mensis martii proxime futuri. Et in ditto tempore fideliter et absque aliqua fraude se exercere prout eidem impositum fuerit per dittum laurentium. Et ex alia parte dittus Vittorius promisit et convenit ditto benozio ipsum benozium in ditto laborerio durante ditto tempore retinere et eidem dare solvere et pagare pro suo salario provisione et mercede pro primo anno dictorum trium annorum flor. sexaginta auri et pro secundo anno dittorum trium annorum, flor. settuaginta auri et pro tertio et ultimo anno dittorum trium annorum flor. ottuaginta auri. . . .[97]

DOC. 95, 1448, April 6, EAST DOOR, Dig. 264

Calimala, vol. 20, Deliberazioni de Consoli . . . 1447, die V jan. al 1451,[98] c. 12
Die VI aprilis. Suprascripti consules omnes simul congregati ut supra servatis servandis providerunt et deliberaverunt Quod retentis et detractis primo de pecunia operae S. Johannis pecuniis depositis pro expensis ordinariis possit solvi de residuo. . . . [sic] laboranti cum Laurentio Bartoluccii in laborerio tertiae januae S. Johannis cum consensu tamen dicti Laurentii usque in florenos triginta auri.[99]

DOC. 96, 1448, April 22, EAST DOOR, Dig. 265

ibidem, c. 14v
Die XXII aprilis. Item modo et forma praedictis deliberaverunt et stantiaverunt Quod depositarius S. Johannis solvat et solvere possit et debeat Laurentio Bartoluccii magistro januae S. Johannis florenos quindecim auri pro eo dandos Bernardo Bartolomei laboranti cum dicto Laurentio in laborerio dictae januae pro parte ejus quod debetur dicto Laurentio pro dicto laborerio.[100]

DOC. 97, 1448, May 18, EAST DOOR, Dig. 266

ibidem, c. 16v
Die XVIII maij. Suprascripti consules omnes simul in loco eorum solitae residentiae congregati pro eorum officium exercendo servatis servandis providerunt deliberaverunt et stanti-

averunt Quod depositarius operae S. Johannis Baptistae de quantacunque pecunia dictae operae ad ejus manus perventae et perveniendae det et solvat et dare et solvere teneatur et debeat solvere et dare Laurentio Bartoli magistro hostiorum januae S. Johannis praedicti florenos quindecim auri eidem debitos pro suo magisterio dictorum hostiorum.[101]

DOC. 98, 1448, July 12, EAST DOOR, Dig. 267

ibidem, c. 27v
Die XII julii. Item simili modo et forma deliberaverunt et stantiaverunt Quod depositarius operae S. Johannis de Florentia solvat et dare et solvere teneatur et debeat Matteo Francisci scarpellatori residuum ejus quod restat habere usque in praesens pro suo labore in laborerio telarii tertiae januae S. Johannis usque in quantitatem librarum octuaginta et non ultra si plus restaret habere et si plus restat habere sint librae LXXX pro parte.[102]

DOC. 99, 1448, July 24, EAST DOOR, Dig. 268

ibidem, c. 27v
Die XXIV julii Consules praefati absente tamen dicto Doffo eorum collega deliberaverunt et stantiaverunt Quod depositarius praedictus det et solvat Simoni Johannis de Fesolis scarpellatori in laborerio telarii supradicti pro parte ejus quod restaret habere pro suo labore scarpellandi dictum telarium libras triginta florenorum parvorum Dominico Antonii scarpellatori supradicti laborerii pro parte ut supra libras triginta.[103]

DOC. 100, 1448, Nov. 15, EAST DOOR, Dig. 269

ibidem, c. 37vff [In margin: pro faciendis expensis et (?) laborerii . . . necessitas]
MCCCCXLVIII Die XV mensis novembris. Suprascripti consules absente tamen dicto Johanne de Canigianis informati qualiter propter expensas extraordinarias quae cotidie non congnitae occurrunt operae S. Johannis Baptistae et maxime praesentibus temporibus eo quod opportet in partibus providere de reficiendo de novo tendam qua hoperitur platea S. Johannis quae est inter ecclesiam S. Johannis et domum operae in quibus opportuerit expendere prout creditur florenos quadringentos et ultra ac item opportet providere de

[97] Milanesi, bibl. 337, p. 90, doc. 107 with misreadings and omissions, mostly insignificant despite the almost illegible handwriting. See also Doc. 71.

[98] The volume ends April 29, 1449.

[99] Brockhaus, bibl. 69, p. 39; Frey, bibl. 532, p. 362, doc. 21.

[100] Brockhaus, bibl. 69, p. 39; Frey, bibl. 532, p. 362, doc. 22.

[101] Brockhaus, bibl. 69, p. 39; Frey, bibl. 532, p. 362, doc. 23.

[102] Brockhaus, bibl. 69, p. 39; Frey, bibl. 532, p. 362, doc. 24.

[103] Brockhaus, bibl. 69, pp. 39f; Frey, bibl. 532, p. 362, doc. 25.

reparando copertam templi S. Johannis versus domum operae cuius expensa non potest immaginari et quod introytus operae non suppetit dictis expensis nisi unum ex duobus fiat videlicet quod aut cantores removeantur aut laborerium januae quae ad praesens fit pro ecclesia S. Johannis suprasedeat pro aliquo tempore. Et advertentes quantae importantiae praedicta sint visum fuit eis consulere homines mercatores artis et propterea requiri fecerunt plures mercatores dictae artis. Ex quibus mercattoribus et se cum dictis consulibus congregaverunt infrascripti videlicet:

Dnus Guiglelminus de Tanaglis
Dnus Geronimus de Machiavellis
Adoardus Lodovici de Acciaiuolis
Oddus Vierii de Altovitis
Ugolinus Niccolai de Martellis
Niccolaus Johannis dni Amerigi de Cavalcantibus
Bartholomaeus Contis de Peruzis
Tommasius Niccolai de Ciampoleschis
Bartolus Bartoli de Tedaldis
Laurentius dni Andreae de Montebuonis
Franciscus Guidetti de Guidettis
Bernardus Francisci Girozii de Bardis
Johannes Filippi de Corbizis
Franciscus Filippi de Nerlis
Franciscus Altobianchi de Albertis
Tommasius Fancisci de Davizis
Johannes Francisci de Riccis
Zenobius Sandri Johannis de Biliottis et
Johannes Niccolai Folchi

Quibus omnibus simul cum dictis consulibus in domo dictae artis congregatis praefati consules exposuerunt et narraverunt omnia et singula suprascripta et eos consulerunt de praedictis et super praedictis. Qui mercatores retenta inter eos lunga pratica super praedictis et demum conclusum fuit inter eos refferre dictis consulibus. Et sic retulerunt et pro eis suprascriptus dnus Guglelminus Tanagle Quod eis videbatur quod dicti consules eligant et eligere et deputare debeant quattuor aut usque in sex mercatores et artifices dictae artis quos voluerint et eis visum fuerit qui videant et examinent exitum et expensas ac introytus et redditus operae S. Johannis et examinent si dictus introitus et redditus suppetat dictis expensis. Et si repertum fuerit sufficere provideatur suprascriptis defectibus. Sin autem non sufficeret recurratur ad dominos priores et procuretur si possibile est habere adliquod adjutorium a comuni Florentiae ac vadant ad

officiales montis et procurent quod dicti officiales dent dictae operae pagamentum pro supplendo necessitatibus dictae operae. Et si opportuerit dicti sic eligendi et deputandi possint ponere hominibus artis aliquam taxam. Et quod nullo modo removeantur cantores neque desistatur laborerio januae quia redundaret unum alterum in non modicam verecundiam artis et hominibus dictae artis.

Qui consules incontinenti servatis servandis providerunt eligerunt et deputaverunt ad omnia suprascripta relata per suprascriptos mercatores egregios et nobiles viros

Dnum Guglelmino de Tanaglis
Dnum Geronimum de Machiavellis
Adovardum Lodovici de Acciaiuolis
Daniellum Loygii de Canigianis
Angelum Nerii de Vettoriis

Qui sic electi habito primo inter eos colloquio et tractato super commissis die XX dicti mensis novembris retulerunt dictis consulibus Quod ipsi prout melius potuerunt examinaverunt expensas tam ordinarias quam extrahordinarias operae S. Johannis ac introytus et exitus. Et quod eis nullo modo videbatur quod expensae dictae operae essent inhutiles sed utiles et necessarias. Et quod deminuendo ipsas expensas cederetur in dedecus dictae artis ac dictae operae et consulum praedictorum. Et quod nullo modo videbatur eis posse dictas expensas defalcari. Et quod opportebat dictis consulibus si volebant reparare ruinae ecclesie S. Johannis et necessitatibus operae unum ex duobus facere aut removere camptores aut desistere in laborerio januarum pro aliquo tempore. [104]

DOC. **101**, 1449, April 28, EAST DOOR, Dig. 270

ibidem, c. 63v

Die XXVIII mensis aprilis. Praescripti consules absente tamen dicto Ghirigoro eorum collega in suprascripto loco pro eorum officium exercendo providerunt declaraverunt et stantiaverunt Quod possit solvi Laurentio Bartoluccii floreni viginti quinque auri pro parte laborerii hostiorum januae S. Johannis quae fiunt per eum.[105]

DOC. **102**, 1449, April 29, EAST DOOR, Dig. 271

ibidem, c. 64v

Die XXVIII mensis aprilis. Item modo et forma praedictis deliberaverunt et stantiave-

[104] Brockhaus, bibl. 69, p. 42, with erroneous indication of c. 37, 38; Frey, bibl. 532, p. 343, doc. 65, excerpts only.

[105] Brockhaus, bibl. 69, p. 44; Frey, bibl. 532, p. 362, as first part of his doc. 26.

runt scarpellatoribus laborantibus super telario januae S. Johannis unam pagam unius mensis pro quolibet eorum.[106]

DOC. 103, 1423, MATRICULATION, Dig. 103

ASF, Arti, Accademia del Disegno, vol. 1, Matricola della Compagnia de' Pittori di San Luca. c. 11v

Lorenzo di bartolo orafo populi s.o Anbruogo MCCCCXXIII.[107]

DOC. 104, 1426, Dec. 20, MATRICULATION, Dig. 126

ASF, Arti, Maestri di Pietra e Legname, vol. II, Matricole dell'Arte, 1388-1518, c. 32v

Anno millesimo CCCCXXVI . . . Laurentius Bartoluccij michaelis scultor pp. s.ambrosij de florentia die 20 decembris 1426[108]

DOC. 105, 1432, Oct. 29, LINAIUOLI ALTAR, Dig. 174

ASF, Arti, Rigattieri, Linaiuoli, e Sarti, vol. 20, Campione dei debitori e creditori, 1418-1511, c. 98v (in margin: Tabernacolo del Arte cioe legname)

MCCCCXXXII a di XXIX dottobre. Ricordo chome detto di E sopradetti Operaj avendo alloghato a Jacopo vo [vocato] papero di piero legnaiuolo a fare e legname del tabernacolo grande di detta arte dove oggi e dipinta la figura di nostra donna. Avendo fattone fare di tutto uno modello per mano di Lorenzo di bartoluccio e paghatolij di sua faticha fl. III di oro e paghato per ferramenti e maschietti di detto tabernacolo l. XVII, s. IIII pagharono a detto papero per parte di detto tabernacolo l. XXX. Et dipoi a di VI. daprile. 1433. gli promisono dare di detto tabernacolo di sua manifattura. quello fussi giudicato et cosi rimasono dacordo. Et a di II di luglio 1433 gli paghorono l. III per resto di detto tabernacolo Chome di tutto appare desto(?) fornito al libro de partiti di detta arte s[egnat]o. D 169, 198, 213 - - - - fl. — 1.82 —.[109]

DOC. 106, 1433, Aug. 11, LINAIUOLI ALTAR, Dig. 174

ibidem: c. 98v. (in margin: Tabernacolo di marmo del arte)

MCCCCXXXIII. adi. XI dagosto.
Ricordo chome detto di . E sopradetti Operaj alogorono a Jacopo di bartolo da settignano et Simone di Nanni da fiesole a fare e intagliare di marmo el tabernacolo dove debbe stare nostra donna Indorato etc (?) dalteza di br. 6 1/6 e largheza di br. 3 1/3 con cornice e fogliamj. Et dio padre di mezo rilievo di sopra nel frontone con due serafini e con altrj ornamentj chome apare per uno disegno fatto di mano di Lorenzo di bartoluccio a ogni sua [above line: loro] spesa per loro ferramenti e [pid . . . ?] per pregio di fl. LXX doro. Et dettero mallavadori chome di tutto appare a libro de partiti di detta arte s[egnat]o. D 218, 223 . . .   fl. 70.[110]

DOC. 107, 1425, April 2, SAINT STEPHEN, Dig. 114

ASF, Arti, Lana, vol. 49, Deliberazioni dei Consoli, 1408, October 27-1427, August 25, c. 109v (in margin: Quod figura sci stefani fiat de bronzo et ornetur tabernaculum)

Die II mensis aprilis. Supradicti Consules in palatio dicte artis pro ipsorum offitio exercendo in sufficienti numero more solito collegialiter congregati absente tamen Ugolino Francisci de Oricellariis advertentes et considerantes cum diligentia ad legem firmatam per Capitaneos societatis beatae Virginis Mariae Sancti Michaelis in Orto disponentem in effectu quod pro ornamento Oratorii quelibet Ars civitatis Florentie ex viginti una artibus in loco eis et cuilibet earum assignato per Capitaneos dicte Societatis certo termino ut in dicta lege latius continetur deberet fecisse seu construi et fabricari fecisse eorum tabernacula bene et diligenter ornata maxime pro honore civitatis et ornamento Oratorii prelibati. Et considerantes prefati domini Consules quod omnes artes eorum tabernaculis dederunt integraliter complementum. et maxime considerantes tabernacula fabricata per artem Calismale Cambii et aliarum artium que in pulcritudine et ornamento tantum excedunt tabernaculum artis Lanae quod verisimiliter posset comuniter dici quod predicta cederent in non modicum honorem artis Lane attenta maxime magnificentia dicte artis que omnium aliarum artium semper voluit esse domina et magistra. Et volentes prefati domini consules pro magnificentia et evidente honore dicte artis in hoc providere de remedio salutari[;] ideo servatis primo et ante omnia solepnitatibus servari debitis et requisitis secundum formam statutorum et ordinamentorum dicte

---

[106] Brockhaus, bibl. 69, p. 44, with erroneous date of April 28; Frey, bibl. 532, p. 362, as last part of his doc. 26.

[107] Referred to by Baldinucci, *Notizie dei professori,* ed. D. Manni, Florence 1767ff, III, p. 1, note 1; published by Mather, bibl. 308, p. 60; the words *Ambruogo*

and the date 1423 appear to be added later.

[108] Vasari-Milanesi, bibl. 533, II, p. 260; and Mather, bibl. 308, p. 60.

[109] Gualandi, bibl. 196, p. 109, summary.

[110] Gualandi, bibl. 196, p. 109, summary.

artis vigore eorum offitii auctoritatis et balie eis concesse per quecumque ordinamenta dicte artis omnique modo via et jure quibus magis et melius potuerunt providerunt ordinaverunt et solemniter deliberaverunt quod presentes domini Consules et eorum in offitio succesores et due partes eorum aliis absentibus etc. hinc ad per totum mensem augusti proxime futuri auctoritate presentis provisionis teneantur et debeant pilastrum seu tabernaculum et figuram seu imaginem beati Stefani protomartiris ac protectoris et defensoris inclite artis Lane et ad eius honorem et reverentiam Dei de novo reficere et construi et fabricari facere illis modis et formis prout eis et duabus partibus eorum videbitur fore honorabilius magnificentie dicte artis[;] dummodo dictum pilastrum vel in pulcritudine et ornamento excedat vel saltem possit in ornamento pulcrioribus adequari[.] In qua constructione figure et tabernaculi possint prefati domini Consules et due partes eorum, aliis absentibus etc, expendere in constructione prefata usque in quantitatem florenorum mille auri. Et possint prefati Domini Consules durante dicto tempore dictam figuram et tabernaculum locare illi seu illis personis et pro eo pretio seu pretiis et cum illis pactis et modis et pro eo tempore et termino quibus eis videbitur fore utilius pro dicta arte[;] providentes insuper quod de redditibus infrascriptis camerarius presens et omnes alii in futurum possint teneantur et debeant solvere pro executione et perfectione omnium predictorum usque in quantitatem florenorum mille auri de redditibus infrascriptis[,] videlicet precedente nicchilominus semper stantiamento dominorum Consulum pro tempore existentium[:] hoc addito presenti provvisioni quod pro executione et efficacia constructionis tabernaculi prelibati omne lucrum factum seu fiendum cum Micchaele Becchi durante societate quam habet cum dicta arte ratione inter eum et artem revisa et calculata intelligatur esse et sit ex nunc dicte constructioni integraliter assignatum. Item pro executione constructionis prefate assignaverunt omnes et singulas quantitates per eum dicte arti debitas a kalendis mensis januarii proxime preteriti MCCCCXXIIII° retro generaliter ex quibuscumque membris minoribus dicte artis et similiter ex tassis lanificum comuniter non exactis. Et similiter omnem quantitatem retrahendam ex figura marmorea beati Stefani et tabernaculo prefato dicte constructioni penitus adsignaverunt et deputa-

verunt. Que quantitates sic adsignate et deputate non possint in aliam causam converti quoquo modo nisi solum et dumtaxat in constructione figure et tabernaculi prelibati. Possint insuper prefati Domini Consules et due partes eorum aliis absentibus etc pro maiori efficacia et effectu omnium predictorum provisiones et ordinamenta facere providere ordinare et deliberare semel et pluries et toties et quoties eis et duabus partibus eorum videbitur et placebit solum dumtaxat pro executione fabrice figure et tabernaculi prelibati. Et facta et gesta provisa et deliberata et ordinata per eos et duas partes ipsorum valeant et teneant et executioni mandentur ac si facta provisa et ordinata forent per totam universitatem prefatam. Cum hac modificatione tantum quod per predicta vel predictorum aliquod prefati domini Consules pro constructione figure et tabernaculi prelibati ullo modo directe vei indirecte tacite vel expresse vel aliquo alio quovis quesito colore non possint lanificibus dicte artis aliquam impositam facere vel indicere nec aliquam quantitatem pecunie pro constructione prefata mutuo vel ad interesse acquirere.[111]

DOC. 108, 1425, April 2, SAINT STEPHEN, Dig. 114

ibidem, c. 110 (in margin: quod eligantur quattuor operarii pro constructione figure s. stefani et tabernaculi eiusdem)
Item secundo modo et forma predictis providerunt ordinaverunt et deliberaverunt ut supra[:] Quod presentes domini Consules et Consules in offitio proxime successores et due partes eorum aliis absentibus etc possint teneantur et debeant per totum presentem mensem auctoritate presentis provisionis eligere et deputare ex artificibus dicte artis unum videlicet pro quolibet conventu videlicet quatuor prudentes et expertos cives et artifices dicte artis pro tempore duorum annorum proxime futurorum in operarios figure et tabernaculi prelibati prout eis videbitur fore utilius pro dicta arte. Et possint et teneantur dicti operarii sollicitare et providere quod dicta constructio dicte figure et tabernaculi bene et sollicite ac perfecte fiat et perficiatur ad honorem artis predicte. Cum hac tamen modificatione et declaratione, quod nullam provisionem vel deliberationem aut stantiamentum facere possint nisi una cum consulibus artis predicte pro tempore in offitio presidentibus.[112]

111 Passerini, bibl. 391, pp. 44f, with erroneous indication of volume as 48.

112 Passerini, bibl. 391, pp. 45f.

DOC. **109**, 1427, May 14, SAINT STEPHEN, Dig. 136

ibidem, c. 127v (in margin: quod eligi debeant operarii ymaginis S. Stephani)
Die XIIIIa maij.
Suprascripti domini Consules in sufficienti numero congregati ut supra considerantes quod electio operariorum seu officialium figure seu tabernaculi Sancti Stefani jam spiravit et volentes de successoribus providere ne ipsum opus remaneat imperfectum sed bene et honorifice perficiatur servatis servandis secundum formam ordinamentorum dicte artis providerunt ordinaverunt et deliberaverunt quod ipsi presentes domini Consules et due partes eorum possint teneantur et debeant eligere nominare et deputare ex artificibus dicte artis quatuor pro quolibet conventu viros prudentes et expertos et ipsos omnes scruptinare et ponere ad partitum inter se ipsos et consiliarios dicte artis ex quibus omnibus sic scruptinandis illi quatuor[,] videlicet unus pro conventu[,] qui obtinuerint partitum ad fabas nigras et albas per duas partes vel ultra[,] dummodo habeant plures fabas nigras omnibus aliis de suo conventu[,] intelligantur esse et sint electi et deputati in operarios et offitiales et offitiales figure et tabernaculi prelibati pro tempore et termino unius anni proxime future a die electionis de eis ut predicitur[,] fiende cum offitio auctoritate et potestate sollicitandi curandi et providendi quod constructio dicte figure et tabernaculi bene sollicite et perfecte fiat et perficiatur ad honorem ipsius artis. Cum hac tamen modificatione[:] quod nullam provisionem deliberationem aut stantiamentum facere possint per se ipsos sed una simul cum Consulibus dicte artis pro tempore in offitio presidentibus[;] et quod dicti offitiales[,] ut supra eligendi[,] pro aliquali remuneratione eorum laboris habeant a dicta arte in fine eorum offitii et anni predicti unum ensenium prout habent consiliarii dicte artis.

DOC. **110**, 1427, May 15, SAINT STEPHEN, Dig. 136

ibidem, c. 128v (in margin: pro electione operariorum figure s. stefanj Electio operariorum predictorum)
Die XVa mensis maij predicti.
Prefati domini Consules in sufficienti numero adunati ut supra. Visa auctoritate eis supra proxime concessa per consilium artis predicte circa modum et formam electionis fiende de offitio operariorum figure seu ymaginis Sancti Stefani que fit de octone pro arte predicta[;] et volentes predicta exequi cum cedere videatur ad honorem et magnificentiam artis eiusdem premisso et celebrato inter eos solempni et secreto scruptinio et obtento partito ad fabas nigras et albas secundum ordinamenta dicte artis elegerunt promoverunt et nominaverunt infrascriptos quatuor cives praticos et expertos dicte artis pro quolibet conventu scruptinandos[,] et qui scruptinari et poni debeant ad partitum inter seipsos dominos Consules ac Consiliarios dicte artis quorum unus pro quolibet conventu remanere et eligi debeat in operarium dicte figure secundum formam supra traditam[;] quorum nomina sunt ista[,] videlicet[:] Gherardus domini Filippi de Corsinis[;] Sander Joannis de Biliottis[;] Tommasus Bartholomei de Corbinellis[;] Joannes Jacobi Bini pro conventu Ultrarni[;] Pierus Cardinalis de Oricellariis[;] Dominicus Jacobi Mazzinghi[;] Franciscus domini Raynaldi de Janfigliazis[;] Taddeus Bartholommei Lorini, pro conventu Sancti Pancratii[;] Antonius Tommasi Ghuccii[;] Stefanus Salvi Filippi[;] Alexander Ugonis de Alexandris et Lapus Joannis Niccolini pro conventu Sancti Petri Scheradii[;] Bindus Gherardi Piaciti[;] Joannes Laurentii de Stufa[;] Andreas ser Landi Fortini et Simon Francisci ser Gini pro conventu Sancti Martini[;] quibus omnibus suprascriptis civibus, positis ad partitum inter ipsos dominos Consules et consiliarios dictae artis in sufficientibus numeris more solitis adunatis in palatio dicte artis dicta die XV maij predicti quomodolibet[,] videlicet eorum singulariter et de per se in suo conventu[,] electi et deputati fuerunt infrascripti quatuor tanquam plures fabas nigras habentes ultra duas partes redditas pro sic[,] videlicet Joannes Jacobi Bini pro conventu Ultrarni[,] Alexander Ugonis de Alexandris pro conventu Sancti Petri Scheradii[,] Pierus Cardinalis ex Oricellaris pro conventu Sancti Pancratii et Bindus Gherardi Piaciti pro conventu Sancti Martini pro tempore et cum offitio auctoritate enseniis et aliis in reformatione suprascripta de predictis disponente latius annotatis.[113]

DOC. **111**, 1427, Aug. 5, SAINT STEPHEN, Dig. 140

ibidem: c. 130v (in margin: quod expense figure S. Stefani fieri possint de qualibet pecunia)
Dicta die V augusti.
Item advertentes domini Consules supradicti ad quandam reformationem editam de mense aprilis MCCCCXXV° disponente inter alia in effectu[,] quod de quibusdam redditibus et

---

[113] Docs. 109 and 110, Passerini, bibl. 391, p. 58, with minor omissions and errors.

introitibus dicte artis in reformatione predicta particulariter annotatis[,] fieret et fieri et construi deberet figura seu ymago S. Stefani Protomartiris enea seu de bronzo modo et forma quibus et prout in eadem reformatione inseritur[;] in qua quidem expendi posset usque in quantitatem florenorum mille auri prout et per dictam reformationem enarratur[;] et attenta locatione facta de dicta figura Laurentio Bartolucci magistro et constructori figure eiusdem[;] consideratoque quod huiusmodi figura per eumdem Laurentium conducta est de terra et cera[,] taliter quod necessarium est ipsam proici et fieri de ottone[,] alias quod actum est destrueretur et sumptus propterea facti perderentur[;] et visa emptione facta per dictam artem et per habentes baliam et auctoritatem ab ea vigore reformationis prefate de libris quatormilibus ottonis ad pondus Venetorum quod dicitur fore necessarium ad proiciendum et perficiendum figuram huiusmodi[.] Et considerato quod ex redditibus prelibatis et ut supra assignatis non est exacta nec exigi posset tanta pecunia que sufficeret ad solutionem et satisfationem pretii ottonis memorati et aliarum expensarum que opportune erunt ad perfectionem operis prelibati nolentesque quod opus predictum remaneat imperfectum[;] ideoque pro honore ipsius artis premisso et obtento partito inter eos ad fabas nigras et albas secundum ordinamenta artis eiusdem et servatis servandis secundum ordinamenta predicta providerunt ordinaverunt deliberaverunt et stantiaverunt[,] quod quicumque camerarius generalis tam presens quam quicumque successor de quacumque pecunia dicte artis ad eius manus perventa et pervenienda ex quibuscumque introitibus et ex quibuscumque causis det et solvat et dare et solvere teneatur et debeat[,] libere et absque eius preiudicio vel gravamine[,] dicto Laurentio et seu aliis quibuscumque personis[,] uni vel pluribus[,] usque in dictam quantitatem florenorum mille uni[,] computato in summa predicta toto eo quod solutum esset et ad exitum reperiretur[,] eo modo et forma tempore et termino ac conditionibus quibus et prout deliberatum et seu stantiatum fuit semel et pluries per Consules dicte artis et operarios dicte figure tam presentes quam qui pro tempore fuerint et duas partes ipsorum pro executione et perfectione omnium premissorum.[114]

DOC. **112**, 1428, June 30, SAINT STEPHEN, Dig. 148

[114] Passerini, bibl. 391, pp. 47f, with minor omissions and errors. Passerini erroneously indicates the *carta*

ASF, Arti, Lana, vol. 50, Deliberazioni dei Consoli, 1427, Dec. 1–1432, Oct. 1, c. 23, 23v
(in margin: Auctoritas stantiandi concessa pro complendo[?] figure s. stefani)
Die ultimo mensis junij dicti anni MCCCCXXVIII ind. VI
Item Intellecto

Quoniam de mense aprilis anno dni MCCCCvigesimo quinto fuerit per tunc dominos consules dicte artis una cum consilio artis eiusdem dispositum et provisum in effectu. Quod [above line: dicti?] domini consules dicte artis eorumque successores tenerentur construi facere figuram et tabernaculum sancti stefani protomartiris gloriosi. Et in dictam causam expendere possent usque in quantitatem et summam florenorum Mille auri de artis redditibus dicte artis in provisione presentis (?). Et statim per aliam provisionem dispositum fuit in effectu Quod per consules eligerentur quattuor offitiales super perfectionem operis supradicti. Et dummodo nichil stantiare vel expendere possent nisi una cum consulibus dicte artis quorum electorum auctoritas duraret duobus annis tunc proxime venturis. Et quod postea de mense maij anno MCCCCXXVII finita auctoritas ipsorum quattuor electorum vigore alterius provisionis in consilio dicte artis firmate alii quattuor electi deputati fuere quorum nomina ista sunt vz

Johannes Jacobi bini	per tempus unius anni finiti die XV mensis maij proximi preteriti cum eadem seu simili auctoritate ipsis primo electis concessa et data. Et quod etiam (?) tempus ipsorum electorum expiravit.
Alexander Ugonis de Alexandris	
Pierus Cardinalis de Oricellariis et	
Bindus Gherardi Piansi (?)	

Et quod ad huc restant fieri stantiamenta et pagamenta pro complemento solutionis tam dicte figure quam eius tabernaculi . . . tam (?) usque in integram quantitatem ipsorum florenorum Mille quam maiorem et quod si aliter (?) provideretur aliquid stantiamentum seu solutio per predictos fieri non possit. Et videntes omnia predicta pro honore dicte artis prout convenit providere. Domini consules dicte artis habita propter huius. . . . (?) deliberacione solempni et demum Int. . . .(?) In . . arum(?) in palatio dicte artis more solito in loco eorum audientie in sufficiente numero congregati et premisso et facto solepni et peracto scruptinio ad fabas nigras et albas et obtento partito secundum formam ordinamentorum artis predicte. Providerunt deliberaverunt et ordina-

as 530v.

verunt quod illa eadem seu similis auctoritas balia atque potestas hactenus ut supra fertur data concessa et attributa ipsi Johanni Jacobi bini et sociis predictis una cum dominis consulibus dicte artis et que finem habuit die XV mensis maij proximi preteriti in stantiando deliberando et solvi facendo tam Laurentio bartolucii aurifici magistro dicti laborerii quam alteri (?) . . (?) que pro predictis habere et capere debenti usque in dictam summam florenorum Mille auri. Et nunc intelligatur eis et sit de novo data concessa et attributa ipsis Johanni jacobi bini et sociis una cum dominis consulibus dicte artis et duabus partibus eorundem usque ad preteritum mensem agusti proximi futuri in stantiando et solvi faciendo de quibuscumque redditibus et introytibus dicte artis tam dicto Laurentio pro eius magisterio et labore quam alteri (?) . . . (?) que pro predictis capere et habere debenti et tam usque in dictam summam florenorum Mille auri quam maiorem prout et sunt et quod . . . (?) ipsis dominis consulibus et dictis Johanni jacobi bini et sociis et duabus partibus eorum predictorum . . . (?) pluries videbitur et placebit. Et quod omnia et singula fienda et deliberanda per predictos dominos consules et dictos quattuor vel duas partes eorum infra dictum mensem agusti rem predictam exequi debeant et executam mandarunt qualibus oppositione et contradicta cessante.[115]

DOC. 113, 1429, Feb. 1, SAINT STEPHEN, Dig. 154

ASF, Arti, Lana, vol. 50, Deliberazioni de Consoli, 1427, Dec. 1–1432, Oct. 1, c. 42, 42v (in margin: Consules possunt vendere res superfluas figure s. stefani)
Die primo mensis februarij dicti anni.
Supra dicti domini consules ut supra more solito in loco eorum audientie in sufficiente numero congregati. Audito qualiter pro constructione figure sci stefani protomartiris gloriosi ipsius artis patroni empte fuerunt certe quantitates et summe ottonis et ferramentorum atque aere Et quod ipsa completa et perfecta superfuerunt ex predictis vz. libre mille octoginta ottonis et libre dugenta ferramentorum et certa quantitas aere. Que res vendi vel alienari non possunt alio non proviso. Et audito atque cognito quod ad presens ars non indiget dictis rebus sed indiget pecuniis quia non integre suffici possit constructioni dicte figure. Et volentes pro utilitate dicte artis providere prom-

isso et facto. Inter eos solepni et peracto scruptinio ad fabas nigras et albas et obtento partito secundum formam ordinamentorum artis predicte providerunt ordinaverunt et deliberaverunt. Quod presentes domini consules dicte artis et due partes eorum aliis etiam absentibus et in requisitis vel presentibus et contradicentibus possint vendere et alienare tradere et concedere dictas res et bona supra expressa. Qui et quibus et pro pretio et pretiis dicte arti solvendo vel solvendis de quo et quibus et prout et sicut ipsis dominis consulibus aut duabus partibus eorum (videbitur [cancelled]) aut cui vel quibus comiserit placuerit et videbitur atque utilius potuerit pro ipsa arte. Et pretium et pretia inde recipienda et solvenda solvi et dari facere camerario dicte artis pro ipsa arte recipienti. Et quod que facta fuerunt per ipsos consules aut duas partes eorum aut per quem vel quos cui vel quibus commisserint . . . (?) valeant et teneant et possint et debeant immutabile (?) observari qualibus contra dicta cessanti.[116]

DOC. 114, 1376, July 30, MATRICULATION OF BARTOLO DI MICHELE

ASF, Arti, Seta, vol. 7, Matricula, 1328–1433, c. 30. Bartolus Michelis aurifex populi s. pauli de florentia quia juravit pro magisterio secundum formam statutorum dicte artis die XXII mensis febr[uarii] a.d. MCCCLXXV existentibus consulibus dicte artis orlandino lapi, bardo corsi, niccolao d'andrea, niccolao bartolj cinj, sandro cambinj et francescho bonacursi alderottj et quia solvit secundum formam sue taxationis dicte artis lb quinque ad flor. ideo matriculatus et descriptus fuit in presenti matricula per me dionisium di ser joh(?) notarium dicte artis die XXX julij a.d. MCCCLXXV tempore consulatus chiarissimi pagnj pergolettj franceschj Bianchi bonsi pauli bartolini pagni luche et pieri gherardi bonsi consulum dicte artis.[117]

DOC. 115, 1409, Aug. 3, FIRST MATRICULATION OF GHIBERTI, Dig. 28

ibidem: c. 115v, Laurentius filius Bartoli olim michelis aurifex populi s. pauli de florentia quia iuravit pro magisterio secundum formam statuti et ordinamentorum dicte artis die III° mensis augusti Anni dm. MCCCCnoni indicionis secunde existentibus consulibus dicte artis Mariano niccolai simonis et eius collegijs et quia habet beneficium ex patre dicti Bartoli

[115] Passerini, bibl. 391, p. 48, gives a brief paraphrase with the erroneous date 1418 and erroneous number of volume, 48.
[116] Passerini, bibl. 391, pp. 48f, gives a brief para-

phrase with the same errors as in the previous one.
[117] Unpublished. Summary in Vasari-Milanesi, bibl. 533, II, p. 259.

eius patris in hac matricula pro magisterio matricolatj ideo matriculatus fuit in presenti matricula per me Lodovicum bertini notarium dicte artis dicta die III° augusti tempore consulatus consulum predictorum.

DOC. 115a, 1444, Apr. 30, CANCELLATION, Dig. 250

The words from Laurentius to s. pauli have been cancelled. (in margin: die 30 aprilis 1444 habetur pro non matriculatus quia non habet dictum beneficium ideo cassatur (?)Ubertus notarius.)[118]

DOC. 116, 1446, June 14, REMATRICULATION, Dig. 257

ASF, Arti, Seta, vol. 8, Matricola, 1433–74, c. 133. Laurentius olim Cionis quondam ser bonachursi abatini de ghibertis vocatus Lorenzo di bartoluccio popoli s. ambrosii de florentia Intalliator et aurifex aurarius Quia juravit pro magisterio secundum formam statutorum dicte artis die XIII maij anno dnj millesimo CCCCXL [sexto cancelled] quarto Ind settima vz. millesimo quattuorcentesimo quadragesimo quarto indict settima Existentibus consulibus dicte artis francescho francisci della luna eiusque collegijs. Et quia solvit dicte arti pretium (?) introitus ad artem camerario artis florinos viginti auri Ideo matriculatus et descriptus fuit in presenti matricola per me Ubertum quondam Martini Bretj(?) de populo Donato in poggis civem (?) et notarium florentinum et nunc scribam dicte artis die XIIII junij anno dnj millesimo CCCCxLsexto ind nona tempore consulatus Caroli de boncianis eiusque collegiorum (?) consulum dicte artis[119]

DOC. 117, 1435, May 28, MATRICULATION OF TOMASO GHIBERTI, Dig. 250

ibidem: c. 214. Thomasus filius Laurentii quondam bartoli michelis alias di Lorenzo di bartoluccio aurifex populi s. anbrosii de florentia Quia . . . (?) consulum juravit pro magisterio secundum formam statutorum dicte artis die xxviii maji anno dnj MCCCC XXXV ind XIIJ Existentibus consulibus dicte artis Parente Johannis pieri parentis eiusque collegis[.] Et quia habet beneficium ex patre dicti eius patris in matricula et per . . . (?) presenti matricula dicte artis pro magisterio matriculati. Ideo matriculatus et prescriptus fuit in presenti matricula per me ubertum martini breti (?) civem et notarium florentinum nunc scribam

dicte artis die . . . (?) et tempore consulatus consulum predictorum.

DOC. 117a, 1444, Apr. 30, CANCELLATION, Dig. 250

The words from Thomasus to Lorenzo have been cancelled. [in margin: 1444 die 30 aprilis cassatur quia fuit matriculatus vigore beneficii patris et pater fuit declaratus non habere beneficium et non habetur matriculatus et . . . (?) juravit Ego Ubertus Martini].[120]

ASF, ARCH. OR S. MICHELE

DOC. 118, 1418, July 30, CANDELABRA, Dig. 59

Vol. 25, Libro delli Atti e Emanati dai Capitani di Or S. Michele, March 3, 1416–July 10, 1417 [recte: May 31, 1419], c. 42

Quod fiant duo candelabra argentea aurata pro altare oratorij et quod in eis possit expendi summa fl. CL vel circa et hoc commiserunt Suino Soderini et Tomasio Corsi quod [above line: Guariento quondam Guarienti aurifici. (?)] fieri facerent prout melius eis videbitur et stantiaverunt dictis fl. CL a denariis corporationis.

DOC. 119, 1418, Aug. 6, CANDELABRA, Dig. 59

ibidem, c. 44v. Die VI mensis augusti . . .
(in margin: locatio candelabrorum pro altarj)
Pateat omnibus Quod

Suinus pieri eucheri Soderini ⎫ duo ex numero
Tomasius Lapi Corsi ⎭ dictorum

Capitanorum vigore commissionis eis factae die XXX Julii proximi praeteriti elapsi de qua commissione plura habita . . . (?) deligati informati et colloquio de re ipsa . . . (?) movende . . . (?) et officii XV die martii praeter . . . (?) premissa (?) quod per [illegible] (?) locaverunt Guarento olim Johanis guarenti aurifici de florentia ad faciendum et fabricandum unum par candelabrorum argenteorum [above line: usque in libras 14 ulterioris] mensure unius brachij et unius quarti vel circa secundum formam eorundem designationis facte per laurentium bartolucij in quodam folio [above line: magno] de papiro cum additione [above line: . . . (?)] de ipso facto per dictum laurentium in quodam petio papirj pro pedistallo dicti designi et promiserunt [above line: . . . (?)] eidem Guarento dare et solvere florenos quattuordecim auri et quartos tres alterius

[118] Unpublished. Summary in Vasari-Milanesi, bibl. 533, II, p. 259.
[119] Unpublished. Referred to by Gaye, bibl. 173, I, p. 150, note.*
[120] Unpublished.

floreni pro qualibet libra dictorum candel-abrorum. Et supra (?) dictus Guarentus prom-isit et convenit dictis Suino et Tomaso [above line: et m.a.] jure et ... dicte artis(?) complere dicta candelabra bene et diligenter facere et fabricare bono et fino argento et cum smaltis in omnibus et per omnia prout et sicut in dicto disegnio continetur ad usum discreti-onem et arbitrium bonj virj sine fraude et malitia [illegible?]. Et ipsa candelabra perficere et dare completa hinc ad per totum mensem novembrem proximum futurum suo argento et magisterio et omnibus suis sumptibus et expensis excepto auro pro auratura desuper fienda. Quae omnia infrascripta promiserunt [several words illegible] observari sub pena duplij fl. pro quibus omnibus sese obligaverunt et renuntiaverunt et cum ... (?)[121]

ASF, CONSIGLI MAGGIORI

DOC. 120, 1444, April 29, DECLARATION OF LEGITIMACY, Dig. 249
Provisioni, Registri, vol. 134, c. 286ff

(In margin: Laurentii Bartoluccii absolutio et habilitas)
Sexto. Provisionem infrascriptam super istam petitionem et omnibus et singulis in ... (?) deliberatam et factam per ipsos dominos priores et vexilliferum gonfalonierorum so-cietatum populi et duodecim bonos viros civi-tatis florentie secundum formam ordinamen-torum dicte civitatis ... (?) quod dicte petiti-onis tenor talis est viz:
Exponitur cum debita reverentia vobis mag-nificis et potentibus dominis dominis prioribus artium et vexillifero iustitiae populi et comu-nis florentini pro parte Laurentii Cionis ser Bonacursi vocati Lorenzo di Bartoluccio civis vestri quod sub die sextodecimo aprilis 1444 conservatores legum et ordinum dicti comunis visa quadam notificatione et seu tamburatione eorum officio facta die 17 mensis martii prox-ime preteriti cuius quidem tamburationis et seu notificationis tenor est talis[:] Lorenzo di Bartolo fa le porte di san giovanni di nuovo tracto al uficio de dodici e inabile a tale ufizio perche non e nato di legittimo matrimonio[;] perche detto Lorenzo fu figliuolo di Bartolo e Mona Fiore, la quale fu sua femmina ovvero fante e fu figliuola d'un lavoratore di Val di Sieve, e maritolla a Pelago a uno chiamato Cione Paltami[,] uomo della persona molto disutile e quasi smemorato il quale non pi-acque alla detta Fiore[:] fuggissi da lui e ven-nesene a Firenze capito nelle mani di Bartolo predetto dell anno 1374 o circa e in quattro

o cinque anni ne ebbe due figliuoli[,] una prima femmina[,] poi questo Lorenzo dell'-anno circa il 1378[;] e quello allevo e inseg-nolli l'arte sua dell Orafo[;] dipoi circa l anno 1406 mori il detto Cione el detto Bartolo tro-vato da certi amici[,] i quali mostrarongli che male era a vivere in adulterio la sposo come di questo e pubblica voce e fama e come per li strumenti di matrimonio. E s[e] egli dicesse esser figliuolo di Cione e non di Bartolo tro-verete che Cione mai ebbe figliuoli della Fiore e che Lorenzo prese e uso i beni di Bartolo e quelli ha venduti e usati come figliuolo e legit-timo erede[:] e perche s[i] e sentito inabile mai ha accettato l'ufizio del Consolato dell'Arte al quale piu volte e stato tratto. Ma sempre per piccola cosa e stato allo specchio a lasciatosi stracciare[:] et pero non consenta la signoria che per lui sappruovi meno diligentia doversi usare in volere gli ufici principali della terra che uno piccolo consolato. E se di tutto vuole la signoria vostra buona informatione pigliate da suoi artefici[,] cioe orafi come intagliatori[,] e saperete la verita. Sievi raccomandato lonore del comune e delle persone vostre. Ricordan-dovi che tutte le dette cose io prima senti da bartolo suo padre col quale piu tempo usai.
Et visa quadam alia notificatione dicta die facta coram dominis officialibus cuius notifi-cationis tenor est talis: Notificasi a voi signori ufitiali e conservatori delle leggi che lorenzo di bartolo che lavora le porte di san giovanni che di nuovo de dodici non puo essere et perche non e legittimo e fu figliuolo di barto-luccio orafo e duna sua femina chiamata monna fiore la quale fu di val di sieve nato duno povero lavoratore maritolla a pelago a uno tristanzuolo il quale in pochi dì ella ricrebbe fuggisi dalui e capito a Firenze alle mani di detto Bartoluccio el quale lungo tempo se la tenne per amica e nei primi tempi che con lui stette che fu circa al 1375 nebbe piu figliuoli femina e maschio lultimo fu questo lorenzo il quale detto bartolo allevo ensegnolli larte sua. Dipoi sendo morto detto cione detto bartolo s'anello alla detta mona fiore del anno 1404 o in quel torno e cosi troverete quando noverete il detto cione non ebbe mai figliuoli della detta fiore come certificatum est (?) per paesani e suoi parenti verete informati. Di Bartolo come suo figliuolo uso e suoi beni e muro in su una casa avea nella via nuova di S. pagolo e dopo la morte di Bartolo la vende come suoi beni patrimoniali e altre ragioni non aveva ne titolo col quale la potesse ven-dere[;] di tutte queste cose ne troverete nella via della scala e nella via nuova assai che sene

---

[121] Docs. 118 and 119 unpublished. Referred to by Vasari-Milanesi, bibl. 533, II, p. 259 with erroneous date 1417.

ricordano e che daloro passati che tutto vidono udirono. Il consolato del arte de maestri ove piu volte e stato tracto mai non a accettato etc. etc.[;] e se volessi pur dire essere figluolo di cione che troverete il contrario cade in un altro inconveniente peroche che negli anni passati e stato piu sua gente mai furono prestantiati in firenze. Lorenzo in suo nome a auto graveza dal 1420 in qua[;] siche ne per luno padre ne per laltro e non puo accettare l'ufficio. Fategli ragione, ricordandovi cheglie molte volte incorso nella pena pero che negli anni passati e stato piu volte del consiglio del popolo e del comune come alle tracte saresti avisati—

Et visis attestationibus plurium et plurium testium examinatorum ex commissione et pro parte dictorum officialium et visa citatione facta de dicto Laurentio notificato ad se excusandum a dictis notificationibus et qualibet earum et visa comparitione dicti Laurentii facta occasione dictarum notificationum et dicte notificationis dicentis in effectum, quod dominus Laurentius fuit et est natus et conceptus de legitimo matrimonio et quod ipse fuit filius legitimus et naturalis Cionis S. Bonacursii de pelago et domine fioris uxoris legitime dicti Cionis et quod constante matrimonio inter predictos Cionem et dominam fiorem natus fuit videlicet de anno 1378[;] et quod non fuit filius nec legitimus nec naturalis dicti bartoli sive bartolucci sed fuit educatus et nutritus et etiam instructus in arte aurificis a dicto bartoluccio tanquam filius a pueritia sua et quod propterea a multis fuit putatus et vocatus filius bartoluccii[;] et etiam quia post mortem domini Cionis sui patris legitimi et naturalis dicta domina fiore eius mater accepit in virum et maritum dictum bartoluccium[;] et quod ipse Laurentius de anno 1413 pro recuperatione bonorum que fuerunt dicti Cionis sui patris fecit quoddam compromissum in dominum Masum de albizis[,] videlicet ipse tamquam filius dicti Cionis vocatus nencio bartoluccii ex una parte et quidam consanguinei dicti Cionis ex alia[;] ex quo secutum fuit quod ipse acquisivit quoddam petium terre quod fuit dicti Cionis et quod ipse ab anno 1413 citra solvit onera et factiones comunis flor[entie] partim sub isto nomine videlicet bartolo di michele orafo el figliuolo et partim sub nomine proprio Laurentii Bartoluccii aurificis[,] videlicet ab anno 1422 citra. Et quod ipse sub dicta descriptione que dicit bartolo de michele orafo el figliuolo tanquam filius putativus dicti bartoli comprehenditur et maxime quia dictus bartolus nullum alium filium legitimum nec naturalem habuit praeterquam dictum Laurentium eius filium pu-

tativum[:] Et demum quod notificationes fuerunt facte per calunpniam et quod contenta in eis non fuerunt et non sunt vera et petens se a dictis notificationibus et qualibet earum absolvi et liberari. Et viso quodam publico instrumento producto per dictum laurentium publice scripto manu domini ser laurentii ser Jannini notarii florentini de anno millesimo trecentesimo septuagesimo et mense aprilis per quod patet qualiter dictus cione et dicta donna per verba de presenti ad invicem et inter se matrimonium legitimum contraxerunt. Et viso etiam alio instrumento per dictum laurentium producto publice scripto manu dicti ser laurentii per quod patet qualiter de anno millesimo trecentesimo septuagesimo et mense septembris dicti anni dominus Cione confessus fuit habuisse in dotem dicte domine fioris libras 85 f. p.[;] et viso instrumento dicti compromissi de quo supra fit mentio scripto et rogato per s. Pierum s. Micaelis Guidonis sub die 5 aprilis anni 1413 in quo instrumento dominus Laurentius promittit ut filius Cionis s. Bonacursi de pelago vocatus Nencio de bartoluccio[;] et visis etiam dictis et actestationibus plurimorum testium pro parte dicte Laurentii productis et ipsis actestationibus diligenter examinatis[;] et visa dicta descriptione facta de dicto bartolo micaelis aurificis de anno millesimo quadragesimo tertio decimo e qua constat in camera actorum (?) communis florentiae in libro distributionum prestantiarum quartiere sce marie novelle incameratarum de dicto anno 1413 ad c. 30. Et viso quod etiam secundum assertionem dicti laurentii non solvit sub suo nomine proprio neque etiam apellativo vc[viz] tanquam filius cionis cuius se asserit fuisse filium onera comunis flor[entie] nisi ab anno 1422 citra et sic non solvit onera comunis flor[entie] debito et requisito tempore secundum formam statutorum et ordinum et reformationum comunis flor[entie;] et viso quod dominus Laurentius ut est notorium electus ad officium duodecim bonorum virorum comunis flor[entie] de anno proxime preterito 1443 et mense decembri dicti anni dictum officium acceptavit et exercuit contra formam dictorum statutorum ordinamentorum et reformationum civitatis florentiae. Et audito pluries et pluries dicto laurentio et quicquid coram dictis conservatoribus dicere et allegare voluit. Et auditis etiam et pluribus et pluribus aliquibus pro dicto laurentio loquentibus et in eius favore. Et visa citatione facta de dicto laurentio et in eius persona ex parte et permissione dictorum offitialium per famulum dicti offitii ad infrascriptam declarationem et damnationem et sententiam audiendum. Et visis consideratis [omnibus quae?] examinanda fuerunt dei nomine invocato pro tribunale sedentes in loco in sententia descripto prestito primo dictis conservatoribus et omnibus coram iuramento per notarium coram offitio secundum formam ordinamentorum civitatis flor[entie] considerantes dictum laurentium se excusare et defendere a dictis notificationibus,—quatenus continent dictum Laurentium non fuisse natum de legitimo matrimonio affirmando se non fuisse filium nec legitimum nec naturalem dicti bartoli sed fuisse filium legitimum et naturalem Cionis ser bonacursi de pelago[;] misso et obtento partito—declaraverunt[:] descriptionem predictam factam de anno 1413 in distributione prestanzonum sub isto nomine videlicet bartolo di michele orafo el figliuolo, nullo modo prodesse vel suffragari posse dicto Laurentio et dictum Laurentium sub dicta descriptione nullo modo potuisse vel posse comprehendi cum asserat se non fuisse filium nec legitimum nec naturalem dicti Bartoli et dictum Laurentium non solvisse debito tempore onera et factiones comunis flor[entie], et exercuisse dictum officium duodecim bonorum virorum comunis flor[entie] contra formam statutorum ordinamentorum et reformationum dicte communis et acceptasse et exercuisse dictum officium duodecim Bonorum virorum comunis florentie contra formam statutorum ordinamentorum et reformationum comunis florentie et propterea incidisse in penam libr. 500 f. p. et dictum Laurentium vocatum nencio di bartoluccio intagliatorem in lib. 500 f. p. dandis et solvendis generali camerario comunis flor[entie] pro ipso comuni recipiendis infra unum mensem tunc proxime futurum sub pena quarti pluris si infra dictum terminum non solveret condemnaverunt[;] ab aliis autem antedictis notificationibus—dictum Laurentium absolverunt et liberaverunt. Et quod ipse Laurentius ideo dictum offitium duodecim bonorum virorum acceptavit quia credidit reputari debere ab omnibus ac si nominatim descriptus esset una cum dicto bartolo eius patre putativo in distributione prestanzonis ordinata ut supra de anno 1413 rationibus et occasionibus[;]—sed nuper intellexit a peritissimis viris quemadmodum dicti conservatores secundum scripturas de hac re penes eorum offitium existentes nec non predicta et allegata coram eis non potuerunt facere de stricto iure quominus declararent et condemnarent et absolverunt prout in prefata sententia expressum est[;] et sic et nunc idem Laurentius confitetur et recognoscit per ipsos conservatores sibi ius administratum fuisse. Et quod post dictam

latam sententiam idem Laurentius invenit quod dictus Cione ser bonacursi de pelago olim eius pater legitimus et naturalis fuerat et est descriptus in soldis quinque in destributione septinarum civium civitatis flor[entie] impositarum in anno 1375 in vexillo leonis rubei ad c. 21. ut constat—sub die 17 mensis aprilis[;] et sic si scivisset ad tempus et produxisset coram dominis conservatoribus fidem prefate descriptionis dicti Cionis credit ipsos eum absolvisse ab omnibus contentis in notificationibus et intamburationibus supradictis[;] posito etiam, quod officium habuisset et exercuisset sub nomine ut supra[;] et quod ipse Laurentius ad hoc[,] ut presens eius petitio proponi possit ante nos et nostra collegia solvit baptiste de Guicciardinis capserio camere die 18 aprilis presentis pro soldo uno pro libra solvi debito—in totum flor. sex libr. 3, prout constat de ipsa solutione[;]—et quod ipse cuperet a dicta condennatione liberari excepta tertia parte ut infra quam exceptare iustum putat pro assignamento salarii dictorum conservatorum et eorum ministrorum et aliarum expensarum occurrentium—ut magis ostendatur iustitia facta per eos in casu predicto; et etiam cuperet infrascripta firmari et confidens gratiam invenire decrevit vestram dominationem adire et ab eadem cum consensu nobilium virorum Ianozi bernardi de manettis et bernardi domini baldi della tosa, de nris. ven. collegiis auditorum suorum ad hoc legitime assumptorum postulare quod inferius est descriptum. Quare vobis dominis supradictis pro parte predicta devotissime supplicatur,— quatenus vobis placeat—oportune providere— quod etiam absque aliqua fide aut probatione de supra narratis—ipse Laurentius ex nunc intelligatur esse et sit a dicta condemnatione libr. 500 et quarti pluris et ab omni descriptione et registratione inde secutis vel propterea factis absolutus et plenissime liberatus[;] et possit et debeat de ipsa condennatione—licite et inpune cancellari absque aliqua solutione propterea fienda vel alia substantialitate servanda visa solum reformatione, quae super his facta fuerit[:] etc. etc. hoc salvo, quod predicta absolutio et liberatio non intelligatur neque locum habeat pro lib. 50 dicte condennationis quas solvere teneatur ipse Laurentius.
Item salvis predictis et in suo robore permanentibus, quod dicta sententia, declaratio, condennatio et absolutio et omnia singula— intelligantur esse et sint vigore reformationis quae super his facta fuerit plene et integre approbata et confirmata etc. etc.
Cum hoc tamen addito intellecto ac expresse apposito quia ipse Laurentius magis

cognoscitur sub nomine Laurentii bartoli sive bartolucci, eius patris putativi sub quo obtinuit officia quam sub nomine Laurentii Cionis ser bonacursi eius patris legitimi et naturalis[;] quod ipse Laurentius de cetero quaecunque officia comunis vel pro comuni florentie et alia quelibi ad que ipsum extrahi vel deputari contigerit sub nomine Laurentii bartoli aut bartolucci magistri intagli vel sub alio nomine vel denominatione artis vel exercitii vel sine aliqua denominatione possit acceptare curare et exercere licite et impune ac si dictus bartolus sive bartoluccius vere fuisset eius pater legitimus et naturalis etc etc

Super qua quidem petitione, et omnibus et singulis in ea contentis, dicti domini priores et vexillifer habita super predictis—invicem et una cum officiis gonfaloneriorum societatum populi et duodecim bonorum virorum comunis flor[entie] deliberatione solenni et secreto scrutinio ad fabas nigras et albas providerunt die 28 mensis aprilis 1444[:] quod dicta petitio et omnia et singula in ea contenta procedant firmentur fiant et firma et stabilita esse intelligantur non obstantibus predictis legibus etc etc

Qua provisione lecta et recitata, dictus dominus propositus proposuit, et petiit sibi per omnia bonum et utile consilium impartiri— CLVIIII ex ipsis consiliariis dedisse fabas nigras pro sic et sic secundum formam dicte provisionis obtentum firmatum et reformatum fuit non obstantibus reliquis XXXII ex ipsis consiliariis repertis dedisse fabas albas in contrarium pro non[122]

BMF, A 199 I

DOC. **121**, 1404-1424, NORTH DOOR, Dig. 109
Collezione Gori, after C. Strozzi, Descrizione dell' . . . S. Giouanni, f. 33v Costo il magistero l'ottone, et ogn' altra cosa fl. 12040 e lire 16656.1.2 che fanno la somma di fl. 16204 s. 1 d.2 valutando il fl. 4 come valeva allora[123]

DOC. **122**, 1424-1452, EAST DOOR, Dig. 286
ibidem: f. 33v. (Description of Ghiberti's second door) . . . egli vi potesse tenere a lauorare Vettorio suo figliuolo e Michelozzo di Bartolommeo, e altri tre che non furono sempre

gl'istessi, ma alcuna volta si mutarono. Matteo di Franc.o di Andrea da Settignano. Simone di Nanni da Fiesole. Domenico d'Antonio Salviati di d.o luogo. Franc.o di Papi Buoni. Franc.o di Nanni Buioni, Cristofano di Franc.o, Giov. di Giuliano, e altri furono in questo numero. . . .
Fu la spesa fra Magisterio e altro fl. 12290 l. 9219.4.1 che fanno la somma di fl. 14594.3. 4.1.[124]

DOC. **123**, 1452-1466 (?), SOUTH DOOR, Dig. 302
ibidem: f. 34. Stipiti, cardinale, soglia, architrave . . . della porta principale e di quella dell'Opera furono lavorati per li stessi maestri che lavororno le Porte; et il costo è computato nella valuta di esse; ma quelli della Porta del Battesimo furon fabricati per Lorenzo di Bartolo, e Vettorio suo figliuolo, ma la maggior parte da q.o[questo? quello?]. L'anno 1466 (sic) furono finiti e costarono in tutto fl. 810 lire 10166.d.1 che fanno la somma di fl. 3351. 2.9.4. . . .[125]

DOC. **124**, [1452, after July 13], EAST DOOR, Dig. 284
ibidem: f. 142 (source unnamed)
Piero Donati Orafo pulisce, e forbisce, e rizza la Porta di S. Gio., c. 14[126]

BNF, MAGL.

DOC. **125**, 1414, SAINT JOHN, Dig. 32
BNF, Magl., Cl. IX, 127, f. 187 from *Libro Grande dell'Arte segnato P, 1414*
Al tabernacolo della detta Arte posto a O.S.M. si lavora, c. 236[127]

DOC. **126**, 1442, Aug. 30, CASSA DI S. ZENOBIO, Dig. 236
BNF, Banco Rari, 228 (formerly *Magl., Cl. XVII, 2*), *Zibaldone di Buonaccorso Ghiberti*, c. 27.
. . . la fijura del santo mateo ebene lorenzo fl. 650 doro per suo salaro . . . di tutte i spesse di lorenzo
la sepoltura o vero chasa di bronzo di santo zanobi costo o vero fu giudichatto che lorenzo maestro dessa dovesi avere fl. 1324 . . . fl. 1324[128]

---

[122] Published by Gaye, bibl. 173, I, pp. 148ff with call number, Filza 136 and a number of omissions and misreadings.
[123] Unpublished.
[124] Unpublished.
[125] Unpublished. The terminating date, 1466, is probably a *lapsus calami*, the correct date being 1462-1464. See Doc. 68.
[126] Unpublished. The date results from the corre-

sponding Doc. 73.
[127] The pagination given for the original ms., c. 236, is identical with that indicated for Docs. 3, 4 and 5 in *Strozz.* LI, 1. In *BNF*, Magl. Cl. IX, 127, Doc. 125 follows immediately upon an entry repeating Doc. 3. Frey, bibl. 532, p. 381, doc. 22, again referring to Berti (see above, p. 366, note 8), thought that Doc. 125 was identical with his doc. 20, our Doc. 4.
[128] Unpublished.

AOF

DOC. 127, 1419, May 20, DESIGN FOR PAPAL APARTMENT, Dig. 65

AOF, Delib., LXXVI, c. 29. Quod scalae habitationis papae in sancta maria novella fiant in una . . . (?) in qua non potest vz. ubi nunc est cappella quondam nicolaj et quod scala in apartamento . . . (?) ex latere ex quo non . . . (?) ita quod vadat per . . . (?) et fiant secundum designum quod datur per laurentium bartoluccij aurificem et removeatur murus quod nunc est in dicta . . . (?) ex latere orti et fiat alius murus loco dicti muri descendendi in dicto orto prout expeditur.[129]

DOC. 128, 1419, Aug. 2, BUILDING OF PAPAL APARTMENT, Dig. 65

AOF, Delib., LXXVII, c. 7. Pippus Johannis populi sancti laurentii magister qui ad praesens laborat in ecclesia sci. trinitatis de florentia pro domino palla de Strozzis debeat et teneatur sub pena librarum centum fl. ire ad hedificandum et designandum scalas habituri papae in sca. maria novella, Saint Matthew . . .[130]

AUF

DOC. 129, 1413-1422, SAINT JOHN, Digs. 57, 97

Florence, Uffizi, Arch., Misc., vol. I, 4.
El scto Macteo che fecie fare larte del cambio costo assue (sic) fl. 650 doro fu dimano di Lorenzo di bartoluccio
La fighura di scto. Giovani battista posta nel pilastro dorto scto michele fecela lorenzo di Bartoluccio per larte de merchatanti sino di genaio 1419 (sic) costo fl. 294, l. 931, s. 17, d. 3.
1432-1442, CASSA DI SAN ZENOBIO, Dig. 236
La sepoltura del bronzo di Scto Zanobi o vero Casone entravi dreto [dentro] libre 3277 dottone, libre 350 di cera, libre 122 di rame e ferro, libre . . . (sic) di carbonj fl. 4, l. 94. Costò tutto fl. 1314 doro fecela lorenzo di Bartoluccio.[131]

ODS

DOC. 130, 1417, May 21, SIENA FONT, Dig. 54
ODS, Pergamena, no. 1437: In nomine Domini amen. Anno ab ipsius Domini salutifera incarnatione MCCCCXVII Inditione decima—die vero vigesima prima mensis Maii.—Appareat omnibus et singulis—quod—dominus Caterinus Corsini miles et operarius Ecclesie cathedralis sancte Marie de Senis; dominus Petrus Thome canonicus dicte Ecclesie; Turinus Mathei mercator et Jacobus Jacobi lanifex; tres ex consiliariis dicti operarii, absente Nicolaccio Terocci eorum quarto collega,—locaverunt et concesserunt magistro Laurentio Bartholi, aurifici de Florentia presenti et conducenti, ad faciendum duas de sex historiis, et tabulis historiarum que fient et fieri debent in fonte Baptismi sancti Johannis de Senis, videlicet de attone fino, eo modo et forma et cum illis figuris, de quibus declaratum fuerit eidem magistro Laurentio per dictos operarium et consiliarios, et sub istis modis, conventionibus et capitulis, videlicet:
Imprimis, quod dictus magister Laurentius teneatur et debeat dictas duas tabulas et historias facere de bono attone, et cum figuris bonis et pulcris, tamquam bonus magister, pro illo pretio et salario, de quo vel declaratum fuerit per dictos dominum operarium et consiliarios supranominatos; in quos presentes et acceptantes dictus magister Laurentius plene et libere remissionem et commissionem fecit et promisit eorum declarationi stare tacitum et contentum, absque aliqua contraditione.
Item, quod dictus magister Laurentius teneatur et debeat perfecisse et complevisse unam de dictis tabulis et historiis infra decem menses proxime venturos, omni perfectione ipsius, et figurarum: quam sic factam et completam, ostendere debeat dictis operario et consiliariis suis, antequam ipsam tabulam deauret; et postea ipsam deauratam, idest prius sine auro et postea cum auro, ut possint ipsam videre et examinare si placeat eis, et si habeat omnem perfectionem suam, et super ipsam habere illam informationem, de qua eis placuerit. Et sic visis et examinatis omnibus, habeant, et teneantur declarare precium et salarium debitum eidem magistro Laurentio, tam pro ipsa prima tabula, quam pro alia: et secundum quod per eos fuerit declaratum, poni debeat ad executionem. Et quod ipse magister Laurentius, teneatur quando deaurabit eas, ipsas deaurare ad nuotum, et non cum panellis.
Item, quod dictus magister Laurentius teneatur et debeat, postquam dicta prima tabula fuerit facta et visa et pretium declaratum ut supra, infra decem menses tunc proxime secuturos, facere aliam tabulam seu historiam cum figuris et forma sibi per predictos datis et traditis, de bono attone et bonis figuris ad similitudinem prime, et melius, si fieri potest, ut bene stet sicut prima, et melius.

---

[129] Unpublished. **Referred to by Vasari-Milanesi,** bibl. 533, II, p. 260.

[130] Poggi, bibl. 409, p. 7.
[131] Fabriczy, bibl. 147.

Item, quod dictus dominus Caterinus et consiliarii prefati non possint nec debeant, antequam fiat et videatur dicta prima tabula et historia, et declaretur pretium ut supra, locare alicui sex figuras, que fieri debent in dicto fonte Baptismi.

Item, quod dictus dominus Caterinus teneatur et debeat de presenti eidem magistro Laurentio, prestare centum flor: auri; ut possit sibi providere de rebus opportunis et in fine operis ipsum integraliter accordare de debito suo absque aliqua contraditione vel lite: et interim etiam facere sibi illas prestantias de quibus fuerint in concordia.

Item, quod predicta omnia et singula intelligantur et sint ad bonam et puram fidem et intellectum[,] omni fraude seu cavillatione, vel mala interpetratione remotis.

Que omnia et singula etc.

Actum Senis in Opera seu in domo opere sancte Marie de Senis, coram Johanne Turini aurifice de Senis, Juliano Honofrii de Florentia, Doccio Jacobi[,] et Antonello Gori de Sen: testibus.

Ego Castellanus Utinelli Castellani de Sen: notarius scripsi et publicavi.[132]

DOC. 131, 1416 [between June 28 and July 17], SIENA FONT, Dig. 44

ODS, Memoriale di Domenico di Mariano speciale (1416-1417), c. 5v. MCCCCXVI Maestro Lorenzo di Bartolo, Giugliano e Bartolomeo maestri d'intaglio da Firenze die' dare per le spese fatte di sotto— li quali maestri mandaro per loro misser Caterino e suoi chonseglieri per edifichare el Battesimo in S. Giovanni- prima, contanti le demo per detto di misser Caterino Hoparaio e per detto de conseglieri, le demo lire dodici per le spese della loro venuta, e per pigione, polastri e per malvagia, pane, aranci e altri cose, per far lor onore, come ci asegnio' Doccio, lire tre soldi diciotto e piu ci asegnio' de soldi 36 al'abergatore del Gallo, per spese d'uno loro ronzino tenne, e le dette cose e spese faciemo di consentimento di misser Chaterino e de' suoi conseglieri. In tutto fior. O, lib. XVII, sol. XIIII, den. VI. Messi a nostra Uscita fo. 53.[133]

DOC. 132, 1417 [prior to Mar. 3], SIENA FONT, Dig. 50

ibidem, c. 16v. MCCCCXVI. Le spese della casa.

E die dare soldi otto pagamo al camarlengho delle some per cabella d'una storia d'atone fecie venire misser Caterino e consiglieri da Firenze per lo fatto del Battesimo.

E die dare per la vettura d'essa storia a Michele vetturale di qui a Firenze soldi XVJ.[134]

DOC. 133, 1417, Mar. 11, SIENA FONT, Dig. 51

ibidem, c. 16v. MCCCCXVI. Le spese della Casa.

E a di XI di marzo lire sei soldi tredici per presto di ronzino e per spese feci quando andai a Firenze per lo fatto del Batesimo. . . .[135]

DOC. 134, 1416 [between July 11 and 17], SIENA FONT, Dig. 44

ODS, Entr. Usc. di Domenico di Mariano, (1416), c. 52v. A maestro Lorenzo di Bartolo intagliatore da Firenze lire diecisette soldi quatordici den. sei per più spese se li fece quando miss. Caterino e chonseglieri el feciero venire da Firenze per edificare el Battesimo apare al nostro memoriale a fo. 5.[136]

DOC. 135, 1416, Dec. 18, SIENA FONT, Dig. 45

ODS, Libro di Spese di Doccio di Jacopo fattore (1416). c. 10. MCCCCXVI Ancho spesi a di' XVIII dicembre quando Giovanni di Turino orafo ando a Fiorenza a maestro Lorenzo per lo fatto del Batesimo, lire IIII.[137]

DOC. 136, 1417, Jan. 1, SIENA FONT, Dig. 49

ibidem, c. 10v. MCCCCXVI Ancho spesi a dì primo di genaio per biada e per pescio per fare onore a maestro Lorenzo da Fiorenza che venne per lo fatto del Batesimo lire II.[138]

DOC. 137, 1417, May 20, SIENA FONT, Dig. 53

ibidem, c. 15v. MCCCCXVII Ancho spesi a di (sic) maggio per fare onore a maestro Lorenzo da Fiorenza quando venne a Siena a tollare le fighure de l'atone del Batesimo, per biada e strame e uno mezzo chapretto e per uova e chacio e due oncie di pepe e per pesegli e per uno pescio arrostito e bacegli e pesegli lire IIJ, soldi V.[139]

DOC. 138, 1417, July 9, SIENA FONT, Dig. 55

ODS, Memoriale d'Antonio di Cristofano (1417), c. 6v. Maestro Lorenzo di Bartalo da

---

[132] Milanesi, bibl. 336, II, pp. 89ff, doc. 61; Lusini, bibl. 283, pp. 96ff, doc. 3; Bacci, bibl. 31, pp. 109f.

[133] Bacci, bibl. 31, p. 96; Milanesi, bibl. 336, II, p. 91, note, as c. 6v; Lusini, bibl. 283, p. 40, note 3.

[134] Bacci, bibl. 31, p. 101.

[135] *ibid.*, p. 107.

[136] Bacci, bibl. 31, p. 98; Milanesi, bibl. 336, II, p. 91, note; Lusini, bibl. 283, p. 40, note 3.

[137] Bacci, bibl. 31, p. 99.

[138] *ibid.*, pp. 99f.

[139] *ibid.*, p. 109.

Firenze die' dare a di 9 di luglio lire dugiento chontanti i quali denari pagho per noi Ghucio di Ghalgano Bichi e chonpagni banchieri chome apare a Liro rosso a fo. 98 e a mia entrata a fo. 3, e i detti denari porto Papi di Bartalomeio suo garzone e i detti denari si pagaro per detto di misser Chaterino Hoparaio e i detti denari sono per parte di paghamento de le storie del Batesimo le quagli s'e alogate da misser Chaterino. Messi a Libro rosso a fo. 137 e a nostra uscita a fo. 57.
Entr. Usc. (1417), c. 57[140]

DOC. **139**, 1420, Nov. 13, SIENA FONT, Dig. 80

ODS, Debitori e Creditori (1420-1444), *Libro giallo, vol. 393*, c. 3v. Maestro Lorenzo di Bartalo da Firenze die dare lire treciento e qua danari ane auti da Antonio di Cristofano e Ghabriello di Giannino Gucci chamarlenghi stati a la detta hopera come apare a liro Rosso in due partite che debi dare[;] e sbatuti la e messi qui a fo. 137.
E a di XIII di novembre fl. centoquaranta d'oro i quali ebbe per noi da Luca di Piero Rinucci in Firenze per some . . . (?) a fo. 52 cigliemo allibre l. 564 s. 13 d. 4.
Et die dare insino a di'detto . . . (?) l. otto s. nove, d. sei e quali si spesero per vetura d uno chavallo e altre spese quando io Pietro di Nofrio speciale kamarlengo vo andai a solecidare le dette storie e sono . . . iscritte a fo. 29.
E die dare l. quatro s. due d. sei i quali pagamo per lui a ser Castellino d' Utinelli notaio per chagione che fu rogato dell'alogazione del Batesimo tolsi a fare dal Uopera per la sua parte come appare inscritto da me Pietro di Nofrio kamerlengo a fo. 29 in soma di l. otto, s. cinque a Ser Castelino detto.[141]

DOC. **140**, 1425, June 28, SIENA FONT, Dig. 119

ibidem, c. 3v. E debe dare a di 28 di giugnio 1425 soldi quarantacinque paghamo contanti per lui a Michele vetturale da San Donato, per detto di misser Bartalomeio nostro Operaio, furo per vettura d'una storia del Batesimo di santo Giovanni mando a vedere all' Operaio[;] paghali io Pietro di Marcho camarlingo e sonno a mia uscitta a f. 61.[142]

DOC. **141**, 1427, Oct. 30, SIENA FONT, Dig. 143

ibidem, c. 240. Maestro Lorenzo di Bartalo da Firenze orafo e sculptore die' avere a dì 30 d'ottobre lire mille seciento ottanta so[no] per due historie d'attone dorate ci a fatto e consegnate el di detto in Firenze a me Berto d'Antonio camarlengo dell'Uopera per lo sacratissimo Batesmo si die fare in san Giovanni[;] l'una contiene[:] QUANDO SAN GIOVANNI BATEZO JESU CHRISTO NEL GIORDANO l'altra[:] QUANDO E RE HERODE COMANDA E FA METTARE SAN GIOVANNI predetto DA LA FAMEGLIA SUA IN PREGIONE. E questo per fiorini dugento dieci l'una[,] a lire 4 fiorino[,] che so[no] frammendue recati a lire in tutto lire 1680.
Del qual prezo di lire 1680 per amendune historie fumo d'accordo in Firenze el detto m.° Lorenzo da l'una parte e io Berto a vice e nome dell' Uopera dall'altra. E questo per commissione pienamente fattami da misser Bartolomeo di Giovanni Cechi Operaio nostro e Giovanni di Francino Patrici[,] Nanni di Piero di Guido e ser Bindotto di Giovanni notajo[,] al presente conseglieri del detto miss. l'Operaio e sopra el detto Batesmo. Et cosi el sopradetto miss. l'Operaio e suoi conseglieri[,] absente misser Giorgio Talomei lor quarto compagno[,] anno avuto rato e confermato nella mia tornata. E qui o acceso il detto m.° Lorenzo creditore di lor buon consentimento e volonta.[143]

DOC. **142**, 1425 [between March 1 and 10], SIENA FONT, Dig. 112

ODS, Memoriale di mess. Bartolomeo operaio (1423-1427), c. 7 (in margin: Firenze)
A di . . . di marzo si delibero—harta per mano di ser Franciescho del Barbuto—che i denari che ano avutti i maestri da Firenze he fano le store del Batesimo si riabino hocio sia hosa so pasatti tutti i termini che le dovesono fare e no l' ano fatte.[144]

DOC. **143**, 1427, April 17, SIENA FONT, Dig. 134

ODS, Entrata—Uscità di Antonio di Jacomo (1426-1427), c. 83v. A M[aestr]o Lorenzo di . . . da Fiorenza orafo (?) adi 17 d'aprile l[ire] dugiento e quegli deve per noi giovanni di giovanni pieri e compagni banchieri esso [e sono?] a lui al monito (?) di messer Antonio

---

[140] *ibid.*, pp. 110f.
[141] Milanesi, bibl. 336, p. 91, note, with large omissions and minor misreadings; Lusini, bibl. 283, p. 40, note 4, after Milanesi.
[142] Doc. 140 continues Doc. 139 in different handwriting. Bacci, bibl. 31, p. 161; Milanesi, bibl. 336, II,

pp. 91f, note; Lusini, bibl. 283, p. 41, note 4.
[143] Bacci, bibl. 31, p. 183f; Milanesi, bibl. 336, p. 92, note. See Docs. 148, 149, 150.
[144] Bacci, bibl. 31, p. 158. For the precise date see Doc. 154.

camerlengo nostro (?) deve dare. E detti denari si mandano[a] Antonio di Jacomo Pieri e compagni banchieri di Fiorenza per che gli desse al detto m[aestr]o Lorenzo perche el detto m[aestr]o Lorenzo dorasse due storie d'attone fatte per lo batessimo di san giovanni nostro. E detti denari si mandano per giovanni pieri per Michele di . . . veturale da san Donato per detto di messer Bartolomeo (cancelled) operaio e di Nanni di Francino e compagni per (?) el batesimo dan . . . (?) esso che maestro Lorenzo debe dare a di' sopradetto.[145]

DOC. 144, 1427, April 23 [Feb. 27-March 7], SIENA FONT, Dig. 130

ibidem, c. 84v. A'ntonio di Jacomo di Dota adi 23 d'aprile l[ire] vinti e questo per una andata fecie a fiorenza per comandamento e volonta di mis[ser] Bartalomeio Oparaio e di Checco Rosso[,] Nanni di Piero di Ghuido e ser Bindotto mandato per li detti a m.° Lorenzo di (. . . . .) per le tav[o]le e storie fatte per lo batesimo[;] ando a di 27 di feraio e torno a di 3 di marzo con due cavaglj stato dì cinque, per soldi quaranta di per ciashuno, cavalo e huomo; fatto questo salario per lo detto miss. Bartelomeio, Nanni di Francino, Nanni di Piero di Ghuido e ser Bindotto.[146]

DOC. 145, 1427, March 1-7, SIENA FONT, Dig. 130

ibidem, c. 85. Alle spese fatte in fiorenza per Antonio di Jacomo mandato di mis[ser] Ser Bartolomeio e Checho Rosso[,] Nanni di Piero di Giudo e Ser Bindetto lire quatro soldi due denari 6 per due casse di legno chostono lire 10 d. 2[;] per lire 3 daghuti per esse casse felle in fiorenza maestro ghino di pietro m[aestr]o di legniame a dì primo di marzo per mettarvi dentro le dette storie che venno da fiorenza le quali fa m[aestr]o Lorenzo di[. . .] Ese che le dette spese debino dare al l[ibr]o giallo a fo. Alle dette spese fatte in questo dì detto di sopra s[oldi] tre d[enari] 6 per fune per magliare (?) le dette casse di muovere dentro le dette storie d'atone
Alla detta spesa a dì 3 di marzo s[oldi] quattro a Nani di Cichanello portatore per recare le dette storie dalla cabella a l'Uopera. . . .
Alla dette spese fatte l[ire] dodici e questo per vetura di recare e portare le dette tavole e sono da Fiorenza a Siena e portare da Siena a Fio-

renza: a Michele veturale da San Donato pesano l[ibre] 600 onc. (?) 20 che monta lire 12 porto insino a di' 7 di marzo a Fiorenza . . .[147]

DOC. 146, 1427, July 14, SIENA FONT, Dig. 139.

ODS, Entrata-Uscita di Berto d'Antonio (1427-1428), c. 63. A ser Jacomo di Nuccino notajo a di 14 di luglio l[ire] quatro le quagli so[no] per una carta ricogliemo da lui del contratto dell'alogagione di due historie d'attone per lo Batismo si die' fare in San Giovanni fatto a maestro Lorenzo di Bartalo orafo da Firenze del quale fu rogato ser Castellano d'Utinello. El detto ser Jacomo a le sue imbreviature.[148]

DOC. 147, 1427, Sept. 26, SIENA FONT, Dig. 141

ibidem, c. 63. A m.° Lorenzo di Bartalo da Firenze fa due storie nostre del Batesmo a di 26 di septembre l[ire] cento otto s[oldi] otto den. otto gli facemo dare a Firenze per fiorini vinticinque di camera[,] gli dè Esau Martellini per lettera di Giovanni Pini e Mariano banchieri per dorare le dette storie.[149]

DOC. 148, 1427, Oct. 30, SIENA FONT, Dig. 143

ibidem, c. 64. A Maestro Lorenzo di Bartalo da Firenze orafo e sculptore a dì 30 di ottobre l[ire] cento novantaquatro. So[no] per parte del prezzo delle due historie ci a fatte per lo batesimo di Siena de quali denari contanti in sua mano in fiorini d'oro 44 che montano . . . (?) per s[oldi] 8 d[enari] 2 l'uno l[ire] 194 in Fiorenza quando vi fui mandato da Misser Bartolomeo e conseglieri suoi per le dette due historie . . .
c. 64v
A maestro Lorenzo di Bartalo soprascripto a dì 30 di ottobre l[ire] trecento otto s[oldi] quindici d[enari] sei e quagli so[no] per resto di l[ire] mille secento ottanta doveva avere per le due historie dell'attone ci fece per lo batesimo si diè fare in san giovanni. E per noi glil de[diede] in Fiorenza Luca di Piero Rinieri banchiere da Fiorenza . . .[150]

DOC. 149, 1427, Oct. 30, SIENA FONT, Dig. 143

ibidem, c. 64v. Ala cabella dele porti di Fiorenza a dì 30 detto l[ire] quarantacinque so[no]

145 Unpublished. Bacci, bibl. 31, p. 170, excerpt only.
146 Unpublished. Summary, Bacci, bibl. 31, pp. 164f.
147 Unpublished. Summary, Bacci, bibl. 31, pp. 165ff.
148 Bacci, bibl. 31, p. 181, as c. 63v.
149 Bacci, bibl. 31, pp. 181f. Quoted by Milanesi, bibl. 336, II, p. 92, note and by Lusini, bibl. 283, pp. 41f, note 5 as *Libro Giallo de Deb. e Cred.*, c. 239v and as immediately preceding our Document 141. Repeated checks have failed to turn up this document.
150 Unpublished. Summary, Bacci, bibl. 31, p. 186.

per cabella dele sopradette due historie dell'atone per lo batesimo pagamo in Fiorenza quando le feci venire per commissione di Mis[ser] Bartolomeo operaio nostro e suoi conseglieri. Et per me le pago Antonio di Jacomo Pieri da Fiorenza.[151]

DOC. 150, 1427, Nov. 2, SIENA FONT, Dig. 143
ibidem, c. 64v. A Berto d'Antonio camarlengo nostro a dì 2 di novembre l[ire] trentadue so[no] per la sua andata e salaro quando ando a Fiorenza con due cavagli a s[oldi] quaranta per cavallo come è usanza per dì otto in tutto cioe partì di Siena a dì 25 d'ottobre sabato e torno l'altro sabato dì primo di novembre el dì dognisanti. E questo per commissione di Mis[ser] bartolomeo operaio nostro e di Giovanni di Francino Parucci (?) e di Ser Bindotto di Giovanni notaio e Nanni di Piero consiglieri del detto operaio e sopra el detto batesimo. Perche non si potevano avere le dette historie dal detto maestro Lorenzo essendovisi scripto piu e piu volte . . .[152]

DOC. 151, 1427, Nov. 15, SIENA FONT, Dig. 144
ibidem, c. 64v. A Antonio di Domenico fameglio de nostri M[agnifici] S[ignori] col rotelino a dì 15 di novembre s[oldi] cinquantacinque. so[no] per suo salaro quando fu mandato da l'oparaio e conseglieri predetti a me quando ero a Fiorenza con lettere che dovessi a ogni modo veder di conduciare le dette historie a Siena commetendomi pienamente el far patto col detto M[aestr]o Lorenzo.[153]

DOC. 152, 1427, Nov. 15, SIENA FONT, Dig. 144
ibidem, c. 64v. A Antoniello e uno compagno portatori a dì detto s[oldi] quatro perche recaro le dette due historie da la cabella nostra di Siena a l'Uopara.[154]

DOC. 153, 1427, Nov. 15, SIENA FONT, Dig. 144
ibidem, c. 64v. A Michele da San Donato vetturale a dì 15 detto l[ire] sei s[oldi] 8 per vettura dele dette due historie dell'attone da Firenze a Siena e alcuno aguto e funella disse messe di suo perche bisogno . . . erarle (?)[155]

DOC. 154, 1425, March 10, SIENA FONT, Dig. 113
ODS, Libro di Documenti Artistici, no. 52
Adi X di Marzo 1424: Honorevole magiore etc. E suto a me Agnolo di Jacomo vostro fattore el quale m'arecho una lettera[:] ami informato Agnolo di vostra intentione intorno al fatto delle storie, le quali esso a vedute[:] son presso che finite[;] le quali sarebono chosta compiute se non fosse stata la moria[;] pero ch'io mi parti[:] andai a Vinegia e ancora tutti miei lavoranti si partirono. E questa e suta la cagione dello indugio d'esse. Per tutto el mese di Giugno aremo finito el vostro lavorio. Altro non c'e a dire. Christo ci conservi in pacie.
Per lo vostro Lorenzo di Bartolo orafo in Firenze.
Egregio chavaliere messer Bartolomeo di Giovanni honorevole operaio nella Chiesa chattedrale di Siena.[156]

DOC. 155, 1425, April 16, SIENA FONT, Dig. 115
ibidem (unnumbered at present; formerly no. 54)
Jhesus—Honorevole amicho etc. Ebi tua lettera a di XIIII d'Aprile la quale vidi come di charo e fedele amicho oltre accio di tuo star bene[:] la qual chosa . . . grolia. Anchora del tuo buono animo in verso di me, el quale ai auto sempre[:] cioe, se bisogno fosse tu m'aiutassi nettare una di queste storie[;] di[ci] che lo faresti volentieri[:] la qual cosa so che non nasce se non per buono amore, del quale Idio ti benifichi per me. Sappi caro amicho le storie sono presso a finite[:] l'una a ne' le mani Giuliano di ser Andrea, l'altra o io[:] e al tempo ch' i' o promesso a messer Bartolomeo saranno finite[:] et sarebono state finite e gia gran tempo se non la 'ngratitudine di quelli che pel pasato sono stati miei conpagni da' quali non o ricevuto solo una ingiuria ma molte. Colla gratia di Dio io sono fuori delle loro mani[:] el quale io lodo senpre Dio, considerato in quanta liberta a me pare esser rimaso.
Al tutto sanza compagnia dilibero stare e volere essere el maestro della bottega mia e pottere ricettare ongni mio amico con buona e lieta cera. Ringratioti della tua buona e perfetta volonta in verso di me. Prieghoti charissimamente mi raccomandi a messer Bartolomeo.
Ancho ti priego charissimamente se modo

151 Unpublished. Summary, Bacci, bibl. 31, p. 186.
152 Unpublished. Summary, Bacci, bibl. 31, p. 185.
See also Doc. 41.
153 Unpublished. Summary, Bacci, bibl. 31, pp. 185f.

154 Unpublished. Summary, Bacci, bibl. 31, pp. 185f.
155 Unpublished. Summary, Bacci, bibl. 31, pp. 185f.
156 Milanesi, bibl. 336, II, pp. 119f, doc. 85, I; Lusini, bibl. 283, p. 99, doc. 5; Bacci, bibl. 31, p. 58.

veruno ti puoi adoperare ch' io riabi le charte delli ucielli ch' io prestai a Ghoro.[a] So che non ti sara faticha pregare Domenicho[b] che intagla di legname, che me le rimandi pero ch' io sento quelli et ogni altra chosa che era nelle mani del detto Ghoro è rimaso nelle mani di maestro Domenicho. E anchora mi saluta lui da mia parte et maestro Francesco di Valdambrina[;] e se per me si puo fare qua alcuna chosa, son senpre a picieri [sic] tuoi. Altro non ci e a dire. Christo ti conservi in pace. Fatta a di XVI d'Aprile 1425.
Per lo tuo Lorenzo di Bartolo, orafo in Firenze amicho tuo caro.

Prudente et honorevole huomo
Giovanni Turini orafo in Siena data.[157]

DOC. **156**, 1425, June 26, SIENA FONT, Dig. 118

ibidem, no. 54. Honorevole maggior mio etc. E suto a me per vostra parte Giovanni di Turino ami [ha mi] detto come v'e suto scritto come in su el vostro lavorio non si lavora. Di questo non vo' che ne faccia relatione se non Giovanni. Sapiate, quella storia venne chosta è quasi finita[;] l'altra vi mando chome mi mandate a chiedere per Giovanni. E subito sara fatta perche io vi lavoro su. Quanto piu tosto potete me la rimandate E mandatemi a dire se volete si dorino chosta o qui; perche a me sarebe molto piu chomodo a doralle qui per le chose che a simile matera bisogna ci sono in punto spetialmente a queste e così grandi. Non dimeno mi contento di quello chon voi. Altro non c'è a dire. Christo vi conservi in pace. Fatta adi XXVI di giugno 1425.
Per lo vostro Lorenzo di Bartolo orafo in Firenze
Egregio kavaliere messer Bartolomeo operaio del Duomo di Siena.[158]

DOC. **157**, 1425, Aug. 2, SIENA FONT, Dig. 121

ibidem (present no. 55; formerly no. 56)
Honorevole magior mio etc. La chagione di questa si è[:] come voi sapete e fu qua per vostra parte Giovanni Turini e chiesemi come voi vi contentavi ch' io mandassi chosta la storia del Battesimo[:] prieghovi che me la rimandiate accioch' io le possa dar fine pero ch' io o finita ogimai l'altra e ancora sono solecitato dalla ghabella[;] pero ch' io promisi a' maestri della ghabella di rimeterlla qui in

tre settimane. E pasato el termine ch' io promisi loro[;] se non viene tosto, saro stretto a paghare la gabella. Penso come sara finita questa mandarvela[:] e rispondetemi al fatto del dorarle, se vi contentate si dorino costa o volete si dorino qua. Di questo ne seghuiro el volere vostro. Altro non c'e a dire. Christo vi conservi in pace. Fatta adi II d'Aghosto 1425.
Per lo vostro Lorenzo di Bartolo orafo in Firenze.
Magnifico ed egregio kavaliere mesere Bartolomeo venerabile operaio del Duomo di Siena.[159]

DOC. **158**, 1427 [after March 17], SIENA FONT, Dig. 131

ibidem: (unnumbered at present; formerly no. 53)
Honorevole magiore. Adi 17 di Marzo o ricevute le storie, m' avete mandate per Michele da Santo Donato[;] et chon esse una vostra lettera dove domandate è bene si levi la ghabella e l'obrigho fatto per voi da Lucha di Piero Rinieri.
Io sono stato alla ghabella, et vegio che per fretta non v' esendo gli uficiagli si presono dal proveditore, che tornando e non tornando si dovesse paghar la ghabella ma meno tornando che no[:] chome de' sapere il vostro camarlingho. Della quale 'npromessa o patto mi sono diliberato d'essere all'uficio e preghargli che la cancellino. Et penso per ongni rispetto la leveranno via. Et se non valesse alla prima, tornarvi tante volte che lo faccino[:] et pero penso che si raunino oggi. Sara la risposta come potro presto.
Aparechiato senpre avostri piaceri.
Lorenzo di Bartolo orafo in Firenze.
Nobili viro messer Bartolomeo di Giovanni oparaio dell'Opera di Siena.[160]

DOC. **159**, 1427 [April 11-20], SIENA FONT, Dig. 133

ibidem (at present no. 64; formerly no. 56)
E suto qua Antonio di Jachomo vostro chamarlingo el quale a veduto come l' una delle storie et (sic) conpiuta[:] l'altra sara finita a Pasqua come per Giuliano vi fu promesso. Bisognaci l'oro per dorarle[:] che in su amendue le storie andra d'oro circha di fior. ottanta o piu. Mandate siamo serviti di fior. cento. Sono senpre aparechiato a vostri piacieri. Christo vi conservi in pace.

[157] Milanesi, bibl. 336, II, pp. 119f, doc. 85, II; Lusini, bibl. 283, pp. 99f, doc. 6; Bacci, bibl. 31, pp. 159f. Milanesi, *loc. cit.*: (a) di Neroccio; (b) di Niccolo.
[158] Milanesi, bibl. 336, II. p. 121, doc. 85, III; not in Lusini; Bacci, bibl. 31, p. 160.

[159] Milanesi, bibl. 336, II, pp. 121f, doc. 85, IV; Lusini, bibl. 283, pp. 100f, doc. 7.
[160] Milanesi, bibl. 336, II, p. 122, doc. 85, V, dated March 1425-1426 (?); Lusini, bibl. 283, pp. 101f, doc. 9, dated March 1426.

Per lo vostro Lorenzo di Bartolo orafo in Firenze.
El magnifico et prudente khavaliere messer Bartolomeo operaio del Duomo di Siena.[161]

DOC. 160, 1427, May 12, SIENA FONT, Dig. 135

ibidem (unnumbered at present; formerly no. 57)
Karissimo magiore mio. Le vostre storie son finite e in questa mattina a di XII di Magio cominciamo a dorare la storia del Battesimo[:] l'altra e finita non manca se none el dorarlla. Mandateci l'oro. Potremo mandarle amendue insieme. Non dimeno seghuiremo la vostra volonta di quello che volete si faccia. Altro altro [sic] non c'e a dire. Christo vi conservi in pace.

Per lo vostro Lorenzo di Bartolo
orafo in Firenze
El egregio kavaliere messere Bartolomeo
operaio del Duomo di Siena.[162]

DOC. 161, 1427, May 31, SIENA FONT, Dig. 137

ibidem, no. 58.
Ricevetti vostra lettera a di ventotto di magio nella quale mi scrivete avere ricevute due mie lettere el tenor d'esse[:] come le vostre istorie sono finite e n'e dorata una. Mandavi a chiedere l'oro per dorarlle amendue[;] mandasti per una. Essa e dorata[:] mandate altrettanto d'oro e doreremo l'altra pero che da me io non o el modo[:] sello avessi la dorerei. O achattato da Antonio di Jachopo Pieri nostro banchiere per mie niscista [sic] e fare finire il vostro lavorio a lato a dugiento fior. e convimi [sic] el resto ch' io resto avere da voi darllo allui. Pertanto mandate qua el vostro chamarlingo in modo ch'io possa dorare la vostra istoria e contentare el detto Antonio che m' a servito. Chi vera (verra) in un dì ne potra mandare le vostre storie pero che in un dì sara dorata. Altro [non] ci è a dire. Christo vi conservi in pace. Fatta a di XXXI di Maggio 1427.

Per lo vostro Lorenzo di Bartolo
orafo in Firenze
Etgregio (sic) kavaliere messer Bartolomeo
Giovanni honorevole operaio in Siena.[163]

DOC. 162, 1427, October, SIENA FONT, Dig. 142

ibidem (unnumbered at present; formerly no. 59)
Honorevole magior mio etc. La chagione di questa si è[:] per vostra lettera e stato fatto chomessione [a] Antonio di Jacopo Pieri nostro banchiere mi siano dati fior. 25 per dorare l'altra storia. E dorata e son finite. Mandate per esse a ogni vostro piacere. Si veramente fate contento della cantita [sic] ch'io resto avere Antonio di Jacopo Pieri nostro banchiere. E per chagione non si perdano troppe parole ponete mente in su el Memoriale di messer Chaterino segnato +[:] e lungo el detto quaderno. Ancora domandate e' detto [sic] operai che in quello tenpo erano, e ragionamenti avemo. In la verita fu questa che messer Chaterino mi volle dare dell' una delle dette storie fior. 220[;] a questo non fui mai contento[;] volevo d' esse fior. 240. Esso mi promisse ch'io le faciessi e che mi contenterebe. Ancor tolsi a far colle dette storie figure quatro[:] d'esse non si fece merchato[:] se vi contentate io le faccia, farolle volentieri in brieve tenpo. Altro non ci e a dire. Christo vi conservi in pacie.

Per lo vostro Lorenzo di Bartolo
orafo in Firenze
Etgregio (sic) kavaliere messere Bartolomeo
honorevole operaio del Duomo di Siena.[164]

DOC. 163, 1414, Dec. 1, SAINT JOHN, Dig. 36

Lost document, in 1681 in the possession of Cristofano Berardi, lawyer of the Collegio de' Nobili.
Giornale di Lorenzo di Cione di ser Buonaccorso di Firenze orafo nel quale iscrivero ogni mia faccenda di giorno in giorno e così in su esso faro ricordo d'ogni mia cosa cominciando a di primo di maggio 1403. Segnato A
A dì primo di dicembre 1414.
Qui appresso farò ricordo di ciò che io spenderò in gettare la figura di S. Gio. Battista. Tolsi a gettarla alle mie spese; se essa non venisse bene io mi dovessi perder le spese: io la gettassi, e venisse bene, mi rimasi nell'arte di calimala, che i consoli e gli operai, che in quel tempo fussono, usassono inverso di me quella discrezione, che essi usassono in' d'un altro maestro, per cui essi mandavano, che la gettassono. A dì d. comincerò a far ricordo di tutte le spese si faranno nel getto.[165]

161 Milanesi, bibl. 336, II, p. 123, doc. 85, VI dates the letter 1426; Lusini, bibl. 283, p. 101, doc. 8, 1425; Bacci, bibl. 31, p. 167, note, with correct date.
162 Milanesi, bibl. 336, II, p. 123, doc. 85, VII; Lusini, bibl. 283, p. 102, doc. 10.
163 Milanesi, bibl. 336, pp. 123f, doc. 85, VIII; Lusini, bibl. 283, p. 102, doc. 11.
164 Milanesi, bibl. 336, pp. 124f, doc. 85, IX, with date 1427 (?); Lusini, bibl. 283, p. 104, doc. 13; Bacci, bibl. 31, p. 182.
165 Quoted after Baldinucci, bibl. 35, I, pp. 254f.

1. 1378-1381. Docs. 81-86. Date of Ghiberti's birth (Tax declarations 1427-1442)

2. 1400-1401. Ghiberti at Pesaro (Ghiberti-Schlosser, bibl. 178, I, p. 45)

3. 1401-1402. Ghiberti participates in the competition for a bronze door to be set up at the Baptistery in Florence (Ghiberti-Schlosser, bibl. 178, I, p. 46)

4. 1402. Doc. 1. The consuls of the *Calimala* decide to entrust the bronze door of the Baptistery to Ghiberti, "Nencio di Bartoluccio Orafo."
ASF, Strozz. LI, 1, f. 2 from: *Libro Grande Calimala C, 1402,* c. 255 (Frey, bibl. 532, p. 353, doc. 2, with date 1403)

5. 1402. Doc. 80. Payment by the *Arte di Calimala* of 30 florins to Ghiberti, "Nencio di Bartoluccio," possibly for work on the competition relief.
ASF, Strozz. LI, 3, f. 153 (index) from: *Libro Grande Calimala C, 1402,* c. 270

6. no date, possibly 1402-1403. Doc. 33. Ghiberti's competition relief is gilded. Later it is decided to represent on the new door the New Testament and to save this relief for the other door "if there the Old Testament should be represented."
ASF, Strozz. LI, 1, f. 80v from: *Libro seconda e terza porta* (Frey, bibl. 532, pp. 356f, doc. 8, erroneously, June 5, 1407; for the correct date see above, p. 103)

7. 1403, Sept. 3. Doc. 60. The consuls of the *Calimala* decide to place the new bronze door at the main portal of the Baptistery facing the Cathedral.
ASF, Strozz. LI, 1, f. 184 from: *Delib. Cons. Calimala, 1401-1414,* c. 35

8. 1403, Nov. 23. Docs. 26, 61. Contract of the *Calimala* with "Lorenzo di Bartolo and Bartolo di Michele, his father, . . . for the second door of S. Giovanni"; they are to invest only their labor, all the rest is the business of the guild; they must finish three reliefs each year, beginning December 1; and they are granted up to 200 florins annually on account. A committee of the guild is elected to supervise the work.

ASF, Strozz. LI, 1, f. 79 from: *Libro seconda e terza porta*; cp. *ibid.,* f. 184 from: *Delib. Cons. Calimala, 1401-1414,* c. 38

9. 1403 (after Nov. 23). Doc. 80. Payment of 100 florins from the *Calimala* to Ghiberti.
ASF, Strozz. LI, 3, f. 153 (index) from: *Libro Grande Calimala D, 1403,* c. 128

10. 1404, Jan. 30. Doc. 65. The *Officiali del Musaico* of the *Calimala* make (final) arrangements with Ghiberti for work on the door.
ASF, Strozz. LI, 1, f. 185v from: *Delib. Off. Musaico,* c. 113

11. early 1404. Doc. 80. The *Calimala* pays small expenses for work on the bronze door, amounting to roughly 25 florins.
ASF, Strozz. LI, 3, f. 153 (index) from: *Libro Grande Calimala D, 1403,* c. 183

12. 1404, Nov. 10. Ghiberti acts as member of a committee of consultants to give an opinion on buttressing and windows for main apse of the Cathedral.
AOF, Delib. XLIX, c. 26 (Guasti, bibl. 199, doc. 425)

13. 1404, prior to Dec. Ghiberti designs window of the *Assumption of the Virgin* for the center oculus on the façade of the Cathedral (Ghiberti-Schlosser, bibl. 178, I, p. 51)

14. 1404, Dec. 10-1405, June 30. Working (?) design and execution of this window by Niccolo Pieri, without Ghiberti's name being mentioned.
AOF, Delib. XLIX, c. 31, 35v, 36; *L,* c. 19ff (Poggi, bibl. 413, docs. 516-521; Paatz, bibl. 375, III, p. 497, note 244)

15. 1405, after Aug. 31; before Feb. 11, 1406. Doc. 62. Ghiberti works on the bronze door for the Baptistery. His assistants are listed.
ASF, Strozz. LI, 1, f. 184v from: *Delib. Cons. Calimala, 1401-1414,* c. 65

16. 1405. Doc. 80. Deliberations of the *Calimala* regarding their pilaster at Or San Michele.
ASF, Strozz. LI, 3, f. 153 (index) from: *Libro Grande Calimala F, 1405,* c. 97

17. 1405. Doc. 2. Giuliano di Ser Andrea is mentioned as assistant (*discepolo*) to Ghiberti, evidently on the door of the Baptistery.

---

[1] The Florentine year ran from March 25 to March 24 of the following year. We have translated the Florentine date into that now in common usage wherever the month is given. When only the year is indicated the date may range from March 25 to the following March 24. Documents giving the year only are inserted at the end of the year, those covering a longer period under the last year referred to.

ASF, Strozz. LI, 1, f. 3 from: *Libro Grande Calimala F, 1405,* c. 171

18. 1406, Jan. 12. Small payment from *Opera del Duomo.*

AOF, scaffale LXXXVI, Quinterno di Cassa a di primo di Gennaio 1405, f. 3 (lost, quoted after Rumohr, bibl. 454, p. 444)

19. 1406, Feb. 16. Ghiberti and others are discharged as consultants of the *Opera del Duomo.*

AOF, Delib. LI, c. 6v (Guasti, bibl. 199, doc. 434)

20. 1406. Death of Cione di ser Buonaccorso (see Doc. 120)

21. 1407, Mar. 14. Ghiberti has to refund 3 florins received for advice and salary as consultant for a window in the main apse of the Cathedral.

AOF, Delib. LIII, c. 5 (Guasti, bibl. 199, doc. 438)

22. 1407, June 1. Doc. 27. A new contract is signed for work on the door of the Baptistery with "Lorenzo di Bartoluccio alone . . . ," made necessary because he failed to observe the stipulations of the first contract. Precise regulations of working conditions: he is not allowed to take on any other work without the permission of the consuls of the *Calimala,* and after completion of the door he has to wait one year in case the guild wants to entrust any other work to him. He is to be paid 200 florins annually for his labor. "He must work with his own hand every working day like any journeyman and in case of idleness this is to be noted down in a ledger kept for that purpose. He has to work in wax and bronze, in particular those parts which require greatest perfection, such as hair, nudes, and the like." He is to hire the workmen, but their salary is fixed by the consuls. All materials and tools are to be furnished by the *Calimala.* (For list of collaborators see Dig. 41 and Doc. 31)

ASF, Strozz. LI, 1, f. 79, 79v from: *Libro seconda e terza porta* (Frey, bibl. 532, pp. 354ff, doc. 71 with date June 5)

23. 1407, on or before June 3. Doc. 63. Decision of the consuls of the *Calimala* to decorate their pilaster at Or San Michele and to appoint a committee *ad hoc.*

ASF, Strozz. LI, 1, f. 185 from: *Delib. Cons. Calimala, 1401-1414* c. 77

24. 1404-1407. Doc. 28. Strozzi's summary referring to wages paid to Ghiberti and his collaborators for work on the door "throughout the time of the first contract" amounting to 882 florins, 260 lire, 66 denari, totaling over 950 florins; his credit is still 200 florins. His assistants during this period are listed, numbering eleven, among them Giuliano di Ser Andrea and Donatello.

ASF, Strozz. LI, 1, f. 79f from: *Libro seconda e terza porta* (Frey, bibl. 532, pp. 354ff, doc. 7 with erroneous date June 5, 1407)

25. 1408, Jan. 7. Ghiberti and six assistants are permitted to be on the street at night (Baldinucci, bibl. 36, 1, p. 372, from: *Libro di Ser Nofri di Ser Paolo Nemi;* lost)

26. 1408, after Dec. 24; before May 2, 1409. Doc. 64. Reference to a list of workmen employed on the door of the Baptistery.

ASF, Strozz. LI, 1, f. 185v from: *Delib. Cons. Calimala, 1401-1414,* c. 95

27. 1408, after Dec. 24; before May 2, 1409. Doc. 64. Free hours of workmen regulated.

ASF, Strozz. LI, 1, f. 185v from: *Delib. Cons. Calimala, 1401-1414,* c. 109

28. 1409, Aug. 3. Doc. 115. Ghiberti matriculated in the goldsmiths' guild.

ASF, Arti, Seta, vol. 7, matricola, 1328-1433, c. 115v

29. 1412 (?). Ghiberti designs two oculi for the façade of the aisles of the Cathedral (Ghiberti-Schlosser, bibl. 178, 1, p. 51); execution by Nicolo di Piero, 1412-1415, without Ghiberti's name appearing in the documents.

AOF, Delib. LXIV, c. 37; *LXV,* c. 13; *LXVI,* c. 12v, 13v, 17v; *LXVII,* c. 3, 5; *Stanz. QQ,* c. 66, 84v, 91, 93v, 96 (Poggi, bibl. 413, docs. 522-531)

30. 1413, April 5. Ghiberti reaches an agreement concerning the contested inheritance of Cione di Ser Buonaccorso (Baldinucci, bibl. 35, 1, p. 360, and note 1 from: lost document of notary ser Pietro di ser Michele Guiducci).

31. 1413. Doc. 54. Work is under way on a figure for the pilaster of the *Calimala* at Or San Michele.

ASF, Strozz. LI, 1, f. 93 from: *Uscità Calimala, 1413,* c. 5

32. 1414, Aug. 7. Doc. 125. Work is under way on the niche of *Saint John* at Or San Michele.

BNF, Magl. Cl. IX, 127, f. 187 from unmentioned document, probably *Libro Grande Calimala P, 1414,* c. 236

33. 1414. Doc. 3. Payments to Giuliano di Arrigo Pesello and partners for work on tabernacle of *Saint John* at Or San Michele.

ASF, Strozz. LI, 1, f. 5 from: *Libro Grande Calimala P, 1414*, c. 236

34. 1414. Doc. 4. Payments to Frate Bernardo di Stefano for mosaic he is to execute for niche at Or San Michele.

ASF, Strozz. LI, 1, f. 5 from: *Libro Grande Calimala P, 1414*, c. 236

35. 1414. Doc. 5. Material for mosaic of niche at Or San Michele bought from *Operai* of the cathedral of Pisa.

ASF, Strozz. LI, 1, f. 5 from: *Libro Grande Calimala P, 1414*, c. 236

36. 1414, Dec. 1. Doc. 163. Ghiberti begins casting the *Saint John* for Or San Michele. (Baldinucci, bibl. 35, I, p. 354, from a lost *Giornale di Lorenzo di Cione di Ser Buonaccorso orafo . . . cominciando a dì primo di Maggio 1403, segnato A*)

37. 1414. Doc. 3. Reference to painting (*sic*) done for the niche of *Saint John* at Or San Michele.

ASF, Strozz. LI, 1, f. 5 from: *Libro Grande Calimala P, 1414*, c. 417, 423

38. 1414-1415. Doc. 80. Numerous entries referring to the statue or niche of *Saint John* at Or San Michele.

ASF, Strozz. LI, 3, c. 153 (index) from: *Libro Grande Calimala P, 1414; Q+, 1415, passim*

39. 1404-1415. Doc. 29. Account for 5564 pounds of bronze purchased for the work on Ghiberti's first door of the Baptistery.

ASF, Strozz. LI, 1, f. 79v from: *Libro seconda e terza porta* (Frey, bibl. 532, pp. 354ff, doc. 7, with erroneous date June 5, 1407)

40. no date, 1404-1415 (?). Doc. 66. Reference to Ghiberti's workmen on the door of the Baptistery.

ASF, Strozz. LI, 1, f. 185v from: *Delib. Off. Musaico*, c. 114-123

41. after 1407, presumably before 1415. Doc. 31. Wage accounts for Ghiberti's assistants on his first door after 1407 and presumably before 1415, among them Giuliano di Ser Andrea, Bartolo di Michele, Donatello, Ciuffagni and Uccello.

ASF, Strozz. LI, 1, f. 80 from: *Libro seconda e terza porta* (Frey, bibl. 532, pp. 354ff, doc. 7, with erroneous date June 5, 1407)

42. 1415. Doc. 55. Albizzo di Piero is paid for work on the tabernacle for *Saint John* at Or San Michele.

ASF, Strozz. LI, 1, f. 101 from: *Uscità S. Giovanni, 1415*, c. 12

43. 1416, May. The stone work of the Baptismal Font in Siena, including steps, niches, etc., is commissioned from three stone masons, among them Giacomo di Corso detto Papi di Firenze.

ODS, (Libro doc. art., 37) (Milanesi, bibl. 336, II, pp. 74ff, doc. 48; Lusini, bibl. 283, pp. 93ff, doc. 1; Bacci, bibl. 31, pp. 92ff)

44. 1416, June 28-July 17. Docs. 131, 134. Expense account for visit to Siena, made by Ghiberti, Giuliano (di Ser Andrea[?]) and Bartolomeo (di Michele[?]) for consultation regarding the "building of the Baptismal Font."

ODS, Memoriale di Domenico Mariano, 1416, c. 5v and *ibid., Entr. Usc. di Domenico di Mariano 1416*, c. 52v

45. 1416, Dec. 18. Doc. 135. Giovanni Turini is sent by the *Opera del Duomo* in Siena to Florence to see Ghiberti regarding the Baptismal Font.

ODS, Libro di Spese di Doccio di Jacopo fattore, 1416, c. 10

46. 1416. Doc. 6. Frate Bernardo di Stefano works on the mosaic for the niche of *Saint John* at Or San Michele.

ASF, Strozz. LI, 1, f. 5v from: *Libro Grande Calimala Q, 1416, n.c.*

47. 1416. Doc. 47. Giuliano di Arrigo Pesello works on the mosaic frieze in the niche of *Saint John* at Or San Michele.

ASF, Strozz. LI, 1, f. 5v from: *Libro Grande Calimala Q, 1416, n.c.*

48. 1416. Doc. 53. Work on the niche of *Saint John* at Or San Michele under way; Bernardo di Stefano is paid for mosaic work. *Saint John* is set up (see, however, Dig. 56).

ASF, Strozz. LI, 1, f. 91 from: *Uscità Calimala, 1416*, c. 7; *LI, 2*, c. 115v (Frey, bibl. 532, pp. 380f, doc. 16, quoted from *LI, 2*, but with erroneous date 1412; also *ibidem*, doc. 25, last part only, with correct date 1416)

49. 1417, Jan. 1. Doc. 136. Expenses paid for a second trip of Ghiberti's to Siena regarding the Baptismal Font.

ODS, Libro di Spese di Doccio di Jacopo fattore, 1416, c. 10v

50. 1417, prior to Mar. 3. Doc. 132. Shipment of a bronze relief of Ghiberti's to Siena and back to Florence as sample for work on the Baptismal Font.

ODS, Memoriale di Domenico di Mariano, 1416-1417, c. 16v

51. 1417, Mar. 11. Doc. 133. Domenico di Mariano discusses the Siena Font in Florence.
ODS, Memoriale di Domenico di Mariano, c. 16v

52. 1417, Apr. 16. Quercia and the Turini firm, father and son, are commissioned to execute, from drawings furnished them, two reliefs each for the Baptismal Font in Siena.
ODS, (Libro doc. art., 39) (Milanesi, bibl. 336, II, pp. 86f, doc. 58; Lusini, bibl. 283, pp. 95f, doc. 2; Bacci, bibl. 31, p. 108)

53. 1417, May 20. Doc. 137. Expenses are paid for Ghiberti "who had come to Siena to take on (*tolare*) the bronze *figures* [sic] of the Font."
ODS, Libro di Spese di Doccio di Jacopo fattore, 1416, c. 15v

54. 1417, May 21. Doc. 130. Contract commissioning Ghiberti to execute for the Baptismal Font in Siena two of the six bronze reliefs "with the figures and in the form" handed to him, to be delivered within ten and twenty months respectively. He has to present the reliefs for inspection before and after gilding (fire gilding). He has to furnish the bronze and the price is to be established upon delivery (see Dig. 42). He is conceded an option to execute six figures for the font after delivering the first relief. He is granted an advance of 100 florins.
ODS, Pergamena, no. 1437

55. 1417, July 9. Doc. 138. Ghiberti receives 200 lire as an advance for work on the Siena Font.
ODS, Memoriale di Antonio di Cristofano, 1417, c. 6v

56. 1417, Nov. 28. Doc. 56. Payment of 5 florins to Ghiberti for gilding the *Saint John* at Or San Michele.
ASF, Strozz. LI, I, f. 101 from: *Uscità S. Giovanni 1417,* c. 20 (Frey, bibl. 532, p. 381, doc. 261 without month and day)

57. 1413-1417. Doc. 129. Cost (Ghiberti's fee?) for the *Saint John* at Or San Michele given as 530 florins.
Florence, Uffizi, Archivio, Misc. vol. 1, no. 4

58. about 1417. Docs. 81-84. Tommaso Ghiberti born.
Tax declarations 1427-1442

59. 1418, July 30 and Aug. 6. Docs. 118, 119. Guariente di Giovanni Guariento is commissioned to execute two silver candlesticks for Or San Michele after Ghiberti's design.
ASF, Or San Michele, vol. 25, Libro delli Atti . . . (dei) Capitani di Or San Michele,

March 3, 1416-May 31, 1419, c. 44v (referred to by Milanesi-Vasari, bibl. 533, II, p. 259 with erroneous date)

60. 1418, Aug. 19. A competition is opened for submitting models for the dome of the Cathedral.
AOF, Delib. LXXV, c. 9v (Guasti, bibl. 198, doc. 11)

61. 1418, Sept. 23. Ghiberti has four workmen assigned to help him in making a model for the dome of the Cathedral.
AOF, Delib. LXXV, c. 20 (Guasti, bibl. 198, doc. 29)

62. 1418, Dec. 13. The models for the dome of the Cathedral are submitted.
AOF, Delib. LXXV, c. 31; also *Stanz. RR,* c. 36 (Guasti, bibl. 198, docs. 14, 15)

63. about 1418. Docs. 81-84. Vittorio Ghiberti is born. Tax declarations of 1427-1442 (the birthdate is given erroneously as 1415 by Schlosser, bibl. 178, II, p. 54)

64. 1419, Feb. 26-1420, Sept. 8. Pope Martin V stays in Florence; Ghiberti designs a miter and morse for him (Ghiberti-Schlosser, bibl. 178, I, p. 47; Bartolomeo del Corazza, bibl. 105, pp. 256ff, 271f)

65. 1419, May 20. Docs. 127, 128. Ghiberti's design of a staircase for the papal apartment in the convent of S. Maria Novella is accepted by the *Opera di S. Maria del Fiore.*
ODF, Delib. LXXVI, c. 29
Other drawings by Giuliano d'Arrigo Pesello (*ASF, Strozz. Repertorio . . . laiche XX, 49*) and Pippo di Giovanni, who builds the staircase beginning Aug. 2, 1419 (*ODF, Delib. LXXVII,* c. 7, 8v, 11, 11v; Poggi, bibl. 409)

66. 1419, June 19. The consuls of the *Arte del Cambio* decide to set up on the pilaster at Or San Michele, assigned to them, a bronze statue of Saint Matthew and elect a committee of four *Operai,* among them Cosimo de' Medici, to implement the decision.
ASF, Arti, Cambio, vol. 18, Libro del Pilastro, c. 4ff (Doren, bibl. 133, pp. 20ff); cf. also *BNF, Magl. II, IV, 378 (=Cl. XXV, 259), p. 436*

67. 1419, June 22. The *Signoria* formally confirms the cession by the bakers' guild of their pilaster at Or San Michele to the *Arte del Cambio.*
ASF, Arti, Cambio, vol. 18, Libro del Pilastro, c. 5v ff (Doren, bibl. 133, pp. 23ff)

68. 1419, July 8-July 28. Ghiberti on August 26 receives several small payments for preparatory work done from July 8 through July 28 for the form of the *Saint Matthew*, including the digging and facing of the foundry ditch, the erection of scaffolding and armature, and the purchasing of clay.

ASF, Arti, Cambio, vol. 18, Libro del Pilastro, c. 11ff (Doren, bibl. 133, pp. 30f)

69. 1419, July 21. The Consuls of the *Arte del Cambio* and the *Operai* decide to commission the *Saint Matthew* and the niche from Ghiberti.

ASF, Arti, Cambio, vol. 18, Libro del Pilastro, c. 7f (Doren, bibl. 133, pp. 25f)

70. 1419, Aug. 11. Ghiberti receives a payment from the *Opera del Duomo* for materials and help employed in preparing models of the dome of the Cathedral, one of them "in small bricks."

AOF, Delib. LXXVII, c. 47v and *Stanz. RR*, c. 54v (Guasti, bibl. 198, doc. 30; similarly [Manetti], bibl. 294, under August 15, 1419)

71. 1419, Aug. 26. Contract of the *Arte del Cambio* with Ghiberti for the *Saint Matthew* at Or San Michele. It is agreed upon that the statue is to be at least as large in size as the *Saint John*, to consist of one or two pieces (body and head) and to weigh not more than 2,000 pounds, to be gilded wholly or in part. The statue is to be completed in three years beginning July 21 by Ghiberti himself, with the assistance of masters good and true. His pay and that of his assistants is left to the good graces of the committee and not to be based on the annual advance received for the *Saint John* or any other work. The guild is to defray expenses for materials and to make advances at their discretion.

ASF, Arti, Cambio, vol. 18, Libro del Pilastro, c. 7v ff, 11f (Doren, bibl. 133, pp. 26ff, 30f)

72. 1419, Oct. 3. Payment of 300 lire to Ghiberti and assistants, among them a carpenter Bartolomeo, for work on models for the dome of the Cathedral.

(Manetti), bibl. 294, p. 44 from: *Libro [di uscità] di Migliore di Tommaso*; the amount of 300 florins is certainly erroneous.

73. 1419, Aug. 26-1420, Dec. 5. Ghiberti on Jan. 29, 1421 (see below, Dig. 83) receives payment for purchases of 362 pounds of wax, clay, copper, and charcoal, made between Aug. 26, 1419, and Dec. 5, 1420, for the *Saint Matthew*.

ASF, Arti, Cambio, vol. 18, Libro del Pilastro, c. 13f (Doren, bibl. 133, pp. 32ff; see also Gaye, bibl. 174, I, p. 108, note **)

73a. 1420, Jan. 4. Ghiberti and Cola di Niccola Spinelli are among the supervisors for the execution of the woodwork in the Strozzi Chapel in S. Trinità.

ASF, Carte Strozzi-Uguccioni (Milanesi, bibl. 357, pp. 75ff; Poggi, bibl. 395, pp. 16f)

74. 1420, Mar. 27-Apr. 3. Final competition (?) opened for the dome of the Cathedral between Ghiberti and Brunelleschi only (?).

AOF, Delib. LXXVIII, c. 29v, 31 (Guasti, bibl. 198, docs. 44, 45)

75. 1420, Mar. 8-Apr. 22. Minor payments to Ghiberti and assistants for the (new?) model for the dome of the Cathedral.

AOF, Stanz. RR, c. 79v (Guasti, bibl. 198, doc. 50)

76. 1420, Apr. 16. Brunelleschi, Ghiberti, and Battista d'Antonio are appointed supervisors for the construction of the dome of the Cathedral at 3 florins each monthly, with Giuliano d'Arrigo Pesello and Giovanni di Gherardo da Prato as substitutes.

AOF, Delib. LXXVIII, c. 34f (Guasti, bibl. 198, doc. 71); cp. also *ASF, Arti, Lana, Partite 148*, c. 61 (Doren, "Zum Bau der Florentiner Domkuppel," *Repertorium fuer Kunstwissenschaft*, XXI [1898], pp. 249ff; XXII [1899], pp. 220f)

77. 1420, April 24. Brunelleschi and Ghiberti are paid 10 florins each for working on a model for the dome and for advice given from Nov. 20, 1419.

AOF, Delib. LXXVIII, c. 66 and *Stanz. RR*, c. 77 (Guasti, bibl. 198, docs. 48, 49)

78. 1420, May 7. The *Arte del Cambio* authorizes the payment to Giovanni di Bicci de' Medici of 296 florins for 3000 pounds of bronze bought in Venice.

ASF, Arti, Cambio, vol. 18, Libro del Pilastro, c. 12 (Doren, bibl. 133, pp. 31f)

78a. 1420, Aug. 7. Ghiberti receives 600 florins (as a loan?) from the banking house of Palla di Nofri Strozzi to pay for the purchase of two farms from the *Capitani* of Or San Michele.

ASF, Carte Strozzi-Uguccioni, vol. 285 (Libro d'Entr. e uscità dal 1420 al 1423), c. 10v and 110v

79. 1420, Oct. 29. Salaries paid to both Ghiberti and Brunelleschi for four months and ten days work as supervisors of dome.

AOF, Stanz. RR, c. 90v, 91v (Guasti, bibl. 198, docs. 72, 73). See below Dig. 120.

80. 1420, Nov. 13. Doc. 139. Ghiberti has thus far received on account for work on the Siena Font 140 florins and 300 lire; the treasurer of the *Opera* in Siena goes to Florence to urge completion of the reliefs.

ODS, Libro deb. cred., 1420-1444, vol. 393, c. 3v

81. no date (*ca.* 1420). Doc. 34. Michelozzo assists Ghiberti for some time on his first door for the Baptistery at 75 florins a year.

ASF, Strozz. LI, 1, f. 80v from *Libro seconda e terza porta* (Frey, bibl. 532, p. 357, doc. 9, with erroneous date June 5, 1407 [?])

82. 1420. Dated inscription on the *Saint Matthew* at Or San Michele.

83. 1421, Jan. 29. Payment to Ghiberti for working expenses including cost of wax and clay (see also Dig. 73), plus an advance of 80 florins for work on the *Saint Matthew*.

ASF, Arti, Cambio, vol. 18, Libro del Pilastro, c. 15v ff (Doren, bibl. 133, pp. 35ff)

84. 1421, May 9. The *Arte del Cambio* authorizes the payment of 40 florins to Ghiberti as reimbursement for advances made in connection with building the casting furnace during the month of May for the *Saint Matthew*.

ASF, Arti, Cambio, vol. 18, Libro del Pilastro, c. 14 (Doren, bibl. 133, p. 34)

85. 1421, May 10-Aug. 23. Ghiberti, on Jan. 29, 1422, is reimbursed for numerous minor expenses paid between May 10 and Aug. 23, 1421, in connection with the armature, form, and casting of the *Saint Matthew*, among them payments to Michelozzo, Jacopo di Piero (Papero?) and "Pagolo" (Uccello?), an assistant of Michelozzo.

ASF, Arti, Cambio, vol. 18, Libro del Pilastro, c. 15v ff (Doren, bibl. 133, pp. 35ff)

86. 1421, July 16. The cast of the *Saint Matthew* has failed in part, and the *Arte del Cambio* decides, upon Ghiberti's suggestion, to have certain parts recast and to compensate Ghiberti for lost time by an advance of 30 florins.

ASF, Arti, Cambio, vol. 18, Libro del Pilastro, c. 14v (Doren, bibl. 133, pp. 34)

87. 1422, Jan. 30. The *Operai* accept the report of Cosimo Medici to the effect that the cast of the *Saint Matthew* is completed, and allot 200 florins for the cleaning, chasing, and setting up of the statue and the decoration of the niche. They propose to the consuls raising an additional 200 florins through a loan levied on the members of the guild, to be repaid in part by diverting income from a charity fund (see Doren, bibl. 133, pp. 39f, note 5).

ASF, Arti, Cambio, vol. 18, Libro del Pilastro, c. 17v ff (Doren, bibl. 133, pp. 38ff)

88. 1422, Feb. 13-Apr. 22. Listing of levies on members of the *Arte del Cambio* to raise 200 florins towards cost of the *Saint Matthew*.

ASF, Arti, Cambio, vol. 18, Libro del Pilastro, c. 19ff, 23f, 25f (see also Digs. 92, 95) (Doren, bibl. 133, pp. 41ff, 43f, 45)

89. 1422, Feb. 28-Apr. 22. Ghiberti is reimbursed for advances totaling 40 florins paid for the *Saint Matthew*.

ASF, Arti, Cambio, vol. 18, Libro del Pilastro, c. 24, 24v, 25, 26 (Doren, bibl. 133, pp. 44ff)

90. 1422, Apr. 22. The stonemasons Jacopo di Corso and Giovanni di Niccolo are paid 35 florins as reimbursement for work on the niche "where the statue of Saint Matthew is to be placed."

ASF, Arti, Cambio, vol. 18, Libro del Pilastro, c. 26 (Doren, bibl. 133, pp. 45f)

91. 1422, May 2. Contract with the stonemasons Jacopo di Corso and Giovanni di Niccolo to execute by August, after Ghiberti's design and specifications, the niche for the *Saint Matthew* at a price of 75 florins plus a block of marble.

ASF, Arti, Cambio, vol. 18, Libro del Pilastro, c. 27v ff (Doren, bibl. 133, pp. 46f)

92. 1422, May 9-13. Additional listings of levies for the *Saint Matthew* (see also Dig. 87)

ASF, Arti, Cambio, vol. 18, Libro del Pilastro, c. 26v f, 29v f, 30v f (Doren, bibl. 133, pp. 46, 48f)

93. 1422, May. The contract with the stonemasons (Dig. 91) is approved by the Consuls of the *Arte del Cambio*.

ASF, Arti, Cambio, vol. 18, Libro del Pilastro, c. 28v (Doren, bibl. 133, pp. 47f)

94. 1422, May 13. Advances of 15 florins to Ghiberti for work on the *Saint Matthew* and reimbursement of 17 florins for 200 pounds of tin purchased in July, 1421.

ASF, Arti, Cambio, vol. 18, Libro del Pilastro, c. 31 (Doren, bibl. 133, p. 49)

95. 1422, July 17. Additional listings of levy on members of the guild for the *Saint Matthew* as in Digs. 87 and 92.

ASF, Arti, Cambio, vol. 18, Libro del Pilastro, c. 31ff (Doren, bibl. 133, pp. 49f)

96. 1422, July 17. Discussion of a payment (though not effected) for the *Saint Matthew*.

ASF, Arti, Cambio, vol. 18, Libro del Pilastro, c. 33 (incomplete) (Doren, bibl. 133, p. 50)

97. 1422, Dec. 17. The consuls of the *Arte del Cambio* establish as Ghiberti's honorarium for the statue of Saint Matthew 650 florins, of which 338 have been advanced to him personally, on condition that he remake the base of the statue and fasten the figure to it.

ASF, Arti, Cambio, vol. 18, Libro del Pilastro, c. 33v f (Doren, bibl. 133, pp. 50f). See also Doc. 129.

98. 1422, Dec. 17-1423, Mar. 8. New levy is decided on and carried through by *Arte del Cambio* to pay debts for the *Saint Matthew*.

ASF, Arti, Cambio, vol. 18, Libro del Pilastro, c. 33v, 34, 34v, 35, 35v, 36ff, 37ff (Doren, bibl. 133, pp. 50f, 53ff)

99. 1423, Mar. 6. Final accounting for the *Saint Matthew*.

ASF, Arti, Cambio, vol. 18, Libro del Pilastro, c. 35 (Doren, bibl. 133, pp. 53f)

100. 1419-1422. Michelozzo, in his tax declaration of 1427, lists a claim of 13 florins against the *Arte del Cambio* for the *Saint Matthew* "when I was a partner" of Ghiberti.

ASF, Catasto, 1427, Quartiere S. Giovanni Gonf. Drago, vol. 54, c. 210 (Gaye, bibl. 173, I, p. 117)

101. 1423, Mar. 30. Doc. 92. The consuls of the *Calimala* decide to have Ghiberti's first door of the Baptistery gilded.

ASF, Arti, Calimala, vol. 17 bis, Petizioni e Deliberazioni 1422-1518, no pagination

102. 1423. Doc. 58. Architrave and jambs for Ghiberti's first door are executed according to his design.

ASF, Strozz. LI, 1, f. 118v from: *Filza seconda, Partiti e Deliberazioni dei Consoli 1425-1438*

103. 1423. Doc. 103. Ghiberti is matriculated with the *Compagnia dei Pittori*.

ASF, Arti, Accademia del Disegno, vol. I, Matricola della Compagnia de'Pittori di S. Luca, c. 11v

104. 1424, Apr. 4. Ghiberti designs two stained glass windows, *Expulsion of Joachim* and *Death of the Virgin*, to be executed for the first bay of the nave of the Cathedral by Fra Bernardino.

AOF, Delib. LXXXV, c. 12v (Poggi, bibl. 413, doc. 549)

105. 1424, Apr. 19. Docs. 32, 35. Ghiberti's first door is finished and set up at the east portal of the Baptistery opposite the Cathedral.

ASF, Strozz. LI, 1, f. 80v, from: *Libro seconda e terza porta* (two entries)

106. 1424, (June ?). Doc. 52. Leonardo Bruni submits to Niccolo da Uzzano a program for the third door of the Baptistery suggesting twenty Old Testament scenes and eight prophets.

ASF, Strozz. LI, 1, f. 82f with copy of Bruni's letter, from: *Libro seconda e terza porta* (Brockhaus, bibl. 69, p. 37; Frey, bibl. 532, pp. 357ff, doc. 3, erroneously dated 1425); for the correct date see letter of Ambrogio Traversari to Niccolo Niccoli, June 21, 1424, bibl. 526, II, cols. 371ff)

107. 1424, possibly May to Oct. Doc. 154. Ghiberti goes to Venice to escape epidemic in Florence (see Dig. 113)

108. 1404-1424 (?). Doc. 30. Expenses for the materials of Ghiberti's first Baptistery door are listed as 831 florins, 11 lire for bronze (evidently incomplete), 57 florins, 1344 lire, 4 denari for coal and wood; 1738 pounds of wax had been used and an additional 69 pounds given to the workmen for personal use.

ASF, Strozz. LI, 1, f. 79v from: *Libro seconda e terza porta* (Frey, bibl. 532, pp. 354ff, doc. 7, with date June 5, 1407)

109. 1404-1424. Doc. 121. Cost of labor, bronze and all other expenses for Ghiberti's first door given as 16,204 florins, 1 lire, 2 soldi.

BMF, Coll. Gori, A, 199 I, f. 33v after: *C. Strozzi, Descrizione dell'* . . . *S. Giovanni*

110. 1425, Jan. 2. Doc. 36. Contract of the *Calimala* with Ghiberti giving him commission for the third door of the Baptistery. He is to receive on account 200 florins a year. Michelozzo is to be paid 100 florins.

ASF, Strozz. LI, 1, f. 81 from: *Libro seconda e terza porta*

111. 1425, Jan. 12-29. Controversy between Ghiberti and Fra Bernardino regarding the design of the two windows for the dome [sic] of the Cathedral.

AOF, Delib. LXXXVII, c. 1v, 3v (Poggi, bibl. 413, docs. 551, 552, with correct reference to windows of nave)

112. 1425, prior to Mar. 10. Doc. 142. The *Operaio* and counselors of Siena cathedral decide to ask for reimbursement of advances made to the Florentine masters who had been commissioned to make the reliefs for the Baptismal Font and who have not kept a single deadline.

ODS, Memoriale di Messer Bartolomeo operaio, 1423-1427, c. 7

113. 1425, Mar. 10. Doc. 154. Ghiberti confirms receipt of a letter from the *Operaio* in Siena. The two reliefs for Siena, delayed by his escape to Venice (see Dig. 107) are in the process of completion. Letter of Ghiberti to the *Operaio* in Siena.

ODS (Libro doc. art., 52)

114. 1425, April 2. Docs. 107, 108. Decision of the *Arte della Lana* to replace the marble *Saint Stephen* in their niche at Or S. Michele by a new bronze figure and tabernacle, and appointment of a supervisory committee.

ASF, Arti, Lana, vol. 49, Delib. Cons. 1408-1427, c. 109v, 110

115. 1425, Apr. 16. Doc. 155. Ghiberti thanks Giovanni Turini for his offer to help in chasing one of the reliefs for the font and maintains that the two reliefs are almost finished; one is in the hands of Giuliano di Ser Andrea, the other in his own. The delay was caused by arguments with his partners from whom he has separated. Letter of Ghiberti to Giovanni Turini.

ODS (Libro doc. art.; at present unnumbered, formerly 54)

116. 1425, April. Specific instructions of the *Arte della Lana* regarding the new *Saint Stephen* for Or S. Michele. (Document lost, but referred to in Doc. 111, Dig. 140.)

117. 1425, Spring or Summer. The *Arte della Lana* commissions the *Saint Stephen* from Ghiberti. (Document lost, but referred to in Doc. 111, Dig. 140.)

118. 1425, June 26. Doc. 156. Ghiberti mentions a prior visit of Giovanni Turini, on behalf of the *Operaio* of the Cathedral of Siena, to expedite the completion of the reliefs for the Baptismal Font; he announces shipment of one relief which is "almost finished" to Siena for inspection and promises to send the other which "will be done in no time." He asks whether the plaques should be gilded in Florence or in Siena. Letter of Ghiberti to the *Operaio*.

ODS (Libro doc. art., 54)

119. 1425, June 28. Doc. 140. Payment is made for shipment of one relief to Siena.

ODS, Libro deb. cred., vol. 393 (1420-1444), c. 3v

120. 1425, June 28. Ghiberti's salary as supervisor of the dome of the Cathedral is suspended, beginning July 1, despite his re-election.

AOF, Delib. LXXXVII, c. 25v (Guasti, bibl. 198, doc. 74). Payments had continued from October 1420 to this date (Guasti, bibl. 198, doc. 73, note).

121. 1425, Aug. 2. Doc. 157. Ghiberti asks the *Operaio* of the Cathedral of Siena to return his relief for completion; the other relief is finished and he promises to send it for inspection. Letter of Ghiberti to the *Operaio*.

ODS (Libro doc. art., 55, formerly 56)

122. 1425, Oct. 12. Payment to Ghiberti for five bronze winches for the construction of the main apse of the Cathedral.

AOF, Stanz. SS, c. 108 (Guasti, bibl. 198, doc. 141)

123. 1426, Jan. 24. Ghiberti, Brunelleschi, and Battista d'Antonio submit a joint report on the procedure proposed for building the dome.

AOF, Delib. 1425-1436, c. 170v, 171 (Guasti, bibl. 198, doc. 75; see also Baldinucci-Moreni, bibl. 36, pp. 220ff)

124. 1426, Feb. 4. The Committee of the *Opera* and the Consuls of the *Arte della Lana* accept the preceding report; Brunelleschi's salary for full-time work on the dome is fixed at 100 florins annually, Ghiberti's for part-time work remains at 3 florins monthly.

AOF, Delib. 1425-1436, c. 170v, 171 (Guasti, bibl. 198, doc. 75; Baldinucci-Moreni, bibl. 36, pp. 220ff)

125. 1426, Mar. 11-12. Decision to have Brunelleschi and Battista d'Antonio continue work on the dome; Ghiberti is not mentioned.

AOF, Delib. 1425-1436, c. 23; also AOF, Stanz. Termini e Malleverie, c. 32v (Guasti, bibl. 198, doc. 76)

126. 1426, Dec. 20. Doc. 104. Ghiberti is matriculated in the *Arte di Pietra e Legname*.

ASF, Arti, Maestri di Pietra e Legname, vol. II, Matricole dell'Arte, 1388-1518, c. 32v

127. 1426, after Apr. 26, immediately before Dec. 29. Doc. 10. The lintel of the East portal of the Baptistery is to be made of three pieces of marble.

ASF, Strozz. LI, 1, c. 38v (accompanied by drawing) from: Filza di più sorte scritture dell' Arte de Mercatanti 1414-1433 (Frey, bibl. 532, p. 357, doc. 1, with erroneous date of April 22, 1423)

128. 1425-1427. Tomb of Leonardo Dati in S. Maria Novella (d. March 16, 1425; Ghiberti-Schlosser, bibl. 178, II, p. 55, with erroneous date 1423), completed before July 9, 1427, when a final payment of 10 florins is still due.

Libro segreto di Gregorio Dati, ed. C. Gargiolli, Bologna, 1869 (*Scelta di Curiosità letterarie, 102*) p. 106. See also Ghiberti's tax declaration, Dig. 138.

129. 1427, Jan. 28. Brunelleschi and Ghiberti are re-elected supervisors for the dome for the year beginning March 1, 1427, Brunelleschi at 100 florins annually, full-time, Ghiberti at 3 florins monthly, part-time.

AOF, Delib. 1425-1436, c. 171v (Guasti, bibl. 198, doc. 77)

130. 1427, Feb. 27-Mar. 7. Docs. 144, 145. The *Camerlingo* of the Sienese *Opera* is reimbursed for a trip made to Florence, from February 27 to March 3, to see Ghiberti about the Siena reliefs. Ghiberti has the plaques boxed and sent to Siena. They arrive March 3 and are returned March 7. Their weight is given as 600 odd *libre*. Small accounts in connection with this transaction.

ODS, Entr. Usc. di Antonio di Jacomo, 1426-1427, c. 84v, 85

131. 1427, after Mar. 17. Doc. 158. Ghiberti acknowledges the receipt on March 17 of both reliefs which have been returned from Siena for completion. Letter of Ghiberti to the *Operaio del Duomo*.

ODS (Libro doc. art., at present unnumbered, formerly 53) (Milanesi, bibl. 536, II, p. 122, doc. 85, v, dated March 1425-1426 [?]; Lusini, bibl. 283, pp. 101f, doc. 9, dated March, 1426)

132. 1427, Apr. 7-11. The *Camerlingo* of the *Opera* of Siena calls on Donatello; as evident from Dig. 133, he also sees Ghiberti. He urges the two artists to complete the stories for the Baptismal Font.

ODS, Entr. Usc. di Antonio di Jacomo, 1426-1427, c. 84v (Bacci, bibl. 31, p. 16)

133. 1427, Apr. 11-20. Doc. 159. One of the Siena reliefs is finished. Ghiberti promises to have the other finished by Easter. The sum of 80 florins is wanted for gilding. Letter of Ghiberti to the *Operaio* with reference to his visit (see preceding digest).

ODS (Libro doc. art., 64, formerly 56). Milanesi (bibl. 336, II, p. 123, doc. 85, VI) dates the letter 1426; Lusini (bibl. 283, p. 101, doc. 8) 1425

134. 1427, Apr. 17. Doc. 143. Ghiberti re-

ceives 200 lire on account for the gilding of the Siena reliefs.

ODS, Entr. Usc. di Antonio di Jacomo, 1426-1427, c. 83v

135. 1427, May 12. Doc. 160. The Siena reliefs are completed; Ghiberti starts gilding one and asks for gold for the other. Letter of Ghiberti to the *Operaio*.

ODS (Libro doc. art., at present unnumbered, formerly 57)

136. 1427, May 14-15. Docs. 109, 110. A new committee is appointed by the *Arte della Lana* to supervise work on the *Saint Stephen* for Or San Michele.

ASF, Arti, Lana, vol. 49, Delib. Cons. 1408-1427, c. 127v, 128v

137. 1427, May 31. Doc. 161. Ghiberti renews his request for material to gild the second Siena relief. The gilding will take one day. He asks the *Operaio* to reimburse his banker for an advance of 200 florins which he has drawn against the rest of his fee. Letter of Ghiberti to the *Operaio*.

ODS (Libro doc. art., 58)

138. 1427, July 9. Docs. 81, 81a. Ghiberti's tax declaration (*denuncia de' beni*). In addition to a house in Florence for his own use and a piece of land at S. Donato di Fronzano and an account of 714 florins in the Monte, Ghiberti declares the following credits: for two bronze reliefs for the Baptismal Font in Siena a final payment of 110 florins on an estimated total of 400 florins; for the bronze shrine for Cosimo de' Medici (Cassa dei SS. Proto, Giacinto, e Nemesio) a final payment of 65 florins on an estimated total of 200 florins (these two works are still in the workshop); for the tomb of Leonardo Dati a final payment of 10 florins from the Frati di S. Maria Novella. Among his creditors appear Papero di Meo da Settignano, Simone di Nanni da Fiesole, and Cipriano di Bartolo da Pistoia, "my helpers (*garzoni*)" in the workshop, with a total of 48 florins.

ASF, Catasto, 1427, Quart. S. Giov., Gonf. Chiavi, portata, vol. 58, c. 199, 199v; *campione, vol. 80*, c. 423v

139. 1427, July 14. Doc. 146. The *Camarlingo* of the Cathedral of Siena pays a notary for a copy of the original contract with Ghiberti.

ODS, Entr. Usc. di Berto d'Antonio, 1427-1428, c. 63

140. 1427, Aug. 5. Doc. 111. The model (form?) of the *Saint Stephen* for Or S. Michele is completed; the treasurer of the guild is empowered, with reference to earlier decisions, to purchase 4000 pounds of bronze.

ASF, Arti, Lana, vol. 49, Delib. Cons. 1408-1427, c. 130v

141. 1427, Sept. 26. Doc. 147. Ghiberti is credited with 25 florins for materials to gild the Siena reliefs.

ODS, Entr. Usc. di Berto d'Antonio, 1427-1428, c. 63

142. 1427, October. Doc. 162. Ghiberti has gilded the second relief for Siena. Both are ready for shipment if the *Operaio* will reimburse Ghiberti for the amount drawn against the rest of his claims. He refers to his original demand of 240 florins per relief and the *Operaio's* promise of 220. Ghiberti also reminds the present *Operaio* that the commission of four statues had been promised him. Letter of Ghiberti to the *Operaio*.

ODS (Libro doc. art., at present unnumbered, formerly 59) (Milanesi, bibl. 336, II, pp. 124f, doc. 85, IX, with date 1427 [?])

143. 1427, Oct. 25-Nov. 1. Docs. 141, 148, 149, 150. The *Camarlingo* of the Cathedral of Siena is sent to Florence since Ghiberti is withholding the reliefs for the Baptismal Font. A settlement is reached regarding the fee for the two reliefs, fixing it at 1,680 lire or 210 florins per relief. Adjustments are paid and Ghiberti hands over the reliefs.

ODS, Libro deb. cred., c. 240; Entr. Usc. di Berto d'Antonio, 1427-1428, c. 64, 64v

144. 1427, Nov. 15. Docs. 151, 153. Small payments are made for carrying Ghiberti's two reliefs from Florence to Siena and from the customhouse in Siena to the *Opera*.

ODS, Entr. Usc. di Berto d'Antonio, 1427-1428, c. 64v

145. 1427. The tomb of Lodovico degli Obizi (d. 1424) in S. Croce, designed by Ghiberti (Ghiberti-Schlosser, bibl. 178, I, p. 47) and executed by Filippo di Cristofano, has not yet been paid for in full. Money is still due the latter.

ASF, Catasto, 1427, Quart. S. Maria Novella, Gonf. Lione Rosso, portata, vol. 43, c. 722; see also campione, vol. 76, c. 292 (Brockhaus, bibl. 68, col. 222)

146. After 1427. Bartolomeo Valori's tomb (d. 1427) in S. Croce is executed by the stonemason Filippo di Cristofano after Ghiberti's design.

ibid. (Ghiberti-Schlosser, bibl. 178, I, p. 47; Brockhaus, bibl. 68, col. 222, quoting Filippo's tax declaration)

147. 1428, May 21. Brunelleschi and Ghiberti are re-elected at previous salaries as supervisors for the dome of the Cathedral.

AOF, Delib. 1425-1436, c. 173 (Guasti, bibl. 198, doc. 78)

148. 1428, June 30. Doc. 112. The *Saint Stephen* is in the process of completion. The supervisory committee of the *Arte della Lana* is continued in office and empowered to make payments not exceeding 1,000 florins.

ASF, Arti, Lana, vol. 50, Delib. Cons. 1427-1432, c. 23 (summary in Passerini, bibl. 391, p. 48, with erroneous date 1418)

149. 1428, July 15. The consuls of the *Arte della Lana* refer to a preliminary discussion held by a committee with a group of experts, among them, as outstanding, Brunelleschi and Ghiberti, and to an ensuing discussion to choose a chapel for S. Zenobius and to place in it a shrine of marble or bronze with the figure of the Saint.

ODF, Delib. 1425-1436, c. 173v, 174 (Poggi, bibl. 413, doc. 898)

150. 1428, Sept. 1. Doc. 93. The *Opera* of S. Giovanni attempts to raise funds to cover its great expenses but is refused by the City Council.

ASF, Arti, Calimala, 17 bis, Petizioni e Deliberazioni, 1422-1518, no pagination

151. 1428. The Shrine of Saints Protus, Hyacinth, and Nemesius, donated by Cosimo and Lorenzo de' Medici, is set up at S. Maria degli Angeli. The inscription on the base carrying the shrine is lost, but reported by Vasari (Vasari-Milanesi, bibl. 533, II, p. 234; see also Dig. 138).

152. 1428 (?). Ghiberti mounts a cornelian with the Flaying of Marsyas (Ghiberti-Schlosser, bibl. 178, I, p. 47; Anonimo Magliabecchiano, bibl. 22, pp. 275f).

153. 1429, Jan. 7. Brunelleschi and Battista d'Antonio are empowered to build the masonry chain of the dome of the Cathedral after the design of Brunelleschi, Ghiberti, and Battista d'Antonio.

AOF, Delib. 1425-1436, c. 98v (Guasti, bibl. 198, doc. 193)

154. 1429, Feb. 1. Doc. 113. The *Saint Stephen* is completed, and the supervising committee is empowered to sell the remaining bronze.

ASF, Arti, Lana, vol. 50, Delib. Cons. 1427-1432, c. 42f

155. 1429, July 21. Brunelleschi and Ghiberti are re-elected for one year at the usual salaries as supervisors of the Cathedral.

AOF, Delib. 1425-1436, c. 175 (Guasti, bibl. 198, doc. 79)

156. 1429, Sept. 22. Brunelleschi and Ghiberti are ordered to commission a model of the entire Cathedral, including apses and façade.

AOF, Delib. 1425-1436, c. 112v (Guasti, bibl. 198, doc. 61)

157. 1429. Docs. 87, 88. The *Arte di Calimala* in its tax declaration, mentions two points of interest concerning Ghiberti's work for the Baptistery: a loan of 1,800 florins plus interest was contracted "when the frame (*telaio*) of the door of S. Giovanni was cast, for bronze and other expenses"; running expenses "for the third door which has been begun . . . and the cost of which cannot be estimated; the master alone is paid 200 florins per year."

ASF, Catasto, 1429, Beni di Compagnie e Arti, portata, vol. 291, c. 5, 6, 6v, 24, 24v, and *campione vol. 293,* c. 4, 5, 5v, 10v

158. 1429. Doc. 8. The two (porphyry) columns at the Baptistery are moved further to either side of the east gate.

ASF, Strozz. LI, 1, f. 6v from: *Libro Grande I, 1429,* c. 176

159. 1430, Jan. 2, Mar. 15. Two letters of Aurispa to Traversari refer to Ghiberti's wish to borrow an Athenaios ms. from the former (Sabbadini, bibl. 457, pp. 67, 69).

160. 1430, Dec. 14. Only Brunelleschi is re-elected as supervisor of the dome.

AOF, Delib. 1425-1436, c. 176v (Guasti, bibl. 198, doc. 80)

161. 1430. Trip to Venice (?)

(G. Fiocco, bibl. 160, based, according to a friendly note of Mr. Fiocco's, on communication made to him orally by the late O. Paoletti).

162. 1431, Jan. 26. Doc. 82. Ghiberti's tax declaration (*denuncia de' beni*). Aside from the real estate owned in 1427 and an account in the Monte of as much as 1,300 florins, he enumerates a credit of 280 florins with the *Arte di Calimala* "which I have advanced them." In the *campione* he also mentions a debt to the *Opera di S. Croce* for a tomb he has bought.

ASF, Catasto 1431, Quart. S. Giov., Gonf.

Chiavi, portata, vol. 386, c. 192, 192v; revised copy, *vol. 388,* c. 170, 170v (with greater detail); *campione, vol. 409,* c. 191v, 192

163. 1431, June 23. Brunelleschi and Ghiberti are re-elected on customary conditions as supervisors of the dome.

AOF, Delib. 1425-1436, c. 177 (Guasti, bibl. 198, doc. 83)

164. 1432, Feb. 22. The *Operai* of the Cathedral of Florence open a competition for designing a sepulcher for the relics of Saint Zenobius.

AOF, Delib. 1425-1436, c. 155 (Poggi, bibl. 413, doc. 903)

165. 1432, Mar. 3. The *Operai* of the Cathedral discuss a report regarding the sepulcher to be designed for the chapel of Saint Zenobius in the Cathedral, submitted by a committee of "outstanding citizens . . . masters of painting and sculpture . . . and theologians." On this basis they decide to commission the shrine to the sculptor (!) Ghiberti and the altar to Brunelleschi and to arrange for the purchase from the *Arte della Lana* of bronze left over from casting the figure of Saint Stephen at Or San Michele.

AOF, Delib. 1425-1436, c. 155 (Poggi, bibl. 413, doc. 905)

166. 1432, Mar. 4-23. Contract of the *Operai* of the Cathedral with Ghiberti concerning the Shrine of Saint Zenobius, giving details, salary, and working conditions: it is to be of bronze, 3 *braccia* long and 1½ high, with stories from the life of the Saint, and of a maximum weight of 5,000 pounds. The *Operai* furnish the materials and pay the wages for the workshop; Ghiberti himself is to receive 15 florins monthly, regardless of the time spent. Delivery is exacted by April 1435, and in case of failure the *Operai* may reassign the commission within six weeks.

AOF, Allogazioni 1438-1475, insert (Poggi, bibl. 413, doc. 906)

167. 1432, Mar. 18. Brunelleschi and Ghiberti are paid for models of the sepulcher of Saint Zenobius.

AOF, Stanz. CC, c. 28v (Poggi, bibl. 413, doc. 907)

168. 1432, Mar. 23. Guarantors, named by Ghiberti for the Zenobius Shrine, are accepted by the *Operai*.

AOF, Delib. 1425-1436, c. 156v (Poggi, bibl. 413, doc. 908)

169. 1432, Mar. 23. 1,661½ pounds of bronze for the Shrine of Saint Zenobius are bought from the *Arte della Lana* for 100 florins.

AOF, Stanz. CC, c. 29v, 46v, and *Delib. 1425-1436*, c. 156 (Poggi, bibl. 413, docs. 908, 911)

170. 1432, Apr. 9. Two assistants (*discepoli*) are hired for Ghiberti, to work on the Shrine of Saint Zenobius on a day-to-day basis at approximately 75 florins a year.

AOF, Delib. 1425-1436, c. 164 (Poggi, bibl. 413, doc. 910)

171. 1432, June 27-Aug. 12. Brunelleschi, Ghiberti, and Battista d'Antonio are to make a wooden model for the key ring of the dome of the Cathedral.

AOF, Delib. 1425-1436, c. 163, 167; also *Ricordi Proveditore 1432-1433*, c. 4 (Guasti, bibl. 198, docs. 247, 248)

172. 1432, Aug. 20. Refund of 40 florins authorized on an advance of 80 florins made by former provisor for sepulcher of Saint Zenobius.

AOF, Delib. 1425-1436, c. 168 (Poggi, bibl. 413, doc. 912)

173. 1432, Aug. 22. Brunelleschi and Ghiberti are re-elected as supervisors for building the dome.

AOF, Delib. 1425-1436, c. 178 (Guasti, bibl. 198, doc. 84, with correction of note on p. 188)

174. 1432, prior to Oct. 29. Docs. 105, 106. Ghiberti designs the model for an altar of the *Arte dei Linaiuoli*. Payments are made on Oct. 29, 1432, and on Aug. 11, 1433, to the woodcarvers Jacopo (Papero) di Piero and the stonemasons Jacopo di Bartolo da Settignano and Simone di Nanni da Fiesole for the execution of the wooden and marble frames after Ghiberti's design.

ASF, Arti, Rigattieri, Linauoli e Sarti, vol. 20, campione dei debitori e creditori 1418-1511, c. 98

175. 1432, Oct. 30. Brunelleschi (alone) makes a new model for the key ring of the lantern.

AOF, Delib. 1425-1436, c. 189v; also *Ricordi Proveditore, 1432-1433*, c. 13 (Guasti, bibl. 198, doc. 250)

176. 1432, Dec. 9. Further refunds authorized for advance made to Ghiberti and Brunelleschi for the sepulcher of Saint Zenobius.

AOF, Delib. 1425-1436, c. 192 (Poggi, bibl. 413, doc. 913)

177. 1433, Jan. 30. Regular payment to Ghiberti as supervisor of the dome of the Cathedral.

AOF, Ricordi Proveditore, 1432-1433, no page (Guasti, bibl. 198, doc. 84, note and p. 188)

178. 1433, May 27. Ghiberti is named as arbitrator in Donatello's contract for the Prato pulpit.

(Baldanzi, bibl. 34, pp. 78, 274ff)

179. 1433, May 29. Doc. 83. Ghiberti's tax declaration (*denuncia de'beni*). The real estate has increased through the lease for life of a farm at Careggi from the *Calimala*, against payment of 370 florins. His account in the Monte has correspondingly decreased but he enumerates a credit of 100 florins advanced to the *Arte di Calimala*. Among his creditors appear Giuliano di Ser Andrea (last time mentioned), Filippo di Nicholo da Fiesole, *iscarpellatore*, Simone di Nanni da Fiesole "who works with me," and Papero di Meo da Settignano.

ASF, Catasto 1433, Quart. S. Giov., Gonf. Chiavi, portata, vol. 481, c. 149, 149v; second copy *vol. 479*, c. 143, 143v (Mather, bibl. 308, pp. 57f with misreadings)

180. 1433, July 10. Payment of 25 florins to Ghiberti for work on the Shrine of Saint Zenobius.

AOF, Stanz. CC, c. 58v (Poggi, bibl. 413, doc. 916)

181. 1433, Dec. 30-1434, Apr. 14. Discussion whether Ghiberti's cartoon of a *Coronation of the Virgin* for a stained-glass oculus for the dome of the Cathedral should be commissioned for execution.

Of two designs, submitted by Ghiberti and Donatello respectively, for this oculus, that of Donatello is chosen for execution.

AOF, Delib. 1425-1436, c. 208v, 214v (Poggi, bibl. 413, docs. 717, 719)

182. 1434, Apr. 10. Two windows in the chapel of Saint Zenobius are to be designed by Ghiberti and executed by Bernardo di Francesco.

AOF, Delib. 1425-1436, c. 215 (Poggi, bibl. 413, doc. 605)

183. 1434, June 9. Ghiberti is paid 100 florins for work on the Shrine of Saint Zenobius.

AOF, Stanz. CC, c. 75v (Poggi, bibl. 413, doc. 917)

184. 1434, Oct. 22. For casting two reliefs for the Shrine of Saint Zenobius 500 pounds of bronze are bought, to be given to Ghiberti.

AOF, Stanz. CC, c. 81v (Poggi, bibl. 413, doc. 918)

185. 1434, Dec. 31. Ghiberti is paid 12 lire for a design for the choir screen of the Cathedral.

AOF, Stanz. CC, c. 85v (Poggi, bibl. 413, doc. 1173)

186. 1435, Jan. 24. The *Opera* of the Cathedral closes Ghiberti's (and Luca della Robbia's) accounts.

Delib. 1425-1436, c. 226 (Poggi, bibl. 413, doc. 1260)

187. 1435, Mar. 19. Ghiberti receives 15 florins for his rejected design for the oculus of the dome (see Dig. 181).

AOF, Stanz. CC, c. 91v (Poggi, bibl. 413, doc. 723)

188. 1435, May 6. A new committee is elected for supervising the Shrine of Saint Zenobius.

AOF, Delib. 1425-1436, c. 233 (Poggi, bibl. 413, doc. 919); see also Dig. 186

189. 1435, Sept. 30. The *Operai* of the Cathedral direct the *Offiziali* of the Sacristy to have a bronze shrine made for the body of Saint Zenobius.

AOF, Delib. 1425-1436, c. 241v (Poggi, bibl. 413, doc. 920); see Dig. 188

190. 1435, Nov. 15. Both Brunelleschi and Ghiberti are commissioned to design the arrangement of new altars in the chapels of the three apses of the Cathedral.

AOF, Delib. 1425-1436, c. 243 (Poggi, bibl. 413, doc. 1065)

191. 1435, Nov. 26. The *Operai* discuss the project for the new choir of the Cathedral as submitted by Ghiberti, Brunelleschi, and Agnolo d'Arezzo. The commission goes to Brunelleschi.

AOF, Delib. 1425-1436, c. 244, 244v (Poggi, bibl. 413, doc. 1176)

192. 1436, June 30. Last payment to Ghiberti for supervising work on the dome of the Cathedral.

AOF, Stanz. CC, c. 130v (Guasti, bibl. 198, correction of note to doc. 84, p. 188)

193. 1436, Aug. 14. Ghiberti has a model made for a lantern for the dome designed in competition with Brunelleschi and others.

AOF, Delib. 1436-1442, c. 2v (Guasti, bibl. 198, doc. 269)

194. 1436, Aug. 14. Ghiberti is pressed to furnish the design for a stained-glass window with a scene from the Life of the Virgin for the eastern apse of the Cathedral, to be executed by Bernardo di Francesco.

AOF, Delib. 1436-1442, c. 2v (Poggi, bibl. 413, doc. 614)

195. 1436, Oct. 32 (*sic*). Final payment is made to Ghiberti for designs of four windows for the chapel and apse of Saint Zenobius.

AOF, Stanz. CC, c. 137v (Poggi, bibl. 413, doc. 615)

196. 1436, Dec. 31. Ghiberti's model for the lantern of the dome and those of four others are rejected in favor of Brunelleschi's.

AOF, Delib. 1436-1442, c. 10v (Guasti, bibl. 198, doc. 273)

197. 1437, Feb. 14. The *Operai* of the Cathedral pay 196 florins for bronze purchased for the Shrine of Saint Zenobius.

AOF, Stanz. DD, c. 4 (Poggi, bibl. 413, doc. 922)

198. 1437[?], Apr. 4. Doc. 23. Ten stories for Ghiberti's second bronze door for the Baptistery and 24 pieces of frieze have been cast and the nettoyage is to be started by Ghiberti, one of his sons, and Michelozzo.

ASF, Strozz. LI, 1, f. 62 from: *Ricordi Proveditore, K, 1435-1440*, c. 87 with presumably erroneous date 1436

199. 1437, April 9-18. The consuls of the *Arte della Lana* and the *Operai* of the Cathedral declare Ghiberti in default for not having finished the Shrine of Saint Zenobius by April 1435. His contract is canceled and a new supervisory committee is appointed (see Dig. 188).

Ghiberti's account regarding the Shrine of Saint Zenobius is ordered closed (see Dig. 186).

AOF, Delib. 1436-1442, c. 15v, 17 (Poggi, bibl. 413, docs. 924, 925)

200. 1437. Doc. 37. Ghiberti may employ for work on his second door of the Baptistery his son Vittorio, Michelozzo, and three others, at 100 florins a year.

ASF, Strozz. LI, 1, f. 81 from: *Libro seconda e terza porta*

201. 1438, May 24. Ghiberti is paid for a drawing of four figures for a stained-glass window for the apse of Saint Zenobius.

AOF, Stanz. DD, c. 34 (Poggi, bibl. 413, doc. 622)

202. 1439, Mar. 8. A committee, among them Leonardo Bruni, reports to the *Arte della Lana* on the projected arrangement of the sepulcher, altar, and Shrine of Saint Zenobius, and suggests, among other things, that the bronze shrine designed by Ghiberti should be placed below the altar with the main story facing the rear and an inscription facing to the front.

AOF, Delib. 1436-1442, c. 60v, 61 (Poggi, bibl. 413, doc. 927)

203. 1439, Mar. 18. The Shrine of Saint Zenobius is returned to Ghiberti for completion.

AOF, Delib. 1436-1442, c. 64v (Poggi, bibl. 413, doc. 928)

204. 1439, Mar. 26. Ghiberti is commissioned to complete the Shrine of Saint Zenobius by January 1440.

AOF, Delib. 1436-1442, c. 66 (Poggi, bibl. 413, doc. 929)

He receives an advance of 50 florins.

AOF, Stanz. DD, c. 51v (Poggi, bibl. 413, doc. 929)

205. 1439, Apr. 3. The *Operai* confirm the recommissioning of the Shrine of Saint Zenobius.

AOF, Delib. 1436-1442, c. 69 (Poggi, bibl. 413, doc. 930)

206. 1439, Apr. 18. Ghiberti receives a new contract from the *Operai* of the Cathedral for the Shrine of Saint Zenobius. It is to have three reliefs, including the Resurrection miracle in front (*sic*), the two other miracles already begun, and in the rear an inscription by Leonardi Bruni. The deadline for the completion is set for January 1440.

AOF, Allog., c. 5 (Poggi, bibl. 413, doc. 931)

207. 1439, Apr. 18. Ghiberti has received on account for his labor on the Shrine of Saint Zenobius over 700 florins; the main story of the shrine for which he has received the bronze, must be delivered within three months.

AOF, Stanz. EE, c. 73 (Poggi, bibl. 413, doc. 931)

208. 1439, July 4. Doc. 24. A new agreement is made with Ghiberti regarding further work on his second door for the Baptistery. He is to be paid 180 florins for work done by him, his son and other helpers during the period between January 1438 and June 1439. The state of work is as follows:

Cain and Abel	"really finished"
Moses	little missing
Jacob and Esau	finished
Joseph	half finished
Solomon	thus far completed: the architectural settings, a part at the bottom and the figures to the right, about one quarter.

For two of the compartments (*spiagie*) only the foliage is ready.

ASF, Strozz. LI, 1, f. 63v from: *Ricordi Proveditore K, 1435-1440,* c. 103 (Brockhaus, bibl. 69, pp. 39f with erroneous date)

209. 1439, July 18. Docs. 59, 25. Tinaccio di Piero and Piero di Francesco are commissioned to prepare the armature for the casting of the frame of Ghiberti's second door.

ASF, Strozz. LI, 1, f. 123 from: *Filza 4a di Petizioni e altre scritture Calimala, 1434-1461,* c. 255

Similar entry: the armature of Ghiberti's second door is commissioned.

ASF, Strozz. LI, 1, f. 64 from: *Ricordi Proveditore K, 1435-1440,* c. 103

210. 1439, July 31. Ghiberti receives 40 florins as a partial payment for work on the Shrine of Saint Zenobius.

AOF, Stanz. DD, c. 66v (Poggi, bibl. 413, doc. 940)

211. 1439, Nov. 23. Ghiberti receives 25 florins for work on the Shrine of Saint Zenobius.

AOF, Stanz. DD, c. 69 (Poggi, bibl. 413, doc. 943)

212. 1439, Dec. 18. Ghiberti receives 50 florins for work on the Shrine of Saint Zenobius.

AOF, Stanz. DD, c. 69v (Poggi, bibl. 413, doc. 944)

213. 1440, Feb. 22. Ghiberti receives 100 florins for work on the Shrine of Saint Zenobius.

AOF, Stanz. DD, c. 75 (Poggi, bibl. 413, doc. 947)

214. 1440, Mar. 8. Bruni's inscription for the Shrine of Saint Zenobius is accepted and the *Operai* decide to have it placed in a garland on the back of the shrine.

AOF, Delib. 1436-1442, c. 101v (Poggi, bibl. 413, doc. 948)

215. 1440, Nov. 8. Ghiberti receives a small payment for a drawing for a stained-glass window.

AOF, Stanz. DD, c. 87v (Poggi, bibl. 413, doc. 647)

216. 1440, Dec. 5. Ghiberti receives 50 florins for work on the Shrine of Saint Zenobius.

AOF, Stanz. DD, c. 90 (Poggi, bibl. 413, doc. 953)

217. 1440, after Dec. 7; before Jan. 4, 1441. Doc. 70. The doors of S. Giovanni (probably the armature of the frame) are in the process of being made.

ASF, Strozz. LI, 1, f. 200 from: *Delib. Cons.*

Calimala, 1439-1440, c. 47 (Brockhaus, bibl. 69, p. 40; Frey, bibl. 532, p. 360, doc. 10, with the erroneous date of Dec. 7, 1439)

218. 1440, Dec. 29. Ghiberti is paid for drawings for four stained-glass windows.
AOF, Stanz. DD, c. 91v, 92 (Poggi, bibl. 413, doc. 648)

219. 1440. Doc. 38. Deliberations to buy 17,000 pounds of fine bronze in Flanders for Ghiberti's second Baptistery door.
ASF, Strozz. LI, 1, f. 81 from: *Libro seconda e terza porta*

220. 1441, Jan. 27. Ghiberti receives 100 florins for work on the Shrine of Saint Zenobius.
AOF, Stanz. DD, c. 95 (Poggi, bibl. 413, doc. 956)

221. 1441, Sept. 26. Ghiberti receives a small payment for a drawing for a window in Saint Peter's chapel in the Cathedral.
AOF, Stanz. EE, c. 2v (Poggi, bibl. 413, doc. 655)

222. undated, perhaps late in 1441. Ghiberti works a miter for Pope Eugene IV during his second sojourn in Florence, Jan. 22, 1439-Mar. 7, 1443. (Ghiberti-Schlosser, bibl. 178, I, p. 228; Muentz, bibl. 350, p. 62, quotes a document of Dec. 7, 1441, according to which pearls were paid for in Florence for a miter for the Pope).

223. 1442, Jan. 5. Ghiberti receives small payments for drawings for stained-glass windows in and above the chapel of Saint Matthew in the Cathedral.
AOF, Bast. ser Niccolo di ser Diedi, III, c. 1v ff (Poggi, bibl. 413, doc. 658)

224. 1442, Jan. 5. Ghiberti purchases an estate at Settimo.
Ghiberti, Libro di Ricordanze A, Florence, Coll. Ginori-Conti. (Ginori-Conti, bibl. 181)

225. 1442, Jan. 20. Ghiberti, as a member of a commission of experts, gives his opinion on the display of stained-glass windows for the drum of the dome of the Cathedral and on decorating the sacristy.
AOF, Bast. ser Niccolo di ser Diedi, III, c. 3f (Guasti, bibl. 198, doc. 202)

226. 1442, Jan. 22. It is decided (by the *Operai*) to have the Shrine of Saint Zenobius varnished.
AOF, Bast. ser Niccolo di ser Diedi, III, c. 3v (Poggi, bibl. 413, doc. 957)

227. 1442, Feb. 10. Ghiberti receives a small payment for the drawing of a window for the chapel of Saint Thomas in the Cathedral.

AOF, Bast. ser Niccolo di ser Diedi, III, c. 7 (Poggi, bibl. 413, doc. 660)

228. 1442, Feb. 28. Ghiberti receives a small payment for the drawing of a window for the chapel of Saint Bartholomew in the Cathedral.
AOF, Bast. ser Niccolo di ser Diedi, III, c. 9 (Poggi, bibl. 413, doc. 663)

229. 1442, Mar. 5. Ghiberti receives small payments for drawings of windows for the chapels of Saint Andrew and Saint Stephen in the Cathedral.
AOF, Bast. ser Niccolo di ser Diedi, III, c. 10v (Poggi, bibl. 413, doc. 664)

230. 1442, May 12. Ghiberti receives small payments for the drawings for two windows for the chapels of Saint John the Evangelist and Saint Anthony Abbot in the Cathedral.
AOF, Bast. ser Niccolo di ser Diedi, III, c. 19v (Poggi, bibl. 413, doc. 667; Paatz, bibl. 375, III, p. 521, note 314)

231. 1442, June 14. Ghiberti receives a small payment for the drawing of a window for the chapel of Saint John the Evangelist in the Cathedral.
AOF, Bast. ser Niccolo di ser Diedi, III, c. 26v (Poggi, bibl. 413, doc. 671)

232. 1442, July 6. Ghiberti receives a small payment for the drawing of a window for the chapel of Saints James and Philip in the Cathedral.
AOF, Bast. ser Niccolo di ser Diedi, III, c. 31 (Poggi, bibl. 413, doc. 674)

233. 1442, July 31. Ghiberti receives a small payment for drawing for the chapel of Saint Barnabas in the Cathedral.
AOF, Bast. ser Niccolo di ser Diedi, III, c. 34 (Poggi, bibl. 413, doc. 677)

234. 1442, Aug. 14. Ghiberti receives a payment of 100 florins for work on the Shrine of Saint Zenobius.
AOF, Bast. ser Niccolo di ser Diedi, III, c. 34v (Poggi, bibl. 413, doc. 961)

235. 1442, Aug. 28. Michelozzo is employed in chasing Ghiberti's second door for the Baptistery.
ASF, Catasto, 1442, Quart. S. Giov., Gonf. Drago, portata, vol. 625, c. 79f (Fabriczy, bibl. 145)

236. 1442, Aug. 30. Ghiberti receives a payment of 27 florins and a final payment of 200 florins for work on the Shrine of Saint Zenobius.
AOF, Bast. ser Niccolo di ser Diedi, III, c. 40v (Poggi, bibl. 413, doc. 962)

The total cost amounted to 1,324 florins (Doc. 126), or 1,314 florins (Doc. 129).

BNF, Banco rari 228, formerly Magl. Cl. XVII, 2, c. 27 (Zibaldone di Buonaccorso Ghiberti); Florence, Uffizi, Arch. Misc. vol. I, no. 4

237. 1442, Aug. 20. Doc. 84. Tax declaration (*denuncia de'beni*) by Ghiberti, "*Maestro delle Porte di S. Giovanni.*" He has sold his account in the Monte and owns only real estate; in addition to the older holdings (Digs. 138, 179) and the estate at Settimo, he has added to his land in S. Donato di Fronzano, acquired three lots at Montepiano, these latter only for a short time, and in 1438 a small house adjoining his residence in Florence.

ASF, Catasto, 1442, Quart. S. Giov., Gonf. Chiavi, portata, vol. 627, c. 214, 214v (Mather, bibl. 308, p. 48, with erroneous date 1432 and an erroneous volume number)

238. 1442, Nov. 24. Ghiberti receives a small payment for a drawing for a window in an unnamed chapel in the Cathedral.

AOF, Bast. ser Niccolo di ser Diedi, III, c. 56v (Poggi, bibl. 413, doc. 685)

239. 1442, Dec. 10. Ghiberti receives a small final payment for the drawing of a window in the chapel of Saint James Major in the Cathedral.

AOF, Bast. ser Niccolo di ser Diedi, III, c. 64 (Poggi, bibl. 413, doc. 686)

240. After 1440, before June 24, 1443; possibly 1442. Doc. 39. A monthly salary of 14 lire is granted to Matteo di Francesco d'Andrea da Settignano who works on Ghiberti's door at the Baptistery.

ASF, Strozz. LI, 1, f. 81 from: Libro seconda e terza porta; BMF, coll. Gori, A 199 1, c. 156v (whence date of 1442) (Frey, bibl. 532, p. 360, doc. 11, last part with erroneous date of 1440)

241. 1443, June 24. Doc. 40. New agreement regarding Ghiberti's second door for the Baptistery. Of the ten stories, four remain to be completed. Ghiberti is to receive for his work —wages, and charcoal and wood—1,200 florins at the discretion of the *Offiziali del Musaico* with the obligation of finishing the remaining reliefs within 18 months, assisted by his sons Vittorio and Tommaso and perhaps others.

ASF, Strozz. LI, 1, f. 81 from: Libro seconda e terza porta

242. 1443, July 13. Ghiberti receives 35 lire as a partial payment for the drawing of an *Ascension* for one of the oculi of the drum of the Cathedral's dome.

AOF, Stanz. G, c. 16 (Poggi, bibl. 413, doc. 751; see also doc. 758). An earlier date has been suggested (Paatz, bibl. 375, III, p. 514, note 289).

243. 1443, Sept. 11. Ghiberti receives 65 lire as a final payment for two drawings, one for this window and one for another oculus showing *Christ in the Garden*.

AOF, Stanz. G, c. 21v (Poggi, bibl. 413, doc. 752; see also doc. 749) (Paatz, bibl. 375, III, p. 513, note 288, suggests the possibility of an earlier date.)

244. 1443, Dec. 7. Ghiberti receives 50 lire for the drawing of an oculus with the *Presentation in the Temple* for the drum of the dome.

AOF, Stanz. G, c. 27v (Poggi, bibl. 413, doc. 756; see also doc. 772); (Paatz, bibl. 375, III, p. 513, note 287)

245. 1443, December. Ghiberti is elected to the Office of the Twelve (see Dig. 249)

246. 1444, Jan. 24. Docs. 94, 71. Agreement between Vittorio Ghiberti, in the name of his father Lorenzo "Master of the doors of S. Giovanni" and Benozzo Gozzoli who is to work exclusively on the doors at an annual salary rising from 60 to 80 florins.

ASF, Arti, Calimala, vol. 19, Delib. Cons. 1444, c. 8f; ASF, Strozz. LI, 1, f. 203 (Milanesi, bibl. 337, p. 90; see also Frey, bibl. 532, p. 360, doc. 14, with the date of Jan. 3)

247. 1444, Mar. 17. Doc. 120. Ghiberti is denounced as being of illegitimate birth and hence unable to hold office as one of the Twelve (see Dig. 245)

ASF, Consigli Maggiori, Provisioni, Registri, vol. 134, c. 286ff (Gaye, bibl. 173, I, 148ff with erroneous indication Filza 136 and numerous omissions; Gualandi, bibl. 196, pp. 17ff); also BLF, Cod. $\frac{252}{296}$ Cartella 2a (Aruch, bibl. 25, pp. 117ff)

248. 1444, Apr. 16. The *Consiglio Maggiore* recognizes Ghiberti's legitimate birth; he is fined 500 lire for tax irregularities.
BLF, Cod. $\frac{252}{296}$ Cartella 2a (Aruch, bibl. 25, loc.cit.).

249. 1444, Apr. 29. Doc. 120. Ghiberti's appeal to the *Signoria* against the imposition of the fine is granted and his right to hold office is recognized.

ASF, Consigli Maggiori, Provizioni, Registri,

vol. 134, c. 286ff (Gaye, bibl. 73, I, pp. 148ff; Gualandi, bibl. 196, pp. 17ff)

250. 1444, Apr. 30. Doc. 115a. Ghiberti's matriculation in the *Arte della Seta* is cancelled because of registering falsely as the son of a guild member.

ASF, Arti, Seta, vol. 7, Matricola 1328-1433, c. 115v

Also Tommaso Ghiberti's matriculation in the *Arte della Seta* is cancelled at that time. Tommaso had been matriculated in 1435. Docs. 117, 117a.

ASF, Arti, Seta, vol. 8, Matricola 1433-1474, c. 214

251. 1444, May 19. Ghiberti, Brunelleschi, and others are called on to advise on alterations of the fence of the Capella della Cintola in the Cathedral of Prato.

(Baldanzi, bibl. 34, pp. 258ff)

252. 1445, after Jan. 7 and shortly before June 1. Doc. 18. The *Operai di S. Giovanni* decide to sell 2,000 florins from the Monte to pay for bronze, expected from Bruges, evidently for Ghiberti's second door.

ASF, Strozz. LI, 1, f. 48 from: *Ricordi Proveditore M, 1444 (1445)-1449,* c. 136 (Brockhaus, bibl. 69, p. 40; Frey, bibl. 532, p. 360, doc. 15, with date of Jan. 3)

253. 1445, May 12. Ghiberti's workshop where the doors are being cast is mentioned as situated near S. Maria Nuova.

ASF, Archivio Notarile S 914, c. 61v f (unpublished, referred to by Baldinucci, bibl. 35, I, p. 371)

254. 1445, after June 1 and shortly before Oct. 7. Doc. 19. 14,623 pounds of bronze are shipped from Bruges and the price of 1,135 florins is deposited in Florence.

ASF, Strozz. LI, 1, f. 48v from: *Ricordi Proveditore M 1444 (1445)-1449,* c. 138 (Frey, bibl. 532, p. 360, doc. 16 with date of Jan. 3)

255. After June 24, 1443; before Aug. 7, 1447 (possibly 1445, see Dig. 254). Doc. 41. Francesco di Papi is commissioned to make the frame of Ghiberti's second door.

ASF, Strozz. LI, 1, f. 81 from: *Libro seconda e terza porta* (Frey, bibl. 532, p. 360, doc. 13, with erroneous date of June 26, 1443)

256. 1446, before May. Ghiberti had accepted together with Bonaiuto di Giovanni the commission for a fresco on the façade of the Bigallo, but it was executed by others.

ASF, Bigallo, vol. DCCLVI, Deb. e cred., 1442-1446, c. 7, 10 (Poggi, bibl. 412, p. 189ff)

257. 1446, June 14. Doc. 116. Ghiberti is re-matriculated in the *Arte della Seta*.

ASF, Arti, Seta, vol. 8, Matricola, 1433-1474, c. 133

258. 1447 (after Feb. 28; before March 25). Doc. 85. Ghiberti's tax declaration (*denuncia de'beni*). In addition to his former land holdings, Ghiberti has acquired on Dec 3, 1444, more land at Settimo, on Aug. 15, 1444, a terrain with house in S. Cervazzo di Pelago, and a house with a druggist's shop in Florence as security for the dowry of his daughter-in-law. Vittorio and he have sold an amount of 530 fiorini in the Monte.

ASF, Catasto, 1446, Quart. S. Giov., Gonf. Chiavi, portata, vol. 682, c. 825f

259. 1447, Aug. 7. Docs. 20, 42. The *Arte di Calimala* declares that Ghiberti has finished the ten reliefs of his second door and is to receive the final payment of the agreed amount of 1,200 florins.

ASF, Strozz. LI, 1, f. 49v from: *Ricordi Proveditore M 1444 (1445)-1449,* c. 148 and *LI, 1,* f. 81 from: *Libro seconda e terza porta*

260. 1447, after Aug. 7; before April 22, 1448 (probably 1447). Doc. 21. Tommaso Ghiberti makes two bronze candlesticks, silver plated, for the Baptistery.

ASF, Strozz. LI, 1, f. 49v from: *Ricordi Proveditore M 1444 (1445)-1449,* c. 151 and *ASF, Strozz. LI, 2,* f. 114 from same source with date 1447 (Frey, bibl. 532, p. 370, doc. 43 with date of Aug. 7, 1447)

261. 1447, after Aug. 7; probably before Jan. 24, 1448. Doc. 79. The friezes of Ghiberti's second door are to be recast.

ASF, Strozz. LI, 2, f. 114 from: *Ricordi Proveditore M 1444 (1445)-1448,* c. 151 (Frey, bibl. 532, p. 361, doc. 18, first part, with date of Aug. 7, 1447)

262. 1448, before Jan. 24. Doc. 43. Ghiberti is to receive 125 florins for making the cross-bars for his second door.

ASF, Strozz. LI, 1, c. 81 from: *Libro seconda e terza porta* (Frey, bibl. 532, p. 361, doc. 19, with date of Jan. 28)

263. 1448, Jan. 24. Docs. 22, 44. A new agreement is arrived at with Lorenzo and Vittorio Ghiberti regarding the completion of Ghiberti's second door: 24 compartments (*spiaggie*) which have been cast are to be finished and made ready for gilding, each within three and one half months, by a good assistant under Ghiberti's supervision at a cost of 28 florins each. Twenty-four heads are to be modeled, cast, and finished at a cost of 300 florins; the cornice above the lintel, the threshold, and one of the jambs are to be modeled and cast and one jamb is to be chased at a total cost of 320 florins; 12 compartments (*spiaggie*) each 2⅛ *braccia* long, for the jambs and the architrave are to be modeled and cast with foliage and animals "more beautiful than those on his first door" at a cost of 360 florins. The frieze on the inside of the jambs and the architrave, to be 25½ *braccia* long, is to be chiseled at a cost of 140 florins.

Ghiberti receives 100 florins for having cast the "last (skeleton) frame" of the door.

ASF, Strozz. LI, 1, f. 81, 81v from: *Libro seconda e terza porta* (Frey, bibl. 532, p. 361, doc. 20 under date Jan. 28. Frey assumed erroneously that the agreement of 1448 became active only in 1451, see Dig. 275)

See also in abbreviated form *ASF, Strozz. LI, 1,* f. 49v from: *Ricordi Provveditore M 1444 (1445)-1449,* c. 152, supplemented from *ASF, Strozz. LI, 2, 114* (Frey, bibl. 532, p. 361, doc. 18, with date of Aug. 7, 1447)

264. 1448, Apr. 6. Doc. 95. Payment of up to 30 florins to an unnamed assistant for work on Ghiberti's second door.

ASF, Arti, Calimala, vol. 20, Delib. Cons. 1447 (1448)-1451, c. 12

265. 1448, Apr. 22. Doc. 96. Ghiberti receives 15 florins on behalf of Bernardo di Bartolomeo (Cennini) for work on the door.

ASF, Arti, Calimala, vol. 20, Delib. Cons. 1447 (1448)-1451, c. 14v

266. 1448, May 18. Doc. 97. Ghiberti receives 15 florins for his own work on the bronze door.

ASF, Arti, Calimala, vol. 20, Delib. Cons. 1447 (1448)-1451, c. 16v

267. 1448, July 12. Doc. 98. The stonemason Matteo di Francesco (d'Andrea) da Settignano receives 80 lire as final payment for work on the frame of the Baptistery door.

ASF, Arti, Calimala, vol. 20, Delib. Cons. 1447 (1448)-1451, c. 27v

268. 1448, July 24. Doc. 99. The stonemasons, Simone di Giovanni da Fiesole and Domenico d'Antonio (Salviati) receive final payments of 30 lire each for work on the frame of Ghiberti's second door.

ASF, Arti, Calimala, vol. 20, Delib. Cons. 1447 (1448)-1451, c. 27v

269. 1448, Nov. 15. Doc. 100. The consuls of the *Calimala* discuss the financial difficulties of the *Opera di S. Giovanni*: either work has to be temporarily suspended on Ghiberti's sec-

ond door or the singers have to be discharged. A special committee is elected to seek means to continue work on the door.

ASF, Arti, Calimala, vol. 20, Delib. Cons. 1447 (1448)-1451, c. 37v, 38, 38v

270. 1449, Apr. 28. Doc. 101. Ghiberti receives 25 florins for work on the door.

ASF, Arti, Calimala, vol. 20, Delib. Cons. 1447 (1448)-1451, c. 63v

271. 1449, Apr. 29. Doc. 102. Payment to stonemasons for one month's work on the frame of Ghiberti's second door.

ASF, Arti, Calimala, vol. 20, Delib. Cons. 1447 (1448)-1451, c. 64v (Brockhaus, bibl. 69, p. 42, with erroneous date and page)

272. 1449, Sept. 22. Doc. 89. Ghiberti receives 1000 pounds of wax for work on his second door.

ASF, Arti, Calimala, vol. 17 bis, Petizioni e Deliberazioni, 1422-1518, c. LXXIIIv

273. 1449, Sept. 22. Docs. 90, 91. The stonemasons Matteo di Francesco da Settignano, Simone di Giovanni da Fiesole, and Domenico di Antonio Salviati are rehired by the *Offiziali del Musaico* for the remaining work of chiseling the frame of Ghiberti's second door. Simone receives as payment for work done on the frame 50 lire, and 60 florins (?) credit for future work.

ASF, Arti, Calimala, vol. 17 bis, Petizioni e Deliberazioni 1422-1518, c. LXXIIIv; see also *ASF, Strozz. LI, 1,* f. 206 from: *Delib. Cons. Calimala 1447 (1448)-1451,* c. 73 (Frey, bibl. 532, p. 362, doc. 27, with the date of Sept. 12)

274. 1450, July 30, Sept. 18, Oct. 30, Nov. 27. Payments totaling 14 florins to the firm of Ghiberti and Son for their work on the tabernacle door at S. Egidio.

Arch. S. Maria Nuova, Florence, Quadernuccio di cassa, 1449-1452, c. 30, 36 (Poggi, bibl. 411, pp. 105ff)

275. 1451, Jan. 5 or 16. Docs. 44, last part, and 11. Renewal of the agreement of Jan. 24, 1448 (Dig. 263) with the added obligation that Lorenzo Ghiberti and Vittorio finish within 20 months, starting Feb. 1, 1451, the remainder of the work on the door of the Baptistery, assisted by seven helpers.

ASF, Strozz. LI, 1, f. 81v from: *Libro seconda e terza porta* (Docs. 44 and 11) and *ASF, Strozz. LI, 1,* f. 43 (partly illegible) completed after *BMF, Coll. Gori, A 199 I,* f. 153 from: *Ricordi Provveditore O, 1450-1453,* c. 132

276. 1451, Aug. 14. Doc. 86. Ghiberti's last tax declaration (*denuncia de'beni*). No changes as against 1446.

ASF, Catasto 1451, Quart. S. Giov., Gonf. Chiavi, portata, vol. 718, c. *297; campione vol. 719,* c. *515f*

277. 1451, Aug. 12. The goldsmith Bernardo di Bartolomeo Cennini works as assistant on the doors of the Baptistery.

ASF, Catasto, 1451, Quart. S. Giov., Gonf. Lion D'Oro, portata, vol. 711, c. *94* (?)

The entry on c. 94, quoted by F. Fantozzi, *Memorie biografiche . . . di Bernardo Cennini*, Florence, 1839, p. 8, has been removed from the volume.

278. 1452, Mar. 19. Doc. 45. The door weights for Ghiberti's second door are commissioned to the locksmith Tinaccio di Piero.

ASF, Strozz. LI, 1, f. *81v from: Libro seconda e terza porta.* The exact date in: *BMF, Coll. Gori, A 199 I,* f. *139*

279. 1452, Apr. 2. Doc. 46. Ghiberti's second door is finished and Lorenzo and Vittorio are commissioned to have it gilded against an advance of 100 florins, on condition that it be finished by June 20.

ASF, Strozz. LI, 1, f. *81v from: Libro seconda e terza porta.* The exact date in: *BMF, Coll. Gori, A 199 I,* f. *139*

280. 1452, June 16. Doc. 47. Ghiberti's second door is declared completely gilded and 884 florins, 99 lire, 8 soldi, 3 denari are paid for gold.

ASF, Strozz. LI, 1, f. *81v, 82 from: Libro seconda e terza porta*

281. 1452, after Apr. 18, before Aug. 22 (probably June 16). Doc. 12. The *Arte di Calimala* acknowledges that Ghiberti has gilded his second door well.

ASF, Strozz. LI, 1, f. *44v from: Ricordi Proveditore O, 1450-1453,* c. *147*

282. 1452, after Apr. 18, before Aug. 22 (probably after June 16). Doc. 13. Lorenzo and Vittorio Ghiberti are declared to have entirely finished the third door of S. Giovanni.

ASF, Strozz. LI, 1, f. *44v from: Ricordi Proveditore O, 1450-1453,* c. *149* (Frey, bibl. 532, p. 363, doc. 31, with date of April 13); see also *ASF, LI, 2,* f. *113* with summary of this and previous entry.

283. 1452, July 13. Docs. 73, 48. The consuls of the *Calimala* decide to have Ghiberti's second door set up on the east portal facing the Cathedral, "because of its beauty," and to remove his first door to the north portal.

ASF, Strozz. LI, 1, f. *209 from: Delib. Cons. Calimala, 1451-1454,* c. *17;* see also *ASF, Strozz. LI, 1,* f. *82 from: Libro seconda e terza porta* (Frey, bibl. 532, p. 363, doc. 33, with date of June 16, 1452)

284. 1452, after July 13. Doc. 124. Ghiberti's door is polished and set up by the goldsmith Piero di Donato.

BMF, Coll. Gori, A 199 I, f. *142,* from unnamed source, c. *14*

285. 1452, Dec. 12-18. Docs. 74, 14. The consuls of the *Calimala* decide to have jambs, threshold, cornice, and architrave made for the frame of Andrea Pisano's door to correspond to the two other doors of the Baptistery.

ASF, Strozz. LI, 1, f. *209v from: Delib. Cons. Calimala, 1451-1454,* c. *33* (Frey, bibl. 532, p. 363f, doc. 39, erroneously under Ghiberti's second door.) Also *LI, 1,* f. *45 from: Ricordi Proveditore O, 1450-1453,* c. *154*

286. 1425-1452. Doc. 122. Description of Ghiberti's second door; total cost fl.14,594, l. 3, s. 4; list of assistants, among them three not appearing in other documents, Francesco di Nanni Buoni, Cristofano di Francesco, and Giovanni di Giuliano.

BMF, Coll. Gori, A 199 I, f. *33v from: C. Strozzi, Descrizione dell' . . . S. Giovanni*

287. 1452-1453, after Dec. 12-18; before Feb. 12. Docs. 15, 49. Ghiberti is to be given the house and workshop where the doors had been made, in lieu of his final payment to the amount of 218.3.4 florins.

ASF, Strozz. LI, 1, f. *45 from: Ricordi Proveditore O, 1450-1453,* c. *155* (Frey, bibl. 532, p. 363, doc. 36, with erroneous date of Aug. 22, 1452); see also *Strozz. LI, 1,* f. *82 from: Libro seconda e terza porta* where the final credit is given as fl. 270 (Frey, bibl. 532, p. 363, doc. 34, with erroneous date of June 16, 1452)

288. 1453, Feb. 12. Docs. 16, 50. Ghiberti and Vittorio receive the commission for the jambs, architrave, threshold and step for Andrea Pisano's door.

ASF, Strozz. LI, 1, f. *45 from: Ricordi Proveditore O, 1450-1453,* c. *155;* repeated with wrong date Feb. 12, 1454, *LI, 1,* f. *82 from: Libro seconda e terza porta* (Frey, bibl. 532, p. 364, doc. 40, with erroneous date of June 16, 1452)

289. 1453, Apr. 9-26. Doc. 75. Ghiberti and his son Vittorio are presented with the house where the doors had been cast in lieu of the final payment due of 250 (!) florins.

ASF, Strozz. LI, 1, f. 210 from: *Delib. Cons. Calimala, 1451-1454,* c. 53

290. 1453, after May 9. Doc. 17. A marble frieze is placed around the east gate of the Baptistery.

ASF, Strozz. LI, 1, f. 45 from: *Ricordi Proveditore O, 1450-1453,* c. 158

291. 1453, May 14-26. Doc. 76. The bronze step is transferred from the east gate to the north gate of the Baptistery.

ASF, Strozz. LI, 1, f. 210 from: *Delib. Cons. Calimala, 1452-1454,* c. 58

292. 1454, after Apr. 23; before Apr. 29, 1456. Doc. 67. The consuls of the *Calimala,* the *Officiali del Musaico* and the *Proveditore delle Porte* block all funds for work on S. Giovanni except for ordinary salaries.

ASF, Strozz. LI, 1, f. 191 from: *Libro di Provisioni 1420-1470,* c. 28

293. 1455, Nov. 26 (?). Ghiberti makes his will with the notary Ser Santi di Domenico Naldi.

(Document lost, after Baldinucci, bibl. 35, p. 351, note 1)

294. 1455, Dec. 1. Ghiberti's death and burial at S. Croce.

(Document lost, after Vasari-Milanesi, bibl. 533, II, p. 249)

295. no date, after 1455. Doc. 57. Vittorio Ghiberti receives permission from the *Calimala* to exchange the estate near Careggi leased to his father.

ASF, Strozz. LI, 1, f. 115v from: *Filza dell'Arte de Mercatanti di Partiti e Deliberazioni de Consoli dall 1425 al 1438 [sic]*

296. 1456, Apr. 3 and following months. Doc. 77. Vittorio Ghiberti receives various payments for the jambs, threshold, and step of Andrea Pisano's door.

ASF, Strozz. LI, 1, f. 213v from: *Delib. Cons. Calimala, 1455-1459,* c. 16, 17, 19, 32, 42

297. 1457, Feb. 11. Doc. 51. Partial payments, totaling 150 florins, to Vittorio for work on the frame of Andrea's door.

ASF, Strozz. LI, 1, f. 82 from: *Libro seconda e terza porta*

298. 1458, after Nov. 21, through Apr. 1459. Doc. 78. The consuls of the *Calimala* decide to purchase bronze for the jambs of Andrea's door.

ASF, Strozz. LI, 1, c. 217v from: *Delib. Cons. Calimala, 1455-1459,* c. 192, 215, 221, 228 (Frey, bibl. 532, p. 364, doc. 43, with date of Nov. 21, 1458)

299. 1462, after July 5, before Mar. 13, 1464. Doc. 68. The frame of Andrea Pisano's door is acknowledged to have been finished; payment is to be determined with Vittorio for the jambs, architrave, threshold, and so on.

ASF, Strozz. LI, 1, f. 192v from: *Libro Provisioni, 1420-1470,* c. 48 (Frey, bibl. 532, p. 364, doc. 45, with misreadings, date of July 5, 1462, and reference to the *Porta del Paradiso*)

300. 1462 (?)=1463 (?). Doc. 9. Vittorio Ghiberti is to receive a total of 2,591 florins, 15 soldi for the jambs, threshold and other work on the third [sic] door of the Baptistery.

ASF, Strozz. LI, 1, f. 10v from: *Libro Grande Calimala F, 1461,* c. 219, 241; correct volume G and year 1462 in: *BMF, Coll. Gori, A 199 I,* f. 153. (Frey, bibl. 532, p. 364, doc. 44, with date of 1461. The entry must follow that of Dig. 299)

301. 1464, before Mar. 13. Doc. 69. The *Proveditori delle Porte* have completed their task and it is decided to dissolve this special committee.

ASF, Strozz. LI, 1, f. 192v from: *Libro Provisioni, 1420-1470,* c. 48 (Frey, bibl. 532, p. 364, doc. 46, with date of July 5, 1462)

302. 1452-1464. Doc. 123. The cost of the frame of Andrea Pisano's doors amounted to 3,351 florins.

BMF, Coll. Gori, A 199 I, f. 34f from: *Carlo Strozzi. Descrizione dell . . . S. Giovanni*

119a. 1425, after June 13.

Lorenzo has been paid by the Opera in Siena lire eight hundred seventy nine, soldi ten, denari four.

ODS Libro Giallo, fol. 76ᵛ. (Transcript of this and other payments for the Siena reliefs, received from Mr. John T. Paoletti. Only this is added since the other documents refer to data already known from other documents or referring to only minor payments.)

179a. 1433, July 6.

Lorenzo is required by the Arte della Lana to provide before August the bronze figure of St. Stephen at Or San Michele with gilded embroidery ("cum brustis aureis").

ASF, Arti Lana, Partiti, Atti, etc., *vol. 168* (May 2-August 31), c. 37 (Krautheimer-Hess, bibl. *31, p. 318, App. B.)

255a. 1445, Sept. 4-Dec. 15.

Payments to Lorenzo Ghiberti, transmitted through various members of the workshop for the casting of parts of the second door, including repairs of furnaces and payments for bronze from Flanders. Tommaso di Lorenzo is frequently mentioned.

Archivio dello Spedale degli Innocenti, Estranei, n. 242, Quaderno di cassa . . . d'Andrea Cambini e compagni, c. 231ᵛ, 236ᵛ, 257ᵛ (Mendes Atanasio, bibl. *2, pp. 97ff., Docs. I, II, III.)

255b. 1445, Dec. 15.

Tommaso Ghiberti and his partner, Matteo di Giovanni, receive final installment on a total payment of fl. 169 for their work on the silver tabernacle of the *dossale* for S. Giovanni.

Archivio dello Spedale degli Innocenti, Estranei, n. 242, Quaderno di cassa . . . d'Andrea Cambini e compagni, c. 257ᵛ (Mendes Atanasio, bibl. *2, p. 102, Docs. III, 7.)

292a. 1455, Jan. 17, Feb. 3, and July 9.

Tommaso Ghiberti is still alive and mentioned in a minor real estate transaction.

ASF, Archivio dello Spedale degli Innocenti, Estranei, n. 788. Libro personale di Ricordi di . . . Leonardo Salutati, Vescovo di Fiesole, c. 36 (Mendes Atanasio, bibl. *2, p. 94 and note 6.)

293a. 1455, Nov. 26.

Lorenzo di Ghiberti names his young granddaughters Fioretta, Andreula, and Angelica, daughters of Vittorio, as heirs. Incomplete entry.

ASF, Archivio notarile, Appendice, vol. 75, Registri dei Testamenti, S. Croce, VI, c. 5 (Krautheimer-Hess, bibl. *31, pp. 314, 317, App. A)

303. 1496, Oct. 5 and 29 (1455, November 26).

Lorenzo Ghiberti's will, excerpted in two arbitrations, mentions as part of his estate, alongside with the house and workshop at S. Maria Nuova, its contents, among them bronze, tools for bronzework, blacksmith work, books, writings, marble and bronze sculptures (*intaglio*), drawings and account books; except these latter, all were left to his grandson Buonaccorso.

ASF, Archivio notarile, A 613, c. 52ff, arbitration of Oct. 5, c. 54ᵛ; *ibid., A 614,* cc. 96ff, second arbitration, Oct. 29, c. 98 (Krautheimer-Hess, bibl. *31, pp. 320, 321, App. D)

According to another source, precious stones, cut and uncut, tools for sculpture, painting, goldsmith work, casting and engineering, belonged to the contents of Lorenzo's shop.

Archivio dello Spedale degli Innocenti, series CXLIV, *Estranei, vol. 546, Libro di Ricordanze di Buonaccorso di Vittorio Ghiberti, 1496-1511,* c. 7', 8, 8' (Krautheimer-Hess, bibl. *31, p. 319, App. C)

304. 1496, Oct. 30.

Buonaccorso redeems from the pawnbroker a ring belonging to his grandfather Lorenzo, with a cameo, showing a child standing on a running horse, for lire eight, soldi eighteen, denari eight.

Archivio dello Spedale degli Innocenti, series CXLIV, *Estranei, vol. 546, Libro di Ricordanze di Buonaccorso di Vittorio Ghiberti, 1496-1511,* c. 8ᵛ (Krautheimer-Hess, bibl. *31, p. 319, App. C)

BIBLIOGRAPHY

BIBLIOGRAPHY

1. Accademia della Crusca, *Vocabulario della lingua italiana*, 5th ed., Florence, 1863ff.

2. J. Adhémar, *Influences antiques dans l'art du moyen âge français*, London, 1937.

3. J. B. L. G. Seroux d'Agincourt, *Histoire de l'art par les monumens depuis sa décadence*, Paris, 1823ff.

4. A. M. E. Agnoletti, *Statuto dell'Arte della Lana (R. Deputazione di storia patria per la Toscana, Fonti e studi sulle corporazioni artigiane del medio evo, Fonti I)*, Florence, 1940.

5. L. B. Alberti, *The Architecture of Leon Battista Alberti in Ten Books, Of Painting in Three Books, and Of Statuary in One Book*, transl. J. Leoni, London, 1726.

6. L. B. Alberti, *Della Architettura, della pittura e della statua*, tr. Cosimo Bartoli (1st ed. 1550), Bologna, 1782.

7. L. B. Alberti, *Leonis Baptistae Alberti Opera inedita . . .*, ed. G. Mancini, Florence, 1890.

8. L. B. Alberti, *Leone Battista Alberti's Kleinere Kunsttheoretische Schriften (Della Pittura libri tre; De statua; I cinque ordini Architettonici)*, ed. H. Janitschek (*Quellenschriften für Kunstgeschichte*, ed. R. Eitelberger von Edelberg, XI), Vienna, 1877.

9. L. B. Alberti, *Opere volgari*, ed. A. Bonucci, Florence, 1843ff.

10. L. B. Alberti, *De Pictura*, in: M. Vitruvius Pollio, *De architectura*, Amsterdam, 1649, pp. 165ff.

11. L. B. Alberti, *De Re Aedificatoria*, Florence, 1485.

12. L. B. Alberti, *Zehn Bücher über die Baukunst*, ed. M. Theuer, Vienna, 1912.

13. F. Albertini, *Memoriale di molte statue et picture sono nella inclyta cipta di Florentia*, Florence, 1510; facsimile ed. H. Horne, London, 1909.

14. (R. degli Albizzi), *Commissioni di Rinaldo degli Albizzi. . . . (Documenti di Storia Italiana, I-III)*, Florence, 1867ff.

15. B. Albrecht, *Die erste Tür Lorenzo Ghibertis am Florentiner Baptisterium*, Diss. Heidelberg, 1950 (typescript).

16. U. Aldrovrandi, (*Le statue antiche di Roma*), reprinted in: S. Reinach, *L'album de Pierre Jacques*, Paris, 1902, pp. 23ff.

17. D. C. Allen, *The Legend of Noah (Illinois Studies in Language and Literature, XXXIII, 1949, 3-4)*, Urbana, Illinois.

18. B. Altaner, *Patrologie*, Freiburg/Br., 1938.

19. W. Amelung, *Führer durch die Antiken in Florenz*, Munich, 1897.

20. W. Amelung, *Die Skulpturen des Vatikanischen Museums, s. l.*, 1903ff.

21. (Amsterdam) *Rijksmuseum Amsterdam, Bourgondische Pracht*, Amsterdam (1951).

22. (Anonimo Magliabecchiano), *Il Codice Magliabecchiano, cl. XVII, 17*, ed. K. Frey, Berlin, 1892.

23. G. C. Argan, "The Architecture of Brunelleschi and the Origins of Perspective Theory in the Fifteenth Century," *Journal of the Warburg and Courtauld Institutes*, IX (1946), pp. 96ff.

24. P. Arndt, W. Amelung and others, *Photographische Einzelaufnahmen*, Munich, 1893ff.

25. A. Aruch, "Il ricorso di Lorenzo Ghiberti contra la prima sentenza della Signoria Fiorentina (17 April 1444)," *Rivista d'Arte*, X (1917-18), pp. 117ff.

26. B. Ashmole, *A Catalogue of the Ancient Marbles at Ince Blundell Hall*, Oxford, 1926.

27. A. Avogadrio (Albertus Advogadrius), *De Religione et magnificentia Cosimi Medices Florentini* (ca. 1455) in: G. Lami, *Deliciae eruditorum*, XII, Florence, 1742, pp. 117ff.

28. E. B(abelon), *Le Cabinet des Medailles et Antiques de la Bibliothèque Nationale, Notice historique et guide des visiteurs, I, Les antiques et les objets d'art*, Paris, 1924.

29. E. Babelon and J. A. Blanchet, *Catalogue des Bronzes Antiques de la Bibliothèque Nationale*, Paris, 1895.

30. P. Bacci, *Francesco di Valdambrino*, Siena, 1936.

31. P. Bacci, *Jacopo della Quercia*, Siena, 1929.

32. P. Bacci, *Gli orafi fiorentini e il 2° riordinamento dell'altare di S. Jacopo . . .*, (Pistoia, 1905).

33. C. C. Bailey, "Petrarch, Charles IV and the Renovatio Imperii," *Speculum*, XVII (1942), pp. 323ff.

34. (F. Baldanzi), *Della chiesa cattedrale di Prato*, Prato, 1846.

35. F. Baldinucci, *Notizie dei Professori del Disegno . . .*, Florence, 1845ff (first published 1681).

36. F. Baldinucci, *Vita di Filippo Brunellesco*, ed. D. Moreni, Florence, 1812.

37. A. M. Bandini, *Catalogus Codicum Latinorum Bibliothecae Mediceae-Laurentianae*, II, Florence, 1775.

38. H. Baron, *Leonardo Bruni Aretino (Quel-*

len zur Geistesgeschichte des Mittelalters und der Renaissance, 1), Leipzig, 1928.

39. H. Baron, "A Struggle for Liberty in the Renaissance . . . ," *American Historical Review*, LVIII (1953), pp. 265ff.

40. C. Baroni, *Scultura gotica lombarda*, Milan, 1944.

41. A. Bartoli, *I Monumenti antichi di Roma nei disegni degli Uffizi di Firenze*, Rome, 1914ff.

42. P. S. Bartoli and G. P. Bellori, *Admiranda Romanarum Antiquitatum . . . Vestigia*, Rome, 1693.

43. G. Beani, *L'Altare di Sant' Jacopo Apostolo nella Città di Pistoia*, Pistoia, 1899.

44. G. B. Befani, *Memorie storiche . . . di San Giovanni Battista . . .* , Florence, 1884.

45. B. Berenson, *Italian Pictures of the Renaissance*, Oxford, 1932.

46. B. Berenson, *The Drawings of the Florentine Painters*, Chicago, 1938.

47. E. Berger, *Quellen und Technik der Fresko- Oel- und Temperamalerei des Mittelalters*, Munich, 1912.

48. J. J. Bernoulli, *Griechische Ikonographie*, Munich, 1901.

49. L. Bertalot, "Zwölf Briefe des Ambrogio Traversari," *Römische Quartalschrift*, XXIX (1915), pp. *91ff.

50. E. Bertaux, "La Renaissance en Espagne et en Portugal," in: A. Michel, *Histoire de l'art*, Paris, 1905ff, IV, pp. 817ff.

51. M. Bieber, *Die antiken Skulpturen und Bronzen des . . . Museum Fridericianum in Cassel*, Marburg, 1915.

52. (A. Billi), *Il libro di Antonio Billi*, ed. K. Frey, Berlin, 1892.

53. F. Biondo, *Blondi Flavii Foriulensis De Roma Instaurata libri tres . . . de Italia Illustrata opus . . .* , Venice, 1510.

54. Vespasiano da Bisticci, *Vite di uomini illustri . . .* , ed. A. Mai and A. Bartoli, Florence, 1859.

55. P. H. von Blanckenhagen, "*Flavische Architektur und ihre Dekoration, untersucht am Nervaforum*, Berlin, 1940.

56. F. Bocchi, *Le Bellezze della città di Fiorenza* (first ed. Florence, 1591), ed. M. G. Cinelli, Florence, 1677.

57. W. Bode, *Bertoldo und Lorenzo di Medici*, Freiburg/Br., 1925.

58. W. Bode, "Lorenzo Ghiberti als führender Meister unter den Florentiner Tonbildnern," *Jahrbuch der Preussischen Kunstsammlungen*, XXXV (1914), pp. 71ff.

59. W. Bode, "Ghiberti's Versuche seine Tonbildwerke zu glasieren," *Jahrbuch der Preussischen Kunstsammlungen*, XLII (1921), pp. 51ff.

60. H. Bodmer, "Una scuola di scultura fiorentina nel Trecento," *Dedalo*, X (1929-30), pp. 616ff.

61. E. Boehringer, *Der Caesar von Arcireale*, Stuttgart, 1933.

62. D. Boninsegni, *Storie della Città di Firenze dal . . . 1410 al 1460*, Florence, 1737.

63. J. Borghesi and L. Banchi, *Nuovi documenti per la storia dell'arte senese*, Siena, 1898.

64. G. G. Bottari and St. Ticozzi, *Raccolta di lettere sulla Pittura, Scultura ed Architettura*, Milan, 1822ff.

65. H. Bouchot, *Les réliures d'art à la Bibliothéque Nationale*, Paris, 1888.

66. J. Breck and M. R. Rogers, *The Metropolitan Museum of Art, The Pierpont Morgan Wing*, New York, 1929.

67. O. Brendel, "Symbolik der Kugel," *Archaeologisches Institut des Deutschen Reiches, Roemische Mitteilungen*, LI (1936), pp. 1ff.

68. (H. Brockhaus), Summary of a lecture, *Kunstchronik*, N. F., XVII (1905-06), col. 22. See also *Jahresbericht des Kunsthistorischen Instituts in Florenz*, 1905-06, p. 8.

69. H. Brockhaus, *Forschungen über Florentiner Kunstwerke*, Leipzig, 1902.

70. Ch. de Brosses, *Le président de Brosses en Italie*, Paris, 1858.

71. R. Bruck, *Die Malereien in den Handschriften des Königreichs Sachsen*, Dresden, 1906.

72. G. Brunetti, "Giovanni d'Ambrogio," *Rivista d'arte*, XIV (1932), pp. 1ff.

73. G. Brunetti, "Un opera sconosciuta di Nanni di Banco . . . ," *Rivista d'arte*, XII (1930), pp. 229ff.

74. G. Brunetti, "Ricerche su Nanni di Bartolo 'Il Rosso,' " *Bolletino d'arte*, XXVIII (1934-35), pp. 258ff.

75. G. Brunetti, "Jacopo della Quercia a Firenze," *Belle arti* (1951), pp. 3ff.

76. G. Brunetti, "Jacopo della Quercia and the Porta della Mandorla," *Art Quarterly*, XV (1952), pp. 119ff.

77. Leonardo Bruni, *Commentarii rerum suo tempore gestarum*, in: Muratori, bibl. 345, XIX, 1731, pp. 913ff.

78. Leonardo Bruni, *Epistolarum Libri VIII*, ed. L. Mehus, Florence, 1741.

79. Leonardo Bruni, *La prima guerra punica*, ed. A. Ceruti (*Scelta di curiosità letterarie* 165), Bologna, 1878.

80. H. Bulle, *Der Schoene Mensch im Altertum*, Munich, 1912.

81. M. Schild Bunim, *Space in Mediaeval Painting and the Forerunners of Perspective*, New York, 1940.

82. J. C. Burckhardt, *Der Cicerone . . .* (Basel,

1855), *Neudruck der Urausgabe*, Leipzig, 1930.

83. M. Cagiano de Azevado, *Le Antichità di Villa Medici*, Rome, 1951.

84. A. Callegari, *Il Museo Nazionale Atestino in Este (Itinerari dei musei e monumenti d'Italia*, 59), Rome, 1937.

85. Giovanni Cambi Importuni, *Istorie di Giovanni Cambi*, ed. Ildefonso di San Luigi (*Delizie degli Eruditi Toscani*, XX-XXIII) Florence, 1785ff.

86. E. Carli, "Niccolo di Guardiagrele e il Ghiberti," *L'Arte*, XLII (1939), pp. 144, 222.

87. (E. Carli), *Capolavori d'arte senese*, Florence, 1946.

88. G. Carocci, "Le porte del Battistero di Firenze e l'ornamento imitato della natura," *Arte italiana decorativa e industriale*, V (1896), pp. 69ff.

89. U. Cassuto, *Gli ebrei a Firenze nell' età del rinascimento (Pubblicazioni del R. Istituto di Studi Superiori di Filosofia e Filologia*, 40), 1918.

90. A. Castiglioni, "Il trattato dell'ottica di Lorenzo Ghiberti," *Rivista di Storia Critica delle Scienze Mediche e Naturali*, XII (1921), pp. 51ff.

91. C. J. Cavallucci, *S. Maria del Fiore . . .*, Florence, 1887.

92. Benvenuto Cellini, *I Trattati dell'oreficeria e della scultura*, ed. C. Milanesi, Florence, 1857.

93. Cennino d'Andrea Cennini, *Il libro dell' arte*, ed. D. V. Thompson, New Haven, 1932f.

94. A. Chastel, "La Rencontre de Salomon et de la Reine de Saba dans l'iconographie médiévale," *Gazette des Beaux-Arts*, XXXV (1949), pp. 99ff.

95. A. Chiapelli, "Della vita di Filippo Brunelleschi attribuita a Antonio Manetti," *Archivio storico italiano*, ser. 5, XVII (1896), pp. 241ff.

96. A. Chiapelli, "Due sculture ignote di Filippo Brunelleschi," *Rivista d'Italia*, II (1899), pp. 454ff.

97. L. Chiovenda, *Die Zeichnungen Petrarcas*, Diss. Frankfurt/Main, 1929. Reprint from *Archivum Romanicum* XVI (1933), pp. 1ff.

98. S. Ciampi, *Notizie inedite della Sagrestia Pistoiese*, Florence, 1810.

99. L. Cicognara, *Storia della scultura*, Prato, 1823.

100. (Sir) Kenneth M. Clark, "Architectural Backgrounds in XVth Century Italian Painting," *The Arts*, 1946-1947, I, pp. 13ff; II, pp. 33ff.

101. (Sir) Kenneth M. Clark, "An Early Quattrocento Triptych from Santa Maria Mag-

giore in Rome," *Burlington Magazine*, 93 (1951), pp. 338ff.

102. (Sir) Kenneth M. Clark, "Leon Battista Alberti on Painting," *British Academy Proceedings*, XXX (1944), pp. 283ff.

103. (Cleveland), *The Collection Holden*, Cleveland, 1917.

104. A. M. Colini, *Storia e topografia del Celio nell' antichità (Accademia Romana di Archeologia, Memorie*, VII), Rome, 1944.

105. Bartolomeo del Corazza, "Diario fiorentino . . . (1405-1438)," ed. G. O. Corazzini, *Archivio storico italiano*, ser. 5, XIV (1894), pp. 233ff.

106. H. Cornell, *Biblia Pauperum*, Stockholm, 1925.

107. H. Cornell, *The Iconography of the Nativity of Christ*, Uppsala, 1924.

108. A. Corsano, *Il pensiero religioso italiano*, Bari, 1937.

109. R. Corwegh, "Der Verfasser des Kleinen Codex Ghiberti's," *Mitteilungen des Kunsthistorischen Instituts Florenz*, I (1910), pp. 156ff.

110. "L. Curtius, Der Geist der roemischen Kunst," *Die Antike*, V (1929), pp. 187ff.

111. L. Curtius, "Ikonographische Beitraege zum Portrait der Römischen Republik . . .," *Archaeologisches Institut des Deutschen Reiches, Roemische Mitteilungen*, XLVII (1932), pp. 202ff.

112. O. M. Dalton, *The Royal Cup in the British Museum*, London, 1924.

113. (O. M. Dalton), *British Museum, A Guide to the Medieval Antiquities*, London, 1924.

114. Dante Alighieri, *Le Opere*, ed. E. Moore and P. Toynbee, Oxford, 1924.

115. A. Darcel, *Musée National du Louvre, Notice des émaux et de l'orfèvrerie*, Paris, 1891, *Supplément* (E. Molinier).

116. G. Dati, *Il libro segreto di Gregorio Dati*, ed. C. Gargiolli (*Scelta di curiosità letterarie*, 102), Bologna, 1869.

117. St. Davari, "Ancora della chiesa di S. Sebastiano in Mantova . . .," *Rassegna d'arte*, I (1901), pp. 95ff.

118. R. Davidsohn, *Forschungen zur Geschichte von Florenz*, Berlin, 1896ff.

119. M. Davies, "Lorenzo Monaco's 'Coronation of the Virgin' in London," *Critica d'arte*, VIII (1949), pp. 202ff.

120. B. Degenhart, "Michele di Giovanni di Bartolo: Disegni dall'antico e il camino 'della Iole,'" *Bolletino d'arte*, XXXV (1950), pp. 208ff.

121. B. Degenhart, "Le quattro tavole della leggenda di S. Benedetto," *Arte veneta*, III (1949), pp. 6ff.

122. B. Degenhart, *Pisanello* (Turin, 1945).

123. B. Degenhart, "Unbekannte Zeichnungen Francesco di Giorgio's," *Zeitschrift für Kunstgeschichte*, VIII (1939), pp. 117ff.

124. G. Dehio, "Das Bauprojekt Nikolaus' V und L. B. Alberti," (1886), *Kunsthistorische Aufsätze*, Munich and Berlin, 1914, pp. 163ff.

125. G. B. De Rossi, "Sull' archeologia nel secolo decimo quarto," *Bulletino di corrispondenza archeologica*, 1871, pp. 3ff.

126. E. DeWald, "Pietro Lorenzetti," *Art Studies*, VII (1929), pp. 131ff.

127. A. Dini-Traversari, *Ambrogio Traversari e i suoi tempi* (Florence, 1912).

128. Diodorus Siculus, *Diodorus of Sicily*, ed. C. H. Oldfather (*Loeb Classical Library*), London, 1933ff.

129. F. L. Dionigi (P. L. Dionysius), *Sacrarum Vaticanae Basilicae . . . Monumenta*, Rome, 1773.

130. Dionysius of Halicarnassus, *The Roman Antiquities of Dionysius of Halicarnassus*, ed. E. Cary (*Loeb Classical Library*), Cambridge, Mass. and London, 1937ff.

131. G. ten Doesschate, *De deerde commentaar van Lorenzo Ghiberti*, Diss. Utrecht, 1940.

132. Frater Dominicus Joannis, O. P., *Theotocon*, in: G. Lami, *Deliciae eruditorum*, XII, Florence, 1742, pp. 49ff.

133. A. Doren, *Das Aktenbuch für Ghiberti's Matthäusstatue an Or S. Michele zu Florenz* (*Kunsthistorisches Institut in Florenz, Italienische Forschungen I*), Berlin, 1906, pp. 1ff.

134. A. Doren, *Italienische Wirtschaftsgeschichte*, I, Jena, 1934 (all published).

135. A. Doren, *Studien aus der Florentiner Wirtschaftsgeschichte*: I, *Die Florentiner Wollentuchindustrie*, Stuttgart, 1901; II, *Das Florentiner Zunftwesen*, Stuttgart and Berlin, 1908.

136. H. Duetschke, *Antike Bildwerke in Oberitalien*, Leipzig, 1874ff.

137. P. Durrieu, "Jacques Coene, peintre de Bruges . . . ," *Les Arts anciens de Flandre*, II (1905), pp. 5ff.

138. P. Durrieu, "Michele di Besozzo et les relations entre l'art italienne et l'art française," *Mémoires de l'Académie des Inscriptions et Belles-Lettres*, XXXVIII, 2 (1911), pp. 365ff.

139. H. Egger (C. Hülsen, A. Michaelis), *Codex Escurialensis. . . . (Oesterreichisches Archäologisches Institut . . . Sonderschriften*, IV), Vienna, 1905-1906.

140. R. Ernst and E. von Garger, *Die früh- und hochgotische Plastik des Stefansdom*, Munich, 1927.

141. C. C. Van Essen, "Elementi etruschi nel rinascimento toscano," *Studi etruschi*, XIII (1939), pp. 497ff.

142. C. Eubel, *Hierarchia Catholica Medii Aevi*, Regensburg, 1913.

143. Pamphilus Eusebius, *Eusebii Pamphilii Canon Chronicus interprete S. Hieronymo*, in: Migne, *bibl.* 333, cols. 259ff.

144. J. Evans, "The Duke of Orleans' Reliquary of the Holy Thorn," *Burlington Magazine*, LXXVIII (1941), pp. 196ff.

145. C. von Fabriczy, "Michelozzo di Bartolomeo," *Jahrbuch der Preussischen Kunstsammlungen*, XXV (1904), *Beiheft*, pp. 34ff.

146. C. von Fabriczy, "Neues Zum Leben und Werke des Niccolo d'Arezzo, III," *Repertorium für Kunstwissenschaft*, XXV (1902), pp. 157ff.

147. C. von Fabriczy, "Donatello's Hl. Ludwig . . . ," *Jahrbuch der Preussischen Kunstsammlungen*, XXI (1900), pp. 242ff.

148. C. von Fabriczy, *Filippo Brunelleschi*, Stuttgart, 1892.

149. C. von Fabriczy, "Kritisches Verzeichnis der toskanischen Holz-und Tonstatuen . . . ," *Jahrbuch der Preussischen Kunstsammlungen*, XXX, *Beiheft*, 1909, pp. 1ff.

150. S. L. Faison, Jr., "Barna and Bartolo di Fredi," *Art Bulletin*, XIV (1932), pp. 285ff.

151. I. Falk, *Studien zu Andrea Pisano*, Diss. Zürich, Hamburg, 1940.

152. I. Falk and J. Lanyi, "The Genesis of Andrea Pisano's Bronze Doors," *Art Bulletin*, XXV (1943), pp. 132ff.

153. A. Fanfani, *Città di Castello, guida storico–artistica*, Città di Castello, 1927.

154. L. de Farcy, *Histoire et description des tapisseries de la Cathédrale d'Angers*, Angers, n. d. (*ca.* 1880).

155. V. Fasolo, "Riflessi Brunelleschiani nelle architetture dei pittori," *Atti del I° Congresso di Storia dell'Architettura*, 1936, pp. 197ff.

156. Bartolommeo Fazio (Bartolomeus Fazius), *De Viris Illustribus*, ed. L. Mehus, Florence, 1745.

157. E. Feinblatt, "Un sarcofago Romano inedito nel Museo di Los Angeles," *Bolletino d'arte*, XXXVIII (1952), pp. 193ff.

158. Antonio Averlino Filarete, *Tractat über die Baukunst . . .* , ed. W. von Oettingen (*Quellenschriften für Kunstgeschichte, N. F.*, III), Vienna, 1896.

159. G. Fiocco, "Michele da Firenze," *Dedalo*, XII (1932), pp. 542ff.

160. G. Fiocco, "I Lamberti a Venezia," *Dedalo*, VIII (1927-28), pp. 287ff, 343ff, 432ff.

161. G. Firestone, "The Iconography of the Annunciation in Florentine Painting of the

Third Quarter of the XVth Century," M.A. thesis, Institute of Fine Arts, New York University, 1939 (typescript).

162. V. Follini, *Lezione . . . letta all' adunanza dell'Accademia della Crusca . . . 13 Gennaio 1824*, Florence, 1824.

163. Agostino Fortunio, *Historiarum Camaldolensium Libri Tres*, Florence, 1575.

164. P. Franceschini, *L'oratorio di S. Michele in Orto in Firenze*, Florence, 1892.

165. M. Frankenburger, "Zur Geschichte des Ingolstädter und Landshuter Herzogs-Schatzes," *Repertorium für Kunstwissenschaft*, XLIV (1923), pp. 24ff.

166. G. de Francovich, "Appunti su Donatello e Jacopo della Quercia," *Bolletino d'arte*, IX (1929-30), pp. 145ff.

167. L. Freund, "Studien zur Bildgeschichte der Sibyllen," Diss. Hamburg, 1936.

168. B. Friedmann, "Ghiberti's Verhaeltnis zur Gothik und Renaissance," Diss. Bern, Vienna, 1913.

169. Andrea Fulvio, *L'Antichità di Roma*, Rome, 1588.

170. E. von Garger, *Die Reliefs an den Fürstentoren des Stefansdom*, Vienna, 1926.

171. E. von Garger, "Zwei gotische Statuen in Klosterneuburg," *Kunst und Kunsthandwerk*, XXIV (1921), pp. 106ff.

172. Pomponius Gauricus, *De sculptura seu statuaria libellus . . .*, Antwerp, 1528.

173. G. Gaye, *Carteggio inedito d'artisti . . . Documenti di Storia Italiana*, Florence, 1839.

174. G. Gaye, "Die Bronzetueren des Lorenzo Ghiberti," in: A. Reumont's *Italien*, II, 1840, p. 273.

175. G. B. Gelli, *Vite d'artisti*, ed. G. Mancini, *Archivio Storico Italiano*, ser. IV, XVII (1896), pp. 32ff.

176. M. L. Gengaro, "Precisazioni su Ghiberti architetto," *L'Arte*, XLI (1938), pp. 28off.

177. Lorenzo Ghiberti, *I Commentarii*, R. Università di Firenze, Facoltà di Magistero, Gruppo rionale fascista, Corso di storia dell'arte, Anno 1939-40, Florence, 1940.

178. Lorenzo Ghiberti, *Lorenzo Ghiberti's Denkwuerdigkeiten (I Commentarii)*, 2 vols., ed. J. von Schlosser, Berlin, 1912.

179. Lorenzo Ghiberti, *I Commentarii*, ed. O. Morisani, Naples, 1947.

180. C. Gilbert, "Alberti and Pino," *Marsyas*, III (1946), pp. 87ff.

181. P. Ginori-Conti, "Un libro di ricordi . . . di Lorenzo e Vittorio Ghiberti," *Rivista d'Arte*, XX (1938), pp. 29off.

182. O. Giustiniani (Horatius Justinianus), *Acta Sacra Oecumenici Concilii Florentini*, Rome, 1638.

183. (V. Giustiniani), *Galleria Giustiniani del Marchese Vincenzo Giustiniani*, Rome, 1631.

184. C. Gnudi, "Jacobello e Pietro Paolo di Venezia," *Critica d'arte*, II (1937), pp. 26ff.

185. C. Gnudi, "Nuovi appunti sui fratelli dalle Masegne," *Proporzioni*, III (1950), pp. 48ff.

186. L. Goldscheider, *Lorenzo Ghiberti*, London, 1949.

187. R. Goldwater and M. Treves, *Artists on Art*, New York, 1945.

188. H. Gollob, *Lorenzo Ghiberti's kuenstlerischer Werdegang*, Strasbourg, 1929.

189. E. Gombrich, "Botticelli's Mythologies," *Journal of the Warburg and Courtauld Institutes*, VIII (1945), pp. 7ff.

190. G. Gonelli, *Elogio di Lorenzo Ghiberti*, Florence, 1822.

191. A. F. Gori, *Inscriptionum Antiquarum Graecarum et Romanarum Pars tertia*, Florence, 1743.

192. C. Grayson, "Notes on the texts of some vernacular works of Leone Battista Alberti," *Rinascimento*, III (1952), pp. 211ff.

193. G. Gronau, "Notizie inedite su due bronzi del Museo Nazionale di Firenze," *Rivista d'arte*, V (1907), pp. 118ff.

194. H. Gronau, "The earliest works of Lorenzo Monaco," *Burlington Magazine*, XCII (1950), pp. 183ff, 217ff.

195. A. Gruenwald, "Ueber einige Werke Michelangelo's," *Jahrbuch der Kunsthistorischen Sammlungen des Allerhoechsten Kaiserhauses*, XXVII (1907-09), pp. 125ff.

196. M. A. Gualandi, *Memorie originali italiane risguardanti le belle arti*, ser. IV, Bologna, 1843.

197. Guarino Veronese, *Epistolario di Guarino Veronese*, ed. R. Sabbadini, I-III (*Miscellanea di Storia Veneta*, ed. R. Deputazione Veneta di Storia Patria, ser. 3, VIII, XI, XIV), Venice, 1915ff.

198. C. Guasti, *La cupola di S. Maria del Fiore*, Florence, 1857.

199. C. Guasti, *Santa Maria del Fiore*, Florence, 1887.

200. P. Gusman, *L'art décoratif de Rome*, Paris (1908ff).

201. C. S. Gutkind, "Poggio Bracciolini's geistige Entwicklung," *Deutsche Vierteljahrsschrift für Geistesgeschichte*, X (1932), pp. 548ff.

202. W. Haftmann, "Italienische Goldschmiedearbeiten," *Pantheon*, XXIII (1939), pp. 29ff, 54ff.

203. W. Haftmann, "Ein Mosaik der Ghirlandajo-Werkstatt aus dem Besitz des Lorenzo Magnifico," *Mitteilungen des Kunst-*

historischen Instituts in Florenz, VI (1940), pp. 98ff.

204. A. Hagen, *Lorenzo Ghiberti, Cronaca del Secolo XV* (first published 1831), Italian translation, Florence, 1845.

205. P. G. Hamberg, *Studies in Roman Imperial Art,* Copenhagen, 1945.

206. G. M. A. Hanfmann, *The Season Sarcophagus in Dumbarton Oaks,* Cambridge, Mass., 1951 (1952).

207. J. Havard, *Histoire de l'Orfèvrerie française,* Paris, 1896.

208. W. S. Heckscher, review of Salis, bibl. 459, *American Journal of Archaeology,* LII (1948), pp. 421ff.

209. F. Hermanin, "Gli affreschi di Pietro Cavallino a Santa Cecilia in Trastevere," *Le Gallerie italiana,* V (1902), pp. 6ff.

210. H. J. Hermann, *Die italienischen Handschriften des Ducento und Trecento der Wiener Nationalbibliothek (Beschreibendes Verzeichnis der . . . Handschriften in Oesterreich,* VIII, 5), Leipzig, 1930.

211. L. H. Heydenreich, "Spaetwerke Brunelleschi's," *Jahrbuch der Preussischen Kunstsammlungen,* LII (1931), pp. 1ff.

212. (Sir) George F. Hill, "Some Drawings from the Antique attributed to Pisanello," *Papers of the British School at Rome,* III (1906), pp. 297ff.

213. A. M. Hind, *Early Italian Engraving,* New York and London, 1938.

214. G. Hoffmann, S.J., *Epistolae Pontificiae ad Concilium Florentinum spectantes,* Rome, 1940.

215. G. Hoffmann, S.J., "Die Konzilsarbeit im Ferrara," *Orientalia Christiana Periodica,* III (1937), pp. 110ff, 403ff.

216. G. Hoffmann, S.J., "Die Konzilsarbeit in Florenz," *Orientalia Christiana Periodica,* IV (1938), pp. 157ff, 372ff.

217. P. Hoffmann, *Studien zu Leone Baptista Alberti's . . . De Re Aedificatoria,* Diss. Leipzig, Frankenberg, i. S., 1883.

218. E. G. Holt, *Literary Sources of Art History,* Princeton, 1947.

219. W. Horn, "Das Florentiner Baptisterium," *Mitteilungen des Kunsthistorischen Instituts in Florenz,* V (1938), pp. 100ff.

220. H. Horne, "Andrea dal Castagno," *Burlington Magazine,* VII (1905), pp. 66ff, 222ff.

221. H. Horne, "An Account of Rome in 1450," *Revue Archéologique,* ser. 4, X (1907), pp. 82ff.

222. G. Huard, "Saint Louis et la reine Marguerite," *Gazette des Beaux-Arts,* LXXIV (1932), pp. 375ff.

223. G. Huizinga, *The Waning of the Middle Ages,* London, 1924.

224. P. G. Huebner, "Studien ueber die Benutzung der Antike in der Renaissance," *Monatshefte für Kunstwissenschaft,* II (1909), pp. 267ff.

225. C. Hülsen, *Das Skizzenbuch des Giovanantonio Dosio,* Berlin, 1933.

226. C. Hülsen und H. Egger, *Die römischen Skizzenbücher von Martin van Heemskerk,* Berlin, 1916.

227. C.-A. Isermeyer, *Rahmengliederung und Bildfolge in der Florentiner Malerei des 14. Jahrhunderts,* Diss. Goettingen, Würzburg, 1937.

228. W. M. Ivins, *On the Rationalization of Sight . . . ,* New York, 1938.

229. O. Jahn, "Über die Zeichnungen antiker Monumente im Codex Pighianus," *Berichte der Sächsischen Gesellschaft der Wissenschaften,* XX (1868), pp. 161ff.

230. M. R. James, *Illustrations of the Book of Genesis . . . facs. of the Ms. Brit. Mus. Egerton 1894 (Roxburghe Club,* 177), Oxford, 1921.

231. S. Jansen, "Iconography of the Meeting of Solomon and the Queen of Sheba," M.A. thesis, Institute of Fine Arts, New York University, 1934 (typescript).

232. H. W. Janson, "The Sculptured Works of Michelozzo di Bartolommeo," Ph.D. thesis, Harvard University, Cambridge, Mass., 1941 (typescript).

233. John of Salisbury, *Joannis Sarisberiensis Historiae quae supersunt,* ed. R. L. Poole, Oxford, 1927.

234. H. S. Jones, *A catalogue of the ancient sculptures in the municipal collections of Rome:* I, *The sculptures of the Museo Capitolino,* Oxford, 1912; II, *The sculptures of the Palazzo dei Conservatori,* Oxford, 1926.

235. H. S. Jones, "Notes on Roman Historical Sculptures," *Papers of the British School at Rome,* III (1905), pp. 213ff.

236. R. Jones and B. Berenson, *Speculum Humanae Salvationis,* Oxford, 1926.

237. H. Kauffmann, *Donatello, eine Einfuehrung in sein Bilden und Denken,* Berlin, 1935.

238. H. Kauffmann, "Florentiner Domplastik," *Jahrbuch der Preussischen Kunstsammlungen,* XLVII (1926), pp. 141ff, 216ff.

239. H. Kauffmann, "Eine Ghibertizeichnung im Louvre," *Jahrbuch der Preussischen Kunstsammlungen,* L (1929), pp. 1ff.

240. H. Keller, "Die Entstehung des Bildnisses am Ende des Hochmittelalters," *Römisches Jahrbuch für Kunstgeschichte,* III (1939), pp. 227ff.

241. R. W. Kennedy, *The Renaissance Painter's Garden,* New York, 1948.

242. G. J. Kern, "Das Dreifaltigkeitsfresko von S. Maria Novella," *Jahrbuch der Preussischen Kunstsammlungen*, XXXIV (1913), pp. 36ff.

243. F. Kimball, "Luciano Laurana and the High Renaissance," *Art Bulletin*, X (1927-28), pp. 125ff.

244. A. Kleinclausz, "Les peintres des Ducs de Bourgogne," *Revue de l'art ancien et modern*, XX (1906), pp. 161ff, 253ff.

245. H. Kohlhausen, *Gotisches Kunstgewerbe*, in: H. T. Bossert, *Geschichte des Kunstgewerbes*, V, Berlin, 1932, pp. 367ff.

246. R. Krautheimer, "Ghiberti," in: *Les sculpteurs célèbres*, ed. P. Francastel, Paris, 1954, pp. 212ff.

247. R. Krautheimer, "Ghiberti and Master Gusmin," *Art Bulletin*, XXIX (1947), pp. 25ff.

248. R. Krautheimer, "Ghiberti architetto," *Allen Memorial Art Museum, Oberlin College, Bulletin*, XII (1955), pp. 48ff.

249. R. Krautheimer, "Ghibertiana," *Burlington Magazine*, LXXI (1937), pp. 68ff.

250. R. Krautheimer, "Santo Stefano Rotondo a Roma e la Chiesa del Santo Sepolcro . . . ," *Rivista di archeologia cristiana*, XII (1935), pp. 51ff.

251. R. Krautheimer, "The Tragic and Comic Scene of the Renaissance: The Baltimore and Urbino Panels," *Gazette des Beaux-Arts*, XXXIII (1948), pp. 327ff.

252. R. Krautheimer, "Zur Venezianischen Trecentoplastik," *Marburger Jahrbuch für Kunstwissenschaft*, V (1929), pp. 94ff.

253. T. Krautheimer-Hess, review of R. S. Loomis, *Arthurian Legends in Medieval Art*, in: *Art Bulletin*, XXIV (1942), pp. 102ff.

254. E. Kris, *Meister und Meisterwerke der Steinschneidekunst in der italienischen Renaissance*, Vienna, 1929.

255. P. Kristeller, "Un ricordo della gara per le porte del Battistero di Firenze . . . ," *Bolletino d'arte*, IV (1910), pp. 297ff.

256. J. Labarte, *Histoire des arts industriels au moyen age et à l'epoque de la Renaissance*, Paris, 1864ff.

257. J. Labarte, *Inventaire de Charles V. Collection de documents inédits sur l'histoire de France*, ser. 6, XVI, Paris, 1879.

258. A. de Laborde, *Etude sur la Bible Moralisée illustrée*, Paris, 1911ff.

259. M. de Laborde, *Notice des Emaux . . . du Louvre*, II, Paris, 1853.

260. H. Ladendorf, *Antikenstudium und Antikenkopie (Abhandlung der sächsischen Akademie der Wissenschaften in Leipzig, Bd. 46 Heft 2)*, Berlin, 1953.

261. R. Lanciani, *Storia degli scavi di Roma*, Rome, 1902ff.

262. A. Lane, "Florentine painted glass and the practice of design," *Burlington Magazine*, XCI (1949), pp. 43ff.

263. J. Lanyi, "Problemi di critica Donatelliana," *Critica d'arte*, IV (1939), pp. 9ff.

264. J. Lanyi, "Il Profeta Isaia di Nanni di Banco," *Rivista d'arte*, XVIII (1936), pp. 137ff.

265. J. Lanyi, "Quercia Studien," *Jahrbuch für Kunstwissenschaft*, II (1930), pp. 25ff.

266. P. Lasinio, *Raccolta di sarcofagi . . . nel Campo santo di Pisa*, Pisa, 1814.

267. E. Lavagnino, "Masaccio: Dicesi è morto a Roma," *Emporium*, XLIX (1943), pp. 97ff.

268. M. Lazzaroni and A. Muñoz, *Filarete scultore e architetto del Secolo XV*, Rome, 1908.

269. G. Ledos, "Fragment de l'inventaire des joyaux de Louis I, duc d'Anjou," *Bibliothèque de l'Ecole des Chartes*, L (1889), pp. 168ff.

270. K. Lehmann, "The *Imagines* of the Elder Philostratus," *Art Bulletin*, XXIII (1941), pp. 16ff.

271. P. W. Lehmann, *Statues on Coins*, New York, 1946.

272. A. Lejard, *Les tapisseries de l'Apocalypse de la Cathédrale d'Angers*, Paris, 1942.

273. H. Lerner-Lehmkuhl, *Zur Struktur und Geschichte des Florentiner Kunstmarktes im 15. Jahrhundert (Lebensräume der Kunst, 3)* Diss. Münster, Wattenscheid, 1936.

274. A. Levi, "Rilievi di sarcofagi nel Palazzo Ducale di Mantova," *Dedalo*, VII (1926), pp. 205ff.

275. A. Liebreich, *Claus Sluter*, Brussels, 1936.

276. S. Loessel, "Santa Maria in Vescovio," M.A. Thesis, Institute of Fine Arts, New York University, 1942 (typescript).

277. R. Longhi, "Fatti di Masolino e di Masaccio," *Critica d'arte*, V (1940), pp. 145ff.

278. W. Lotz, Review of Planiscig, bibl. 403, in: *Rinascità*, IV (1941), pp. 289ff.

279. W. Lotz, *Der Taufbrunnen des Baptisteriums zu Siena (Der Kunstbrief)*, Berlin, 1948.

280. B. Lowry, "Letter to the Editor," *Art Bulletin*, XXXV (1953), pp. 175ff.

281. F. P. Luiso, "Ricerche cronologiche per un riordinamento dell'epistolario di A. Traversari," *Rivista delle biblioteche e degli archivi*, VIII (1897), pp. 35ff, 148ff; IX (1898), pp. 74ff; X (1899), pp. 73ff, 105ff.

282. A. Lumachi, *Memorie storiche dell'antichissima Basilica di San Giovanni Battista in Firenze*, Florence, 1782.

283. V. Lusini, *Il San Giovanni di Siena . . .*, Florence, 1901.

284. J. Lutz and P. Perdrizet, *Speculum humanae Salvationis*, Leipzig, 1907ff.

285. E. B. MacDougall, "Nicolas V's Plan for Rebuilding St. Peter's, the Vatican Palace and the Borgo," M.A. Thesis, Institute of Fine Arts, New York University, 1955 (typescript).

286. Timoteo Maffei, *In magnificentiae Cosmi Medicei detractores*, in: Lami, *Deliciae Eruditorum*, XII (1742), pp. 150ff.

287. L. Magherini-Graziani, *L'arte a Città di Castello*, Città di Castello, 1890.

288. T. Magnuson, "The Project of Nicholas V for Rebuilding the Borgo Leonino in Rome," *Art Bulletin*, XXXVI (1954), pp. 89ff.

289. G. Mancini, *Vita di Leon Battista Alberti*, 2nd ed., Florence, 1911.

290. G. Mancini, "Il bel S. Giovanni e le feste patronali . . . descritte nel 1475 . . . da Piero Cennini," *Rivista d'arte*, VI (1909), pp. 195ff.

291. G. Mancini, "Nuovi documenti e notizie sulla vita . . . di Leon Battista Alberti," *Archivio storico italiano*, ser. 4, XIX (1887), pp. 190ff.

292. E. Mandowsky, "Some notes on the early history of the Medicean Niobides," *Gazette des Beaux-Arts*, XLI (1953), pp. 251ff, 288ff.

293. Antonio Manetti, *Uomini singholari*, in: *Operette istoriche*, ed. G. Milanesi, Florence, 1887.

294. (Antonio Manetti), *Vita di Filippo Brunelleschi*, ed. E. Toesca, Rome, 1927.

295. Gianozzo Manetti, *De dignitate et excellentia hominis Libri IIII*, Basel, 1532.

296. G. Mansi, *Sacrorum Conciliorum nova et amplissima collectio*, ed. P. Labbaeus, G. Cossartius, N. Coleti, Florence, 1739ff.

297. M. Marangoni, "Rilievi poco noti nella seconda Porta del S. Giovanni in Firenze," *Rassegna d'arte*, XI (1911), pp. 31f.

298. G. Marchini, "Aggiunte a Michelozzo," *Rinascità*, VII (1944), pp. 24ff.

299. G. Marchini (and others), "Note brevi su inediti toscani," *Bolletino d'arte*, XXXVII (1952), pp. 173ff.

300. V. Mariani, *Michelangelo e la facciata di San Pietro*, Rome, 1943.

301. R. Van Marle, *The Development of the Italian Schools of Painting*, The Hague, 1923ff.

302. A. Marquand, *Luca della Robbia (Princeton Monographs in Art and Archaeology*, III), Princeton, 1914.

303. A. Marquand, "A Terracotta Sketch by L. Ghiberti," *American Journal of Archaeology*, IX (1894), pp. 207ff.

304. A. Marquand, "Two Windows in the Cathedral of Florence," *American Journal of Archaeology*, N. S., IV (1900), pp. 197ff.

305. J. J. Marquet de Vasselot, *Musée du Louvre, Catalogue sommaire de l'orfèvrerie . . .*, (Paris, 1914).

306. H. M. R. Martin, *La miniature française du XIIIᵉ au XVᵉ siècle*, Paris, 1923.

307. G. Martini (J. Martinius), *Theatrum Basilicae Pisanae*, 2nd ed. *Appendix*, Rome, 1728.

308. R. G. Mather, "Documents Mostly New Relating to Florentine Painters and Sculptors of the Fifteenth Century," *Art Bulletin* XXX (1948), pp. 20ff.

309. H. Mattingly, *Coins of the Roman Empire in the British Museum*, London, 1923ff.

310. F. Matz, Über eine dem Herzog von Coburg-Gotha gehörige Sammlung alter Handzeichnungen nach Antiken," *Monatsberichte der Berliner Akademie der Wissenschaften, Phil.-Hist. Klasse*, 1871, pp. 445ff.

311. F. Matz and F. von Duhn, *Antike Bildwerke in Rom*, Leipzig, 1881ff.

312. A. L. Mayer, "Giuliano Fiorentino," *Bolletino d'arte*, ser. II, vol. II (1922-23), pp. 337ff.

313. G. Mazzatinti, *Inventari dei manoscritti delle biblioteche d'Italia*, IX (*Firenze*), Forli, 1899.

314. J. Meder, *Die Handzeichnung*, Vienna, 1923.

315. M. Meiss, "Italian Style in Catalonia and a Fourteenth Century Italian Workshop," *Journal of the Walters Art Gallery* IV (1941), pp. 45ff.

316. M. Meiss, "London's New Masaccio," *Art News*, LI (1952), pp. 24ff.

317. M. Meiss, *Painting in Florence and Siena after the Black Death*, Princeton, 1951.

318. M. Meiss, "The Problem of Francesco Traini," *Art Bulletin*, XV (1933), pp. 97ff.

319. A. Melani, "I fascioni dell' imposte di Andrea da Pontedera," *Arte e Storia*, XVIII (1899), p. 128.

320. A. Mercati, *Per la cronologia della vita e degli studi di Niccolo Perotti (Studi e Testi*, 44), Rome, 1925.

321. Giovanni Cardinal Mercati, *Ultimi contributi alla Storia degli Umanisti (Studi e Testi*, 90), Città del Vaticano, 1939.

322. Mrs. Merrifield, *Original Treatises . . . on the Arts of Painting*, London, 1849.

323. J. Mesnil, "La data della morte di Masaccio," *Rivista d'arte*, VIII (1912), pp. 31ff.

324. J. Mesnil, "Die Kunstlehre der Fruehrenaissance im Werke Masaccio's" *Vorträge der Bibliothek Warburg*, 1925-26 (1928), pp. 122ff.

325. J. Mesnil, "Masaccio and the Antique," *Burlington Magazine*, XLVIII (1926), pp. 91ff.

326. A. G. Meyer, "Lorenzo Ghiberti," *Museum*, V (1900), pp. 17ff.

327. A. Meyer-Weinschel, *Renaissance und Antike (Tuebinger Forschungen zur Archäologie und Kunstgeschichte*, 12), Reutlingen, 1933.

328. A. Michaelis, "Monte Cavallo," *Roemische Mitteilungen*, XIII (1898), 248ff.

329. P. H. Michel, *La Pensée de L. B. Alberti*, Paris, 1930.

330. U. Middeldorf, Review of H. Kauffmann, bibl. 237, in: *Art Bulletin*, XVIII (1936), pp. 570ff.

331. U. Middeldorf, "Zur Goldschmiedekunst der toskanischen Fruehrenaissance," *Pantheon*, XVI (1935), pp. 279ff.

332. L. Migliori, *Firenze . . . illustrata*, Florence, 1684.

333. J. P. Migne, *Patrologiae Cursus Completus Series Graeca*, Paris, 1854ff, quoted as *P.G.*

334. J. P. Migne, *Patrologiae Cursus Completus Series Latina*, Paris, 1844ff, quoted as *P.L.*

335. Milan Cathedral, *Annali della fabbrica del Duomo di Milano*, Milan, 1877ff.

336. G. Milanesi, *Documenti per la storia dell'arte senese*, Siena, 1854ff.

337. G. Milanesi, *Nuovi documenti per la storia dell'arte toscana*, Florence, 1901.

338. Ministero della Pubblica Istruzione, *Documenti Inediti per servire alla storia dei musei d'Italia*, Rome, 1878ff.

339. P. Misciatelli, "Un' Eva Lorenzettiana nel Museo del Louvre," *Diana*, V (1930), pp. 215ff.

340. I. B. Mittarelli and A. Costadoni, *Annales Camaldulenses*, VI, Venice, 1761.

341. E. Molinier, *Musée National du Louvre, Catalogue des ivoires*, Paris, 1896.

342. T. Mommsen, "Petrarch and the Story of the Choice of Hercules," *Journal of the Warburg and Courtauld Institutes*, XVI (1953), pp. 178ff.

343. T. Mommsen, "Petrarch's Conception of the Dark Ages," *Speculum*, XVII (1942), pp. 226ff.

344. R. Morçay, *Chroniques de Saint-Antonin, Fragments . . . du titre XXII (1378-1459)*, Paris, 1913.

345. H. Moranvillé, *Inventaire de l'orfèvrerie et des joyaux de Louis I, duc d'Anjou*, Paris, 1906.

346. J. Morelli, "De Joanne Dondio," *Operette*, II, 1820, pp. 285ff.

347. C. R. Morey, *The Sarcophagus of Claudia Antonia Sabina and the Asiatic Sarcophagi (American Society for the Excavation of Sardis, Publications*, V, 1), Princeton, 1924.

348. O. Morisani, *Studi su Donatello*, Venice, 1952.

349. D. A. Mortier, *Histoire des maîtres généraux . . . des frères prêcheurs*, Paris, 1903ff.

350. E. Muentz, "Les Arts à la Cour des Papes," I, *Bibliothèques des Ecoles Françaises d'Athènes et de Rome*, IV (1878).

351. E. Muentz, *Les Collections des Médicis au XV Siècle . . .*, Paris, 1888.

352. E. Muentz, "Essai sur l'Histoire des collections italiennes d'antiquitées . . .," *Revue archéologique*, LXIX (1879), pp. 45ff, 84ff.

353. E. Muentz, *Les précurseurs de la Renaissance*, Paris and London, 1882.

354. E. Muentz et Prince d'Essling, *Petrarque*, Paris, 1902.

355. I. von Müller, *Handbuch der Altertumswissenschaft*, I (1886).

356. L. A. Muratori, *Annali d'Italia*, Florence, 1827.

357. L. A. Muratori, *Rerum Italicarum Scriptores*, Milan, 1723ff; *Supplement*, ed. G. M. Tartini, Florence, 1748ff.

358. idem, new series, ed. G. Carducci and others, Città di Castello, 1900ff.

359. F. Nardini, *Roma antica* (1st ed., 1660), Rome, 1771.

360. Ugo Nebbia, *La Scultura nel Duomo di Milano*, Milan, 1908.

361. G. di Nicola, "Alcuni dipinti di Lippo Vanni," *Rassegna d'arte senese*, VI (1910), pp. 39ff.

362. Nicolaus de Lyra, *Postilla in universa Biblia*, Rome, 1471-72.

363. Dorothea F. Nyberg, "A Study of Proportions in Brunelleschi's Architecture," M.A. Thesis, Institute of Fine Arts, New York University, 1953 (typescript).

364. R. Oertel, *Filippo Lippi*, Vienna (1942).

365. R. Oertel, "Masaccio's Frühwerke," *Marburger Jahrbuch für Kunstwissenschaft*, VII (1933), pp. 1ff.

366. R. Oertel, review of K. Steinbart, *Masaccio*, in *Zeitschrift fur Kunstgeschichte*, XIV (1951), pp. 167ff.

367. R. Oertel, "Wandmalerei und Zeichnung in Italien," *Mitteilungen des Kunsthistorischen Instituts in Florenz*, V (1937-40), pp. 217ff.

368. R. Offner, "Four Panels, a Fresco and a Problem," *Burlington Magazine*, LIV (1929), pp. 224ff.

369. R. Offner, "Niccolo di Pietro Gerini, A List of Works by Niccolo di Pietro Gerini," *Art in America*, IX (1921), p. 238.

370. R. Offner, *A Critical and Historical*

Corpus of Florentine Painting, New York, 1930ff.

371. L. Olschki, *Geschichte der neusprachlichen wissenschaftlichen Literatur, I, Die Literatur der Technik und der angewandten Wissenschaften vom Mittelalter bis zur Renaissance*, Heidelberg, 1919.

372. H. A. Omont, *Miniatures des plus anciens manuscrits grecs de la Bibliothèque Nationale du VIᵉ au XIVᵉ siècle*, Paris, 1929.

373. H. A. Omont, *Les Miniatures du Psautier de Saint Louis*, Leyden, 1902.

374. S. Orsati (Ursatus), *Monumenta Patavina*, Padua, 1653.

375. W. and E. Paatz, *Die Kirchen von Florenz, ein kunstgeschichtliches Handbuch*, Frankfurt/Main, 1940ff.

376. O. Paecht, "Early Italian Nature Studies and the Early Calendar Landscapes," *Journal of the Warburg and Courtauld Institutes*, XIII (1950), pp. 13ff.

377. M. Palmieri, *Matthei Palmerii Liber de Temporibus (AA 1-1448) . . . Appendice: Matthei Palmerii Annales*, ed. A. Scaramilla in: Muratori, bibl. 358, XXVI, 1.

378. M. Palmieri, *Matthaei Palmerii opus de Temporibus suis*, in: Muratori, bibl. 357, *Supplement*, I, cols. 235ff.

379. E. Panofsky, *The Codex Huygens and Leonardo da Vinci's Art Theory*, (Studies of the Warburg Institute, 13), London, 1940.

380. E. Panofsky, *Early Netherlandish Painting*, Cambridge, Mass., 1953.

381. E. Panofsky, "Das erste Blatt aus dem Libro Giorgio Vasari's," *Staedeljahrbuch*, VI (1930), pp. 25ff.

382. E. Panofsky, "The Friedsam Annunciation," *Art Bulletin*, XVII (1935), pp. 433ff.

383. E. Panofsky, *Galileo as a Critic of the Arts*, The Hague, 1954.

384. E. Panofsky, "Imago Pietatis," *Festschrift für Max I. Friedlaender*, Leipzig, 1927, pp. 261ff.

385. E. Panofsky, "Die Perspektive als symbolische Form," *Vorträge der Bibliothek Warburg*, 1924-25, Leipzig and Berlin, 1927, pp. 258ff.

386. E. Panofsky, "Das perspektivische Verfahren Leone Battista Alberti's," *Kunstchronik*, XXVI (1914-15), p. 508.

387. E. Panofsky, "Renaissance and Renascences," *Kenyon Review*, VI (1944), pp. 201ff.

388. E. Panofsky and F. Saxl, *Classical Mythology in Mediaeval Art (Metropolitan Museum Studies, IV, 2)*, New York, 1933.

389. (R. Papini), *Il Camposanto (Catalogo delle cose d'arte e di antichità d'Italia, Pisa, II)*, Rome, 1932.

390. R. Paribeni, "La colonna Traiana in un codice del Rinascimento," *Rivista del R. Istituto d'Archeologia e Storia dell'Arte*, I, (1929), pp. 9ff.

391. L. Passerini, *Curiosità storico-artistiche Fiorentine, I, La Loggia di Or S. Michele*, Florence, 1866.

392. T. Patch (A. Cocchi) and F. Gregori, *La porta principale del Battistero di S. Giovanni*, Florence, 1773 (reprinted in: E. Muentz, *Les Archives des arts, I*, Paris, 1890, pp. 15ff).

393. C. Perkins, *Ghiberti et son école*, Paris, 1886.

394. C. Perkins, "Lorenzo Ghiberti," *Gazette des Beaux-Arts*, XXV (1868), pp. 457ff.

395. Francesco Petrarca, *Le familiari*, ed. V. Rossi, Florence, 1933ff.

396. Francesco Petrarca, *Opera omnia*, Basel, 1584.

397. A. Pica, "La cupola di S. Maria del Fiore e la collaborazione Brunellesco-Ghiberti," *Emporium*, XCVII (1943), pp. 70ff.

398. P. Pieri, *Intorno alla Storia dell'Arte della Seta in Firenze*, Bologna, 1927.

399. A. L. Pietrogrande, "Descrizione del sarcofago decorato ed esame della scena bacchica," *Notizie Scavi*, XII (1934), pp. 230ff.

400. W. Pinder, *Die deutsche Plastik vom ausgehenden Mittelalter bis zum Ende der Renaissance, I (Handbuch der Kunstwissenschaft)*, Wildpark-Potsdam (1924ff).

401. M. Pittaluga, *Masaccio*, Florence, 1935.

402. L. Planiscig, "I profeti sulla porta della Mandorla," *Rivista d'arte*, XXIV (1942), pp. 125ff.

403. L. Planiscig, *Lorenzo Ghiberti*, Vienna (1940).

404. L. Planiscig, *Lorenzo Ghiberti*, Florence, 1949.

405. L. Planiscig, *Nanni di Banco*, Florence, 1946.

406. L. Planiscig, "Geschichte der Venezianischen Skulptur im XIV Jahrhundert," *Jahrbuch der Kunsthistorischen Sammlungen des Allerhoechsten Kaiserhauses*, XXXIII (1916), pp. 31ff.

407. L. Planiscig, "Die Bildhauer Venedigs in der ersten Hälfte des Quattrocento," *Jahrbuch der Kunsthistorischen Sammlungen in Wien*, N. F. IV (1930), pp. 47ff.

408. Pliny (Caius Plinius Secundus), *Natural History*, ed. H. Rackham (*Loeb Classical Library*), Cambridge, Mass. and London, 1938ff.

409. G. Poggi, *La Capella e la tomba di Onofrio Strozzi*, Florence, 1902.

410. (G. Poggi), *Catalogo del Museo dell'Opera del Duomo*, Florence, 1904.

411. G. Poggi, "Il Ciborio di Bernardo Ros-

sellino nella chiesa di S. Egidio," *Miscellanea d'arte*, I (1903), pp. 105ff.

412. G. Poggi, "La Compagnia del Bigallo," *Rivista d'arte*, II (1904), pp. 189ff.

413. G. Poggi, *Il Duomo di Firenze* (Kunsthistorisches Institut in Florenz, Italienische Forschungen, II), Berlin, 1909.

414. G. Poggi, *La Porta del Paradiso di Lorenzo Ghiberti*, Florence, 1949.

415. G. Poggi, "Il reliquario 'del libretto' nel battistero fiorentino," *Rivista d'arte*, IX (1916-18), pp. 238ff.

416. G. Poggi, "La ripulitura delle porte del Battistero Fiorentino," *Bolletino d'arte*, XXXIII (1948), pp. 244ff.

417. G. Poggi, L. Planiscig, B. Bearzi, *Donatello, San Ludovico*, New York (1949).

418. Poggio-Bracciolini, *Epistolae*, ed. T. de Tonellis, Florence, 1831ff.

419. Poggio-Bracciolini, *Poggii Bracciolini ... Historiae De Varietate Fortunae Libri IV*, ed. D. Georgius, Paris, 1723.

420. Polybius, *The histories . . .*, ed. W. R. Paton (*Loeb Classical Library*), London and New York, 1922ff.

421. J. Pope-Hennessy, *The Complete Work of Paolo Ucello*, London and New York, 1950.

422. J. Pope-Hennessy, *Donatello's Relief of the Ascension*, London, 1949.

423. (A. E. Popham), *Old Master Drawings from the Albertina* (London), 1948.

424. F. Poulsen, *Catalogue of Ancient Sculpture in the Ny Carlsberg Glyptothek*, Copenhagen, 1951.

425. F. D. Prager, "Brunelleschi's Inventions and the Renewal of Roman Masonry Work," *Osiris*, IX (1950), pp. 457ff.

426. U. Procacci, "Gherardo Starnina," *Rivista d'arte*, XV (1933), pp. 151ff; XVII (1935), pp. 333ff.

427. U. Procacci, "Niccolo di Piero Lamberti . . . e Niccolo di Luca Spinelli," *Il Vasari*, I (1927-28), pp. 300ff.

428. U. Procacci, "Sulla cronologia delle opere di Masaccio e di Masolino tra il 1425 e il 1428," *Rivista d'arte*, XXVIII (1953), pp. 3ff.

429. G. Pudelko, "The maestro del Bambino Vispo," *Art in America*, XXVI (1938), pp. 47ff.

430. G. Pudelko, "The Stylistic Development of Lorenzo Monaco," *Burlington Magazine*, LXXIII (1938), pp. 237ff; LXXIV (1939), pp. 76ff.

431. G. Pudelko, "The early works of Paolo Ucello," *Art Bulletin*, XVI (1934), pp. 231ff.

432. G. Pudelko, "The Minor Masters of the Chiostro Verde," *Art Bulletin*, XVII (1935), pp. 71ff.

433. C. L. Ragghianti, "Apologo storico su vecchio e nuovo," *Il Mondo Europeo*, July 15, 1947 [mystification].

434. I. Ragusa, "The re-use . . . of Roman Sarcophagi during the Middle Ages and the Early Renaissance," M.A. Thesis, Institute of Fine Arts, New York University, 1951 (typescript).

435. S. Reinach, *Répertoire de Reliefs Grecs et Romains*, Paris, 1909ff.

436. S. Reinach, *Répertoire de la Statuaire Grecque et Romaine*, Paris, 1897ff.

437. M. Reymond, "L'arc mixtiligne florentin," *Rivista d'arte*, II (1904), pp. 245ff.

438. M. Reymond, "Lorenzo Ghiberti," *Gazette des Beaux-Arts*, 3rd ser., XVI (1896), pp. 125ff.

439. M. Reymond, "La porte de la Chapelle Strozzi," *Rivista d'arte*, I (1903), pp. 4ff.

440. M. Reymond, *La sculpture florentine*, Florence, 1897ff.

441. C. Ricci, *Il Tempio Malatestiano*, Milan and Rome, 1925.

442. P. G. Ricci, "Ambrogio Traversari," *Rinascità*, II (1939), pp. 578ff.

443. G. Richa, *Notizie istoriche delle chiese fiorentine*, Florence, 1754ff.

444. G. M. Richter, *The Metropolitan Museum of Art, Greek, Etruscan and Roman Bronzes*, New York, 1915.

445. Ristoro d'Arezzo, *Mappa Mundi*, in: V. Nannucci, *Manuale della Letteratura . . . Italiana*, Florence, 1857.

446. G. E. Rizzo, "Sculture antiche del Palazzo Giustiniani," *Bulletino della Commissione Archeologica Communale*, 1904-05.

447. D. M. Robb, "The Iconography of the Annunciation in the Fourteenth and Fifteenth Centuries," *Art Bulletin*, XVIII (1936), pp. 480ff.

448. C. Robert, *Die antiken Sarkophagreliefs*, II, III, 1-3, Berlin, 1890ff (see also Rumpf, bibl. 455).

449. C. Robert, "Über ein dem Michelangelo zugeschriebenes Skizzenbuch auf Schloss Wolfegg," *Archäologisches Institut des Deutschen Reiches, Roemische Mitteilungen*, XVI (1901), pp. 209ff.

450. A. Rosenberg, "Lorenzo Ghiberti," in: R. Dohme, *Kunst und Kuenstler*, Abt. II, 1 (1877), pp. 35ff.

451. G. Rosini, *Storia della pittura italiana*, Pisa, 1848ff.

452. F. Rossi, "The Baptistery Doors in Florence," *Burlington Magazine*, LXXXIX (1947), pp. 334ff.

453. G. Rowley, "The Gothic Frescoes at Monte Siepi," *Art Studies*, VII (1929), pp. 107ff.

454. K. F. von Rumohr, *Italienische Forschungen*, Berlin, 1827.

455. A. Rumpf, *Die antiken Sarkophagreliefs*, v, Berlin, 1935 (see also Robert, bibl. 448).

456. G. McN. Rushforth, "Magister Gregorius De Mirabilibus Urbis Romae . . . ," *Journal of Roman Studies*, IX (1919), pp. 14ff.

457. R. Sabbadini, *Carteggio di Giovanni Aurispa (Fonti per la storia d'Italia pubblicate dall' Istituto Storico Italiano*, LXX), Rome, 1931.

458. R. Sabbadini, *Le scoperte dei codici latini e greci*, Florence, 1914.

459. A. von Salis, *Antike und Renaissance*, Erlenbach-Zurich, 1947.

460. M. Salmi, "Aggiunte al Tre e al Quattrocento fiorentino, II," *Rivista d'arte*, XVI (1934), pp. 168ff.

461. (M. Salmi), *Mostra d'arte sacra . . . Arezzo*, Arezzo, 1950.

462. M. Salmi (and others), *Mostra di quattro maestri del primo Rinascimento*, Florence, 1954.

463. M. Salmi, *Paolo Uccello, Andrea del Castagno, Domenico Veneziano*, Paris (1939).

464. Roberto Salvini, *L'arte di Agnolo Gaddi*, Florence, 1936.

465. Coluccio Salutati, *De laboribus Herculis*, ed. B. L. Ullman, Zurich, 1951.

466. P. Sanpaolesi, "Aggiunte al Brunelleschi," *Bolletino d'arte*, XXXVIII (1953), pp. 225ff.

467. P. Sanpaolesi, *Brunellesco e Donatello nella Sacrestia Vecchia . . .* , Pisa (1950).

468. P. Sanpaolesi, "Il concorso del 1418-20 per la cupola di S. Maria del Fiore," *Rivista d'arte*, XV (1936), pp. 301ff.

469. P. Sanpaolesi, "Le prospettive architettoniche di Urbino, di Filadelfia e di Berlino," *Bolletino d'arte*, XXXIV (1949), pp. 322ff.

470. F. Sartini, *Statuti dell'arte dei rigattieri e linaiuoli di Firenze (R. Deputazione di Storia patria per la Toscana. Fonti e studi sulle corporazioni artigiane del medio evo, Fonti*, II), Florence, 1940.

471. F. Saxl, "The Classical Inscription in Renaissance Art and Politics," *Journal of the Warburg and Courtauld Institutes*, IV (1940-41), pp. 19ff.

472. A. Van Schendel, *Le dessin en Lombardie*, Brussels (1938).

473. J. von Schlosser, "Die aeltesten Medaillen und die Antike," *Jahrbuch der Kunsthistorischen Sammlungen des Allerhoechsten Kaiserhauses*, XVIII (1897), pp. 64ff.

474. J. von Schlosser, " 'Armeleutekunst' in alter Zeit," *Praeludien* (Vienna, 1927), pp. 304ff.

475. J. von Schlosser, "Geschichte der Portraitbildnerei in Wachs," *Jahrbuch der Kunsthistorischen Sammlungen des Allerhoechsten Kaiserhauses*, XXIX (1911), pp. 255ff.

476. J. von Schlosser, "Kuenstlerprobleme der Fruehrenaissance," 3. Heft. v. Stueck, "Lorenzo Ghiberti," *Akademie der Wissenschaften in Wien, Philosophisch-historische Klasse*, CCXV, 4 (1934), pp. 3ff.

477. J. von Schlosser, *Leben und Meinungen des Florentinischen Bildners Lorenzo Ghiberti*, Basel, 1941.

478. J. von Schlosser, "Lorenzo Ghiberti's Denkwuerdigkeiten, Prolegomena zu einer kuenftigen Ausgabe," *Kunstgeschichtliches Jahrbuch der K. K. Zentralkommission*, IV (1910), pp. 105ff.

479. J. von Schlosser, "Ueber einige Antiken Ghiberti's," *Jahrbuch der Kunsthistorischen Sammlungen des Allerhoechsten Kaiserhauses*, XXIV (1903), pp. 25ff.

480. J. von Schlosser, "Ein Veroneser Bilderbuch der höfischen Kunst des XIV. Jahrhunderts," *Jahrbuch der Kunsthistorischen Sammlungen des Allerhoechsten Kaiserhauses*, XVI (1895), pp. 144ff.

481. J. von Schlosser, "Die Werkstatt der Embriachi," *Jahrbuch der Kunsthistorischen Sammlungen des Allerhoechsten Kaiserhauses*, XX (1899), pp. 200ff.

482. A. Schmarsow, "Ghiberti's Kompositionsgesetze an der Nordtuer des Florentiner Baptisteriums," *Kgl. Saechsische Gesellschaft der Wissenschaften, Abhandlungen der Philosophisch-Historischen Klasse*, XVIII, 4, Leipzig, 1899, pp. 1ff.

483. A. Schmarsow, *Italienische Kunst im Zeitalter Dantes*, Augsburg, 1928.

484. A. Schmarsow, "Juliano Florentino, ein Mitarbeiter Ghiberti's in Valencia," *Sächsische Akademie der Wissenschaften, Abhandlungen der Philosophisch-Historischen Klasse*, XXIX, 3 (1911), pp. 1ff.

485. A. Schmarsow, "Die Statuen an Or San Michele," *Festschrift zu Ehren des Kunsthistorischen Instituts in Florenz*, Leipzig, 1897.

486. A. Schmarsow, "Vier Statuetten in der Domopera zu Florenz," *Jahrbuch der Preussischen Kunstsammlungen*, VIII (1887), pp. 137ff.

487. F. Schottmueller, *s. v.* Ghiberti, Lorenzo, in: Thieme-Becker, bibl. 517, XIII, pp. 541ff.

488. P. Schubring, *Cassoni*, Leipzig, 1915.

489. M. Semrau, "Notiz zu Ghiberti," *Repertorium für Kunstwissenschaft*, L (1929), pp. 151ff.

490. L. Serra, *L'Arte nelle Marche*, Pesaro, 1929.

491. B. S. Sgrilli, *Descrizione e studj della . . . fabrica di S. Maria del Fiore . . .* , Florence, 1733.

492. F. R. Shapley and C. K. Kennedy, "Brunelleschi in Competition with Ghiberti," *Art Bulletin*, v (1922-23), pp. 31ff.

493. D. C. Shorr, "The Mourning Virgin and St. John," *Art Bulletin*, XXII (1940), pp. 61ff.

494. G. Sinibaldi, "Come Lorenzo Ghiberti sentisse Giotto e Ambrogio Lorenzetti," *L'Arte*, XXXI (1928), pp. 8of.

495. O. Sirén, "Ghiberti's förste Bronzeporte," *Tilskueren*, xxv (1908), pp. 834ff.

496. O. Sirén, *Don Lorenzo Monaco*, Strasbourg, 1905.

497. O. Sirén, "Due Madonne della bottega del Ghiberti," *Rivista d'arte*, v (1907), pp. 48ff.

498. O. Sirén, *Studier i Florentinsk Renässansskulptur . . .* , Stockholm, 1909.

499. A. H. Smith, *A Catalogue of Sculpture in the Department of Greek and Roman Antiquities in the British Museum*, III, London, 1904.

500. (Sopraintendenza alle Gallerie . . . di Firenze, Arezzo e Pistoja), *Mostra di opere d'arte trasportate a Firenze . . . e di opere d'arte restaurate . . .* , Florence, 1947.

501. C. Spicq, *Esquisse d'une histoire de l'exégèse latine au moyen-âge (Bibliothèque Thomiste, XXVI)*, Paris, 1944.

502. C. von Stegmann and H. von Geymueller, *Die Architektur der Renaissance in Toscana*, Munich, 1885ff.

503. H. Steigemann, *De Polybii olympiadum ratione et oeconomia*, Breslau, 1885.

504. A. Stix and L. Froehlich-Bum, *Beschreibender Katalog der Handzeichnungen in der . . . Albertina*, III, *Die Zeichnungen der Toskanischen, Umbrischen und Römischen Schulen*, Vienna, 1932.

505. A. Stix, *Handzeichnungen aus der Albertina, N. F. II. Italienische Meister des XV bis XVI Jahrhunderts*, v, Vienna, 1928.

506. A. Stix, "Eine Zeichnung von Lorenzo Ghiberti," *Kunstchronik und Kunstmarkt*, N. F. XXXV (1925-26), pp. 139ff.

507. L. Stornaiolo, *Le miniature della Topografia Cristiana di Cosma Indicopleuste*, Milan, 1918.

508. K. van Straelen, *Studien zur Florentiner Glasmalerei des Trecento und Quattrocento (Lebensräume der Kunst, v)*, Diss. Münster, Wattenscheid, 1938.

509. E. Strong, *Art in Ancient Rome*, New York, 1928.

510. E. Strong, "Six Drawings from the column of Trajan with the date 1467 and a note on the date of Giacomo Ripanda," *Papers of the British School at Rome*, VI (1913), pp. 174ff.

511. F. Susemihl, *Geschichte der griechischen Literatur der Alexanderzeit*, Leipzig, 1892.

512. G. Swarzenski, "A bronze statuette of St. Christopher," *Bulletin of the Museum of Fine Arts* (Boston), XLIX (1951), pp. 84ff.

513. G. Swarzenski, "Der Kölner Meister bei Ghiberti," *Vorträge der Bibliothek Warburg*, 1926-27, Leipzig, 1930, pp. 22ff.

514. G. Swarzenski, "Insinuationes Divinae Pietatis," *Festschrift Adolph Goldschmidt*, Leipzig, 1923, pp. 65ff.

515. K. M. Swoboda, *Peter Parler*, Vienna, 1943.

516. H. Taine, *Voyage en Italie*, 17th ed., Paris, n.d.

517. U. Thieme and F. Becker, *Allgemeines Lexikon der bildenden Künstler . . .* , Leipzig, 1907ff; quoted as *Thieme-Becker*.

518. H. Tietze ed., *Österreichische Kunsttopographie*, XXIII; *Geschichte und Beschreibung des St. Stephansdomes in Wien*, Vienna, 1931.

519. E. Tietze-Conrat, "Botticelli and the Antique," *Burlington Magazine*, XLVII (1925), pp. 124ff.

520. P. Toesca, *La pittura e la miniatura lombarda*, Milan, 1912.

521. P. Toesca, "Michelino di Besozzo e Giovannino de' Grassi," *L'Arte*, VIII (1905), pp. 321ff.

522. P. Toesca, *Il Trecento*, Turin (1951).

523. N. Tommaseo, *Dizionario della lingua italiana*, Turin, 1861ff.

524. A. Della Torre, *Storia dell'Accademia Platonica di Firenze (Pubblicazione del R. Istituto di Studi Superiori . . . in Firenze, Sezione di Filosofia e Filologia, 28)*, Florence, 1902.

525. G. B. Toschi, "Le Porte del Paradiso," *Nuova Antologia di science, lettere ed arti*, ser. 2, xv (1879), pp. 449ff.

526. Ambrogio Traversari (Ambrosius Traversarius), *Latinae Epistolae . . .* , ed. P. Cannetus and L. Mehus, Florence, 1759.

527. C. L. Urlichs, *Codex Urbis Romae topographicus*, Würzburg, 1871.

528. P. Vaccarini, *Nanni di Banco* (Florence, 1950).

529. W. R. Valentiner, *Studies of Italian Renaissance Sculpture*, London, 1950.

530. B. Varchi, *Storia Fiorentina*, Cologne, 1721.

531. Giorgio Vasari, *Le Vite de' piu eccellenti architetti, pittori et scultori Italiani*, Florence, 1550, reprint, ed. C. Ricci, Milan and Rome, 1927.

532. Giorgio Vasari, *Le vite de' piu eccellenti pittori, scultori ɔ architettori*, ed. K. Frey, I, 1, Munich, 1911; quoted as *Frey*.

533. Giorgio Vasari, *Le vite de' piu eccellenti pittori, scultori ed architettori* (*Le opere di G. Vasari*: I-VII, *Le Vite*; VIII, *I ragionamenti e lettere*), Florence, 1878ff; quoted as *Vasari-Milanesi*.

534. A. Venturi, *Storia dell'arte italiana*, Milan, 1901ff.

535. L. Venturi, "Lorenzo Ghiberti," *L'Arte*, XXVI (1923), pp. 233ff.

536. U. Verini, *De illustratione urbis Florentiae libri tres*, Florence, 1636.

537. O. Vessberg, *Studien zur Kunstgeschichte der roemischen Republik* (*Acta Instituti Romani Regni Sveciae,* VIII), Lund and Leipzig, 1941.

538. G. Villani, *Istorie fiorentine . . .* (*Classici italiani,* X-XVII), Milan, 1802ff.

539. C. Vincenzi, "Di tre foglie di disegni quattrocenteschi dall'antico," *Rassegna d'arte*, X (1910), pp. 6ff.

540. M. Vitruvius Pollio, *Vitruvius on Architecture*, ed. F. Granger (*Loeb Classical Library*), London and New York, 1934ff.

541. G. Voigt, *Die Wiederbelebung des Classischen Alterthums*, 3rd ed., Berlin, 1893.

542. J. J. Volkmann, *Historisch-Kritische Nachrichten von Italien* (first published 1770), Leipzig, 1777.

543. M. Wackernagel, *Der Lebensraum des Künstlers in der Florentinischen Renaissance*, Leipzig, 1938.

544. E. Walser, *Poggius Florentinus, Leben und Werke.* (*Beiträge zur Kulturgeschichte des Mittelalters und der Renaissance,* 14), Leipzig and Berlin, 1914.

545. A. Warburg, *Gesammelte Schriften*, Leipzig and Berlin, 1932.

546. (Sir) George Warner, *Queen Mary's Psalter*, London, 1912.

547. K. Wegner, "Bemerkungen zu den Ehrendenkmälern des Marcus Aurelius," *Deutsches Archaeologisches Institut, Archaeologischer Anzeiger*, LIII (1938), cols. 155ff.

548. G. Weise, "Gli archi mistilinei di provenienza islamica nell'architettura gotica italiana . . . ," *Rivista d'arte*, XXIII (1941), pp. 1ff.

549. A. S. Weller, *Francesco di Giorgio*, Chicago (1943).

550. (P. Wescher), *Beschreibendes Verzeichnis der Miniaturen . . . des Kupferstichkabinetts der staatlichen Museen Berlin . . .* , Leipzig, 1931.

551. A. Wesselski, *Angelo Poliziano's Tagebuch*, Jena, 1929.

552. J. White, "Developments in Renaissance Perspective," *Journal of the Warburg and Courtauld Institutes*, XII (1949), pp. 58ff; XIV (1951), pp. 42ff.

553. (W. von Hartel and) F. Wickhoff, *Die Wiener Genesis*, Vienna, 1895.

554. H. Wieleitner, "Zur Erfindung der verschiedenen Distanzkonstruktionen," *Repertorium für Kunstwissenschaft*, XLII (1920), pp. 249ff.

555. E. Wind, "The Revival of Origen," *Studies in Art and Literature for Belle Da Costa Greene*, Princeton, 1954, pp. 412ff.

556. F. Winkler, "Paul de Limbourg in Florence," *Burlington Magazine*, LVI (1930), pp. 95f.

557. R. Wittkower, *Architectural Principles in the Age of Humanism*, London, 1949.

558. R. Wittkower, "Brunelleschi and 'Proportion in Perspective,'" *Journal of the Warburg and Courtauld Institutes*, XVI (1953), pp. 275ff.

559. O. Wulff, "Ghiberti's Entwicklung im Madonnenrelief," *Amtliche Berichte der Berliner Museen* (*Beiblatt zum Jahrbuch der Preussischen Kunstsammlungen*), XLIII (1922), pp. 91ff.

560. O. Wulff, "Giovanni d'Antonio di Banco," *Jahrbuch der Preussischen Kunstsammlungen*, XXXIV (1913), pp. 99ff.

561. M. Ziegelbauer, *Centifolium Camaldulense*, Venice, 1750.

562. G. Zippel, "Paolo II e l'arte," *L'Arte*, XIII (1910), pp. 241ff.

563. G. Zocchi, *Scelta di XXIV vedute . . . di Firenze*, Florence, 1754.

ADDITIONAL BIBLIOGRAPHY

1. Anonymous Reviewer, *Times Literary Supplement*, XXVI (April 26, 1957), p. 254.
2. M. C. Mendes Atanasio, "Documenti inediti riguardanti la Porta del Paradiso e Tommaso di Lorenzo Ghiberti," *Commentari* (1963), pp. 92ff.
3. K. Bloom, "Lorenzo Ghiberti's Space in Relief: Method and Theory," *Art Bulletin*, LI (1969), pp. 164-169.
4. M. Boskovits, "Quello ch'e dipintor oggi dicono prospettiva, Contribution to 15th Century art theory," *Acta Hist. Artium*, VIII (1962), pp. 241-260 and IX (1963), pp. 139-162.
5. G. Brunetti, *Ghiberti*, Florence, 1966.
6. A. Carandini, *Vibia Sabina, la funzione politica, l'iconografia dell'Augusta e il problema del classicismo adrianeo*, Florence, 1969.
7. M. Ciardi-Dupré, "Sulla collaborazione di Benozzo Gozzoli a la porta del Paradiso," *Antichità Viva*, VI (1967), pp. 6off.
8. A. Chastel, "L' 'Etruscan Revival' du XVe siècle," *Revue Archéologique*, series 3, I (1959), pp. 165-180.
9. A. Chastel, "Mésure et demésure dans la sculpture florentine au XVe siècle," *Critique* (1958), pp. 960-975.
10. K. Clark, review, *Burlington Magazine*, C (1958), pp. 175-178.
11. M. Dalai, "La questione della prospettiva," *L'Arte*, Rassegna, n.s. I (1968), pp. 96-105.
12. E. De'Negri, "Un libro sul Ghiberti," *Critica d'Arte*, XXX (1958), pp. 489-496.
13. B. Degenhart and A. Schmitt, "Gentile da Fabriano in Rom und die Anfänge des Antikenstudiums. Antikennachzeichnung," *Münchner Jahrbuch für Bildende Kunst*, II (1960), pp. 59-151.
14. B. Degenhart and A. Schmitt, *Corpus der italienischen Handzeichnungen*, Berlin, 1968.
15. G. Fiocco, "Le porte d'oro del Ghiberti," *Rinascimento*, VII (1956), pp. 3-11.
16. C. Gilbert, "The Archbishop and the Painters of Florence, 1450," *Art Bulletin*, XLI (1959), pp. 75-87.
17. C. Gilbert, "When Did a Man in the Renaissance Grow Old?" *Studies in the Renaissance*, XIV (1967), pp. 7-32.
18. D. Gioseffi, "Complementi di prospettiva," *Critica d'Arte*, XXIII-XXIV (1957), pp. 468-488; XXV-XXVI (1958), pp. 102-149.
19. D. Gioseffi, *Perspectiva artificialis. Per la Storia della Prospettiva, spigolature e apunti*, Trieste, 1957.
20. E. Gombrich, "The Renaissance Concept of Artistic Progress and its Consequences," *Actes du XVIIe Congrès International d'Histoire de l'Art, Amsterdam, 23-31 juillet 1952*, The Hague, 1955, pp. 291-307.
21. E. Gombrich, review, *Apollo* (July, 1957), pp. 306-307.
22. E. Gombrich, *Norm and Form, Studies in the Art of the Renaissance*, London, 1966.
23. C. Grayson, "L. B. Alberti's 'costruzione legittima'," *Italian Studies*, XIX (1964), pp. 14-27.
24. F. Hartt, "The Earliest Works of Andrea del Castagno," *Art Bulletin*, XLI (1959), pp. 159-181 and 225-236.
25. H. W. Janson, *Donatello*, Princeton, 1957.
26. H. W. Janson, review, *Renaissance News*, X (1957), pp. 103-105.
27. H. W. Janson, "Donatello and the Antique," *Donatello e il suo tempo*, Florence, 1968, pp. 77-96.
28. J. Jantzen, "Kleinplastische Bronzeportraits des 15. bis 16. Jahrhunderts und ihre Formen," *Zeitschrift des Deutschen Vereins für Kunstwissenschaft*, XVII (1963), pp. 111-112.
29. R. Krautheimer, "Terracotta Madonnas," *Parnassus*, VIII, 7 (1936), pp. 5-8, and *Collected Essays*, New York (1969), pp. 315ff.
30. R. Krautheimer, "Die Anfänge der Kunstgeschichtsschreibung in Italien," *Repertorium für Kunstwissenschaft*, L, pt. 2 (1929), pp. 49-63, and as "The Beginnings of Art Historical Writing in Italy," *Collected Essays*, New York, 1969, pp. 257ff.
31. T. Krautheimer-Hess, "More Ghibertiana," *Art Bulletin*, XLVI (1964), pp. 307-321.
32. O. Kurz, review, *Gazette des Beaux-Arts* (1958), p. 364.
33. S. Lang, " 'De Lineamentis'—L. B. Alberti's use of a technical term," *Warburg and Courtauld Journal*, XXVII (1965), pp. 331-335.
34. E. Loeffler, "A Famous Antique: A Roman Sarcophagus at the Los Angeles Museum," *Art Bulletin*, XXXIX (1957), pp. 1ff.
35. W. Lotz, review, *Saturday Review* (March 16, 1957), pp. 13-14.
36. B. Lowry, review, *College Art Journal*, XVIII (1959), pp. 184-187.

37. G. Marchini, *Italian Stained Glass Windows*, New York, 1957.

38. G. Marchini, "Ghiberti Ante Litteram," *Bollettino d'Arte*, 50, III-IV (1965), pp. 181-193.

39. F. Matz, *Die Dionysischen Sarkophage*, II, Berlin, 1968.

40. U. Middeldorf, "L'Angelico e la Scultura," *Rinascimento*, VI (1955), pp. 179-194.

41. U. Middeldorf, "Su alcuni bronzetti all'antica del Quattrocento," *Il mondo antico nel Rinascimento (Atti del V convegno internazionale di studi sul rinascimento, Firenze, 2-6 settembre, 1956)* Florence, 1958, pp. 167-177.

42. Geza von Österreich, *Die Rundfenster des Lorenzo Ghiberti*, Ph.D. thesis, Fribourg, 1965.

43. E. Panofsky, *Renaissance and Renascences in Western Art*, Stockholm, 1960, pp. 118-145.

44. A. Parronchi, "La Croce dei Pisani," *Studi su la dolce Prospettiva*, Milan, 1964, pp. 156-181.

45. A. Parronchi, "Le misure dell'occhio secondo il Ghiberti," *Paragone*, 123 (1961), pp. 18-48.

46. J. Pope-Hennessy, *Catalogue of Italian Sculpture in the Victoria and Albert Museum*, London, 1964, vol. 1, 8th-15th centuries.

47. J. Pope-Hennessy, *An Introduction to Italian Sculpture*, 3 parts, London, 1955-1962.

48. L. Portier, review, *Revue des études italiennes*, nn. 2-3 (1959), pp. 222-224.

49. C. Ragghianti, review, *Sele Arte*, 40 (1959), pp. 38-56.

50. C. Ragghianti, "Aenigmata Pistoriensia," *Critica d'Arte*, V (1954), pp. 423-438.

51. M. Salmi, "Lorenzo Ghiberti e Mariotto di Nardo," *Rivista d'Arte* (1955), pp. 147-152.

52. M. Salmi, "Lorenzo Ghiberti e la pittura," *Scritti di storia dell'arte in onore di Lionello Venturi*, Roma, 1956, pp. 223-237.

53. G. Scaglia, "Drawings of Brunelleschi's Mechanical Inventions for the Construction of the Cupola," *Marsyas*, X (1960-1961), pp. 45-63.

54. G. Scaglia, *Studies in the 'Zibaldone' of Buonaccorso Ghiberti*, thesis, unpubl., New York University, Institute of Fine Arts, 1960.

55. G. Scaglia, "Drawings of Machines for Architecture from the Early Quattrocento in Italy," *Journal of the Society of Architectural Historians*, XXV (1966), pp. 90-114.

56. C. Seymour, "The Younger Masters of the First Campaign of the Porta della Mandorla," *Art Bulletin*, XLI (1959), pp. 1-17.

57. C. Seymour, *Sculpture in Italy, 1400-1500*, Harmondsworth and Baltimore, 1966.

58. C. Seymour, "Some Aspects of Donatello's Methods of Figure and Space Constructions. Relationships with Alberti's 'De Statua' and 'Della Pittura'," *Donatello e il suo tempo*, Florence, 1968, pp. 195-206.

59. W. Smith, "Definitions of Statua," *Art Bulletin*, L (1968), pp. 263-267.

60. J. Spencer, "Volterra, 1466," *Art Bulletin*, XLVIII (1966), pp. 95-96.

61. E. Steingräber, "A Madonna Relief by Michele da Firenze," *The Connoisseur* (1957-1958), pp. 166ff.

62. E. Steingräber, "The Pistoia Silver Altar, a Re-examination," *The Connoisseur* (1955-1956), pp. 152ff.

63. E. Steingräber, review, *Zeitschrift für Kunstgeschichte*, XXI (1958), pp. 271-274.

64. F. Taylor, review, *New York Herald Tribune Literary Magazine*, April 21, 1957, p. 3.

65. M. Trachtenberg, "An Antique Model for Donatello's Marble David," *Art Bulletin*, L (1968), pp. 268-269.

66. L. Vayer, "*L'imago pietatis* di Lorenzo Ghiberti," *Acta Hist. Artium*, VIII (1962), pp. 45-53.

67. C. Vermeule, *European Art and the Classical Past*, Cambridge, 1964.

68. J. White, *The Birth and Rebirth of Pictorial Space*, 2nd ed., Boston, 1967.

69. M. Wundram, "Albizzo di Pietro, Studien zur Bauplastik von Or San Michele in Florenz," *Das Werk des Künstlers, Festschrift H. Schrade*, 1960, pp. 161-176.

70. M. Wundram, *Die Künstlerische Entwicklung im Reliefstil Lorenzo Ghibertis*, Ph.D. thesis, Göttingen, 1952.

71. M. Wundram, "Der Meister der Verkündigung in der Domopera zu Florenz," *Festgabe für H. R. Rosemann*, Munich, 1960, pp. 109-121.

72. M. Wundram, "Niccolo di Pietro Lamberti und die Florentiner Plastik um 1400," *Jahrbuch der Berliner Museen* (1962), pp. 78-115.

73. M. Wundram, *Die Paradiestür*, Stuttgart, 1962.

INDEX

Adam, John and Robert, 294

Adam of Eaton, Bishop of Hertford, 358n

Adonis sarcophagus, *see* Roman sculpture, sarcophagi

Agincourt, Seroux d', 22

Alamandi, Ludovico, Archbishop of Arles, 358n

Albani Collection (former), *see* Rome, Capitoline Collections, *Kneeling Son of Niobe*

Albergati, Cardinal Niccolo, 317-18, 321

Alberti, Leone Battista, 28, 150, 236, 240n, 246, 248, 267n, 268n, 269-71, 274, 276-77, 288, 293, 304, 310, 315-34, 346; linear perspective of, 244n, 245-47, 248n, 252-53, 273; appointed to Priorate of S. Martino in Gangalanda, 318

    Architecture: Florence, S. Maria Novella, 272n; Mantua, S. Andrea, 272; Mantua, S. Sebastiano, 272; Rimini, S. Francesco, 270n, 271, 272n, 317

    Writings: *De commodis litterarum atque incommodis*, 317n; *De Equo animante*, 269n; *Della Famiglia*, 270n, 274, 310, 315-16, 317n; *Della Pittura*, 229, 232, 234, 244-45, 247, 250-51, 273, 301n, 311, 313, 315-17, 319-20, 322-26, 328-29, 331-34; *De Re Aedificatoria*, 230, 232, 268-71, 273-74, 311, 313, 317n, 324, 330; *Descriptio urbis Romae*, 315-16, 322n; *De Statua*, 311, 322n; *Intercoenales*, 269n; *Ludi mathematici*, 269n; *Philodoxis*, 317n, 318; *see also* antiquity, architecture; antiquity, art of; terminology

Albertini, Francesco, 18

Albizzi family, 33

Albizzo di Piero, 74n

Alcherius, Johannes, 58

Alcuin Bible, *see* Paris, Bibliothèque Nationale

Alexander the Great, portrait type, 341

Alhazen, 307

all 'antica, see antiquity, art of

Altenburg, Staatliches Museum, *Reclining Eve, see* Lorenzetti, Ambrogio, and Iconography; *Flight into Egypt, see* Monaco, Lorenzo

Altoetting, *Golden Roessel*, 65

Altoviti family, 365

Ambrose, Saint, 175, 177-80, 187, 216; *De Abraham*, 174n, 176; *De bono mortis*, 176; *De Cain et Abel*, 175-76; *De fuga saeculi*, 176; *De Isaac et anima*, 176; *De Jacob et vita beata*, 176; *De Joseph Patriarcha*, 176; *De Noe et Arca*, 176; *De Paradiso*, 175; *De Virginitate*, 174n; *Hexaemeron*, 175

Amiens Cathedral, foliage decoration of nave, 61

Amsterdam, formerly Gutmann Collection, *imago pietatis* reliquary, 65

Andrea da Firenze, 139n, 219; Pisa, Camposanto, frescoes, 221; Florence, S. Maria Novella, Spanish Chapel, frescoes, *Via Veritatis, Crucifixion, Way to Calvary*, 215, 221-22, 224, 258n

Angelico, Fra, 181; Florence, Museo San Marco, Linaiuoli Altar (frame design by Ghiberti), 6, 261n, 264, 361

Angelo d'Arezzo, 256

Angers, Tapestries of the Apocalypse, 56, 60, 63; *Saint John Eating the Book*, 60; *Dragon Threatening the Woman*, 60

Anonimo Magliabecchiano, 19-20, 39, 62n, 75n, 87n, 306, 354, 357

antiquity, architecture, influence of: on Alberti, 269-75; on Brunelleschi, 262-63, 273; on Donatello, 263-64, 273; on Ghiberti, 258-60, 262, 264-65, 273, 330, 334. *See also* Roman architecture

antiquity, art of, 25n, 279, 287, 293, 316; early revival in Venice, 278; impression made on Ghiberti, 278, 301, 314; known to the Renaissance, 337-57; Renaissance, image of, 90; Renaissance tool, 89. *See also* Roman art; Roman sculpture; Trecento, influence on Ghiberti; *influence*: on Alberti, 272-74, 315, 322, 324, 330; on Nanni di Banco, 83, 86, 90, 91, 100; on Brunelleschi, 45, 53, 273, 281-83; on city representations, 198, 267n; on Donatello, 90, 91, 273; on Florentine artists, 208, 273, 279, 304-5, 323;

on Vittorio Ghiberti, 212; on Hercules master, 52-53, 281-83; on Lorenzetti workshop, 218; on medals of Duc de Berry, 59; on Middle Ages, 297-98; on Pisanello, 288, 337, 349, 351; on Porta della Mandorla, 279, 280, 281; on Trecento 225, 286, 290, 292, 342, 343; on Lorenzo Ghiberti, 28, 49, 137, 260, 275, 277-93, 337-52; competition relief, 53, 281, 283-84; East Door, 210, 218, 225; architectural settings, 258, 262, 265, 273, 330, 334; figures and draperies, 181, 195, 332; North Door, 92, 127, 283-84; *Saint Matthew*, 87-89, 92; Roman trips, influence of, 288, 330, 332

Antonine, Saint, *Summa Theologica*, 187n, 188n

Antonio di Tommaso, 110n

Apelles, 309

Apuleius, 325

Aragazzi, Bartolomeo, 321

Arbois, Jean, 58

Arbury Hall, Newgate College, Bacchic sarcophagus, *see* Roman sculpture, sarcophagi

Aretine vases, 298

Arezzo, Museum, *Pax* with *imago pietatis*, 65

Aristotle, *Poetics*, 316

Arnolfo di Cambio, 94n

art nouveau, 26-27

Arte di Calimala, etc., *see* Guilds

Arthurian cycles, 77-78

Assisi, S. Francesco, *see* Lorenzetti, Pietro

Athenaios, Tà 'Οργανικà, 308, 310-12, 332

Athens, Duke of, 33

Augustine, Saint, 173, 175, 178, 185, 216; *De catechizandis rusticis*, 173n; *De Civitate Dei*, 174n, 176; *Enarratio in Psalmos*, 173, 174n

Aurispa, 308, 311-12, 332

Averroës, 307-8

Avicenna, 307

Baboccio (Antonio da Priverno), 62n

Bacchic sarcophagi, *see* Roman sculpture, sarcophagi

Bacon, Roger, 307-8

Badia di Settimo, frescoes, *see* Bonamico (Buffalmacco)

Baerze, Jacques de, *see* Dijon, Museum, Altar

Baese, Arduino del, 261n

Baldinucci, Filippo, 11, 21, 27, 73, 75n, 97, 110, 360, 365

Baldovinetti, Alessandro, Florence, S. Miniato, Chapel of the Cardinal of Portugal, frescoes, 186n

Balduccio da Pisa, Giovanni, Florence, S. Croce, Berlinghieri Tomb, *Annunciation*, 99

Baltimore, Walters Art Gallery, Architectural panel, Luciano di Laurana (attributed), 268-69, 272-73

Bamberg Cathedral, Tomb of Bishop Hohenlohe, 147n; *Visitation*, 297

Banco, Antonio di, Florence Cathedral, Porta della Mandorla, archivolt, 83

Banco, Nanni di, 17n, 52n, 53n, 83, 84n; Florence Cathedral, Porta della Mandorla, Tympanum, 90, 100; *Isaiah*, 83, 90-91; Museo dell'Opera, *Saint Luke*, 71-72, 83; Or San Michele, *Quattro Coronati*, 72, 84, 86, 90-91, 137, 143, *Saint Eligius*, 72, 84, 90-91, *Saint Peter* (with Donatello?), 72, *Saint Philip*, 72, 84, 86, 90-91, 97n; *see also* antiquity, art of

Bandinelli, Baccio, 19

Bandino di Stefano, 108, 110n

Barbarian heads, *see* Roman sculpture, sarcophagi

Barbo, Cardinal Pietro, *see* Paul II, Pope

Barna da Siena, 56, 218, 223, 309

Barnaba di Francesco, 110n

Bartoli, Cosimo, 20, 244n

Bartolo di Fredi, 55; Montalcino, Museo Civico, Altarpiece, *Assumption*, 55, 76, 215; San Gimignano, Collegiata, Old Testament cycle, 175, 176n, 221-23, 225, 345

Bartolo di Michele, foster father of Lorenzo Ghiberti, 3-5, 36, 41, 51, 105, 106, 108, 110n, 121n, 137, 139, 360

Bartolomeo di Luca, father-in-law of Lorenzo Ghiberti, 4

Bartoluccio, *see* Bartolo di Michele

Battista d'Antonio, 254-56

Battle sarcophagi, *see* Roman sculpture, sarcophagi

Baume-les-Messieurs, *Saint Paul*, 79

Beardsley, Aubrey, 26

Bearzi, Cavaliere Bruno, 46n, 75n, 116n, 133n, 139n, 164

Beatrix of Tuscany, tomb of, *see* Pisa, Camposanto, Phaedra sarcophagus and Roman sculpture, sarcophagi

Beau Bréviaire of Charles V, Paris, Bibliothèque Nationale, 61

Becchi, Michele, 93

"bel San Giovanni," *see* Florence, Baptistery

Bellano, Bartolomeo, 18

Bellini, Jacopo, Sketchbook, drawing of Samson, 349

Bellori, Giovanni Pietro, 294

Benevento Cathedral, bronze doors, New Testament cycle, 114n

Benvenuto da Imola, 287n

Berardi, Cristofano, 365

Berenson Collection, *see* Monaco, Lorenzo

Bergamo, Museo Civico, model book, *Boar Hunt*, 59. See also Giovannino de'Grassi

Berlin, Kaiser Friedrich Museum, *Desco di Parto* (perspective construction), 245n

———, Kupferstichkabinett, *see* Dosio, Giovanni Antonio

———, Staatsbibliothek, Hamilton Bible, 39; Codex Pighianus, 338

Bernard of Clairvaux, 185

Bernardino of Siena, 178

Bernardo di Stefano, Fra, 74n, 79n

Beroldo Manuscript, *see* Milan, Biblioteca Visconti

Berry, Jean Duc de, 58, 63, 300

Bertoldo di Giovanni, Florence, Bargello, bronze relief after Roman battle sarcophagus, 341, 349

Besozzo, Michelino da, 58, 79

Bessarion, Cardinal, 184

Biblia Pauperum, 39n, 173-74

Bicci di Lorenzo, 259; New York, Metropolitan Museum of Art, Saint Nicolaus panels, 259n

Bisticci, Vespasiano de', 183, 304

Black Death, *see* Pestilence of 1348

Blenheim Castle, Bacchic sarcophagus, *see* Roman sculpture, sarcophagi

Boccaccio, Giovanni, 310

Bocchi, Francesco, 18, 21, 97

Bode, Wilhelm, 26-27

Bologna, Giovanni da, 71n

Bologna, Museo Civico, Legnano Tomb, 57; S. Maria de' Servi, Manfredi Tomb, 57

Bologna, University of, 315, 317-18

Bonamico (Buffalmacco), 309, 353-54, 357-58; Badia di Set-timo, frescoes (lost), 357; Porta a Faenza, frescoes (lost), 357

Bonannus, Monreale Cathedral, bronze door, Old Testament cycle, 114n, 177n, 218; Pisa, Cathedral, bronze door, *Life of Christ*, 114, 218

Bondol, Jean (Hennequin de Bruges), 55-56, 60

Boninsegni, Domenico, 16

Boston, Museum of Fine Arts, *Saint Christopher*, bronze, 83-84

Botticelli, Alessandro, Florence, Uffizi, *Primavera*, 325, 334, 346; London, National Gallery, *Venus and Mars*, 333, 351; Rome, Sistine Chapel, *Sacrifice of the Leper*, 333

Boucicaut Master (Jacques Coene?), 58n, 78

Bracciolino, Poggio, *see* Poggio Bracciolino, Giovanni

Branda da Castiglione, Cardinal, 320

Broccardi, Mona Caterina (widow of Piero Broccardi, 111, 112, 116n

Broccardi, Piero, 111, 112, 116n

Brockhaus, Heinrich, 26

Broederlam, Melchior, *see* Dijon, Museum, Altar

De Brosses, President Charles, 21

Brunelleschi, Filippo, 5, 7-9, 12, 17, 19, 23, 25, 35-36, 38-42, 50-51, 66, 89, 139n, 234, 256, 263, 267, 272-73, 302, 304, 316, 318-21, 323; and Alberti, perspective method, 229n, 234-48, 251

Works: Florence Cathedral, dome, 15, 254-56, 263, 274, 323; design for choir, 256, 257n; Sepulcher of Saint Zenobius, design of architecture, 141; Hospital of the Innocents, 262, 265-66, 275, 319; Palazzo di Parte Guelfe, 262, 266, 275; Pazzi Chapel, 262, 265; Bargello, competition panel, *Sacrifice of Isaac*, 42-49, 50-53, 66, 278, 281-83, 299; S. Lorenzo, 257n, 262n, 266, 275; Sagrestia Vecchia, 262, 264-65, 268, 275-76; S. Maria degli Angeli, 33, 263; S. Spirito, 35n, 262n, 263, 266, 275; Pistoia, Silver Altar of San Jacopo, Prophets, 59, 90; perspective paintings, 234-48. See also antiquity, architecture; Early Christian basilicas; Manetti, Antonio di Tuccio; *Vita di Brunellesco*

Bruni, Leonardo, 37, 154, 161, 164, 169, 171-72, 174-76, 178,

180, 187, 279, 302n, 310, 321, 332, 363; *Commentarii de Bello Punico*, 356; program for East Door, Florence Baptistery, 114, 159-72, 174-76, 180, 217, 225, 302

Brussels, Bibliothèque Royale, *Brussels Hours*, 78; Musées Royaux, Pelops sarcophagus, *see* Roman sculpture, sarcophagi

Burckhardt, Jacob, 25, 27, 97; *Der Cicerone*, 24

Byzantine style, Ghiberti's discussion of, 309, 357

Cambi, Giovanni, *Istorie*, 16
Campania, School of, 297
Campione, Jacopo da, Milan Cathedral, *Salvator Mundi in His Glory*, 57, 59
Campione, S. Maria de'Ghirli, *Last Judgment*, Franco and Filippolo de'Veris, 79
Capuan workshop, 297
Caravaggio, Polidoro da, Munich, Graphische Sammlung, Drawing after Bacchic sarcophagus, 344, *see* Roman sculpture, sarcophagi, London
Carelli Tomb, *see* Milan, S. Eustorgio
Carracci, the, 294
Carrara herbal, *see* London, British Museum
Carocci, Giovanni, 26
Cassel, Museum, *see* Roman sculpture, Victory statuette, Zeus statuette
Castel del Sangro, reliefs, *see* Florence, Cathedral, Museo dell'Opera
Catasto (Portate al Catasto), 3, 7, 8, 111, 112, 162, 163, 360. *See also* Ghiberti, *Catasto* and Guilds, *Arte di Calimala*
Castiglione d'Olona, frescoes, Masolino, 259n
Cavallini, Pietro, 309; Rome, S. Maria in Trastevere, apse mosaics, 357
Cellini, Benvenuto, 20
Cennini, Bernardo, 232
Cennini, Cennino, 315, 316n
Cennini, Piero, 17
Challante, Antoine de, 358n
Charlemagne, *see* Paris, Louvre, Scepter of Charles V
Charles IV, German Emperor, *see* Vienna, Rathausmuseum, statue of
Charles V, King of France, 63, 133, 297. *See also* Paris, Louvre, statues from the Quinze-Vingt

Charles VI, King of France, 65
chivalric romances, 298
Chrysobergi, Andrea, Archbishop of Colossos, Bishop of Rhodes, 184
Chrysoloras, Manuel, 279
Cicero, manuscripts of, 312n
Cicognara, Luigi, 23-24
Cimabue, 309
Ciompi revolt, 78
Cione Paltami di Ser Buonaccorso Ghiberti, father of Lorenzo, *see* Ghiberti, Cione Paltami
Ciriaco d'Ancona, 300-1, 305
Cité de Dieu, Paris, Bibliothèque Nationale, 61
Città di Castello, Galleria Municipale, reliquary of Saint Andrew, 119, 130n. *See also* Ghiberti, Lorenzo, *Works* (attributed to), statuettes of Saint Andrew and Saint Francis
Ciuffagni, Bernardo di Piero, 84, 109; *Saint Matthew*, 83
classical art, *see* antiquity, art of; Roman art
classical principles in Ghiberti competition relief design, 53; in *Saint Matthew*, 87-89, 92; North Door, 92, 127-28; in Florentine Renaissance, 86, 90-91; in Donatello, 90, 91, 273, 286
classicism, 18th century, 25; 19th century, 22-25
Clement XII, Pope, 339
Clementia Imperatoris, *see* Roman sculpture, reliefs, Arch of Constantine, Aurelian reliefs
Cleveland Museum, *Reclining Eve*, attributed to Siena or Marche, 172n
Coburg, Bavaria, Castle, Codex Coburgensis, 291, 337; drawing of Bacchic sarcophagus, 345; drawing for *Gathering-in of Meleager*, 347; drawing after a Medea sarcophagus, 348; drawings after Bacchic sarcophagi, 350
Coccharelli Manuscript, *see* London, British Museum
Cocchi, Antonio, 22
Cocchi, Raimondo, 22
Codex Berolinensis, *see* Dosio, Giovanni Antonio
Codex Coburgensis, *see* Coburg, Bavaria, Castle
Codex Escurialensis, *see* Escorial
Codex Pighianus, *see* Berlin, Staatsbibliothek
Coene, Jacques (Boucicaut Master?), 58n, 78

Cola di Domenico di Giovanni, 110n
Cola di Nicola, *see* Spinelli
Colle, Simone da, 12, 40
Colonna, Cardinal Francesco, 346
Colonna, Cardinal Prospero 269n, 321
Cone, Jacobus, *see* Coene, Jacques
Constans II, colossal head and hand of, *see* Roman sculpture
Constantine, Emperor, 182, 309, 353, 357; Arch of, *see* Roman sculpture, reliefs
Constantine with three sons, *see* Roman sculpture
"Constantine," *see* Paris, Bibliothèque Nationale
Constantine medal for Jean Duc de Berry, 59. *See also* antiquity, art of, influence on medals of Duc de Berry
Copenhagen, Ny-Carlsberg Glyptothek, Bacchic sarcophagus, *see* Roman sculpture, sarcophagi
Cortona, Cathedral, *see* Roman sculpture, sarcophagi, *Dionysos Battling the Amazons*, lid
Cosenza, Cathedral, Tomb of Isabeau of France, 147n
Council of Basel, 183, 185
Council of Florence, 181-88
Cristiani, Giovanni di Bartolomeo, 51n
cupolone, *see* Florence Cathedral, dome
Cyprian, Saint, 185

Daddi, Bernardo, 217n
Dante Alighieri, 28, 31, 295
Dark Ages, 309
Dati, Leonardo the Younger, 178
Dati, Leonardo, General of Dominicans, 138n. *See also* Ghiberti, Lorenzo, *Works*, Florence, S. Maria Novella, Dati Tomb
David, Jacques Louis, 294
Delli, Dello, 209n; *Blessing of Isaac*, *see* Florence, S. Maria Novella, Chiostro Verde
Desiderio da Settignano, 17, 333
Dijon, Museum, Altar, Jacques de Baerze and Melchior Broederlam, 78; Chartreuse de Champmol, Virgin and donors, Claus Sluter, 55; *Well of Moses*, 78, 85
Diodorus Siculus, *World History*, 356
Dionysius of Genoa, Frater, 58n
Dionysius of Halicarnassus, *Roman Antiquities*, 356

Domenico di Giovanni, 108
Dominicus Johannis, Frater, 16
Donatello, 7, 17-20, 23-24, 27, 36, 40n, 72n, 84n, 93, 100, 109, 138, 140, 152n, 193, 200, 206, 238n, 262-63, 273, 275, 302-4, 311, 318-23, 325, 329, 331-32, 338. *See also* classical elements; antiquity, architecture; antiquity, art

Works: Florence, Bargello, *David*, 84n; *Marzocco*, 90-91, 132, 152; *Saint George* (*see* Or San Michele); Cathedral, *Cantoria*, 106n, 263, 264n; Museo dell'Opera, *Jeremiah*, 90; *John the Baptist*, 90 (both from Campanile), *Saint John the Evangelist*, 83, 90; Porta della Mandorla, 84; S. Croce, Cavalcanti Altar, 263, 264n; *Christ on the Cross*, 120; S. Croce, Museum, *Saint Louis* (from Or San Michele), 5, 74, 87, 93, 95, 152-53; S. Lorenzo, Sagrestia Vecchia, bronze doors, 327; Tondi of *Life of Saint John the Evangelist*, 201; Or San Michele, *Saint George*, 72, 83-84, 86, 90 (*see also* Florence, Bargello), relief, 150, 153, 319; *Saint Louis* (*see* S. Croce, Museum) architecture of niche, 263; *Saint Mark*, 72, 84, 90-92, 137, 152, 319; *Saint Peter* (in collaboration with Nanni di Banco?), 72; alleged competition relief, *Sacrifice of Isaac*, 43n; Lille, Musée Wicar, *Dance of Salome*, 201; London, Victoria and Albert Museum, *Giving of the Keys*, 150, 327; Naples, S. Angelo a Nilo, Brancacci Tomb, *Assumption*, 150, 153; Padua, Santo, High Altar, *Miracle of the Ass*, 25, 264, 268; Rome, St. Peter's, Sacristy, *Tabernacle*, 347; Siena, Cathedral, Baptismal Font, *Salome*, 151-53, 221, 244, 263, 264n, 327-28, Pecci Tomb, 152-53
Dondi, Giovanni, 295-99, 302, 304
Doni, Anton Francesco, 20
Doren, Alfred, 26
Dosio, Giovanni Antonio, Codex Berolinensis, Berlin, Kupferstichkabinett, drawing of Bacchic sarcophagus, 345
Dresden, Secundogeniturbibliothek, *Bible*, 177n
Duccio, 54, 215n, 218, 309; Siena, *Maestà*, 114n, 218
Duccio, Agostino di, 325, 333

Early Christian basilicas, influence on Brunelleschi, 263
Early Christian and Byzantine art, influence on Ghiberti, 286, 325; sarcophagi and pyxides, *Sacrifice of Isaac*, 38n
Egeria, Grotto of, *see* Rome
Embriachi workshop, 58
Empoli altarpiece, *see* Lorenzo Monaco
Endymion sarcophagus, *see* Roman sculpture, sarcophagi
Escorial, Codex Escurialensis, 337
Este, Lionello d', 269n, 270n
Este, Meladusio d', 269n
Este, Museo Nazionale Atestino, *cippus*, *see* Roman sculpture, reliefs
Euclid, 245
Eugene IV, Pope, 5, 13, 67, 183-85, 315, 356
Evander, *see* Rome, Palace of
Eyck, Jan van, 17, 150, 318

Fabriano, Gentile da, 17, 58, 137, 146n, 147, 150, 320; Florence, Uffizi, Epiphany altar (Strozzi altar) from S. Trinità, 146, 285, 326; Quaratesi altarpiece, 80; New Haven, Conn., Yale University Art Gallery, *Jarvis Madonna*, 146
Farnese, Piero, 340
Fazio, Bartolommeo, 16, 85, 269n
Federighi, Antonio, Munich, Graphische Sammlung, drawing of barbarian from Arch of Constantine, 345; drawing of Three Graces, 346
Feo, Niccolo di Luca di, 106
Ficino, Marsilio, 325
Filarete (Antonio Averlino), 234, 236; Paris, Louvre, *Madonna*, 172n; *Treatise*, 267n, 268
Filippo di Ser Ugolino, Ser, 279
Finiguerra, Maso, 17
Fiore, Mona, mother of Ghiberti, 3
Florence, Guilds, *see* Guilds; Taxes, *see* Catasto
——, Accademia, *Annunciation*, Lorenzo Monaco, 80, 81n; Nobili altarpiece, Lorenzo Monaco, 80; *Mount of Olives*, Lorenzo Monaco, 82, 120, 124
——, Baptistery, history, 31, 33; Baptismal Font, 120
——, Baptistery, East Door (*Porta del Paradiso*), and North Door, *see* Ghiberti, Lorenzo
——, Baptistery, South Door, *Life of Saint John the Baptist*,

Andrea Pisano (frame by Vittorio Ghiberti and workshop), 9, 17, 24, 25n, 31n, 32-34, 38, 105, 113, 133-34, 169, 212-13, 215, 216n, 218, 363, 365; *Eve*, Vittorio Ghiberti, 291, 344. *See also* antiquity, art of; Roman sculpture, *Venus Pudica*, Roman sculpture, Bacchic sarcophagus, London
——, Baptistery, Mosaics of the Dome, *Storing of Grain by Joseph*, 171; Tomb of John XXIII, *Virtues*, Michelozzo, 87. *See also* Museo dell'Opera, Silver Altar of Saint John the Baptist
——, Bargello, Battle relief, Bertoldo di Giovanni, 341, 349; Competition relief, *Sacrifice of Isaac*, Brunelleschi, 42-49, 50-53, 66, 278, 281-83, 299; *David*, Donatello, 84n; *Saint George* (from Or San Michele), Donatello, 72, 83-84, 86, 90; *Marzocco*, Donatello, 90, 91, 132, 152; Competition relief, *Sacrifice of Isaac*, Ghiberti, 12, 31-54, 60, 61-67, 71, 76, 82, 113, 117n, 122-23, 132, 137, 143, 214, 278-79, 283, 299, 339, 363; Shrine of SS. Protus, Hyacinth and Nemesius, 5, 10, 12, 13, 100, 138-39, 143, 146-48, 152-53, 206, 286, 319, 329, 331, 343; *Saint Luke*, Niccolo di Piero Lamberti (from Or San Michele), 71, 72n
——, Biblioteca Laurenziana, Biadajolo miniature, 258n; Diogenes Laertius manuscript, 186n; *see also* Traversari
——, Biblioteca Nazionale, Codex, Francesco di Giorgio, 281n; *Vita di San Giovanni Battista*, Zanobi di Pagholo d'Agnolo Perini, 122, 123
——, Bigallo, fresco, 258n
——, Campanile, *Jeremiah*, Donatello, *see* Museo dell'Opera; *Saint John the Baptist*, Donatello, *see* Museo dell'Opera; *Artes*, *Agriculture*, Andrea Pisano, 298, 345
——, Cathedral (S. Maria del Fiore, S. Reparata), 33, 94n, 274; "*Poggio*," 341; *Cantoria*, Donatello, Luca della Robbia, 106n, 211, 263-64, 319; *Saint Stephen* from façade, Arnolfo di Cambio workshop (attributed), *see* Gardens Venturi-Ginori; *Isaiah*, Nanni di Banco, 83, 90, 91; choir, design by

Brunelleschi, 256, 257n; dome, 4-6, 15, 36, design by Brunelleschi, 15, 254-56, 263, 274, 323; Sepulcher of Saint Zenobius, design for architecture, Brunelleschi, 141; choir, design by Ghiberti, 6, 256; model for lantern, Ghiberti, 6; model for dome, Ghiberti, 112; Zenobius Shrine, Ghiberti, 5-6, 8, 12-14, 17, 22-23, 36, 94, 141-43, 146-47, 154-55, 166, 192-95, 200-2, 205-10, 257-59, 272, 276, 291, 331, 348, 351, 352, 360-61, Angels, 142-43, 154; *Miracle of the Cart*, 154, 206, *Resurrection of the Servant*, 154, 206, *Resurrection of a Boy of the Strozzi family*, 142, 154, 205-10, 351-52; stained glass window cartoons by Ghiberti, 4, 6, 203, 361, *Assumption of the Virgin* 15, 54, 76, 82, 122-23, 215, *Ascent of Christ, Mount of Olives, Presentation in the Temple*, 15; *Saint Stephen* from façade, Piero di Giovanni Tedesco, *see* Paris, Louvre; *Saint Stephen* from Or San Michele, Andrea Pisano (attributed to), 94; North Sacristy Door, Luca della Robbia, 7n, 106n, 116n, 117n, 211; Porta della Mandorla, 52, 53, 59, 83-84, 278-81, 299; Tympanum of the Porta della Mandorla Virgin, Nanni di Banco, 90, 100; prophets, Donatello, 84; *Hercules with the Lion Skin*, Hercules Master, 52-53, 60, 67, 89, 280n, 282-83, 299

————, Cathedral, Museo dell'-Opera di S. Maria del Fiore, *Saint Luke*, Nanni di Banco, 71-72, 83; *Saint Matthew*, Ciuffagni, 83; *Jeremiah*, Donatello, 90; *Saint John the Evangelist*, Donatello, 83, 90; *Annunciation* from Porta della Mandorla, Hercules Master, 53, 279, 281; *Saint Mark*, Niccolo Lamberti, 83, Sainted Deacon, attributed to Andrea Pisano, 94n, 95n; Phaeton sarcophagus, 339-40, *see* Roman sculpture, sarcophagi; Prophets, copies after mosaics, 216; Silver Altar of Saint John the Baptist, 50, 258n, 279; six reliefs from Castel di Sangro, 116n

————, Cathedral Treasury, *Libretto*, reliquary, 64

————, Column of S. Zenobius, 167

————, Gardens, Venturi-Ginori, *Saint Stephen* from Cathedral façade, Arnolfo di Cambio workshop (attributed to), 94n

————, Hospital of S. Gallo, 33

————, Hospital of the Innocents, Brunelleschi, 262, 265-66, 275, 319, Galleria, *Saint John the Evangelist*, Jacopo di Piero Guidi (attributed to), 71

————, Medici Chapel, *see* Palazzo Medici

————, Museo Archeologico, bronze Hercules, 280n, 281n

————, Museo S. Marco, Linaiuoli Altar, Fra Angelico (frame design by Ghiberti), 6, 261n, 264, 361

————, Or San Michele, 73, history, 71; *Quattro Coronati*, Nanni di Banco, 72, 84, 86, 90-91, 137, 143; *Saint Eligius*, Nanni di Banco, 72, 84, 90-91; *Saint Peter*, Nanni di Banco (attributed, with Donatello?), 72; *Saint Philip*, Nanni di Banco, 72, 84, 86, 90-91, 97n; *Saint George*, Donatello (copy after, *see* Florence, Bargello), relief, 150, 153, 319; *Saint Louis*, Donatello (*see* S. Croce, Museum), architecture of niche, 263; *Saint Mark*, Donatello, 72, 84, 90-92, 137, 152, 319; *Martyrdom of Saint Lawrence*, Taddeo Gaddi, 258n; Ghiberti, three statues, 7, 11, 17-18, *Saint John the Baptist*, inscription, 3, commission, 4, mentioned, 13, 21, 24, 71-86, 88-90, 92-94, 112, 121, 124-27, 131, 152, 244-47, 260-61, 360, 362, 365, architecture of niche, 260; *Saint Matthew*, commissioned, 5, mentioned, 13, 19, 26, 71, 73-75, 86-97, 99-100, 111-13, 121, 131-32, 137, 144, 149, 152, 208, 283, 286, 292, 319, 331, 342-43, 360-61; architecture of niche, 261n, 262, 264-66; *Saint Stephen*, commission, 5, mentioned, 13, 71, 74, 86, 88n, 93-100, 137, 141, 358, 361, projected architecture of niche, 264-66, 275, preparatory drawing, 95n, 97-99, *see* Paris, Louvre; *Saint John the Evangelist*, Jacopo di Piero Guidi, attributed to, 71n, *see* Florence, Hospital of the Innocents, Galleria; *Saint James Major*, Nicolo di Piero Lamberti, 71; *Saint Luke*, Nicolo di Piero Lamberti, *see* Bargello; *Saint Mark*, commissioned to Nicolo di Piero Lamberti, 72; *Annunciation*, above niche of *Saint Matthew*, attributed to Michelozzo, 87n, 88n; *Tabernacle of the Virgin*, Orcagna, 72

————, Palazzo Medici, Chapel, murals, *Journey of the Magi*, Benozzo Gozzoli, 202, 205-6, 333; two deacons, 95n

————, Palazzo di Parte Guelfa, Brunelleschi, 262, 266, 275

————, Palazzo Pitti, Argenteria, *Pietà* (sardonyx), 65; *Pope Leo X*, Raphael, 39n; Caesar portrait, 341, *see* Roman sculpture

————, Palazzo Ruccellai, 271n

————, Pazzi Chapel, Brunelleschi, 262, 265

————, Porta della Mandorla, *see* Cathedral

————, S. Croce, 33; Convent, 33; Medici Chapel columns, Michelozzo, 265n; Berlinghieri Tomb, *Annunciation*, Giovanni Balduccio da Pisa, 99; Cavalcanti Altar, Donatello, 263, 264n; *Christ on the Cross*, Donatello, 120; Apse frescoes, Agnolo Gaddi, 214n; Castellani Chapel, frescoes, Agnolo Gaddi, 80, 214n; Sacristy, *Crucifixion* and *Sacrifice of Isaac*, Taddeo Gaddi or Niccolo di Piero Gerini, 50n, 282n; Tombs of Bartolomeo Valori and Lodovico degli Obizi, Ghiberti workshop, 6, 13, 203-4; Ghiberti Tomb, 9; Sylvester legend frescoes, Maso di Banco, 224, 259; Museum, *Saint Louis* (from Or San Michele), Donatello, 5, 74, 87, 93, 95, 152-53

————, S. Egidio, Shutter with *God the Father*, Ghiberti, *see* S. Maria Nuova

————, S. Lorenzo, architecture, Brunelleschi, 257n, 262n, 266, 275; Sagrestia Vecchia, architecture, Brunelleschi, 201, 262, 264-66, 268, 275-76; bronze door, Donatello, 327; tondi of the *Life of Saint John the Evangelist*, Donatello, 201

————, S. Maria degli Angeli, architecture, Brunelleschi, 33, 263; Shrine of SS. Protus, Hyacinth and Nemesius, Ghiberti, *see* Ghiberti, Bargello; Nobili altarpiece, Lorenzo Monaco, *see* Florence, Accademia

————, S. Maria del Carmine, Brancacci Chapel, frescoes, Masaccio, *Expulsion*, 344; *Giv-*

ing of the Keys, 201; *Tabitha* fresco, 201, 241-42; *Tribute Money*, 150, 201, 220-21, 326

———, S. Maria Novella, façade, 271; pilasters flanking portal, Alberti (?), 272n; papal apartment, 183, design for staircase by Ghiberti, 256; Chapel of Niccolo Acciaiuolo, murals, 33; Spanish Chapel, fresco cycle of New Testament, Andrea di Firenze, 215, *Way to Calvary*, 257n, *Crucifixion*, *Via Veritatis*, 221-22, 224; Tomb of Leonardo Dati, Ghiberti, 5, 12-13, 138, 143, 147-48, 152-53; *Trinity* fresco, Masaccio, 150, 240, 263, 319; Chiostro Verde, frescoes, *Abraham* scenes, 208-10; Dello Delli, *Blessing of Isaac*, lost, 259; Paolo Uccello and workshop, 178, 208-10, 344; *Creation of Adam*, 208, *sinopia* of *Adam*, 210, 344; *Creation of Eve*, 208n, 209n; *Creation of Animals*, 208, 219n; *Fall of Man*, 208n, *Expulsion*, 208, 209n, 210; *Labors of Man*, 208, 209n

———, S. Maria Nuova, bronze shutter with *God the Father* for tabernacle, Ghiberti, 9, 204, 207, 361. See also S. Egidio

———, S. Miniato, 33; Chapel of the Cardinal of Portugal, frescoes, Baldovinetti, 186n

———, S. Reparata, *see* Cathedral

———, S. Spirito, Brunelleschi, 33n, 262n, 263, 266, 275

———, S. Trinità, Strozzi Tomb Chapel, choir stalls and furnishings, 256, 261n; portal, 261; Epiphany Altar, Gentile da Fabriano, *see* Uffizi

———, Uffizi, Iphigenia *cippus*, 287-88, 290, 347; Niobid statues, 339; *Sacrifice of Isaac*, engraving, 43n; Satyr torso, 339; *Primavera*, Botticelli, 325, 334, 346; Epiphany Altar (Strozzi altar), Gentile da Fabriano, 146, 285, 326; *Coronation of the Virgin*, Fra Filippo Lippi, 202; *Presentation in the Temple*, Ambrogio Lorenzetti, 243-44; *Adoration of the Magi*, Lorenzo Monaco, 259n; *Coronation of the Virgin*, Lorenzo Monaco, 81; (formerly Uffizi), *Hercules and the Hydra*, Piero Pollaiuolo, 333; drawing after Meleager sarcophagus, Villa Doria Pamphili, 348

Forzetta, Oliviero di, 297, 300
Francesco di Giorgio (Martini), 268n, 281n, 337
Francesco di Papi, 167n
Francesco di Valdambrino, *see* Valdambrino, Francesco di
Franchi, Rosello di Jacopo, 98n, 181
French 14th century art, 54-67, 76, 122. *See also* International Style; realism

Gaddi, Agnolo, 219; Florence, S. Croce, Castellani Chapel frescoes and apse frescoes, 80, 214n
Gaddi, Monsignor Giovanni, 305n, 339
Gaddi family, 339
Gaddi, Taddeo, 50n, 77, 215, 309; Florence, Accademia, *Christ among the Doctors*, 214, 215; S. Croce, *Crucifixion* (attributed to), 50n; Or San Michele, *Martyrdom of Saint Lawrence*, 258n
Gates of Paradise, origin of phrase, 18; *see* Florence, Baptistery, East Door
Gauricus, Pomponius, 18
Gelli, Giambattista, 10, 20
Gentile da Fabriano, *see* Fabriano, Gentile da
Gerini, Niccolo di Piero, 219; S. Croce, *Crucifixion* (attributed to), 50n
GHIBERTI, LORENZO di Cione di Ser Buonaccorso (Lorenzo Ghiberti, Lorenzo di Bartolo di Michele, Lorenzo di Bartoluccio, Nencio di Bartoluccio), account book, 360; collection of antiques, 28, 305; death, 365; diaries or journals, 10-11; drawings, 95n, 97-99, 129-30; from the antique, 207, 284; knowledge of Greek and Latin, 312; legitimacy, 3-4; letters, 360; model books, 207-12, 288, 291, 333; *Portate al Catasto* (tax declarations), 3, 7-8, 111, 162, 163, 360; real estate holdings, 7-9, 11, 142n, 261n, 360; tomb, 9; trips to Pesaro, 4, 31, 51, 82, Pisa, 284, Rome, 6, 275, 284, 288, 321, 330, 332, 353-54, 357-58, Siena, 4, 117n, 140, Venice, 5, 140; use of antique, 28, 49, 137, 207, 277-93, 337-52; workshop, 203-13
Commentarii: 6, 10-11, 17, 20, 26, 34-36, 40-42, 51, 53, 62, 65-66, 73, 87n, 95n, 105, 112, 171-72, 199-200, 214, 219-20, 223-25, 230-32, 253, 305-13, 332,

353-54, 356, 360; attitude toward antiquity, 309, 313, 357; toward humanism, 310-13; perspective, 309; Sienese painting, 219-20, 309; Trecento, 219-20, 313; Autobiography, 12-15, 171, 203, 254, 360; *see also* terminology

WORKS

Designs for goldsmith work, 4, 203; molds for terracotta Madonnas, reliefs, and statues, 7, 26-27, 203-4; Medici Cornelian, *Flaying of Marsyas*, mounting, 5, 11, 13, 67, 146-47, 278, 300, 312; sketches in wax and clay, 7; papal miters and morses, 5, 13, 67
Città di Castello, Galleria Municipale, *Saint Andrew* and *Saint Francis*, attributed to Ghiberti workshop, 119-20, 130
Florence, Baptistery, East Door, 5, 6, 8-12, 16-22, 24-25, 27, 42, 66, 87, 96, 100, 109n, 111-12, 114-16, 149, 153, 155, 159-214, 218, 220-22, 225, 233, 272, 274, 282, 286-88, 293, 305, 307, 313, 328-32, 334, 343-45, 354, 358, 361-63, 365; program, 159-70, 217, 225, 301; iconography, 14-15, 172-74, 176-88, 217, 292; inscription, 4. *See also* Antiquity, art of, influence on Ghiberti
Frame: 146, 166, 204, 212, 349-51, 365; architrave, 166; figures of frame, 168, 204-5, 207, 211, 223, 289-92, 333; heads, 166; self portrait, 9-10; frieze, 11, 165-66, 168; jambs, 11, 146, 166; iconography, *Parents of Mankind*, 172, Prophets and Old Testament heroes, 172-74
Panels: *Abraham*, 163n, 173, 175-76, 190-91, 193, 195, 208-10, 222, 232n, 248-49, 346-47; architectural settings, 257-59, 265-66, 269, 272-73, 275-76; *Cain and Abel*, 163n, 165, 174-76, 191-97, 201, 204-5, 208, 222-23, 232n, 248, 290-93, 345; *David*, 153, 173, 175, 180, 191, 197-99, 202, 204, 222, 258, 289, 349; *Genesis*, 23, 130n, 163n, 168, 174-76, 189-95, 201, 204-5, 208-11, 222, 248, 289-91, 293, 328-29, 332, 343-45; *Isaac*, 165, 174-76, 190-91, 196-97, 201-2, 204-5, 210-11, 223-24, 229, 233, 249-52, 257-59, 265, 273, 290-92, 323, 328-29, 331, 334; *Joseph*,

165, 175-76, 180, 189, 191, 196-99, 201-2, 204-6, 208-11, 224, 229, 233, 249, 251-52, 257-58, 265-68, 273, 290-91, 323, 328, 331-32, 347-48; *Joshua*, 173, 175, 180, 191, 197-99, 202, 204-6, 222, 258, 289, 291-92, 348-49; *Moses*, 165, 171, 173, 175, 180, 189, 191, 197-99, 204-6, 208, 210, 222-23, 225, 232n, 289-91, 328, 348; *Noah*, 173-76, 190n, 191-95, 201, 204-7, 222-23, 288-90, 292-93, 328-29, 331, 345-46; *Solomon*, 165, 168, 174-75, 177, 180, 190-92, 197-99, 202, 204-6, 229, 232-33, 249, 252-53, 257-58, 265-66, 273, 326, 331

————, North Door, 3, 5, 9-10, 12-13, 16-18, 23-24, 26, 60-61, 66, 73, 87, 103-12, 127, 137, 142, 199, 203, 207, 212, 260, 265, 288, 299, 339-42, 361-63; commission, 105-6; competition for, 4, 11; competition relief, *Sacrifice of Isaac, see* Bargello; iconography, 38-39, 216; inscription, 3; program, 103, 105, 114; realism in, 60

Frame: 60-62, 103-6, 113, 122, 132-33; prophets' heads, 103, 121n, 132-33, 145, 216-17, 284, 340-342; self portrait, 9-10

Jambs: floral decoration, 138, 143-45, 147-48, 285 .

Panels: *Adoration of the Magi*, 81, 103, 115n, 117, 121n, 123, 131-32, 214-15; *Annunciation*, 81, 103, 115n, 121-23, 131n, 215; *Arrest*, 92, 103, 115n, 121n, 127-28, 132, 143, 147, 215n, 217n, 218, 284; *Baptism of Christ*, 82-83, 103, 115n, 120-21, 123, 125, 130n, 131, 215; *Christ among the Doctors*, 83, 103, 115n, 117-18, 121n, 124-25, 131n, 132, 215; *Christ before Pilate*, 92, 103, 115n, 121n, 126-27, 131, 144, 214, 215n, 217n, 261, 340; *Christ in the Storm*, 103, 117, 121n, 127, 132, 215; *Church Fathers*, 103, 121n, 125, 215n; *Crucifixion*, 81, 103, 115n, 116n, 120, 121n, 124-25, 215n, 217n; *Entry into Jerusalem*, 92, 103, 115n, 121n, 126-28, 131, 215n, 217, 283, 340; *Evangelists*, 103, 115n, 117-18, 121n, 125, 132, 215n; *Expulsion of the Money Changers*, 103, 115n, 121n, 126-27, 131n, 215n, 283, 340; *Flagellation*, 92, 103, 114, 115n, 121n, 127-32, 143, 215n, 217, 261, 275;

Last Supper, 103, 115n, 121n, 125-26, 131n, 132, 215n, 217; *Mount of Olives*, 76, 82, 103, 115n, 120, 121n, 123-24, 128, 215n; *Nativity*, 81-82, 103, 115n, 117, 121n, 122-23, 126-27, 214-15, 283, 339-40; *Pentecost*, 103, 116n, 121n, 127-28, 131n, 215; *Raising of Lazarus*, 23, 81, 92, 103, 115n, 117, 121n, 125-27, 132, 215n; *Resurrection*, 103, 116n, 121n, 127, 215; *Temptation*, 76, 83, 103, 121n, 124, 126, 215n; *Transfiguration*, 103, 115n, 117, 121n, 124-26, 128, 132, 215n; *Way to Calvary*, 92, 103, 115n, 116n, 119, 121n, 127-28, 131-32, 143, 149, 215n, 217

————, South Door, Frame, Vittorio Ghiberti and workshop, 9, 17, 24, 212-13, 291, 344, 363, 365

Florence, Bargello, Competition relief, *Sacrifice of Isaac*, 12, 31-54, 60, 66-67, 71, 76, 82, 113, 117n, 122-23, 132, 137, 143, 214, 278-79, 283, 299, 339, 363; Shrine of SS. Protus, Hyacinth and Nemesius, 5, 10, 12-13, 100, 138-39, 143, 146-48, 152-53, 206, 286, 319, 329, 331, 343

————, Cathedral, design for choir, 6, 256; dome, 15, Ghiberti appointed supervisor, 5-6, 255, model for, 112, model for lantern, 6; cartoons for stained glass windows, 4, 6, 203, 361, *Ascension of Christ* window, 15, *Assumption of the Virgin*, 15, 54, 76, 82, 122-23, 215, *Mount of Olives*, 15, *Presentation in the Temple*, 15; Zenobius Shrine, 5-6, 8, 12-14, 17, 22-23, 36, 94, 141-43, 146-47, 154-55, 166, 192-95, 200-2, 205-10, 257-59, 272-74, 276, 291, 331, 348, 351-52, 360-61, Angels, 142-43, 154, *Miracle of the Cart*, 154, 206, *Resurrection of the Servant*, 142, 154, 206, *Resurrection of a boy of the Strozzi Family*, 142, 154, 205-10, 351-52

————, Museo S. Marco, design for frame of Linaiuoli Altar, 6, 261n, 264, 361

————, Or San Michele, three statues, 7, 11, 17-18; *Saint John the Baptist*, inscription, 3; commission, 4; mentioned, 13, 21, 24, 71-86, 88-90, 92-94, 112, 121, 124-27, 131, 152, 244-47,

260-61, 360, 362, 365, architecture of niche, 261; *Saint Matthew*, commission, 5, 13, 19, 26, 71, 73-75, 86-97, 99-100, 111-13, 121, 131-32, 137, 144, 149, 152, 208, 283, 286, 292, 319, 331, 342-43, 360-61; architecture of niche, 261n, 262, 264-66; *Saint Stephen*, presentation drawing, Paris, Louvre, 95n, 97-99, 130n; *Saint Stephen*, statue, commission, 5; mentioned 13, 71, 74, 86, 88n, 93-100, 137, 141, 358, 361; architecture of niche (projected), 264-66, 275

————, S. Croce, Tombs of Bartolomeo Valori and Lodovico degli Obizi, 6, 13, 203-4.

————, S. Egidio, *see* S. Maria Nuova

————, S. Maria degli Angeli, Shrine of SS. Protus, Hyacinth and Nemesius, *see* Ghiberti, Bargello

————, S. Maria Novella, Dati Tomb, 5, 12-13, 138, 143, 147-48, 152-53; papal apartment, design for stairway, 5, 256

————, S. Maria Nuova, *God the Father*, on small bronze shutter, 9, 204, 207

————, S. Trinità, Strozzi Tomb Chapel, choir stalls and furnishings, influence on, 256, 261n; portal, 261

Paris, Louvre, Cabinet des Estampes, Presentation Drawing for *Saint Stephen* at Or San Michele, 95n, 97-99, 130n

Princeton University, Museum, *Moses*, terracotta relief attributed to Ghiberti follower, 191n

Siena Cathedral, Baptistery of S. Giovanni, Baptismal Font reliefs, 4-5, 112, 139-41, 149, 199, 329; *Baptism of Christ*, 13, 100, 144, 150-55, 190, 192-93, 200-1, 331; *John the Baptist before Herod*, 13, 108, 117n, 118, 130n, 132, 143-44, 146-47, 151, 153, 207, 248, 261, 264, 283-84, 343, 360

Vienna, Albertina, Drawing for *Flagellation*, Baptistery, North Door, 129-30

See also antiquity, architecture, influence of; antiquity, art, influence of; Early Christian and Byzantine art; terminology; Trecento, influence of

Ghiberti, Buonaccorso di Vittorio,

grandson of Lorenzo, 305; *Zibaldone*, 142, 360

Ghiberti, Cione Paltami di Ser Buonaccorso, father of Lorenzo Ghiberti, 3-4, 36, 365

Ghiberti, Mona Marsilia, wife of Lorenzo Ghiberti, 4, 9

Ghiberti, Tomaso, son of Lorenzo Ghiberti, 5, 6-8, 166, 360

Ghiberti, Vittorio, son of Lorenzo Ghiberti, 5, 6-9, 17-18, 165-67, 305n, 333; tax declaration, 17n; Florence Baptistery, South Door, frame, 212-13, *Eve*, 291, 344

Ghiberti, Vittorio di Buonaccorso, great-grandson of Lorenzo Ghiberti, 130n

Ginori-Conti, Piero, *see* Ghiberti, account book

Giotto, 10, 16, 21, 24, 62, 215, 218, 231, 309-10; Padua, Arena Chapel, 215n, 217n, 258n

Giovanni d'Ambrogio, 52n, 53

Giovanni da Milano, 219

Giovanni di Francesco, 108

Giuliano del Facchino, 118n

Giuliano di Giovanni, 118n

Giuliano di Monaldo, 118n

Giuliano di Ser Andrea, 108, 118n, 132, 139-40, 144n, 165

Giustiniani, Leonardo, 178

Goethe, Johann Wolfgang, 22

Gonzaga, Cardinal Federigo, 272n

Gonzaga, Giovanni Francesco, 316

Gonzaga, Lodovico, 272n

Gori, Francesco Antonio, 161, 362; *Historia Florentinae Basilicae et Baptisterii S. Johannis*, 161n; engravings after sarcophagi, 338; notes, 364-65

Governatori, *see* guilds, etc., *Arte della Lana, Operai di S. Maria del Fiore*

Gozzoli, Benozzo, 6, 212, 362-63; Florence, Palazzo Medici, Chapel, murals, *Journey of the Magi*, 202, 205-6, 333

Gran, Cathedral, *Calvary*, 65

Grassi, Giovanni de', 58-59, 61, 62n

Grassi, Salomone di, 79n

Greek authors, 330

Greek art, 280; 4th century sculpture and competition relief, 279. *See also* Hellenistic art

Greek orator figures and *Saint Matthew*, 286, 342

Greek revivalists, 19th century, 23

Gregory the Great, letters, 184

Grenoble, Museum, *Flagellation*,

Pietro Lorenzetti workshop, 224n

Gualandi, Pistoia, Reliquary of Saint Eulalia, 117n, 120n; Vignole, S. Sebastiano, Cross, 117n, 120n

Guardiagrele, Niccolo di, Teramo, Cathedral, *Paliotto*, 116n

Guarienti, Guariento, 361

Guasconi, Biagio, 301n

Guglielmo da Cremona, Fra, 295n, 296n

Guidi, Jacopo di Piero, 52n, 53n; Florence, Hospital of the Innocents, Galleria, *Saint John the Evangelist* from Or San Michele (attributed to), 71n

Guidoni, Ser Pietro di Ser Michele, 365

Guilds (committees, confraternities):

Armourers' Guild (*Arte dei Corrazzai*), 72, 86

Arte del Cambio (Bankers' Guild), 5, 32, 72, 74, 86-88, 93, 95-96, 361; *Libro del pilastro*, 86, 361

Arte di Calimala (Merchants' Guild), 4-5, 7-8, 31-34, 36, 38, 41, 43, 46, 71-73, 84-87, 93, 95, 103, 105-7, 111-13, 126, 133-34, 142, 159, 161, 163-64, 166, 169, 171, 189, 299, 355, 364-65; *Deliberazioni e partiti de' consoli*, 159, 360-62; *Libri Grandi*, 72, 73n, 74, 103, 110, 111n, 361, 364; *Libri (Quaderni) del Proveditore*, 164, 166n, 360; *Libro della seconda e terza porta*, 22, 106, 108-9, 161, 165, 362-63; *Offiziali del Musaico (Governatori di S. Giovanni*, Regents, Committee of the Regents), 12, 35, 37-41, 106, 361-62; *Opera di S. Giovanni*, 163, 167; *Uscita dell'Arte*, 361; *Portata al catasto* (tax declaration), 111-12

Arte dei Giudici e Notai (Lawyers' Guild), 71

Arte della Lana (Wool Guild), 5, 13, 32-33, 36, 71-72, 74, 93-99, 141, 361; *Deliberazioni dei Consoli*, 361; *Operai di S. Maria del Fiore*, 6, 7n, 13, 35-37, 41, 73, 94, 140-41, 254-56, 361

Arte dei Linaiuoli e Rigattieri (Linen Weavers' and Rag Dealers' Guild), 72, 86; *Deliberazioni de' Consoli*, 361

Arte dei Medici e Spetiali (Druggists', Doctors' and Paint-

ers' Guilds), 41, 71, 109

Arte dei Mercatanti di Calimala, see *Arte di Calimala*

Arte Mercatoria, see *Arte di Calimala*

Arte di Pietra e Legname (Carpenters' and Stone Masons' Guild), 72, 360; Ghiberti joins, 6

Arte della Seta (Silk Weavers', Levant Dealers' and Goldsmiths' Guild), 7, 32, 41, 61n, 71-72, 105, 109n, 360; *Statuti*, 7n

Arte di Por S. Maria, see *Arte della Seta*

Arte dei Vaiai e Pelliciai (Tanners' and Furriers' Guild), 71

Bakers' Guild, 86

Blacksmiths' Guild, 72

Butchers' Guild (*Arte dei Beccai*), 72

Capitani di Or San Michele, 261n, 361

Cobblers' Guild (*Arte dei Calzolai*), 72, 86

Compagnia dei Pittori (Confraternity of Painters; *Compagnia di S. Luca*), 361; Ghiberti joins, 6

Lawyers' Guild, see *Arte dei Giudici e Notai*

Linen Weavers' and Rag Dealers' Guild, see *Arte dei Linaiuoli e Rigattieri*

Opera di San Giovanni, see *Arte di Calimala*

Operai di S. Maria del Fiore, (*Opera del Duomo*), see *Arte della Lana*

Operaio of Siena Cathedral, 9, 140-41, 360, *Libro di documenti artistici*, 360; *Libri gialli*, 360

Parte Guelfa, 5, 74, 93, 95

Tanners' and Furriers' Guild, see *Arte dei Vaiai e Pelliciai*

Gusmin, *see* Master Gusmin

Hamilton Bible, *Sacrifice of Isaac, see* Berlin, Staatsbibliothek

Heemskerk, Marten van, drawing, 350

Helena, Empress, 182

Hellenistic art, 285, 286. *See also* Greek art, Roman art

Hennequin de Bruges, *see* Bondol, Jean

Henry of Winchester, 297

Hercules Master, 52-53, 60, 67, 89, 280n, 281, 282-83, 299;

Florence Museo dell'Opera, *Virgin Annunciate*, 279, 281; Porta della Mandorla, *Hercules with the Lion Skin*, 52-53, 60, 67, 89, 280n, 282-83, 299

Hermanin, Federigo, 353-55

hermaphrodite, found in Rome, *see* Roman sculpture, examples mentioned

Hilarius, Saint, 174n, 178; *Tractatus in Psalmos*, 119

Hildesheim, St. Michael, door, Old Testament cycle, 114n

Honnecourt, Villard de, 297

Horace, 294, 316; *Ars Poetica*, 316

Hrabanus Maurus, *Commentarius in Genesim*, 177n

Hugh of St. Victor, 177; *De Arca Noe Morali* and *De Arca Noe Mystica*, 177n

humanism, 17, 332; Florentine in the Renaissance, 52n, 278-80, 294-305, 312, 320-21, 331, 358; Roman in the Quattrocento, 332; of Alberti, 275; aspirations of Ghiberti, 28, 310-14; attitude towards art, 294-305

iconography; Florence, Baptistery, East Door, 14-15, 172-73, 176-88, 217, 292; *Noah* panel, 176-79, 187n; *Parents of Mankind*, 172; Prophets and Old Testament heroes, 172-74; Rebecca as prefiguration of the Church, 173; *Solomon* panel, 180-87, 188n, Queen of Sheba as prefiguration of Marriage and the Coronation of the Virgin, 180; alluding to Union of Churches, 181-84, 187; *Reclining Eve*, 172; *Sacrifice of Isaac* (Competition relief) as prefiguration of Crucifixion, 38-39; North Door, 216-17

Impruneta, near Florence, Silver Crucifix from, 116n

Innocent II, Pope, 357

International Style, 17, 56, 67, 76-85, 88-89, 91, 113, 120, 121n, 123-24, 126-27, 137, 202, 207, 283; *see also* French 14th century art; Siena, Trecento art

Isidor of Seville, *Allegoriae*, 174n

Jacopo di Piero Guidi (attributed to), *see* Florence, Hospital of the Innocents

Jacquerie, 78

Japan, art of, 26

Jefferson, Thomas, 294

Jerome, Saint, continuation of Eusebius' *Chronicle*, 355; translation of Origen's *Homilies*, 179; *Vulgate*, 178

Johannes da Modena, 58n

John of Monte Nigro, 185

John VIII Palaeologos, Byzantine Emperor, 182-85

Julià lo Florentì, 118n, 127; Valencia, Alabaster reliefs, *Pentecost, Resurrection, Samson*, 118

Justitia Imperatoris, *see* Roman sculpture, Arch of Constantine, Aurelian reliefs

Kalakas, *Treatise on the Errors of the Greeks*, 183-84

Klosterneuburg, two female saints, 78

Laertius, Diogenes, *De Vita et Moribus Philosophorum*, 178, 186

Lamberti, Niccolo di Piero, 12, 36, 43n, 52n, 53n, 71n, 81n, 83, 88n, 210n; Florence, Bargello, *Saint Luke*, from Or San Michele, 71, 72n; Museo dell'Opera, *Saint Mark*, from Cathedral, 83; Or San Michele, *Saint Mark*, commissioned to, 72; *Saint James Major*, 71; *Annunciation*, above Ghiberti's *Saint Matthew*, formerly attributed to, 87n

Lamberti, Piero di Niccolo, 72n

Laurana, Luciano di, Baltimore and Urbino panels, attributed to, 268n, 269, 272-73

Lavagna, Cardinal Guglielmo di, 340

Leonardo da Vinci, 18

Liberalitas Augusti, 284

Lille, Musée Wicar, *Dance of Salome*, Donatello, 201; Witter Collection, Franco-Flemish Bible, 39n

Limbourg Brothers, 77-78, 137, 150; *Très Riches Heures du Duc de Berry, Adoration of the Magi*, 59n, 77, *Coronation of the Virgin*, 59

Lippi, Filippino, 333

Lippi, Fra Filippo, Coronation altarpiece, *see* Florence, Uffizi

Livy, *Decades*, 297

London, British Museum: Aspertini Sketchbook, 337n; Bacchic sarcophagus, from Rome, S. Maria Maggiore, 344, 348; Carrara herbal, from Padua, 62n;

Coccharelli Manuscript, 62; Lothar Crystal, 64n; Reliquary of the Holy Thorn, 65; Royal Cup of France, 64

——, National Gallery: *Coronation of the Virgin*, Lorenzo Monaco, 81; *Venus and Mars*, Alessandro Botticelli, 333, 351

——, Victoria and Albert Museum: *Giving of the Keys*, Donatello, 150, 327

Lorenzetti, Ambrogio, 54, 66, 77, 99, 214, 216n, 217n, 223, 287n, 309-10; Altenburg, Staatliches Museum, *Reclining Eve* (attributed to), 172n; Florence, Uffizi, *Presentation in the Temple*, 243-44; Paris, Louvre, *Reclining Eve* (School of), 172n; Siena, S. Francesco, lost murals, 219-20; Siena, Palazzo Pubblico, *Good and Bad Government*, 219-21, 258n, 313, 343, *Pax*, 298

Lorenzetti, Pietro, 217-18, 223, 259; Assisi, S. Francesco, *Entry into Jerusalem*, 217; Grenoble, *Flagellation* (Workshop), 224n; Montefalcone, S. Agostino, fresco (School), 172n; Siena, Accademia, Carmine altarpiece, predella, *Saint Albert Consigning the Order of the Carmelites to Saint Broccardo*, 224; *Dream of Sebach*, 224

Lorenzetti, the, 172, 224; workshop, 218; Monte Siepi, San Galgano, fresco (School), 172n

Lorenzo di Bartolo di Michele, *see* Ghiberti, Lorenzo

Lorenzo di Bartoluccio, *see* Ghiberti, Lorenzo

Lorenzo di Cione, *see* Ghiberti, Lorenzo

Lorenzo di Niccolo, 209n

Los Angeles County Museum, Sarcophagus with Life of Roman official, 207, 287, 289, 290, 346-47, 350

Loschi, Antonio, 303, 321

Louis I, Duc d' Anjou, 60, 62-64, 357

Louis I, Duc d'Orleans, 65

Lupa, 277, 294, *see* Roman sculpture, Rome

Lysippos, 282, 339

Maestro del Bambino Vispo, 80

Maffei, Timoteo, 300

Magione, Church, *Reclining Eve*, fresco by Cola di Petrucciuoli, 172n

Magister Gregorius, 297

Maitre aux Boqueteaux, 55

Malatesta, Sigismondo, 270n, 271

Malpaghini, Giovanni, 279

Mancini, Girolamo, 315n

Manetti, Antonio di Tuccio, 35, 319n; *Uomini singholari*, 35, 234; *Vita di Brunellesco* (attributed to), 17n, 19-20, 27, 35-36, 40-43, 45, 234, 254, 256

Manetti, Gianozzo, 20

Mantua Cathedral, façade, 260n

Mantua, S. Andrea, Alberti, 272; S. Sebastiano, Alberti, 272

Marcanova Manuscript, 267n

Marine Sarcophagi, *see* Roman sculpture, sarcophagi

Marsuppini, Carlo, 279

Martin V, Pope, 5, 13, 63, 67, 139n, 183, 320, 354

Martini, Giuseppe, Pisa, Camposanto, engravings of Roman sarcophagi, 338

Martini, Simone, 54, 56, 77, 232n, 309-10; illustrations for Petrarch's *Virgil*, 298

Masaccio, 100, 138, 273, 304, 318, 320-21, 323, 327, 329, 332; death, 319; Berlin, Kaiser Friedrich Museum, Altar predella from Pisa, 150, 151n; Florence, S. Maria del Carmine, Brancacci Chapel, *Tabitha* fresco, 201, 241-42 (*see also* Masolino); *Tribute Money*, 150, 201, 220-21, 326; *Expulsion*, 344; S. Maria Novella, *Trinity* fresco, 150, 240, 242, 263, 319; Rome, S. Clemente, Branda Chapel, frescoes, 320 (*see also* Masolino); S. Maria Maggiore Altar, 320

Masegne brothers, 56; workshop, 260n; Bologna, S. Maria de'-Servi, Manfredi Tomb (circle), 57

Masegne, Jacobello, 56n, 57; Bologna, Museo Civico, Legnano Tomb, 57; Venice, Museo Correr, *Doge*, 57; S. Mark's, *Apostles*, 57, 59

Masegne, Pier Paolo, 56n; Venice, Palazzo Ducale, South Window, 79

Maso di Banco, 309; Florence, S. Croce, frescoes of *Sylvester* legend, 224, 259

Maso di Bartolomeo, 7n, 110n, 319n

Maso di Cristofano, 108, 109n, 110n. *See also* Masolino

Masolino, 108, 109n, 137-38, 241n, 320; *Bremen Madonna*, 80; Castiglione d'Olona, 259n;

Florence, S. Maria del Carmine, Brancacci Chapel, 319; Naples, *Miracle of the Snow*, from S. Maria Maggiore altarpiece, 150, 200, 202, 241, 243, 320; Rome, S. Clemente, Branda Chapel, frescoes, 241-42, 320, *Disputation of Saint Catherine*, 242-43, *Death of Saint Ambrose*, 242. *See also* Masaccio

Master of the Annunciation, *see* Hercules Master

Master of the Bamberg Visitation, 297

Master of the Bargello Tondo, 209n

Master Gusmin, 62-67, 76, 83, 231, 309, 353-57

Master of Rimini, 62n, 83n

Master of Saint Cecilia, *see* Bonamico (Buffalmacco)

Matteo di Donato, 108

Matteo di Francesco da Settignano, 166, 167

Medea Sarcophagus, *see* Roman sculpture, sarcophagi

Medici family, 39, 183, 300, 347

Medici, Cosimo, 5, 133, 134n, 138-39, 184n, 278-79, 300-1, 320-21

Medici, Lorenzo the Elder, 5, 138, 139n, 279, 300, 320

Medici, Piero, 134n, 186, 278, 300

Mehus, Giovanni, 300n, 301n, 302n

Meleager relief, Rome, *see* Roman sculpture, sarcophagi

Meleager sarcophagus, *see* Roman sculpture, sarcophagi

Memmi, Lippo, 99

Menabuoi, Giusto da, Padua, frescoes, *Sacrifice of Isaac*, 38n

Mengs, Anton Raphael, 22

Meyer, Alfred Gotthold, 26

Michelangelo, 18, 21

Michele da Firenze, Verona, S. Anastasia, Pellegrini Chapel, terracotta reliefs, 108, 116n

Michele di Giovanni di Bartolo (attributed to), drawings, Paris, Louvre, Cabinet des Estampes, 337

Michele di Nicolai, *see* Michele da Firenze

Michelozzo di Bartolommeo, 7n, 17, 19, 87, 109-11, 152, 164-67; Montepulciano, Aragazzi Tomb, 88n; Florence Baptistery, Tomb of John XXIII, *Virtues*, 87; Florence, Or San Michele, *Saint Matthew* (col-

laborator of Ghiberti), 6, 87, *Annunciation*, *see* Florence, Or S. Michele; S. Croce, Medici Chapel, capitals, 265n

Migliori, Leopoldo, 18

Milan, Biblioteca Ambrosiana, drawing after Bacchic sarcophagus, 344

———, Biblioteca Visconti, Beroldo Manuscript, 79n

———, Cathedral, Annunciation Window, 79; *Salvator Mundi in His Glory*, Jacopo da Campione, 57, 59; foreign sculptors, 58. *See also* Coene, Jacques; Monich, Walter; Raverti, Matteo

———, fabrica del Duomo, 58

———, S. Eustorgio, Carelli Tomb, 79

Mirabilia Urbis Romae, 295

Modrone, Library of Duke Visconti, *Uffiziuolo of Gian Galeazzo Visconti*, manuscript, 58n

Molini, Cardinal Gaspare, 321

Monaco, Lorenzo, 77, 80, 118n, 125, 137, 181, 259; Altenburg, *Flight into Egypt*, 81; Empoli Collegiata altarpiece, 80-81; Florence, Accademia, *Annunciation*, 80-81n, *Mount of Olives*, 82, 120, 124, Nobili altarpiece from S. Maria degli Angeli, 80; Bargello, *Diurnale* from S. Marco, 81; Uffizi, *Adoration of the Magi*, 259n, *Coronation of the Virgin*, 81; London, National Gallery, *Coronation of the Virgin*, 81; Montoliveto altarpiece, 82; Paris, Louvre, Diptych, *Mount of Olives*, 81, 82; Raczinsky Collection (formerly), *Adoration of the Magi*, 81; Settignano, Berenson Collection, *Madonna dell' Umiltà* (1405), 80-81, 122

Monich, Walter, Milan Cathedral, *Saint Stephen*, 79

Monreale Cathedral, bronze door, Old Testament cycle, Bonannus, 114n, 177n, 218; Mosaic cycle, Old Testament, 176n

Montalcino, Museo Civico, *Assumption*, Bartolo di Fredi, 54, 76, 215

Montalto *Pax*, 65n

Montefalcone, S. Agostino, *Reclining Eve*, fresco, Pietro Lorenzetti School, 172n

Montepulciano, Aragazzi Tomb, *see* Michelozzo

Monte Siepi, S. Galgano, *Reclin-*

ing Eve, fresco, Lorenzetti School, 172n

Montoliveto altarpiece, *see* Lorenzo Monaco

Munich, Glyptothek, hermaphrodite, 277n; *Ilioneus*, 339

————, Graphische Sammlung, drawing of Trajan relief from Arch of Constantine, 345; and drawing of Three Graces, Antonio Federighi, 346; drawing after a Bacchic sarcophagus, Polidoro da Caravaggio, 344

————, Private collection, Zeus statuette, 349

————, Staatsbibliothek, *Psalter of Queen Isabeau*, 39n

Naldi, Ser Santi di Domenico, 365

Nane, Ippolito delle, *Vita di San Zanobi*, 142n

Nanni di Bartolo il Rosso (Giovanni Rosso il Fiorentino), 88n; Verona, S. Fermo, Brenzoni Tomb, 116n

Naples, Museo Nazionale, Bacchic sarcophagus, 345; *Miracle of the Snow*, S. Maria Maggiore altarpiece, *see* Masolino

————, S. Giovanni a Carbonara, Tomb of Gianni Carracciolo del Sole, 139

————, S. Angelo a Nilo, Brancacci Tomb, *Assumption*, Donatello, 150, 153

Nazarenes, 23-24

Nemi, Nofri di Ser Paolo, 110n, 365

Nencio di Bartoluccio, *see* Ghiberti, Lorenzo

Neo-Attic reliefs, influence on Agostino di Duccio, 325. *See also* Roman sculpture

Nero, *see* Rome, *Macellum Magnum*

New Haven, Yale University Art Gallery, Jarvis Collection, *Solomon and the Queen of Sheba*, Virgil Master, 259n; *Madonna*, Gentile da Fabriano, 146

New York (formerly Duveen), *Saint Francis, the Fire Test*, Sassetta, 259n

————, Metropolitan Museum of Art, Saint Nicolaus panels, Bicci di Lorenzo, 259n; Caesar portrait, 341; Saint Catherine (from Clermont-Ferrand), 65; Zeus statuette, 349

————, Robert Lehmann Collec-

tion, *Reclining Eve*, Paolo di Giovanni Fei, 172n

Niccoli, Niccolo, 159, 161, 171, 178-79, 184n, 187, 279, 300n, 301-4, 311, 320, 322

Niccolo d'Arezzo, *see* Spinelli, Niccolo di Luca

Nicolaus V, Pope, 267n, 268, 269n, 356

Niobe group, *see* Roman sculpture

Niobe, Kneeling son of, *see* Roman sculpture

Numa, 294

Officiali del Musaico, *see* guilds, committees, confraternities, *Arte di Calimala*

Olympiads, Ghiberti's calendar, 353-58

Orcagna, Andrea, 51, 62, 99n, 309; Florence, Or San Michele, *Tabernacle of the Virgin*, 71

Orcagna brothers, 309

Origen, 177n, 178; *Homilies*, 179, 187; second homily *In Genesim*, 177

Orsini, Giordano, Cardinal, 321

Orvieto Cathedral, Reliquary of the SS Corporale, enamels, Ugolino da Vieri, 114n, 129-30, 217-18

Ovid, 294, 325

Oxford, Bodleian Library, French Psalter, 14th century, 39n

————, Ashmolean Museum, *Hunt*, Uccello, 202; Sketchbook, drawing of Endymion sarcophagus, attributed to Jacopo Ripanda, 347

Padua, Arena Chapel, Tomb of Enrico Scrovegni, Giovanni Pisano School, 147n (*see also* Giotto); Baptistery, *Sacrifice of Isaac*, fresco, Giusto Di Menabuoi, 38n; Carrara herbal, *see* London, British Museum; S. Antonio (Il Santo), tomb *gisants*, 56; High Altar, *Miracle of the Ass*, Donatello, 25, 264, 268

Paganino da Sala, 268n

Pagolo di Dono, *see* Uccello, Paolo

Palmieri, Matteo, 178; *De temporibus suis*, 16

Paolo di Giovanni Fei, New York, Robert Lehmann Collection, *Reclining Eve*, 172n

Papero di Meo, 165

Paris, Bibliothèque Nationale, Cabinet des Medailles, "Con-

stantine," from Sainte Chapelle, 64, 66; *Jupiter and the Eagle*, 64n; *Zeus*, 349

Department of Manuscripts: Alcuin Bible, 114, *Beau Breviaire* of Charles V, 81; *Bible of Jean de Sy*, 38n; *Cité de Dieu*, 64; *Creator Mundi*, 58n; *Eulogy for Gian Galeazzo Visconti*, 79n; *Homilies of Gregory of Nazianz*, 38n; *Lancelot du Lac*, 57n; *Psalter of Saint Louis, Sacrifice of Isaac*, 38n; *Taccuinum Sanitatis*, 57n

————, Louvre, *Annunciation*, 65n; *Charles V and Jeanne de Bourbon*, from the Quinze-Vingts, 55; *Parament de Narbonne*, 55; Reliquary of the Holy Spirit, 65; Scepter of Charles V, 56, 64n, 66; Silver *Madonna* of Jeanne d'Evreux from St. Denis, 54; *Virgin Annunciate*, 65; *Madonna*, Filarete, 172n; *Reclining Eve*, attributed to Ambrogio Lorenzetti School, 172n; Diptych, *Mount of Olives*, Lorenzo Monaco, 81, 82; *Saint Stephen*, from Florence Cathedral, façade, Piero di Giovanni Tedesco, 95n, 99; Remnants of a Proserpina sarcophagus, 351 Cabinet des Estampes, preparatory drawing for Ghiberti's *Saint Stephen*, 97-99, 130n; drawings (attributed to) Michele di Giovanni di Bartolo, 337; perspective drawing, Pisanello, 240

————, Notre Dame, *Vierge Blanche*, 54

Parlers, the, 55

Parma, Pinacoteca, *Reclining Eve*, 172n

Pasti, Matteo de, 270n

Patch, Thomas, *see* Cocchi, Antonio

Paul II, Pope, 65, 300n, 349, 356

Pavino, Antonio, 300n

Peckham, John, 307-8

Pelops sarcophagus, *see* Roman sculpture, sarcophagi

Perini, Zanobi di Pagholo d'Agnolo, *Vita di S. Giovanni Battista*, 120, 123

Perkins, Charles, 24

Perrotti, Niccolo, 356

perspective, aerial, 138; linear, 138, 199, 229-53, 323, 331; Ghiberti's scientific, 305, 329. *See also* Alberti, Brunelleschi, Ghiberti, Masaccio, Masolino

Perugia, Fountain, *Expulsion*, Niccolo Pisano, 344; Museum, San Domenico altarpiece, Taddeo di Bartolo, 79

Pesello, Giuliano di Arrigo, 74n, 75n

Pestilence of 1348, 33, 299; of 1400, 34; of 1424-1425, 140

Peter and Paul Master, Rheims, 297

Petrarch, 28, 61, 295, 298-99, 301, 303, 310, 316; concept of antiquity, 294; *Labors of Hercules*, 280; *De Remediis, De Vasis Corinthiis*, 61n; *Virgil*, 298

Petrucciuoli, Cola di, *see* Magione Church fresco

Phaedra sarcophagus, *see* Roman sculpture, sarcophagi

Phidias, 16, 311, 324

Philip, Duke of Burgundy, 58, 63

Piccolomini, Cardinal Francesco, 346

pictorial relief, 25, 137-55, 168, 201-2, 286

Piero della Francesca, 268n, 328n

Piero di Giovanni Tedesco, 51n, 52n, 53n; Florence, Or San Michele, *Saint John the Evangelist* (formerly attributed to), 71n; Paris, Louvre, *Saint Stephen*, 95n, 99

Pietro di Pavia, Frate, 61

Pippo di Benincasa, 51n. *See also* Brunelleschi, Filippo

Pirgotile, 13

Pisa, Cathedral, bronze doors, Bonannus, 114, 218; pulpit, *Prudentia*, Giovanni Pisano, 287n

————, Camposanto, San Ranieri frescoes, 258n; Genesis scenes, Piero di Puccio, 175n, 210, 221-23, 225, 343; *Trionfo della Morte* and *Thebais*, Francesco Traini, 221-23, 225; Job frescoes, Francesco da Volterra, 258n; Roman monuments, 287; Caesar portrait type, 341; decorative sculpture, 278; sarcophagi collection, 278, 342-43; sarcophagus of T. Aelius with victories, 343; Battle sarcophagus, 341-43; Endymion sarcophagus, lid with victories, 343; Gaia and Oceanus sarcophagus with victories, 343; Muse sarcophagus, 342-43; Phaedra sarcophagus, 132, 284-85, 340-41, 350; sarcophagus with victories, from S. Pietro in Vinculi, 343. *See also* Berlin,

Kaiser Friedrich Museum, Masaccio, altar predella

Pisanello, 17, 320, 337, 349, 351-52; Paris, Louvre, perspective drawing, 240

Pisano, Andrea, 31-32, 62, 71n, 106, 309, 353-55, 357; Florence Baptistery, South Door, *Life of Saint John* (frame by Vittorio Ghiberti and workshop), 9, 17, 24, 25n, 31n, 32-34, 38, 105, 113, 133-34, 169, 216n, 218, *Baptism*, 215; Florence Campanile, *Artes* reliefs, 298, 346, *Agriculture*, 298, 345; Florence, Cathedral, *Saint Stephen* from Or San Michele (attributed to), 94; Museo dell'Opera, *Sainted Deacon* (attributed to), 94n, 95n

Pisano, Giovanni, 54n, 56, 62, 98, 173, 309; Pisa, Cathedral, pulpit, *Prudentia*, 287n

Pisano, Niccolo, 297, 340; Perugia Fountain, *Expulsion*, 344

Pistoia Cathedral, Silver Altar of San Jacopo, 51n, 59, 84, Brunelleschi, 50; Prophets, Brunelleschi, 59, 90; Reliquary of Santa Eulalia, Gualandi, 117n, 120n; Reliquary of San Jacopo, 120-21

Pistoia, Francesco di, 303

Pius II, Pope, 65n

Pliny, 230-31, 308, 310-11; *Naturalis Historia*, 61, 315, 353, 355-56

Poggibonsi, Giuliano di Giovanni da, *see* Julià lo Florentì

Poggio, Bracciolino Giovanni, 178, 279, 300n, 332, 356; approach to art, 302-4, 312, 322; *De Varietate Fortunae*, 277, 303, 316

Policreto, 13

Poliziano, Angelo, 325

Pollaiuolo, Antonio, 17, 19, 213

Pollaiuolo, Piero, 17; *Hercules and the Hydra*, ex-Uffizi collection, 333

Polybius, *Roman History*, 356

Polycletus (Polykleitos, Policreto), 13, 303-4, 305n; canon, 230

Pompey, 294

Ponte, Giovanni del, 80

Ponte S. Angelo, *see* Rome

Porta a Faenza, lost frescoes, Bonamico (Buffalmacco), 357

Porta (Porte) del Paradiso, *see* Florence Baptistery, East Door

Portate al Catasto, see *Catasto*

Porzellas, Alberto, 58n

Poussin, Nicolas, 294

Pozzo, Dal, Collection, *see* Windsor Royal Library

Prague Cathedral, Imperial portrait busts, 55

Praxiteles, 303-4

Pre-Raphaelites, 23, 25; Rome, Casino Massimi, murals, 24

Princeton University, Museum, terracotta relief, *Moses*, attributed to Ghiberti, 191n

Proserpina sarcophagus, *see* Roman sculpture, sarcophagi

Protogenes, 309

Provence, School of, 297

Puccio, Piero di, Pisa Camposanto, Genesis scenes, 175n, 210, 221-23, 225, 343

Pucelle, Jean, 54, 56, 61

Quercia, Jacopo della, 12, 25, 40, 53n, 140, 151n; competition panel for North Door, 43n; Siena, Fonte Gaia, 121n, 143, *Expulsion*, 143; Cathedral, Baptismal Font, *Annunciation to Zacharias*, 117n

Quintilian, *Institutiones*, 316

Raczinsky Collection (formerly), *Adoration of the Magi*, see Lorenzo Monaco

Rape of the Palladium, see Roman sculpture, reliefs

Raphael, 23-24, 294; Florence, Pitti Palace, *Portrait of Pope Leo X*, 39n; Vatican, *School of Athens*, 25

Ravenna, Roman putto relief from S. Vitale, *see* Venice, Museo Archeologico

Raverti, Matteo, *Saint Babila*, *see* Milan, Cathedral

realism, 14th century, 54n, 55, 58-59, 100; 14th century Florentine, 90-91; 14th century French, 56, 76-77, 85; 19th century rediscovery, 24, 27; in Brunelleschi, 49; in Ghiberti, competition panel, 45, *Saint John*, 76, *Saint Matthew*, 88-89

Renaissance style, 21, 92-93, 100, 137; in Ghiberti, 89 and *passim*

Reymond, Marcel, 26

Rheims Cathedral, Peter and Paul Master, Visitation Master, 297

Richa, Giovanni, 21, 365

Rienzo, Cola di, 295

Rimini, S. Francesco, Alberti, 270n, 271, 272n, 317

Rinio herbal, Venice, Biblioteca Marciana, 61, 62n

Ripanda, Jacopo (attributed to), Oxford sketchbook, Endymion sarcophagus drawing, 347

Ristoro d'Arezzo, 28, 298

Robbia, Luca della, 7, 17, 19, 119n, 302, 304, 311, 318, 320, 323; Florence Cathedral, North Sacristy door, 106n, 116n, 117n, 211; *Cantoria*, 211, 319

Robert, Carl, 337

Roman architecture, influence on Brunelleschi, 263, 273; on Alberti, 272-73, 275; on Donatello, 273; on Ghiberti, 258, 262, 265, 273, 330, 334; on Masaccio, 273

Roman architecture: Basilica of Constantine (*Tempio della Pace*), 275; Colosseum, 275; *Macellum Magnum* of Nero, 267n; Pantheon, 31, 275; S. Stefano Rotondo, 267n, 268n

Roman art, 132, 146, 196, 330, 332-33; *see also* antiquity; Greek art; Hellenistic art

Roman relief sculpture, 331; shallow relief technique, 286

Roman sculpture: known to the Quattrocento, 90-91, 277-78, 287; in Ghiberti's collection, 28, 305; influence on Ghiberti, 6, 21, 28, 49, 132, 137, 277-93, 337-52; motifs in Ghiberti, 210; ceremonial compositions, 286, 289; medals, gems, coins, 278, 299; decorative sculpture, 146, 285-86; monuments known to Ghiberti, 132, 277-93, 330, 337-52. *See also* Roman sculpture; reliefs; sarcophagi

Roman sculpture (including copies after Greek originals): Rome, Villa Ludovisi, *Aesculapius*, 343; Caesar portrait, 132; Florence, Pitti, Caesar Portrait, 341; Pisa, Camposanto, Caesar Portrait, 341; Rome, Vatican, Caesar Portrait, 341; Rome, Capitoline Collections, *Camillus* from Lateran, 277; Rome, Capitoline Collections, Colossal head and hand of Constans II from Lateran, 277; Paris, Bibliothèque Nationale, Cabinet des Medailles, "Constantine," 64, 66; Rome formerly Quirinal, Constantine with Three Sons, 277n; Florence, Museo Archeologico, *Hercules*, statuette, 280n, 281n; Vienna, Kunsthistorisches Museum, *Hercules*, statuette, 280n;

hermaphrodite excavated with Ghiberti as witness, 277, 313; Munich, Glyptothek, hermaphrodite, 277n; Rome, Villa Borghese, hermaphrodite, 277n; Venice, *Horses of San Marco*, 59n; Rome, Quirinal, *Horse tamers*, 277; Munich, Glyptothek, *Ilioneus*, 339; Rome, Capitoline Collections, *Lupa* from Lateran, 277, 294; Rome, Capitoline, *Marcus Aurelius* from Lateran, 277, 278; Rome, Capitoline Collections, *Marforio* formerly near S. Martina, 277, 351; Niobid group, 279; Florence, Uffizi, Niobid group, 339; Rome, Capitoline Collections, *Kneeling Son of Niobe*, 279, 339; Rome, *Pasquinio*, 277n; Rome, Capitol, formerly Quirinal, River Gods, 277; Florence, Uffizi, Satyr torso, 339; Rome, Vatican, Portrait of Socrates, 132, 341; Socrates Head, 132, 341; Rome, Lateran, *Sophocles*, 343; *Thorn Picker*, 281; Rome, Capitoline Collections, *Thorn Picker (Spinario)*, formerly Lateran, 277, 281, 282n; *Venus Medici*, type, 287n; *Venus Pudica*, type, 287, 291, 344; formerly Padua, *Venus*, 287n; Paris, Louvre, *Venus de Milo*, 287n; formerly Rome, Quirinal, *Venus*, 298; formerly Siena, *Venus*, 287n; Cassel, Museum, *Victory*, statuette, 349; *Zeus*, statuette type, 349; Cassel, Museum, *Zeus*, statuette, 349; Munich, private collection, *Zeus*, statuette, 349; New York, Metropolitan Museum of Art, *Zeus*, statuette, 349

Roman sculpture, reliefs: Arch of Constantine, 281, 282n, 343; Aurelian reliefs from (destroyed) Arch of Marcus Aurelius, 284, 343; Trajanic reliefs, 284, 287, 290; battle reliefs, 285; ceremonial reliefs, 286, 289; Este, Museo Atestino, *Cippus*, 348; Rome, Column of Marcus Aurelius, 278, 337; Column of Trajan, 278, 294, 337; decorative reliefs, 285; Rome, St. Peter's formerly chapel of John VII, decorative reliefs, 280; historical reliefs, 146, 147, 284; Florence, Uffizi, Iphigenia *cippus*, 287, 288, 290, 337; Paris, Bibliothèque Nationale, Cabinet des Medailles, *Jupiter and*

the Eagle, cameo, 64n; formerly Florence, Medici Collection, *Flaying of Marsyas*, 278; Rome, Forum of Nerva, Minerva frieze, 207, 287, 289, 292, 346; Venice, Museo Archeologico, from S. Maria dei Miracoli, formerly S. Vitale in Ravenna, relief with four putti, 297; formerly Florence, Collection Niccolo Niccoli, *Rape of the Palladium*, 278, 301, 314; *Slaughtering of the Pig*, 281, 282n; Rome, Palazzo Sacchetti, ceremonial relief, 340

————, sarcophagi: Asiatic type, 342; Bacchic sarcophagi, 292; Barbarian heads, *see* Battle sarcophagi, Pisa, Rome; Battle sarcophagi, 132, 284-85; Ceremonial sarcophagi, 278, 291, 293, 332; Historical sarcophagi, 278; Mythological sarcophagi, 278, 285; Phaedra sarcophagus, 132; Rome, Palazzo Rospigliosi, Adonis sarcophagus, 270, 287, 293, 343, 348; Arbury Hall, Newdgate College, Bacchic sarcophagus, 349; Blenheim castle, Bacchic sarcophagus, 350; Copenhagen, Ny-Carlsberg Glyptothek, Bacchic sarcophagus, 345; London, British Museum, Bacchic sarcophagus formerly S. Maria Maggiore, 291, 344, 348; Naples, Museo Nazionale, Bacchic sarcophagus, 345; formerly Rome, Palazzo Gentili, Bacchic sarcophagus, lost (?), 349; Rome, Palazzo Rospigliosi, Bacchic sarcophagus (*Indian Triumph*), 345, 347; Rome, Vatican, Bacchic sarcophagus, 349; Rome, Villa Aldobrandini, fragments, Bacchic sarcophagus, 289, 350; Rome, Villa Medici, Bacchic sarcophagus, 345; Pisa, Camposanto, Battle sarcophagus, 284, 341-43, 349; Rome, Villa Borghese, Battle sarcophagus from St. Peter's, 284, 287, 289, 341-42, 349; Cortona, *Dionysos battling the Amazons*, 278, lid with victories, 286, 343; Pisa, Camposanto, Endymion sarcophagus, lid with victories, 343; Rome, Palazzo Colonna (formerly), lost Endymion sarcophagus, 347; Rome, Palazzo Giustiniani, Endymion sarcophagus, 287, 291, 292, 346-47, 350; Rome, S. Lorenzo f.l.m., Fieschi sarcophagus, 283-

84, 289, 340, 345; Pisa, Camposanto, Gaia and Oceanus sarcophagus, with victories, 343; Ince Blundell Hall, *Wounding of Hippolytus*, sarcophagus, 283, 337n, 340; Los Angeles, County Museum, sarcophagus with scenes from Life of Roman General, formerly Rome, St. Peter's, 207, 287, 289, 290, 346-47, 350; Mantua, Palazzo Ducale, sarcophagus with Life of Roman Official, Marriage scene, 340; Florence, Uffizi, sarcophagus with Life of Roman Official, Marriage scene, 340; Florence, formerly Rinuccini Collection, sarcophagus with Life of Roman Official, Marriage scene, 340; *see also*, Rome, S. Lorenzo f.l.m., Fieschi sarcophagus; Rome, Vatican, Marine sarcophagus, 287, 289, 344; Medea sarcophagi, 207, 287; Rome, Museo delle Terme, Medea sarcophagus from SS. Cosma e Damiano, 291, 348, 351-52; Turin, Museum, Medea sarcophagus, fragments, 207, 291, 348; Meleager sarcophagus (relief?) known to Alberti, 324, 330; Rome, Villa Albani, Coffee House, *Death of Meleager*, 347; Villa Doria Panfili, Meleager sarcophagus, 287, 289-90, 292, 348-49; lost Meleager sarcophagus, 287, 290, 347; Muse sarcophagus, 342-43; sarcophagus with orator in shell-topped niche, 286, 287, 342; Rome, Villa Medici, Paris sarcophagus, 350; Brussels, Musées Royaux, Pelops sarcophagus, 279, 283, 287-88, 337n, 339, 348; Pisa, Camposanto, Phaedra sarcophagus, 132, 284-85, 340-41, 350; Florence, Museo dell'Opera, Phaeton sarcophagus, 283, 290, 339-40; lost Ploughman relief, probably from sarcophagus, 345; Rome, Palazzo Giustiniani, Ploughman on season sarcophagus, 345; Paris, Louvre, Proserpina sarcophagus, fragments, 287, 290, 351; Pisa, Camposanto, sarcophagus with victories from cemetery of S. Pietro in Vincuoli, 343; Pisa, Camposanto, sarcophagus of T. Aelius, with victories, 343

Roman authors, 330

Romanesque churches, influence on Brunelleschi, 263

romantics, 19th century, 23n, 24, 26

Rome, Biblioteca Casanatense, *Historia plantarum*, 58n

——, Monuments and Sites: Acqua Vergine, 270n

——, Arch of Constantine, 281, 282n, 343; Aurelian reliefs from Arch of Marcus Aurelius, 284, 343; Trajanic reliefs, 284, 287, 290, 345

——, Arch of Marcus Aurelius, reliefs from, *see* Arch of Constantine

——, Arch of Septimius Severus, 295

——, Basilica of Constantine (*Tempio della Pace*), 275

——, Capitol, *Marcus Aurelius*, 277; *River Gods*, formerly Quirinal, 277; Capitoline Collections, *Camillus*, 277; Colossal Head and Hand of Constans II, 277; *Lupa*, 277, 294; *Marforio*, 351; *Kneeling Son of Niobe*, 339; *Thorn Picker*, 277, 281, 282n

——, Colosseum, 275

——, Column of Marcus Aurelius, 278, 337

——, Column of Trajan, 278, 294, 337

——, Forum of Nerva, Minerva Frieze, 207, 287, 289, 292, 346

——, Grotto of Egeria, 294

——, Lateran, S. Giovanni in Fonte, 31

——, Formerly Lateran, *Camillus*, 277; Colossal Head and Hand of Constans II, 277; *Lupa*, 277, 294; *Marcus Aurelius*, 277; *Thorn Picker*, 277, 281, 282n

——, Lateran Museum, *Sophocles*, 343

——, *Macellum Magnum* of Nero, 267n

——, Museo delle Terme, *Medea* sarcophagus, 291, 348, 351-52

——, Palace of Evander, 294

——, Palazzo Colonna (formerly), lost Endymion sarcophagus, 347

——, Palazzo de' Conservatori, *see* Capitoline Collections

——, Palazzo Gentili (formerly), lost Bacchic sarcophagus, 349

——, Palazzo Giustiniani, Endymion sarcophagus, 287, 291-92, 346-47, 350; Ploughman from Season sarcophagus, 345

——, Palazzo Rospigliosi, Adonis sarcophagus, 270, 287, 293, 343, 348; Bacchic sarcophagus (*Indian Triumph*), 345, 347

——, Palazzo Sacchetti, ceremonial relief, 340

——, Pantheon, 31, 275

——, Ponte S. Angelo, 270n

——, Quirinal, *Horse Tamers*, 277

——, Formerly Quirinal, Constantine with Three Sons, 277n; two river gods, 277; *Venus*, 298

——, S. Clemente, Branda Chapel, frescoes, Masolino and Masaccio, 320; Masolino, 241-42, *Disputation of Saint Catherine*, 242, *Death of Saint Ambrose*, 242

——, Formerly S. Cosma e Damiano, Medea sarcophagus, *see* Roman sculpture, sarcophagi; Rome, Museo delle Terme

——, S. Lorenzo f.l.m., Fieschi sarcophagus, 283-84, 289, 340, 345

——, S. Maria Maggiore, altar, *see* Masaccio and Masolino

——, Formerly S. Maria Maggiore, Bacchic sarcophagus, *see* Roman sculpture, sarcophagi; London, British Museum

——, S. Maria in Trastevere, 12th century mosaics of the façade and apse, 357; apse mosaics, Pietro Cavallini, 357

——, Formerly near S. Martina, *Marforio*, 277

——, S. Paolo f.l.m., Old Testament cycle, 169

——, St. Peter's Sacristy, Tabernacle, Donatello, 347; Roman pilasters, formerly Chapel of John VII, 280

——, Formerly Old St. Peter's, Battle sarcophagus, *see* Roman sculpture, sarcophagi; Rome, Villa Borghese; sarcophagus with Life of Roman General, *see* Roman sculpture, sarcophagi; Los Angeles, County Museum

——, S. Stefano Rotondo, 267n, 268n

——, Vatican, Bacchic sarcophagus, 349; Marine sarcophagus, 287, 289, 344; Caesar Portrait, 341; Socrates Portrait, 132, 341; Pinacoteca, *Thomas Aquinas before the Cross*, Sassetta, 259n; Sistine Chapel, *Sacrifice of the Leper*, Botticelli, 333; Stanze,

School of Athens, Raphael, 25; Vatican Library, *Cosmas Indicopleustes*, *Sacrifice of Isaac*, 38n

————, Villa Albani, Coffee House, *Death of Meleager*, 347

————, Villa Aldobrandini, fragments of a Bacchic sarcophagus, 289, 350

————, Villa Borghese, Battle sarcophagus, 284, 287, 289, 341-42, 349; hermaphrodite, 277n

————, Villa Doria Panfili, Meleager sarcophagus, 287, 289-90, 292, 348-49

————, Villa Ludovisi, *Aesculapius*, 343

————, Villa Medici, Bacchic sarcophagus, 345; Paris sarcophagus, 350

Romulus and Remus, 294

Rosa, Salvatore, Florence, Uffizi, drawing after Meleager sarcophagus, 348

Rossellino, Antonio and Bernardo, 17, 19; workshop, Caesar Portrait, New York, Metropolitan Museum of Art, 341

Rossi, Roberto de', 279

Rosso, Giovanni, il Fiorentino, *see* Nanni di Bartolo il Rosso

Rudolph II of Hapsburg, 28

Rudolph IV of Austria and his wife, *see* Vienna, St. Stephen

Rufinus, 179

Rumohr, Carl von, 23-24

Rustici, Cenci de', 321

Sacchetti relief, *see* Rome, Palazzo Sacchetti

Salutati, Coluccio, 279, 296, 299; *De Laboribus Herculis*, 280

Samson, *see* Bellini, Jacopo

San Gimignano, Collegiata, Bartolo di Fredi, Old Testament cycle, 175, 176n, 221-23, 225, 292, 345; Taddeo di Bartolo, frescoes, 80

Sangallo, Giuliano da 268n

S. Maria in Vescovio, Old Testament cycle, 176n; *Sacrifice of Isaac*, 282n

Sassetta, 259; *Saint Francis, the Fire Test* (formerly Duveen, New York), 259n; Rome, Vatican, Pinacoteca, *Thomas Aquinas before the Cross*, 259n

Scalcagna, Michele, *see* Michele da Firenze

Scarparia, Giacomo da, 279

Scepter of Charles V, *see* Paris, Louvre

Schlosser, Julius von, 10, 23, 25-28, 231, 339, 353-55; *Antiken*,

27-28; *Commentarii*, 27-28, 306, 307n, 308, 310; *Prologomena*, 27-28, 306n

Schoene Madonnen, 78-79

Schmarsow, August, 26

Seal of Louis of Bavaria, 258n

Seneca, 330, 334, 346

Sesto family, 6n

Siena, Accademia, Carmine altarpiece, predella, *Saint Albert Consigning the Order of the Carmelites to Saint Broccardo* and *Dream of Sebach*, Pietro Lorenzetti, 224

————, Cathedral (including Baptistery of S. Giovanni and Museo dell'Opera), *Baptismal Font*, 138-41, reliefs commissioned, 138-41; *Salome*, Donatello, 151-53, 221, 244, 263, 264n, 327-28; Ghiberti reliefs, 4-5, 9, 112, 126, 139-41, 149, 199, 329, 360; *Baptism*, 13, 100, 144, 150-55, 190, 192-93, 200-1, 331; *Saint John before Herod*, 13, 108, 117n, 118, 130n, 132, 143-44, 146-47, 151, 153, 207, 248, 261, 264, 343; *Annunciation to Zacharias*, Jacopo della Quercia, 117n; *Birth of John the Baptist*, Giovanni Turini, 117, 119; *Saint John the Baptist Preaching*, Giovanni Turini, 117-19, 144n; *Juda Maccabi* in pavement, 173; *Maestà*, Duccio, 114n, 218; Tomb of Giovanni Pecci, Donatello, 152-53; *Three Graces*, 346

————, Fonte Gaia, *see* Palazzo Pubblico

————, Palazzo Pubblico, *Good and Bad Government*, Ambrogio Lorenzetti, 219-21, 258n, 313, 343; *Pax*, Ambrogio Lorenzetti, 298; Fonte Gaia, Jacopo della Quercia, 121n, 143; frescoes, Taddeo di Bartolo, 80

————, S. Francesco, lost murals by Ambrogio Lorenzetti, 219-20

————, Trecento art and influence on Ghiberti, 53-54, 214-15, 217, 218-25, 309

Sigismund, Emperor, 185

Simone di Nanni da Fiesole, 165n, 167

Sirén, Osvald, 26

Sixtus V, Pope, 65n

Skopas, 282, 339

Sluter, Claus, 62n, 118n; Chartreuse de Champmol, 55; *Well of Moses*, 78, 85

Socrates Portrait, 132, 341, *see* Roman sculpture

Spano, Pippo, 33

Speculum Humanae Salvationis, 39n, 173

Spinelli, Cola di Nicola, 256, 261n

Spinelli, Niccolo di Luca, 12, 36, 40, 43n

Spinelli, Parri, 80, 129n

Starnina, Gherardo, 21

Stefano, 309

Stefano da Verona (da Zevio), 79

Strasbourg Cathedral, pretended influence of sculpture on Ghiberti, 26

Strozzi, bank, 261n; family, 33, 261n

Strozzi, Carlo, excerpts from documents of Arte di Calimala, 34, 39, 73, 121n, 169, 355, 362-65; Index of Libri Grandi, 106; excerpts from *Libri (Quaderni) del Proveditore*, 164, 166n; from *Libro della Seconda e terza porta*, 22 and *passim*; *Repertorio Generale delle Cose Ecclesiastiche*, 362; *Cose Laiche*, 363

Strozzi, Lodovico, 142n

Strozzi, Palla di Nofri, 105-8, 146, 279, 299

Sulla, 16

Sylvester, Pope, 357

Taddeo di Bartolo, Perugia, Museum, San Domenico altarpiece, 79; San Gimignano, Collegiata, frescoes, 80; Siena, Palazzo Pubblico, frescoes, 80; Triora, Collegiata, *Baptism*, 80

Taine, Hippolyte, 25

Talmudic legend from *Targum II* to the *Book of Esther*, 177, 179, 187

Teramo, Cathedral, *Paliotto*, Niccolo di Guardiagrele, 116n

Terminology: Albertian, 310, 313; *lineamenta*, 230; *piano*, 232; Ghibertian, *casamenti*, 230-33, 247-49; *commentarii*, 230, 310-11; *diligentia*, 313; *disciplina*, 11, 313; *industria*, 313; *lineamenti*, 230-31, 233-34, 293, 310, 311, 313; *misura*, 230-31, 233-34, 310-11; *piani*, 230-34, 310, 313; *prospettiva*, 313; *ragione*, 233; *regole*, 230, 311; *symmetria*, 231; *teorica dell'arte*, 309-11; Plinian, *lineamenta*, 230; *symmetria*, 231; Vitruvian, *commensus e membris*, 231; *firmitas, commoditas, venustas*, 270

Theodericus of Flanders, 58n

Toledo, Spain, Cathedral, *Madonna of the Folding Chair*, 65

Tomaso da Modena, 55

Torquemada, Juan (John), 185

Torriti, Jacopo, Assisi, S. Francesco, fresco, *Sacrifice of Isaac*, 38n

Toschi, Giovanni Battista, 25

Traini, Francesco, Pisa, Camposanto, *Trionfo della Morte, Thebais*, 221-23, 225

Trajan, 294

Traversari, Ambrogio, 279, 300n, 332; approach to art, 301; admiration of Bernardino of Siena, 178; Greek studies and knowledge of Greek Church-fathers, 178; interest in Saint Ambrose, 179, 187; in Origen, 178-79, 187; intermediary between Ghiberti and Aurispa, 311-12; knowledge of Hebrew, 179; neopatristic movement, 178-79; papal adviser on Byzantine affairs and Union of Churches, 183-87; portrait, 186-87, 200; program of Gates of Paradise, 171-80, 183-88; critique of Bruni's, 159, 161, 171; shrine of SS. Protus, Hyacinth and Nemesius, 138-39; translation of Diogenes Laertius, 178, 186

Trecento, influence of art on Ghiberti, 51, 90, 114n, 128, 147-48, 172, 214-25, 258n, 282, 309, 313; crypto-antique elements in, 292; influence on Ghiberti, 225, 286, 290, 342-43; features in Ghiberti's work, 28, 32, 61, 211; North Door, 259-61, *Saint John*, 85, *Saint Stephen*, 98-99; approach to art of antiquity, 298-99; symbols and traditions in perspective, 243-44, 247-48

Triora, Collegiata, *Baptism, see* Taddeo di Bartolo

Turin Museum, Medea sarcophagus, *see* Roman sculpture, sarcophagi

Turini, Giovanni, 9, 127, 140, 207, 360; Siena, Baptismal Font, *Birth of John the Baptist*, 117, 119, *Saint John the Baptist Preaching*, 117-19

Turino di Sano, 117n

Uccello, Paolo, 28, 109, 209-10, 319n, 328n; (and workshop) Florence, S. Maria Novella, Chiostro Verde frescoes, 175, 208-10, 344, *Creation of Adam*, 208, *Sinopia*, 210, 344, *Creation of Eve*, 208n, 209n, *Creation of Animals*, 208, 209n, *Fall of Man*, 208n, *Expulsion*, 208, 209n, 210, *Labors of Man*, 208, 209n, *Deluge*, 201-2; Oxford, Ashmolean Museum, *Hunt*, 202

Ugo di Prete Ilario, 222

Ugolino da Vieri, Orvieto, Cathedral, Reliquary of the SS. Corporale, 114n, 129-30, 217-18

Urbino, Palazzo Ducale, Architectural panel, Laurana, Luciano (attributed to), 267n, 268, 272-73

Uzzano family, 33

Uzzano, Niccolo da, 161, 169

Valdambrino, Francesco da, competition panel, 40, 43n

Valencia, Cathedral, alabaster reliefs, *Pentecost*, 117-19, *Resurrection* and *Samson*, 118, Julià lo Florentì

Valla, Lorenzo, 178

Valle-Rustici Collection, 339

Vanni, Andrea, 172n

Varchi, Benedetto, 18

Varro, 267n

Vasari, Giorgio, 10, 18, 20-22, 24, 27-28, 35-36, 43, 50, 51n, 84, 97, 109n, 130n, 139, 173, 217n, 234, 238, 257n, 263n, 294, 305n, 354

Vatican, *see* Rome, Vatican

Venice, Biblioteca Marciana, Rinio herbal, 61, 62n; Museo Correr, *Doge*, Jacobello Masegne, 57; Palazzo Ducale, Porta della Carta, 139; south window, Pier Paolo Masegne, 79

——, SS. Giovanni e Paolo, Tomb of Raneri Zen, 343

——, S. Marco, Collection of Early Christian and Byzantine sculptures *all'antica*, 278; Horses, 59n; center arch reliefs, *Sacrifice of Isaac* and *Adam*, 210n; rod screen with Apostles, Jacobello Masegne, 57, 59

——, Museo Archeologico, Roman relief with four putti, from S. Maria de' Miracoli, formerly S. Vitale in Ravenna, 297

Venturi, Lionello, 24-25, 27

Verini, Ugolino, 16

Veris, Franco and Filippolo de', Campione, S. Maria de' Ghirli, *Last Judgment*, 79

Verona, S. Anastasia, Pellegrini Chapel, terracotta reliefs, Michele da Firenze, 108n, 116n; S. Fermo, Brenzoni Tomb, Nanni di Bartolo il Rosso, 116n

Veronese, Guarino, 301n

Verrocchio, Andrea, 17-18, 333

Vienna, Albertina, *Flagellation*, drawing, Ghiberti, 129-30

——, formerly Hofmuseum, *Taccuinum sanitatis*, 57

——, Kunsthistorisches Museum, *Hercules*, statuette, *see* Roman sculpture

——, Nationalbibliothek, *Vienna Genesis*, 177; *Codex 1191*, 39n

——, Rathaus Museum, statues of Charles IV and Princes of the Austrian House from St. Stephen, 55

——, St. Stephen, statues of Rudolph IV and his wife; story of St. Paul, 55

Vignole, San Sebastiano, *Cross*, Gualandi, 117n, 120n

Villani, Filippo, 28; *Uomini singholari*, 309

Villani, Giovanni, 31

Virgil, 294, 297, 312n

Virgil Master, New Haven, Yale University Art Gallery, Jarvis Collection, *Solomon and the Queen of Sheba*, 259n

Visconti, Gian Galeazzo, 34-35, 57-58

Visitation Master, *see* Bamberg

Visitation Master, *see* Rheims

Vitruvius, 231, 244n, 247, 268n, 270, 307-8, 310-13

Volkmann, Johann J., 21-22

Volterra, Francesco da, Pisa Camposanto, Job frescoes, 258n

Warburg, Aby, 325, 332

Washington, National Gallery, Widener Collection, *Trinity Morse*, 61, 65

Wat Tyler riots, 78

Weyden, Roger van der, 17

Windsor Royal Library, Dal Pozzo Collection, drawings, 337n, 338, 344-45, 348-49

Winckelmann, Johann Joachim, 277, 294

Witelo, 307

Wolfegg Castle, *Wolfegg Sketchbook*, 337, 344-46, 349, 351

Zafferini, Ser Matteo di Domenico, 360

Zagonara, Battle of, 163

Zeuxis, 16

ADDENDA

p. 19, line 18: H. W. Janson who has read the book in page proof calls my attention to the fact that the Anonimo Magliabecchiano is dated by Schlosser and Kallab 1537 to 1542 as against Frey's date of 1505.

p. 72: H. W. Janson is of the opinion that Niccolo Lamberti was commissioned only to procure a block for the Saint Mark, but not to execute the statue.

p. 90, note 8: H. W. Janson tells me that he has come to accept as irrefutable Lanyi's thesis ("Le statue quattrocentesche dei Profeti nel Campanile e nell'antica facciata di Santa Maria del Fiore," *Rivista d'Arte*, XVII [1935], pp. 121ff; 245ff), that the *Saint John* is identical with a statue documented for Rosso in 1419 to 1420.

p. 147, note 17: The Dati Tomb in 1956 was transferred from its place in the transept into the Ruccellai Chapel, off the right transept arm.

p. 152: While I still cannot help feeling that Ghiberti's bronze technique surpasses Donatello's I should add in fairness the opinion of a great bronze founder, Bruno Bearzi ("Considerazioni di tecnica sul S. Ludovico e la Giuditta di Donatello," *Bollettino d'Arte*, XXXVI [1951], pp. 119ff), who explains Donatello's procedure of piecemeal casting as caused by the impossibility of firegilding a large-scale statue, cast in one piece.

p. 253: H. W. Janson very kindly has called my attention to the suggestion made by Kauffmann, bibl. 237, pp. 64ff, to the effect that Donatello in designing the perspective of the Lille *Salome* presumably in 1434 made use of the procedure expounded by Alberti. If the date is correct, it would only confirm my thesis that Alberti's impact was felt by the Florentine artists even before *Della Pittura* was completed. Needless to say I cannot agree with Kauffmann's view when he presents the perspective procedure of Alberti's as only "codifying thoughts discussed and practiced in the circles of artists gathering around Brunelleschi."

CORRIGENDA

p. 22 omit erroneous statement that Thomas Patch was a pseudonym for Antonio Cocchi (see Kurz, bibl. *32). I was apparently misled by the inclusion of Cocchi's name in parentheses in the title of the Italian edition of 1773.

pp. 64, 66 the bust of "Constantine," crystal with gilded silver trimmings, was not ca. 1370 but ca. 1300. Correction orally supplied by Willibald Sauerländer.

p. 166 line 5 and 4 from bottom. Cancel: "Tomaso apparently died in 1447" (see Dig. 292a).

p. 200 n. 12, line 2. instead of "early in 1424 or even before," read "the year 1428" (see Hartt, bibl. *24, p. 163, note 16)

p. 305 n. 51, line 9, read "great-grandson" instead of "grandson"

p. 312 n. 21, line 7, read "by sending him instead of the manuscript, a Latin translation" instead of "the manuscript of a Latin translation"

p. 345 no. 31, cancel "Ny Carlsberg (Poulsen, bibl. 424, no. 777a), and"; forgery, see Matz, bibl. *39, II, p. 212

p. 348 no. 43b, line 10, instead of "Rome, Museo delle Terme," read "Ancona, Museo Civico"

p. 351 no. 66, line 11, instead of "Museo delle Terme," read "Ancona, Museo Civico"; line 12, after "bibl. 448," add "II"

p. 421 Dig. 293: cancel question mark (see bibl. *31, p. 317 App. A)

ILLUSTRATIONS

WORKS OF GHIBERTI, PLATES 1-137

COLLATERAL MATERIAL, FIGURES 1-146

PLATE 1. Competition Relief. Florence, Bargello

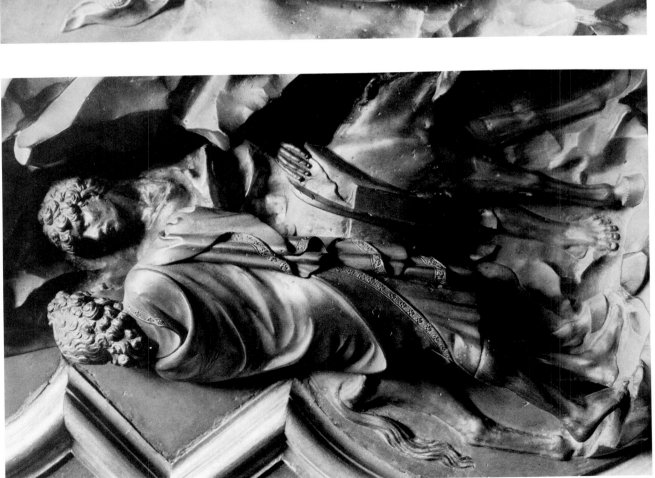

PLATE 2b. Competition Relief, Abraham and Isaac. Florence, Bargello

PLATE 2a. Competition Relief, Servants. Florence, Bargello

PLATE 3. *Saint John the Baptist* and Niche. Florence, Or San Michele

PLATE 4. *Saint John the Baptist*. Florence, Or San Michele

PLATE 5. *Saint John the Baptist*, Head. Florence, Or San Michele

PLATE 6. *Saint Matthew* and Niche. Florence, Or San Michele

PLATE 7. *Saint Matthew.* Florence, Or San Michele

PLATE 8. *Saint Matthew*, Head. Florence, Or San Michele

PLATE 9a. *Saint John the Baptist*, Profile.
Florence, Or San Michele

PLATE 9b. *Saint Matthew*, Profile.
Florence, Or San Michele

PLATE 10b. *Saint Matthew,* Head, Profile.
Florence, Or San Michele

PLATE 10a. *Saint John the Baptist,* Head, Profile.
Florence, Or San Michele

PLATE 11b. *Saint Matthew*, Drapery.
Florence, Or San Michele

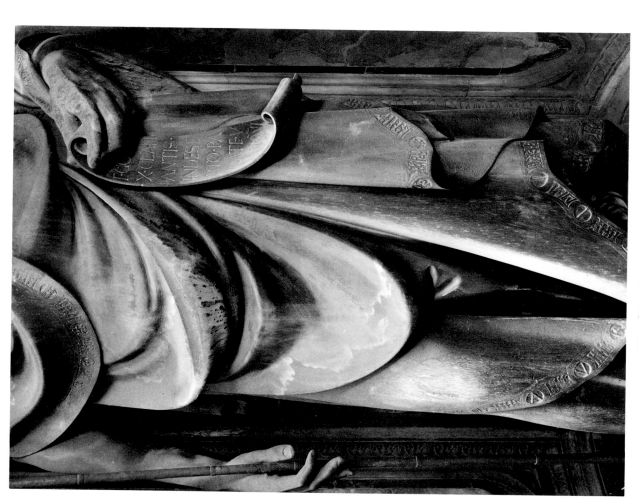

PLATE 11a. *Saint John the Baptist*, Drapery.
Florence, Or San Michele

PLATE 12a. *Saint Matthew*, Hand. Florence, Or San Michele

PLATE 12b. *Saint Stephen*, Hand. Florence, Or San Michele

PLATE 13b. *Saint Matthew*, Foot.
Florence, Or San Michele

PLATE 13a. *Saint John the Baptist*, Foot.
Florence, Or San Michele

PLATE 14. *Saint Stephen*. Florence, Or San Michele

PLATE 15. Ghiberti Workshop: *Saint Stephen*, Presentation Drawing.
Paris, Louvre, Cabinet des Estampes

PLATE 16. *Saint Stephen*, Head. Florence, Or San Michele

PLATE 17. *Saint Stephen*, Detail. Florence, Or San Michele

PLATE 18. North Door. Florence, Baptistery

PLATE 19b. *Saint Jerome.* North Door

PLATE 19a. *Saint Augustine.* North Door

PLATE 20b. *Saint Ambrose. North Door*

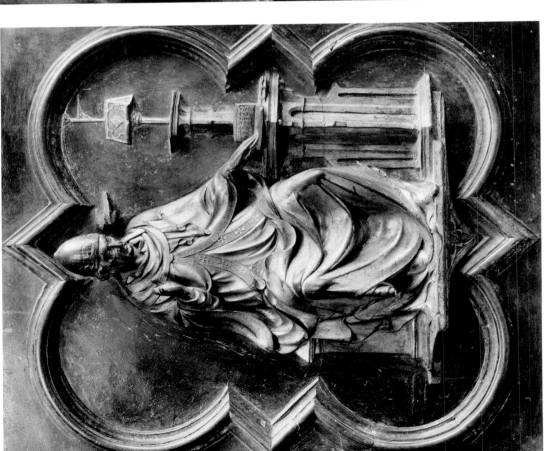

PLATE 20a. *Saint Gregory. North Door*

PLATE 21b. *Saint Matthew.* North Door

PLATE 21a. *Saint John the Evangelist.* North Door

PLATE 22b. *Saint Mark.* North Door

PLATE 22a. *Saint Luke.* North Door

PLATE 23. *Saint John the Evangelist*, Eagle. North Door

PLATE 24. *Saint Matthew*, Detail. North Door

PLATE 25. *Annunciation.* North Door

PLATE 26a. Competition Relief, Isaac.
Florence, Bargello

PLATE 26b. *Annunciation*, Mary. North Door

PLATE 27. *Nativity.* North Door

PLATE 28. *Adoration of the Magi.* North Door

PLATE 29. *Adoration of the Magi*, Holy Family. North Door

PLATE 30. *Christ Among the Doctors.* North Door

PLATE 31. *Christ Among the Doctors*, right half. North Door

PLATE 32. *Baptism of Christ.* North Door

PLATE 33. *Temptation.* North Door

PLATE 34. *Expulsion of the Money Changers.* North Door

PLATE 35. *Expulsion of the Money Changers, Fallen Youth. North Door*

PLATE 36. *Christ in the Storm*. North Door

PLATE 37. *Transfiguration*. North Door

PLATE 38. *Transfiguration*, Apostles. North Door

PLATE 39. *Raising of Lazarus*, Mary Magdalene. North Door

PLATE 40. *Raising of Lazarus.* North Door

PLATE 41. *Entry into Jerusalem.* North Door

PLATE 42. *Last Supper*. North Door

PLATE 43. *Agony in the Garden.* North Door

PLATE 44. *Arrest of Christ.* North Door

PLATE 45a. *Raising of Lazarus*, Man at Left.
North Door

PLATE 45b. *Flagellation*, Christ at the Column.
North Door

PLATE 46. *Flagellation*, Sketch. Vienna, Albertina

PLATE 47. *Flagellation.* North Door

PLATE 48. *Christ before Pilate*. North Door

PLATE 49b. *Christ before Pilate, Pilate. North Door*

PLATE 49a. *Baptism of Christ, Angels. North Door*

PLATE 50. *Way to Calvary.* North Door

PLATE 51a. *Way to Calvary*, Christ. North Door

PLATE 51b. *Way to Calvary*, Mary and Saint John. North Door

PLATE 52. *Crucifixion*. North Door

PLATE 53. *Resurrection.* North Door

PLATE 54. *Pentecost.* North Door

PLATE 55a. *Temptation*, Wing of Satan. North Door

PLATE 55b. *Saint Matthew*, Wing of Angel. North Door

c

f

b

e

a

d

PLATE 56. *Prophets*. North Door

a

b

c

d

e

f

PLATE 57. *Prophets.* North Door

c

f

b

e

a

d

a

b

c

d

e

f

PLATE 59. *Prophets*. North Door

a

b

c

d

e

f

PLATE 60. *Prophets.* North Door

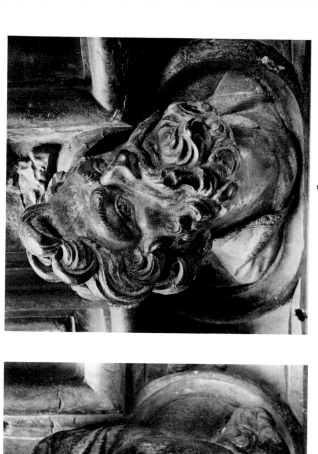

a

b

c

d

e

f

PLATE 61. *Prophets*. North Door

PLATE 62b. *Youthful Prophet.* North Door

PLATE 62a. *Elderly Prophetess.* North Door

PLATE 63a. *Prophet.* North Door

PLATE 63b. *Youthful Prophet.* North Door

PLATE 64b. *Prophet.* North Door

PLATE 64a. *Prophet.* North Door

PLATE 65b. *Youthful Prophetess. North Door*

PLATE 65a. *Youthful Prophet. North Door*

PLATE 66b. *Prophet.* North Door

PLATE 66a. *Youthful Prophetess.* North Door

PLATE 67. *Prophet*. North Door

PLATE 68b. *Tondo*, back frame. Gates of Paradise

PLATE 68a. *Lion's Head*, back frame. North Door

PLATE 69d. Floral Decoration, outer jambs.

PLATE 69c. Floral Decoration, inner jambs.

North Door

PLATE 69b. Foliage, lattice frame.

PLATE 69a. Foliage, lattice frame.

PLATE 70b. Floral Decoration, outer jambs. North Door

PLATE 70a. Floral Decoration, outer jambs. North Door

PLATE 71a. Architrave, Detail. North Door

PLATE 71b. Architrave, Detail. Gates of Paradise

PLATE 72. *Saint John the Baptist brought before Herod*. Siena, Baptistery, Font

PLATE 73. *Baptism of Christ*. Siena, Baptistery, Font

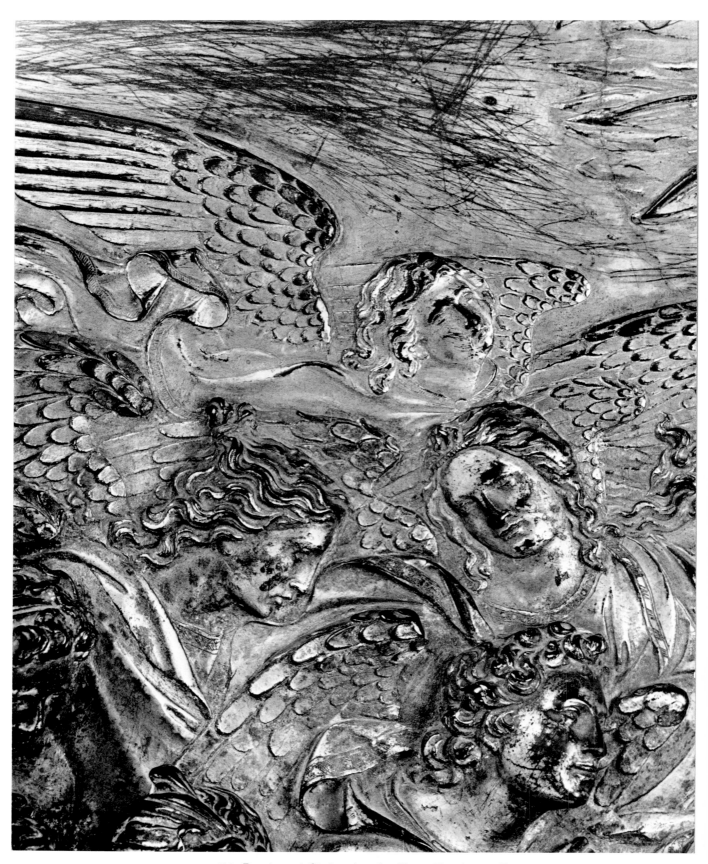

PLATE 74. *Baptism of Christ*, Angels. Siena, Baptistery, Font

PLATE 75. *Tomb of Leonardo Dati.* Florence, S. Maria Novella

PLATE 76. Cassa dei SS. Proto, Giacinto e Nemesio, from S. Maria degli Angeli, front. Florence, Bargello

PLATE 77a. Cassa di S. Zenobio, *Miracle of the Oxcart*. Florence, Cathedral

PLATE 77b. Cassa di S. Zenobio, *Miracle of the Servant*. Florence, Cathedral

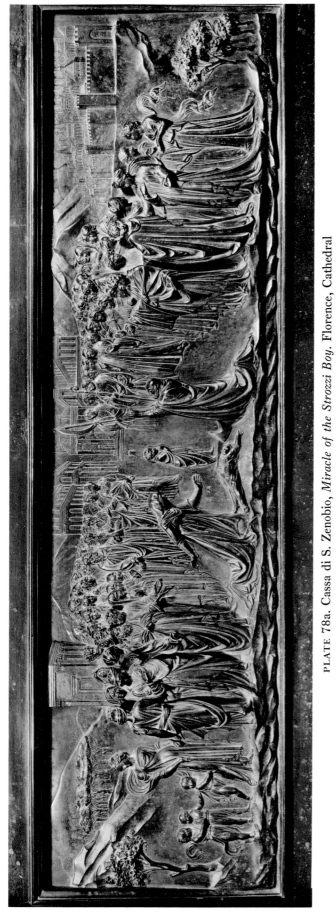

PLATE 78a. Cassa di S. Zenobio, *Miracle of the Strozzi Boy*. Florence, Cathedral

The inscription on the garland reads:

CAPVT
BEATI ZENOBII F
LORENTINI EPISCOPI
IN CVIVS HONOREM
HEC ARCA INSIGNI OR
NATV FABRICATA
FVIT

PLATE 78b. Cassa di S. Zenobio, *Angels with Garland*. Florence, Cathedral

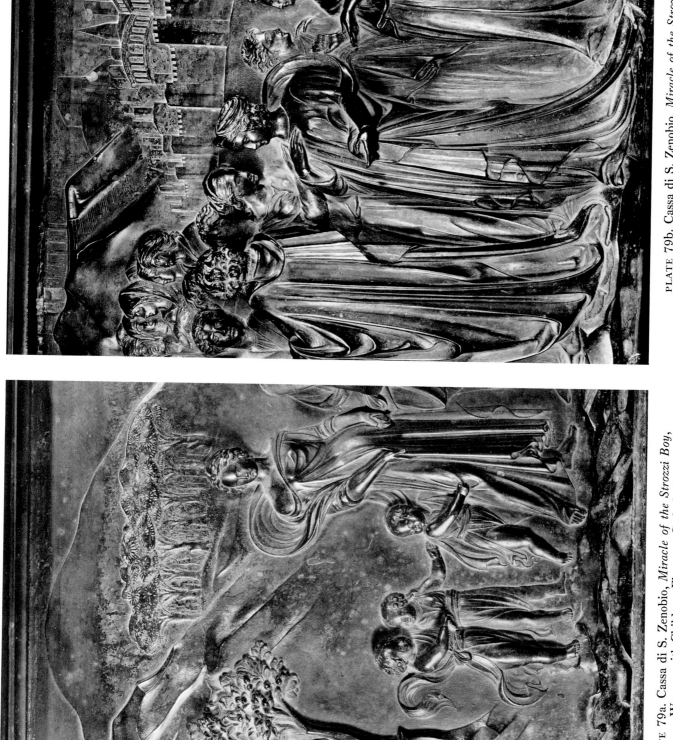

PLATE 79b. Cassa di S. Zenobio, *Miracle of the Strozzi Boy,*
Group at Right. Florence, Cathedral

PLATE 79a. Cassa di S. Zenobio, *Miracle of the Strozzi Boy,*
Woman with Children. Florence, Cathedral

PLATE 80a. Cassa di S. Zenobio, *Angels with Garland*, Detail. Florence, Cathedral

PLATE 80b. Cassa di S. Zenobio, *Miracle of the Strozzi Boy*, Detail. Florence, Cathedral

PLATE 81. Gates of Paradise. Florence, Baptistery

PLATE 82. *Genesis*. Gates of Paradise

PLATE 83a. *Genesis*, Adam. Gates of Paradise

PLATE 83b. *Genesis*, Creation of Eve. Gates of Paradise

PLATE 84. *Genesis*, Expulsion from Paradise. Gates of Paradise

PLATE 85. *Cain and Abel*. Gates of Paradise

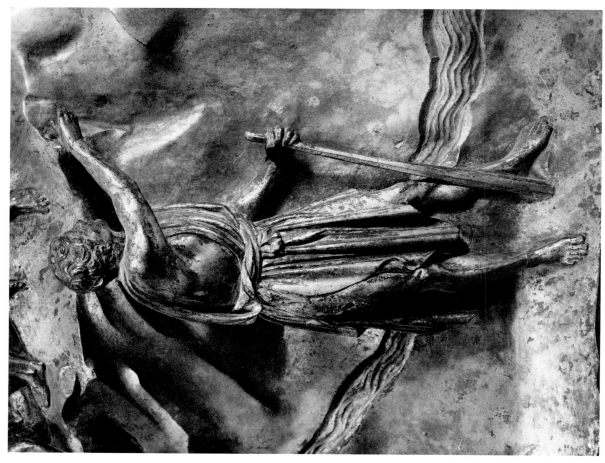

PLATE 86b. *Cain and Abel*, Cursing of Cain. Gates of Paradise

PLATE 86a. *Cain and Abel*, Slaying of Abel. Gates of Paradise

PLATE 87. *Cain and Abel*, Cain Plowing. Gates of Paradise

PLATE 88a. *Cain and Abel*, First parents of Mankind. Gates of Paradise

PLATE 88b. *Noah*, Animals Leaving the Ark. Gates of Paradise

PLATE 89. *Noah*. Gates of Paradise

PLATE 90. *Noah*, Noah's Drunkenness. Gates of Paradise

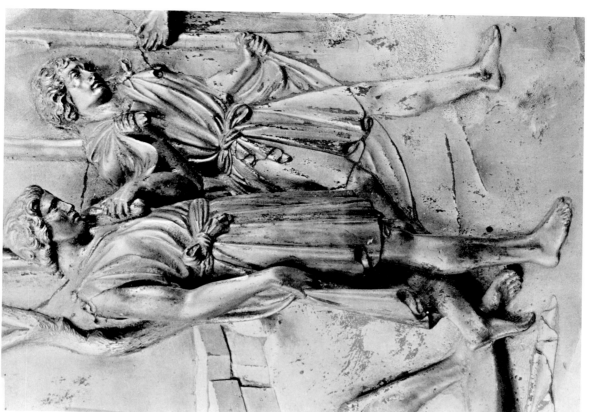

PLATE 91b. *Noah*, Noah's Sons. Gates of Paradise

PLATE 91a. *Abraham*, Servants Waiting. Gates of Paradise

PLATE 92. *Noah*, Noah's Sacrifice, Detail. Gates of Paradise

PLATE 93. *Abraham*. Gates of Paradise

PLATE 94. *Isaac*. Gates of Paradise

PLATE 95. *Isaac*, Rebecca Praying. Gates of Paradise

PLATE 96b. *Solomon*, Falconier with Dog. Gates of Paradise

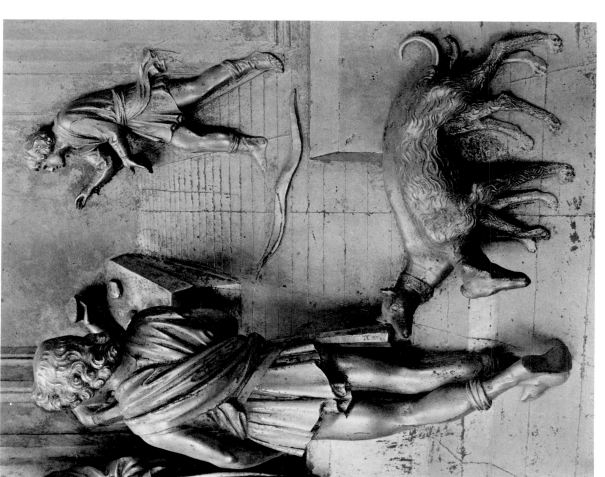

PLATE 96a. *Isaac*, Esau and His Dogs. Gates of Paradise

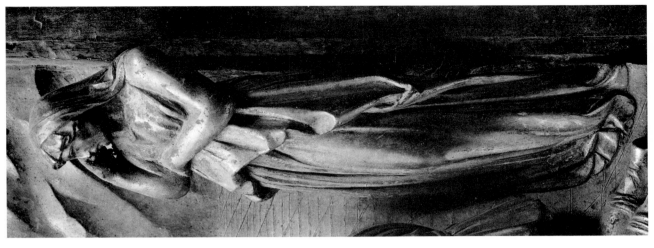

PLATE 97b. *Isaac*, Blessing of Jacob, Rebecca. Gates of Paradise

PLATE 97a. *Isaac*, Visiting Women. Gates of Paradise

PLATE 98. *Joseph*. Gates of Paradise

PLATE 99. *Joseph*, Distribution of Grain. Gates of Paradise

PLATE 100. *Joseph*, Architectural Detail. Gates of Paradise

PLATE 101b. *Joseph*, Two Girls. Gates of Paradise

PLATE 101a. *Joseph*, Joseph Revealing Himself. Gates of Paradise

PLATE 102. *Moses.* Gates of Paradise

PLATE 103. *Moses*, Daughters of Israel. Gates of Paradise

PLATE 104a. *Noah*, Noah and His Family Leaving the Ark. Gates of Paradise

PLATE 104b. *Moses*, The People at Mount Sinai. Gates of Paradise

PLATE 105a. *Genesis*, The Lord with the Angelic Host. Gates of Paradise

PLATE 105b. *Moses*, Moses Receives the Law. Gates of Paradise

PLATE 106a. *Abraham*, Trees. Gates of Paradise

PLATE 106b. *Moses*, Trees. Gates of Paradise

PLATE 107. *Joshua*. Gates of Paradise

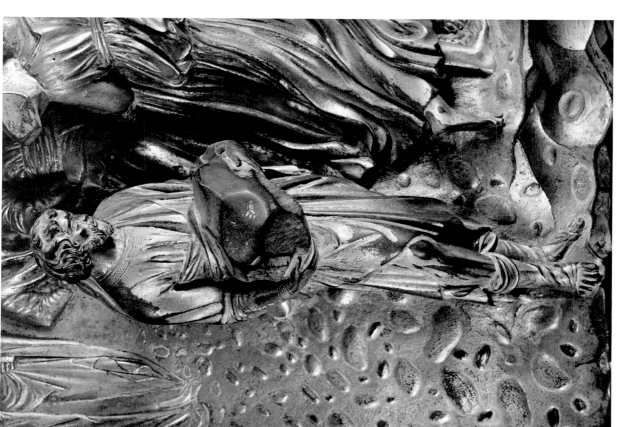

PLATE 108a,b. *Joshua*, The Carrying of the Stones. Gates of Paradise

PLATE 109. *Joshua*, Joshua on Chariot. Gates of Paradise

PLATE 110. *Joshua*, Group. Gates of Paradise

PLATE 111a. *Joshua*, The Walls of Jericho. Gates of Paradise

PLATE 111b. *David*, Jerusalem. Gates of Paradise

PLATE 112. *David*. Gates of Paradise

PLATE 113. *David*, right side. Gates of Paradise

PLATE 114a. *David*, Detail. Gates of Paradise

PLATE 114b. *David*, Entry into Jerusalem. Gates of Paradise

PLATE 115. *David*, Palm Tree. Gates of Paradise

PLATE 116. *Solomon.* Gates of Paradise

PLATE 117. *Solomon*, Solomon and the Queen of Sheba. Gates of Paradise

PLATE 118. *Solomon*, Group upper right. Gates of Paradise

PLATE 119. *Solomon*, Group lower right. Gates of Paradise

PLATE 120a. *Joseph*, Corn Hall. Gates of Paradise

PLATE 120b. *Solomon*, Architectural Detail. Gates of Paradise

PLATE 121b. *Aaron*, Detail. Gates of Paradise

PLATE 121a. *Saint Stephen*, Detail. Florence, Or San Michele

PLATE 122a. *Eve*. Gates of Paradise

PLATE 122b. *Noah*. Gates of Paradise

PLATE 123a. *Adam*. Gates of Paradise

PLATE 123b. *Puarphera*. Gates of Paradise

PLATE 124a. *Ezechiel* (?). Gates of Paradise   PLATE 124b. *Jeremiah* (?). Gates of Paradise

PLATE 125a. *Prophetess*. Gates of Paradise   PLATE 125b. *Joab* (?). Gates of Paradise

PLATE 126a. *Elia* (?). Gates of Paradise   PLATE 126b. *Jonah*. Gates of Paradise

PLATE 127a. *Hannah* (?). Gates of Paradise   PLATE 127b. *Samson*. Gates of Paradise

PLATE 128d. *Prophet.* Gates of Paradise

PLATE 128c. *Prophet.*
Gates of Paradise

PLATE 128b. *Prophetess.*
Gates of Paradise

PLATE 128a. *Prophet.* Gates of Paradise

PLATE 129a. *Miriam.* Gates of Paradise

PLATE 129b. *Aaron.* Gates of Paradise

PLATE 129c. *Joshua.*
Gates of Paradise

PLATE 129d. *Gideon* (?).
Gates of Paradise

PLATE 130d. *Bileam* (?).
Gates of Paradise

PLATE 130c. *Daniel* (?).
Gates of Paradise

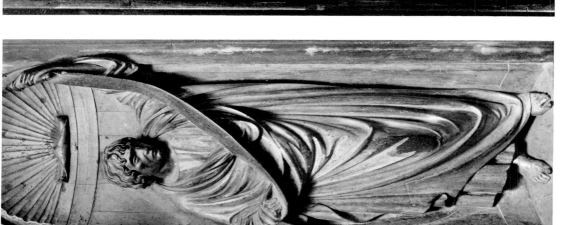

PLATE 130b. *Nathan* (?).
Gates of Paradise

PLATE 130a. *Judith.* Gates of Paradise

c

b

f

a

e

d

PLATE 131. *Prophets' Heads. Gates of Paradise*

a

b

c

d

PLATE 132. *Prophets' Heads*. Gates of Paradise

a

b

c

d

PLATE 133. *Prophets' Heads*. Gates of Paradise

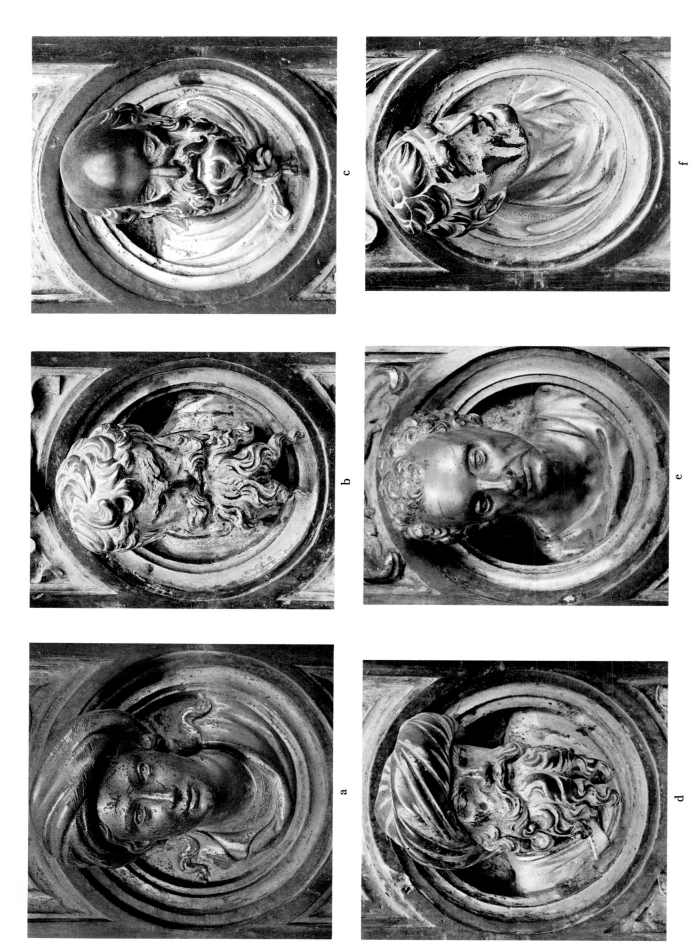

PLATE 134. *Prophets' Heads.* Gates of Paradise

PLATE 135b. Portrait of *Vittorio Ghiberti*. Gates of Paradise

PLATE 135a. *Lorenzo Ghiberti*, Self Portrait, Profile. Gates of Paradise

PLATE 136a. *Lorenzo Ghiberti.* Self Portrait. North Door   PLATE 136b. *Lorenzo Ghiberti,* Self Portrait. Gates of Paradise

a

b

c

d

PLATE 137. Floral Decoration, lattice frame.
Gates of Paradise

PLATE 138a. Floral Decoration, outer jambs. Gates of Paradise

PLATE 138b. Floral Decoration, inner jambs. Gates of Paradise

PLATE 138c. Decoration, outer jambs. Gates of Paradise

PLATE 138d. Decoration, outer jambs. Gates of Paradise

FIG. 1. Brunelleschi, Competition Relief. Florence, Bargello

FIG. 2. Leonardo di Ser Giovanni and Collaborators, Silver Altar of San Giovanni Battista,
Saint John Baptizing the People. Florence, Museo dell'Opera

FIGS. 3-4. Brunelleschi, Silver Altar of San Jacopo, Prophets. Pistoia, S. Jacopo

FIG. 5. Porta della Mandorla, *Abundantia.*
Florence, Cathedral

FIG. 6. Porta della Mandorla, *Hercules.*
Florence, Cathedral

FIG. 7. Ghiberti, *Assumption*, Window.
Florence, Cathedral

FIG. 8. Bartolo di Fredi, *Assumption*, from
Montalcino. Siena, Pinacoteca

FIG. 9. *Parament de Narbonne*, Detail. Paris, Louvre

FIG. 10. Brunelleschi (?), Silver Altar
of San Jacopo, *Church Father.*
Pistoia, S. Jacopo

FIG. 11. Jacobello dalle Masegne, *Doge.*
Venice, Museo Correr

FIG. 12. Jacobello dalle
Masegne, *Apostle.*
Venice, S. Marco

FIG. 13. Jacopo di Campione, *Salvator Mundi in His Glory.*
Milan, Cathedral, North Sacristy Door

FIG. 14. *The Woman and the Dragon,*
Saint John. Angers, Cathedral

FIG. 15. Trinity Morse. Washington, National Gallery of Art, Widener Collection

FIG. 16. *Charles V*, from the Quinze-Vingts, Head. Paris, Louvre

FIG. 17. Scepter of Charles V. Paris, Louvre, Gallerie d'Apollon

FIG. 18. Constantine Bust, Rear view. Paris, Bibliothèque Nationale, Cabinet des Medailles

FIG. 20. Donatello, *Saint Mark*. Florence, Or San Michele

FIG. 19. Nanni di Banco, *Quattro Coronati*. Florence, Or San Michele

FIG. 24. *Madonna.*
Poughkeepsie, Vassar College,
Art Gallery

FIG. 22. *Saint Paul*, Head.
Baume-les-Messieurs,
Abbey Church

FIG. 23. Jacques de Baerze, Broederlam Altar,
Adoration of the Magi. Dijon, Museum

FIG. 21. Taddeo di Bartolo, Altar, 1403. Perugia, Pinacoteca

FIG. 27. Lorenzo Monaco, *Agony in the Garden.*
Paris, Louvre

FIG. 26. Lorenzo Monaco, *Agony in the Garden.*
Florence, Accademia

FIG. 25. Lorenzo Monaco, Coronation Altar, Predella Panel,
Story of Saint Benedict. London, National Gallery

FIG. 28. Lorenzo Monaco, *Adoration of the Magi,* Predella Panel.
Formerly Poznán, Raczinsky Collection

FIG. 29. *Saint Christopher*,
1407. Boston,
Museum of Fine Arts

FIG. 30. Donatello, *Marzocco*.
Florence, Bargello

FIG. 31. Nanni di Banco
Isaiah.
Florence, Cathedral

FIG. 32. Ghiberti, *Saint John
the Baptist*, Head, Rear View.
Florence, Or San Michele

FIG. 33. Ghiberti, *Saint Stephen*,
Head, Rear View.
Florence, Or San Michele

FIG. 34. *Saint Stephen*, formerly façade Florence Cathedral.
Paris, Louvre

FIG. 35. Andrea Pisano, South Door. Florence, Baptistery

FIG. 36. *Adoration of the Magi* and *Presentation in the Temple*
from Castel del Sangro. Florence, Museo dell'Opera

FIG. 37. Julià lo Florentì, *Pentecost*.
Valencia, Cathedral

FIG. 38. Julià lo Florentì, *Samson*.
Valencia, Cathedral

FIG. 40. Giovanni Turini, *Preaching of Saint John.*
Siena, Baptistery, Font

FIG. 39. Giovanni Turini, *Birth of Saint John.*
Siena, Baptistery, Font

FIG. 41. Reliquary of Sant'Andrea.
Città di Castello, Pinacoteca

FIG. 42. Ghiberti Workshop, Reliquary of Sant'Andrea,
Saint Andrew and *Saint Francis*.
Città di Castello, Pinacoteca

FIG. 43. Donatello, *Christ on the Cross*.
Florence, S. Croce

FIG. 44. Ghiberti Workshop, Crucifix.
Impruneta near Florence

FIG. 45. *Baptism of Christ.* Florence, Biblioteca Nazionale, II, 445 (Zanobi di Pagholo d'Angnolo di Pierini, *Vita di San Giovanni Battista*)

FIG. 46. Florentine Goldsmith, Reliquary of San Jacopo, *Prophet.* Pistoia, S. Jacopo

FIGS. 47-48. Florentine Goldsmith, Reliquary of San Jacopo, Angels. Pistoia, S. Jacopo

FIG. 49. Ugolino da Vieri, Reliquary of the SS. Corporale, *Flagellation*.
Orvieto, Cathedral

FIG. 50. Ghiberti, Bracket below *Annunciation*.
Florence, Baptistery, North Door

FIG. 51. Ghiberti, Bracket below *Christ among the Doctors*.
Florence, Baptistery, North Door

FIG. 52. Roman Garland, Ara Pacis, Detail. Rome

FIG. 53. Gentile da Fabriano, Epiphany Altar, Flowers.
Florence, Uffizi

FIG. 54a,b. Ghiberti, Lions' Heads. Florence, Baptistery,
North Door, Back frame

FIG. 55. Ghiberti, Cassa dei SS. Proto, Giacinto, e Nemesio,
from S. Maria degli Angeli, Flank.
Florence, Bargello

FIG. 56. Tomb of Bartolommeo Valori (from cartoon by Ghiberti). Florence, S. Croce

FIG. 57. Filippo di Cristofano, Tomb of Lodovico degli Obizi (from cartoon by Ghiberti). Florence, S. Croce

FIG. 58. Tomb of Ranieri Zen. Venice, SS. Giovanni e Paolo

FIG. 59. Donatello, *Salome*. Siena, Baptistery, Font

FIG. 60. Donatello, Tomb of Giovanni
Pecci. Siena, Cathedral

FIG. 61. Donatello, Relief of Saint George, Right half. Florence, Or San Michele

FIG. 62. Ghiberti Workshop, *God the Father*,
Shutter for Ciborium from S. Egidio.
Florence, Ospedale di S. Maria Nuova

FIG. 63. Window with Saint James
(from cartoon by Ghiberti's Workshop).
Florence, Cathedral

FIG. 64. Ghiberti, *Solomon* Panel, Ambrogio
Traversari (?). Gates of Paradise

FIG. 65. Portrait of Ambrogio Traversari,
De Vita et Moribus Philosophorum. Florence,
Bibl. Medicea-Laurenziana, ms. plut. 65.22, f.1

FIG. 66. Donatello, *Giving of the Keys*. London, Victoria and Albert Museum

FIG. 67. Uccello, *Creation of the Animals*

FIG. 68. Uccello (?), *Expulsion from Paradise*

FIG. 69. Florentine Master, *Abraham and Hagar*

FIG. 70. Uccello, *Creation of Adam*

FIG. 71. Uccello, *Creation of Adam*, Sinopia

FIGS. 67-71. Florence, S. Maria Novella, Chiostro Verde and Capitolo del Nocentino

FIG. 72. Agnolo Gaddi, *Monk in the Desert*.
Florence, S. Croce, Castellani Chapel

FIG. 73. Taddeo Gaddi, *Christ among the Doctors*.
Florence, Accademia

FIG. 74. Ugolino da Vieri, Reliquary of the SS.
Corporale, *Way to Calvary*. Orvieto, Cathedral

FIG. 75. Ugolino da Vieri, Reliquary of the SS.
Corporale, *Last Supper*. Orvieto, Cathedral

FIG. 76. Ambrogio Lorenzetti, *Good Government*, Detail. Siena, Palazzo Pubblico

FIG. 77. Andrea da Firenze, *Via Veritatis*, Detail.
Florence, S. Maria Novella, Spanish Chapel

FIG. 78. Francesco Traini, *Thebais*, Right half. Pisa, Camposanto

FIG. 79. Piero di Puccio, *Creation*. Pisa, Camposanto

FIG. 80. Piero di Puccio, Stories of Cain, Abel, and Lamech.
Pisa, Camposanto

FIG. 83. *Passage through Red Sea*

FIG. 81. *Slaying of Abel*

FIG. 82. *Noah's Drunkenness*

FIGS. 81-83. Bartolo di Fredi. San Gimignano, Collegiata

FIG. 84. Pietro Lorenzetti, Carmine Altar, Predella Panel, *Dream of Sebach.*
Siena, Pinacoteca

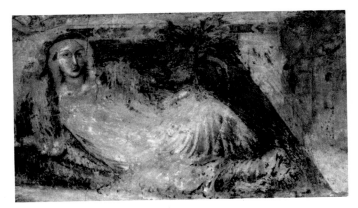

FIG. 86. School of Pietro Lorenzetti, *Coronation of the Virgin*, Eve. Montefalco, S. Agostino

FIG. 85. Maso di Banco, Sylvester Legend, *Wailing Women*. Florence, S. Croce

FIG. 87. Masaccio, Trinity Fresco.
Florence, S. Maria Novella

FIG. 88. Masolino, S. Maria Maggiore
Altar, *Founding of S. Maria della Neve.*
Naples, Museum

FIG. 89. Masolino, *Death of Saint Ambrose.*
Rome, S. Clemente

FIG. 90. Portal of Strozzi Chapel,
Detail. Florence, S. Trinità

FIG. 91. Augustus Altar, Garland, Detail.
Lyons

FIG. 92. Ghiberti, Niche of *Saint Matthew*.
Florence, Or San Michele

FIG. 93. Portal of Strozzi Chapel.
Florence, S. Trinità

FIG. 94. Brunelleschi, Palazzo di Parte Guelfa,
Façade. Florence

FIG. 95. Ghiberti, *Saint John the Baptist before Herod.*
Architectural Detail. Siena, Baptistery, Font

FIG. 96. Donatello, Niche of *Saint Louis.*
Florence, Or San Michele

FIG. 97. Ghiberti, Linaiuoli Altar, Frame.
Florence, Museo di S. Marco

FIG. 98. Simone il Cronaca, S. Stefano Rotondo, Drawing.
Florence, Uffizi, dis. Sant. 161r

FIG. 99. Alberti, S. Sebastiano, Façade.
Mantua

FIG. 100. Luciano Laurana (?), Architectural Setting. Urbino, Palazzo Ducale

FIG. 101. Roman Pilaster, Detail. Rome,
S. Pietro, Grotte Vaticane

FIG. 102. *Niobide*. Rome, Museo Capitolino

FIG. 103. Pelops Sarcophagus, Left part. Brussels, Musées Royaux

FIG. 104. Phaeton Sarcophagus, Left half. Florence, Museo dell'Opera

FIG. 105. Sarcophagus with *Wounding of Hippolytus*, Fallen Hunter.
Ince Blundell Hall

FIG. 106. Fieschi Sarcophagus, Marriage scene. Rome, S. Lorenzo, f.l.m.

FIG. 107. *Julius Caesar*, Bust.
Florence, Pitti, Argenteria

FIG. 108. Antonio Rossellino Workshop (?),
Julius Caesar, Bust. New York, Metropolitan Museum

FIG. 109. Head of Nurse

FIG. 110. Head of Hippolytus

FIG. 111. Head of Slave Girl

FIG. 112. Head of Companion
of Hippolytus

FIGS. 109-112. Phaedra Sarcophagus, Pisa, Camposanto

FIG. 113. Battle Sarcophagus. Rome, Villa Borghese

FIG. 114. Bertoldo di Giovanni, Battle Relief. Florence, Bargello

FIG. 115. Barbarian Head   FIG. 116. Barbarian Head   FIG. 117. Barbarian Head   FIG. 118. Head of Female
                                                                                            Barbarian Prisoner

FIGS. 115-118. Battle Sarcophagus. Rome, Villa Borghese

FIG. 119. Barbarian Chieftain Submitting to the Emperor   FIG. 120. Barbarian Prisoner Brought before the Emperor

FIGS. 119-120. Rome, Arch of Constantine

FIG. 121. Sarcophagus of *Dionysos Battling the Amazons*, Lid with Victories. Cortona, Cathedral

FIGS. 122-123. Adonis Sarcophagus, Details.
Rome, Palazzo Rospigliosi

FIG. 124. Marine Sarcophagus, Detail.
Rome, Vatican, Giardino della Pigna

FIGS. 125-126. Bacchic Sarcophagus from S. Maria Maggiore, Details,
Drawings. Wolfegg Sketchbook, fols. 31v, 32

FIG. 127. Bacchic Sarcophagus from S. Maria Maggiore, Right flank.
London, British Museum

FIG. 128. Vittorio Ghiberti, Eve, Frame.
Florence, Baptistery, South Door

FIG. 129. Minerva Frieze, Detail. Rome, Forum of Nerva

FIG. 130. Plowman from (lost) Relief, Drawing.
Windsor Royal Library, Dal Pozzo Collection

FIG. 131. Trajanic Battle Relief, Detail.
Rome, Arch of Constantine

FIG. 132. Sarcophagus with *Life of Roman Official*,
Right flank, Birth of a Child.
Los Angeles, County Museum

FIG. 133. Sarcophagus with *Life of Roman Official*,
Birth of a Child from Rome, S. Pietro.
Drawing, Wolfegg Sketchbook, fol. 25v

FIG. 135. Endymion Sarcophagus, Selene. Rome, Palazzo Guistiniani

FIG. 134. Cippus with *Sacrifice of Iphigeneia*, Iphigeneia. Florence, Uffizi

FIG. 136. Medea Sarcophagus, Medea and Children, Drawing. Coburgensis, fol. 32. Coburg, Castle, Library

FIG. 137. Sarcophagus with *Indian Triumph of Bacchus*. Rome, Palazzo Rospigliosi

FIG. 138. Meleager Sarcophagus, *Gathering in of Meleager*,
Drawing. Coburgensis, fol. 70. Coburg, Castle, Library

FIGS. 139-140. Bacchic Sarcophagus, Maenads.
Windsor, Royal Library, Dal Pozzo Collection

FIG. 141. Meleager Sarcophagus, *Gathering in of Meleager*. Rome, Villa Panfili

FIG. 142. Proserpina Sarcophagus, Gaia, Drawing.
Wolfegg Sketchbook, fol. 37

FIG. 143. *Zeus* (?), Bronze Statuette.
Munich, Private Collection (?)

FIG. 144. Bacchic Sarcophagus, Drunken Dionysos.
Rome, Vatican, Giardino della Pigna

FIG. 145. Bacchic Sarcophagus,
Tambourine-Playing Maenad,
Coburgensis, fol. 195.
Coburg, Castle, Library

FIG. 146. Medea Sarcophagus, Children of Medea, Drawing.
Coburgensis, fol. 42. Coburg, Castle, Library